THE TAMING OF ROMANTICISM

HARVARD STUDIES IN COMPARATIVE LITERATURE
Founded by William Henry Schofield
37

THE TAMING OF ROMANTICISM

*European Literature
and the
Age of Biedermeier*

VIRGIL NEMOIANU

HARVARD UNIVERSITY PRESS
CAMBRIDGE, MASSACHUSETTS
AND LONDON, ENGLAND
1984

Library of Congress Cataloging in Publication Data

Nemoianu, Virgil.
The taming of Romanticism.
(Harvard studies in comparative literature ; 37)
Includes index.
1. European literature—19th century—History and
criticism.   2. Romanticism—Europe.   3. Biedermeier.
I. Title.   II. Series.
PN751.N45   1984   840′.9′145   84-4604
ISBN 0-674-86802-1

For my dear mother and father

PREFACE

IN the last fifty years or so, romanticism has been the object of many profound and illuminating commentaries. However, consensus has been slow to develop. In this study I should like above all to map out the ground on which the controversies unfold. I do not mean to refute any view, but rather to provide a framework inside which the truths of other scholars can coexist. I assume that theories about romanticism (including my own) are partial truths, approaches to a truth that in its entirety is bound to escape us, much as the tridimensional truth of a spatial figure is bound to escape even the most skillful draftsman.

The particular side of romanticism here explored is its *dynamics,* because I feel that romanticism is often regarded as a fixed quantity rather than as a cultural process. The study is a general one, but if in the course of the investigation some specific items of European literature between 1815 and 1848 come to be seen more clearly, as I hope they will, so much the better.

I also try to discuss romanticism as a genuinely international period process. This is not to deny for a second the overriding importance of national literatures and, of course, individual authors and texts as the ultimate facts to be dealt with. However, since it seems inevitable that we use mediating structures, it is only fair that they too be examined with some care. Perhaps some of the results contradict the opinions of distinguished historians of national literatures. The differences are simply those of perspective: I am trying to describe what things look like from my particular vantage point, that of a European comparatist. It is, I think, a pleasant vantage point—but I admit that it is not the only one. What we can see from it completes, but does not necessarily invalidate, other views.

As a comparatist I feel some affinity to the traditions of cultural morphology, which I have tried to enrich with dialectical and structuralist methodologies. In fact I believe that any broad and serious investigation will ultimately strive toward a sociocultural approach that is stripped as far as possible of ideological biases. This can in turn provide a foundation for the truly aesthetic and axiological analyses of the literary critic.

I like to think of the book as wheel-shaped. The first chapter is the hub of the wheel, and the subsequent chapters are the spokes; ideal readers will return occasionally to the central statement as they explore its significance in different countries and in different forms.

Quotations in the text are given in the original German, French, and Italian; translations may be found in the notes. Quotations from Eastern Europe languages are given in English translation.

The University of California Press kindly consented to my use of some passages of Chateaubriand, *Atala/René,* a new translation by Irving Putter (copyright 1952), and Frederick Ungar permitted the quotation of sections from *C. D. Grabbe: Jest, Satire, Irony and Deeper Significance,* translated by Maurice Edwards (copyright 1966). The Catholic University of America offered timely financial assistance for preparation of the typescript.

A version of the first half of Chapter 4 appeared in German as "Ostmitteleuropäischer Biedermeier. Versuch einer Periodisierung," in *Österreichische Literatur. Ihr Profil im 19ten Jahrhundert,* ed. Herbert Zeman (Graz, Austria: Akademische Druck- und Verlagsanstalt, 1982). The first two chapters contain parts of my article "Is There an English Biedermeier?" published in *Canadian Review of Comparative Literature,* Winter 1979. Parts of Chapter 5 are included in an essay being published in *Romantic Drama,* ed. Gerald Gillespie, in the ICLA comparative history of world literature series. Several paragraphs of Chapter 1 were used in a review published in *Studies in Romanticism,* Winter 1981. Papers based on the ideas of this book were presented between 1977 and 1981 at several universities and conferences.

My study is of course indebted to many scholars. However, Friedrich Sengle and Meyer H. Abrams were of decisive importance; without their landmark works, mine would have been impossible. I see this study as a continuation and completion of theirs.

Among those who encouraged or advised me at crucial points I wish to thank Ruth Angress, Les Chard, Milan Dimić, Fred Garber, Claudio Guillén, Robert Hughes, Ken Johnston, Alphonse Juilland, Henry H. H. Remak, Joseph Sendry, William Slottman, and René Wellek.

The competent professionalism and delicate empathy of Denise Thompson-Smith played a truly important part in improving the manuscript and are gratefully acknowledged. The index was prepared by Nancy Herington. Terry Kennedy, Judy Michalski, Pauline Pappalardo, Cheryl Retta, Paul Rice, and Deborah Schull helped with editing or typing. To Anca and Martin I owe the most.

CONTENTS

THE TAMING OF ROMANTICISM

1

THE DYNAMICS OF THE
ROMANTIC PERIOD

WHAT romanticism was, how long it lasted, when it began, and how wide it spread are questions that have yet to receive satisfactory answers. These questions are not purely academic, because in many ways the nineteenth century and even the twentieth century were shaped by the values or perceptions that emerged in the decades just before and after 1800. The historical realities of those times—from socialism to nationalism, from scientism to imaginative literature—remain a part of our social and cultural environment. Therefore, an understanding of romanticism contributes to our understanding of the contemporary world.

Romanticism eludes definition because of its own rich diversity. Perhaps more than other movements, romanticism reflects the variety of European culture. But perhaps the foremost dichotomy within romanticism is the opposition between the great fantasies and visions of the revolutionary age (high romanticism) and the more perplexed and disappointed musings, sentimentalities, aspirations, and ironies of the post-Napoleonic era. If we can gain insight into what the writings of these periods have in common, then perhaps we will speak more confidently of romanticism.

Two broad hints are helpful in approaching such a task. The first is that if we look around Europe as a whole, not merely at its western half, we find many diverse relations between romanticism's two periods. The second hint is that for one area, the German-speaking center of Europe, scholars developed a set of categories that describe the opposition between high romanticism and its later, moderate stages. These later stages (approximately 1815–1848) were called *Biedermeier*, and its model may prove useful in answering our question.

Of course, the relationship between successive epochs in German literature is not reproduced identically all over Europe. In fact our proposed look at the whole of Europe would soon negate any attempt at absolute generalization. Nevertheless, the abundance and variety of the ties between high romanticism and the German literature of the 1820s, 1830s, and 1840s, as well as the complex identity of the German Biedermeier as a literary and sociocultural period deserve more than local attention. We may ask ourselves whether analogous phenomena appear elsewhere and whether all such phenomena can be subsumed in a broader view of period dynamics in the romantic age. The term *Biedermeier* itself is perhaps somewhat like one of those artifices introduced in algebraic computation that are meant to eliminate themselves in the end result, after helping us solve the problem. Not so the substance; wherever some kind of high romanticism flourished, it was followed by something resembling Biedermeier discourse and mentality.

For example, Karl Immermann's novel *Die Epigonen* (1836) is typical of the writings that came after Germany's high-romantic period.[1] It contains many features that can be recognized in contemporary literature elsewhere, even though it had no influence abroad (it had very little in its own country) and the author was not particularly well versed in European trends. The action revolves around the struggle for an inheritance, but the inheritance in turn hinges on the identity of the main character, who is ostensibly the son of a Bremen patrician, but in fact is the illegitimate offspring of an aristocrat. Hermann has to cope with an increasing burden of inheritance, a multiplicity of parents, and a choice of mates who stand for different existential and sociocultural options. Hermann himself is, like many characters created by Byron or Chateaubriand, obsessed with the fear of incest but, unlike them, also fearful of his own lack of creativity, originality, and purpose. He wanders all over the country and samples, as it were, the choices and diverse activities of his epigonic contemporaries (*die Spätlinge*), who were reliving and reviving in a minor mode the aspirations of previous eras: he views idyllism, glimpses revivals of feudalism, notes the growth of capitalism, converses with intellectuals about aesthetic *Bildung,* and observes revolutionaries in action.[2] The categories seem to express the dilemmas and expectations of the German Biedermeier society in the face of the disintegration of revolutionary and high-romantic ideals. The parable of the wastrel or lost son or brother can be seen as another central image for the mentality captured by Immermann.[3] The structure and general drift of Immermann's novel reminds one of Scott's *Waverley, The Antiquary,* or

Redgauntlet. Gothic horrors are never far away. Tough entrepreneurial characters seem to belong to Balzac; the abundance of museums, collections, skeletons, precious stones, *naturalia,* and mummified bodies remind us of E.T.A. Hoffmann. The idyllic scenes and the wholesome figure of Cornelie seem descended from *Werther,* and echoes of other Goethe characters (Mignon, Euphorion) abound in the novel. The narrator of *Die Epigonen,* even more than its characters, can be categorized with the heroes of Alfred de Musset, Juliusz Słowacki, and Georg Büchner; they have in common capriciousness, disappointed irony, a sense of relativism, and an enjoyment of craziness.[4]

Immermann's novel embodies Biedermeier features, but it also shares a broad range of mentalities, images, and literary strategies with various other contemporary writers. We are entitled to ask what real-life emotions and situations were so faithfully reflected in Immermann's novel. How do the features alluded to above relate to a German and a European historical situation? What is the Biedermeier?

THE INTERRELATIONS that bind together the years between 1815 and 1848 were too obvious in the literature and the culture of German-speaking areas to be missed. True, for a while German literary periodization concentrated on the *Goethezeit* theory (as expounded by Hermann August Korff and others).[5] This theory held that there was a unitary German movement developing in a rational sequence from Gotthold Ephraim Lessing and Christoph Wieland through Johann von Herder, Goethe, and Schiller to idealist philosophy and the great romantics. This conceptual framework vied for supremacy with the more traditional division: Enlightenment—"Sturm und Drang"—and a two-step romanticism, according to the centers of development in Jena and Heidelberg. (Recently Paul Gottfried has suggested that there was a third center around the München-Landshut University).[6] To this movement, the classical or neohumanist movement would simply provide a counterweight in Weimar. Much like their British counterparts, the proponents of both the *Goethezeit* and the traditional periodizations are slightly fuzzy about the decades after 1820, sometimes labeling them "poetischer Realismus."

This fuzziness in turn encouraged a rival theory that held that 1815–1848 in German literature represented a unit that can be called "Biedermeier." This point of view was put forward in the 1920s by

Paul Kluckhohn, Julius Wiegand, and others, and more systematically after 1931 by Günther Weydt and Wilhelm Bietak, who triggered a substantial scholarly debate in the 1930s.[7] The participants seemed to agree that the writings of the period they discussed had a number of common features: inclination toward morality, a mixture of realism and idealism, peaceful domestic values, idyllic intimacy, lack of passion, coziness, contentedness, innocent drollery, conservatism, resignation. The term *Biedermeier* had originally been derogatory (as had *baroque* or even *romantic*). Gottlieb Biedermeier was a character invented by Adolf Kussmaul and Ludwig Eichrodt and introduced to the public in 1855 in the Munich *Fliegende Blätter;* this smug and cozy philistine was a caricature of the old-fashioned petty bourgeois of southern Germany and Austria.[8] *Biedermeier* might be translated roughly as "John Simpleton," though the word carries a connotation of nostalgic, smiling benevolence. By 1900 the term was already being used descriptively by historians of art and fashion for the intimate, pretty, quiet paintings of the period 1815–1848 (Carl Spitzweg, Ferdinand Georg Waldmüller) or for the furniture and dress styles of the same years. The term was then transferred from art to literature. Applying the term *Biedermeier* to the tone and color of an entire age was also to some extent the work of nostalgic-ironic novelists such as Georg Hermann in *Jettchen Gebert* (1906) and Thomas Mann in *Buddenbrooks* (1901).

The debate of the 1930s is now viewed with distrust for three reasons. First, there was widespread suspicion that the reappraisal of the figures of the 1820s and 1830s was nationalistically motivated. The debaters sometimes resorted to ideological arguments meant to bring this period in line with official thinking (for instance underlining that the authors they discussed were "rooted in the native soil" and in small communities).[9] Much earlier Adolf Bartels, an anti-Semitic populist, had tried to use Austrian Biedermeier writers as a weapon against the "degenerate" modernism of pre–World War I literature. Biedermeier writing may well have appealed to the more philistine Nazi *Parteigenossen* for reasons that had little to do with aesthetic values. But in fact the chief literary historians of the period (Walter Linden and Franz Koch, as well as the more serious Paul Fechter or Josef Nadler) do not show much interest in the Biedermeier.[10] It may safely be assumed that obnoxious aspects of the discussion in the 1930s are due to academic opportunism rather than to some intrinsic mystical correspondence over the centuries between the Biedermeier and the political rulers of the day.

Second, there was the suspicion that Biedermeier was just a tedious, idealistic concoction, a fruit of the tireless *geistesgeschichtlich* urge to invent periodizations, define the spirit of the age, and multiply the breed of historical types. This suspicion is not without some justification, but it seems to go a little too far. One may well question the validity of a methodology without actually denying the object of its research. Even if Kluckhohn's approach was wrong, the questions he raised could still be interesting.

The third objection, and probably the weightiest, is that the really dynamic and significant force in the 1830s and 1840s was *Das junge Deutschland*, which like similar contemporary movements (for example, *La giovine Italia*) represented national and radical tendencies. Karl Gutzkow, Heinrich Laube, Heinrich Heine, and Ludwig Börne are associated with it, but in a broader sense so are Anastasius Grün, Georg Herwegh, Ferdinand Freiligrath, Max Schneckenburger, and others. People such as Büchner and Grabbe, some argue, are compatible with this movement and close to it.[11] The young Hegelians, coming slightly later, are seen as its direct continuation and so is the realism of the second half of the nineteenth century. Such a reading of German literary history would make literary-philosophical discourse the spearhead of a general progressive line in nineteenth-century social growth and would reject the Biedermeier as being just the provincial and epigonic movement that, after all, it had always been thought to be. It would be limited to such writers as Eduard Mörike, Franz Grillparzer, Jeremias Gotthelf, Anette von Droste-Hülshoff, Adalbert Stifter, perhaps Nikolaus Lenau and August Graf von Platen, and many secondary figures.

But the scholarship of the 1930s made notable efforts to rescue the Biedermeier from such a restricted scope. Hermann Pongs had observed, for instance, that demonic and grotesque characters and situations abound in these writings.[12] More important, several early scholars, including Wilhelm Bietak and Günther Weydt, had tried to describe the social and philosophical roots of the movement. Even more radical was the claim of Rudolf Majut that the Biedermeier could only be understood as a dialectical whole, covering all the writing of the period, including that of the "progressives." (Majut even speaks about "der problematische Menschentypus," the type of problematic man.[13]) But a fuller response to lingering doubts was provided only in Friedrich Sengle's monumental three-volume *Biedermeierzeit*.[14] According to Sengle, basic shifts in the social psychology of the time, objective historical conditions, and a combination of contrasting literary developments cooperated to create a specific cultural climate, which differs from both the high-romantic period and the post-1850 realistic age. The general precondition for all the writings of the age is, in his opinion, anxiety. The insecurity created by the vast upheavals of revolution and imperial wars led to doubts about the solidity of the ensuing Restoration: it also led to the manic production of systems and countersystems of order and progress. The need to seek refuge in the coziness of home and hearth, garden and family follows naturally, and the wish to proclaim a soothing reform of social and national arrangements is equally escapist and angst-ridden. Sengle concludes that the conservative idyllists and the ironic progressives are dialectically connected: Mörike and Heine are but faces of the same coin. He therefore asserts that the best way to deal with the period is to distinguish between *Biedermeier* and *Biedermeierzeit*. While the first term can be safely maintained for the traditional description of a *current* in German literature, the second can be applied to the whole Restoration period and can accommodate other (even opposing) trends, united only by a broad framework of values and sociohistorical events.

BEFORE TRYING to comment on the dilemmas raised by the Biedermeier debate and before extending the discussion to literatures outside Germany, we should take a quick look at some of the social and intellectual realities of a historical period that managed to avoid major wars but was riddled with outbursts of agitation and rebellion, that was peaceful yet nervous. The feeling of a drastically endangered existence in some ways caused and in some ways was the effect of the rejection of the visionary, all-integrating, titanic claims of high romanticism and led to a partial return to eighteenth-century attitudes. What was striking in the years after 1815 was the coalescence of some romantic and some Enlightenment values into new combinations and networks of practical solutions, into splintered or reduced interpretations of the high-romantic model, or into diminutive prettifications.

This coalescence was perhaps most obvious in aesthetic theory and literary practice. The disciples of Friedrich Schiller are, after 1815, rare birds: few were inclined to accept play and aesthetic creation as privileged areas of humaneness; fewer yet described imagination as the agent of redemption. For example, an aesthetician like J. F. Herbart (1776–1841) was typical. Anti-Kantian and anti-Hegelian, he was an idealist but a pragmatic one: not a formalist but rather a kind of practical, low-level metaphysician. His views as well as those of others were symptomatic of the belief that art has some autonomy (the high-romantic inheritance), but that it should not be regarded as a salvation; on the contrary it should endeavor to adapt itself to reality and provide service. Symbol was thus swallowed by allegory, irony by the grotesque, the preromantic *Empfindsamkeit* and *Weltschmerz* reappeared. Harmony and stability were counteracted by drollery and caricature, by the "ludicrous demon"—all inroads of chaos.[15] The literary production of the age abounds, to use Sengle's terminology, in *Zweckformen* (utilitarian forms): epigrams and aphorisms, didactic poems, fables and parables, satires and epistles, memoirs and travelogues.[16] In addition, the well-established major literary species strive to accommodate tendentiousness: historical and family novels, landscape and historical tableaux, the countless permutations of idyllic structures. At bottom epigonism is placidly accepted, and its benefits are enjoyed: pluralism of styles, the reverence for history, the deliberate contrivance of new forms. It has been argued that a "disappointed pantheism," that is, a retreat from the values of comprehensive creativity, should be seen as an "originary phenomenon" (Lenau, Heine, Immermann, Büchner) dealing in the exploration of negativity.[17] In any case, the didactic and the problematic, retreat from romanticism and renewal of Enlightenment traditions, go hand in hand.

The values expressed by this combination are disseminated by the first systematic, modern network of popularization. In the 1820s, 1830s, and 1840s, in Germany no less than in the rest of Europe, there were massive extensions of publishing houses, collections, libraries and museums, translations, encyclopedias, and newspapers. According to some, Emile Girardin's *La Presse* (1836) must be considered the first modern newspaper.[18] The tremendous spread of encyclopedic popularization by Larousse, Brockhaus, Meyer, Chambers, and dozens of others dates from this time. In Germany the number of published titles hardly rose from 1800 to 1821, but tripled in the next two decades.[19] Almanacs of all kinds constituted for the first time their own genre. Sensational literature flourished as never before. The industry of fairy tales picked up. Several collections of Jacob and Wilhelm Grimm's tales appeared between 1812 and 1826; England was hit slightly later (the translation of Hans Christian Andersen in 1846 and F. E. Paget's *The Hope of the Katzekopfs,* 1844, were the spearhead, though preceded by the Grimms in the 1820s). It would seem that the insights of romanticism into special states of mind and romanticism's yearning for remote times and places were now commercial products, turned out by a large industry for general consumption.

In the sciences of the Restoration we can see the pressure exerted by lowered expectations. The general theories and visionary philosophies were now empirically tested and directed toward practical applications. There was a remarkably consistent and synchronized growth of philology (the movement is away from the broad language philosophies of Johann Georg Hamann, Herder, and Wilhelm v. Humboldt and toward the practical studies of Franz Bopp or Friedrich Diez), geology, and zoology. André-Marie Ampère, Jöns Berzelius, Justus Liebig, Martin Klaproth, Hans Christian Oersted, Georg Ohm, and Joseph Gay-Lussac are figures characteristic of the age, as much as any poet or king. Liebig's main work was an application of chemistry to agriculture; Farraday was intent on transforming the somewhat mystical-poetical powers of magnetism that had so much preoccupied the romantics into prosaic-practical electric power; Ampère, Robert Meyer, and François Arago were pursuing similar aims. In fact the law of energy conservation may be said to have functioned for a while as a spiritual principle heightening the meaning of technology.

We are fortunate enough to have one thorough study explaining in what sense we can speak about an age of Biedermeier in medicine.[20] The idealistic philosophy of nature was waning after 1815, but a causal and experimental approach got the upper hand only after 1850, the author points out. The period in between was characterized by a (theoretically) uneasy empiricism trying (in the case of Liebig for instance) to accommodate James Mill's decidedly empirical views with belated echoes of the "organic vitality" theory. Philippe Pinel, Marie-François Bichat, Michel Lévy in France, no less than Johannes Müller or Johann Lukas Schönlein in Germany, were skeptical of the older theorizing on *materia medica* and put their trust in accumulation of data, classification, and comparison. Many historians regard the change of attitude toward folklore material—from the cavalier and freely creative collection of Achim von Arnim and Clemens Brentano to the much more carefully "folkloristic" effort of the Grimm brothers—as exemplary for the Biedermeier mentality. Another good example is that of Samuel Hahnemann, the father of homeopathy, who took one of the esoteric-mystic principles of occult romanticism and used it to start a curative industry.

In history the universal syntheses of Schelling or Hegel, and the prophetic élan of Novalis, were replaced by Barthold Niebuhr's and by Leopold von Ranke's scruples and by Friedrich Karl von Savigny's efforts at objectivity. The *Monumenta Germaniae Historica* directed by Georg Heinrich Pertz got underway in 1823. August Böckh began the *Corpus Inscriptionum Graecorum* in 1828, while Georg Grotefend and Jean-François Champollion deciphered the texts of Persian and Egyptian civilization (the latter in the 1820s). Comparatist treatments, inspired to some extent by Georges Cuvier, spread in philology, history, and literature. Carl Ritter envisaged history almost as a branch of geology (1817). In 1800 P. C. V. Boiste expanded the range of the terms included in the dictionary of the *Académie Française,* an idea with unmistakable romantic and revolutionary implications. The initiative was widely imitated and quite successfully turned into a well-ordered industry during the Restoration, when dictionaries with 110,000–170,000 entries became popular. Empiricism and application informed Friedrich Fröbel's (1782–1852) work. He decided to test the romantic aspects of play, symbol, natural organicism, relationship between microcosm and macrocosm, "the spheric law," integrity, original purity and the like in one specific area of research and innovation, namely pedagogy. Thus he became in 1840 the initiator of the kindergarten. His theories came from Friedrich Ludwig Jahn, Ernst Moritz Arndt, Fichte, and Pestalozzi, and the illustrations of his books seem rifled from Philip Otto Runge.[21] In industry far-reaching technological innovations were introduced with energetic practicality (the steam engine on the Continent) even while inventions and experiments were still viewed with amused wonderment. At the very time when Robert Fulton's steamship was revolutionizing communications, sailing ships reached, in the forties and fifties, their highest flowering.[22] The tension between stagecoach and railway is symbolic of the Biedermeier age: its denizens from Alfred de Vigny to King Ludwig I of Bavaria were writing eloquent verses against the steam engine, yet in many ways they were encouraging it.

While scientific endeavors moved from general theory to practical application, literature and the arts abandoned the visionary creative outburst for the dispersion of general pleasure. Eight of the major German museums (including the Glyptothek and what is now called the Alte Pinakothek in Munich) were initiated between 1815 and 1855, along with numerous smaller ones.[23] Nor was this diffusion of art limited to a narrow, elite stratum. The middle and lower classes enjoyed the moralizing posters (*Bilderbogen*) often accompanied by texts from romantic poets, that were brought out in editions of over a million by publishers such as Gustav Kühn of Neuruppin.[24] (Their French equivalent was the *images d'Epinal*.) The other great popular art of the Restoration age is caricature. The manneristic fantasy of Grandville; the ironic art of the post-Hogarthians (George Cruikshank, Thomas Rowlandson, James Gillray, and many lesser lights); the continuous barrage of the social grotesque in *Charivari, Fliegende Blätter,* and *Kladderadatsch;* and the comprehensive vision of Honoré Daumier were important forces in the age that established a complex dialectical relationship with romantic ideals.

Opera houses, public orchestras, and conservatories of music were started. Robert Schumann, Franz Schubert, or Stephen Heller, whose small fragmentary melodies displayed fluid growth and transitions and mild crepuscular descents, answered the musical needs of a society based on the intimacy of the home. And, of course, by the time of the Congress of Vienna the bourgeois mansions offered the opportunity for concerts as often as the princely courts. Bankers such as Wurth and Fellner, financiers such as Baron Arnstein, Ludwig Pereira, and Wertheimstein, industrialists such as F.T. v. Hornbostel, Schöller, or Konrad Graf, scholars and public officials such as Joseph von Hammer-Purgstall, Anton Prokesch von Osten, and Kiesenwetter emerged in Vienna as patrons of music.[25] Meanwhile, at a humbler level, music was made to function as a defense against alienation through the initiation and extension of popular amateur singing groups (*Liedertafel, Männergesangvereine*) and indeed through the establishment of the piano as a fixture in bourgeois homes. The cult of the virtuoso performer was a kind of psychological projection of the age's anxieties and solutions onto privileged individuals: Paganini and Chopin achieved their greatest success in the Biedermeier age, and Liszt began his career in those decades; dancers Fanny Elssler and Marie Taglioni were among the first artists to marry into the high aristocracy; sopranos Jenny Lind and Henriette Sontag had huge followings; the salaries of theater directors and actors in Berlin in the 1820s and

1830s could compete with and surpass those of senior government officials.

For the rapidly expanding middle classes everyday life was the locus for applying romantic ideals in a rational, moderate fashion—under Enlightenment auspices, as it were. The imagery of Santa Claus and the coziness of the elaborate sociable Christmas were invented in the age of Biedermeier. Nonpolitical anxieties were relieved in good-natured drinking and feasting.[26] This was also the age of great chefs: Anthelme Brillat-Savarin (1755–1826), Antonin Carême (1784–1833), Grimod de la Reynière (1758–1838), Antoine Beauvilliers (1754–1817), as well as G.A. Escoffier, Alexis Sager, Montmirel, Riquette and others. A popular sentimental middle-brow music developed in the German-speaking areas. The waltz changed now from a dizzying, rapidly revolving dance with body contact into a sedate and elegant ritual, fit for stately ballrooms.[27] Analogously, the free romantic hairstyles, the extravagances of the Parisian *muscadins* and *merveilleux* were tamed into the Regency's balance of tightness and looseness (to use Anne Hollander's phrase)[28] and were replaced by a delicate historic nostalgia for the rococo: the cravat displaced the jabot. Fashion itself, whether male or female, may be seen as the application or even "industrialization" of high-romantic innovations.[29] The dandyism of England, as epitomized by Beau Brummel, was not an isolated phenomenon; in the Vienna of the 1820s the tailor Josef Gunkl was conspicuous for his aesthetic attitude toward clothing and for his ability to channel extravagant impulses in refined, orderly sartorial structures.

Personal hygiene was the outcome of an idyllist culture, home-oriented, disciplined, pious, and enlightened. (In 1826 at Grafenberg, Vincenz Pressnitz initiated the cold water cure.) Biedermeier culture was an age of hypochondria: that is, of the light chronic ailment produced or maintained by the imagination. It was also, at least as much as the century's second half, the age of spas and of walking tours. Swimming and bicycle riding became pastimes. The grand tour of the Alps ceased to be the property of the intense, lonely, and sublime poet and became the object of organized tourism. Imaginative experimenters were followed in the Alps by intellectual hedonists.[30] Experimental balloon flights were symptomatic not only of the search for knowledge and communication but also of the search for controlled adventure.

But adventure could be found closer to home. The emergence of the suburban residence could, according to contemporaries, supply everything needed and would "with a very small portion of the land attached . . . contain all that is essential to happiness, in the garden, park and demesne of the most extensive country residence."[31] The suburban architect promised in effect that a purely and highly individual experience could be owned by everybody, containing idyllic intimacy and broad equality, a compromise between utopianism and bureaucracy. The eminence of Brighton (as Bath was declining) had its own semantics, closely linked to the bourgeois changes in the romantic ideals and similar to suburbia. The semantics of Brighton seemed to imply that seawater and the emotions inspired by the ocean (infinity, danger, power) in moderate dosage could become convenient possessions. Brighton further illustrated how the principles of standard repetition and patterned reduction can be combined with elegance and classicist mannerism. (Versailles by contrast seemed to illustrate uniqueness, centrality and, yes, wholeness.)[32] The famous Apollosaal in Vienna (1810–1819) was like a Brighton pavilion for masses of bourgeois citizens: artificial grottos, groves, and arbors, and a huge circular dining hall with mythological pictures, statues, spouting fountains, Ionic pillars, niches, and mirrors. (As a matter of fact, the owner-entrepreneur, Sigmund Wolfsohn, had been born in London.)[33] Berlin had its own equivalent in the Kolosseum, a huge ballroom and amusement center.[34]

Wrapped around these events was Metternich's system, not the repressive ogre-like enclosure it was made out to be by partisan commentators, but rather a dialectical and sophisticated framework that could preserve stability by absorbing and particularly by expecting opposition from within and without. French commentators had intimated as early as 1845 that, ideally, Mörike and Heine need each other.[35] Can we then not ask whether the eclecticism of Victor Cousin and the moderation of Alexis de Tocqueville and François Guizot result from the political drift of Louis-Philippe's age or whether they are its guiding lights? Even the proliferation of spying after the Restoration can be seen as a disalienating factor, as if the mild pressures of the parental state were meant to do nothing more than achieve the warmth of *Zusammensein,* a boost for communitarian sensations. Imagine Kaiser Franz at the Congress of Vienna, titillated and good-natured, chuckling every morning as he pored over intelligence reports describing mostly the peccadilloes of his crowned colleagues—the sensational press with a circulation of one.[36] Conspiracies and secret societies (the domain of favorite and spoiled offspring)—Carbonari, Babouvists, Decembrists, Philhellenes, Masons—with their often theatrical and verbose agitation were the counterparts of this "friendly" and frantic spying. Jacob Talmon even maintains that the 1848 revolutions were an unsuccessful, downgraded version (a "caricature") of the great French Revolution, an observation that echoes Tocqueville.[37] If we are to believe Donald Charlton and George Boas, the invention of systems of "secular religions" in France (and, we can safely add, in the rest of Europe)—"ideologue," positivist, eclectic (Cousin), indeed even neo-Christian—created "secondary" paradigms, both multiplying and reducing a huge vision now fading into the past.[38] Socially, it was the age of mobility (the age of upstarts and parvenus) and yet one held together by bureaucratic systems and an increased respect for hierarchy. Despite appearances, the parts and the whole seemed to hold together much as a philosophical high romantic might have wished.

Given the period's productions, events, and changes that I have been enumerating almost at random (arts and furniture, the earliest signals of a common period structure, along with politics, have hardly been mentioned), it would be unfair to ignore the theoreticians of the Biedermeier or to dismiss their attempts to explore the coherent stucture and the philosophical motivations of the age. Two hypotheses that oppose their theories have to be rejected out of hand. The first limits the term *Biedermeier* to marginal occurrences, popular and commercial literature, and the like.[39] Of course, as Damáso Alonso once pointed out, the better and more significant a work of literary art is, the more likely it will be to transcend strict temporal limitations (*Faust, Don Quixote*), while a work of lesser value is more likely to be caught up in period stylistics.[40] But this proposition holds good, if it does, for any given historical period, and there is no reason to apply it solely to the 1820s: one might as well deny that George Eliot is a Victorian, and keep the term solely for Mrs. Gaskell, Sheridan Lefanu, and Charles Kingsley. The second hypothesis, that the Biedermeier is merely a trend inside a period, is equally untenable. The term itself, when it came to be applied to broad cultural phenomena (in art, in furniture, in fashion and social habits) was not perceived as an isolated current, rival to others. The writers whom we consider typically Biedermeier never regarded themselves as a group, nor did Mörike and Jeremias Gotthelf or Droste and Grillparzer collaborate. We are talking, therefore, at least about a genuine cultural aspect of a larger whole. This kind of broader interrelationship is a fully legitimate object of research.

Elfriede Neubuhr correctly suggests that the object to be examined is a *Grundgefühl*, that is, a general cultural intentionality or sociocultural prolepsis, rather than a movement.[41] This "basic feeling" cannot be simply labeled, nor should it; like most basic things it will not yield to rational analysis without an irreducible remainder. But there seem to be good reasons to strive for an approximate definition of this state and inclination, whether as a rational system of motives or as a general atmosphere.

The era after 1815 fully acknowledged the social and spiritual shock of the preceding age. A feeling of chaos prevailed and human existence was seen as endangered. The mobility of large masses of people (armies, refugees) over vast areas as well as the vertical mobility of equally large masses (meteoric ascents of low-born talents, precipitous drops of the loftiest personages) altered perspectives radically, while the collapse of regenerative hopes led to the resurgence on a large scale of feelings which, at the end of the previous century, had seemed the lot of only a handful of individuals: disenchantment with the universe, a general tired pessimism, doubt, *Weltschmerz*.[42] Challenging harmony no longer seemed a way of enriching and reinforcing it (as for Friedrich Schlegel)—harmony was now clutched with apprehension, it was both refuge and the site of resignation.[43] Even more generally, time seemed to be replaced by space as a dominant category: local landscapes, familiar objects, home and hearth, animals and plants, woods and gardens were fervently sought. Traditions themselves seemed to have spatial value, insofar as they had withstood time. Destiny and happiness, passion and luck seemed likewise captured in the dialectics of space and time. The elderly gained new attention and respect, and so did children—as those who best epitomized independence from the onslaught of time.[44] But over and above these rose feminine figures. Family relationships became central and positive in opposition to the earlier explosions of eros; "feminine sensitivity" pervaded writings and manners. In many ways, the writing of J. J. Bachofen (chiefly that of the 1840s and 1850s) with its passionate and fanciful description of gynocracy as the genuine state of early humanity epitomized underlying yearnings of the age. The maternal principle suddenly loomed behind the rational processes and behavioral modes of society and was identified with durability, patience, wisdom, and perhaps even eternity; rarely in Western history had the principle of female divinity been adumbrated as in these ages. (The Victorian age and the *Gründerzeit*, as we know, were to change all that.)

Proposals for combatting anxiety, chaos, and the undiscriminating pressure of time were, historically, at odds with one another and accounted for the internal contradictions of the age. But from a morphocultural vantage point these proposals seem almost equivalent: the search for new communities, defenses against uncertainty, the internalization of change.[45] They seem to fall roughly under five headings. The first is the grand order of empire and universal harmony (mostly in Christian terms, though sometimes with occult or agnostic coloration). Continuity is the great catchword for Joseph von Görres, Adam Müller or Friedrich von Gentz, as it had been for Edmund Burke, and as it was for Joseph de Maistre and the Vicomte de Bonald. The second heading is revolutionary and utopian schemes which chose slightly smaller frameworks: the nation that must arise from a centuries-long sleep, the class that must rearrange the priorities of social order, the minority that must be emancipated and will cure the sick body politic. Social revolt and improvement were advocated rather than the absolutely sweeping metamorphoses of Saint-Just's constitutional projects and their poetic counterparts in Blake and Hölderlin. The revival of one national group (in Italy, Bohemia, Poland, and so on) became a feasible and acceptable alternative to global reform. Radical as these changes may be in practical terms, they are nothing but limited versions of Eden, quite similar to the attempts to restore a specific historical past (the Middle Ages or the good old prerevolutionary times) reclaimed by the conservatives in a symmetrical move. What they all have in common is a localizing of regeneration inside limits that can be grasped and handled. Pragmatism replaced idealism.

The third (and perhaps broadest) heading is stability itself as the source of stability. The middle class as a whole—rural and urban, petty bourgeoisie and financial aristocracy, intellectuals, civil servants, and entrepreneurs—was deemed more than sufficient to repulse change and fear. Here were initiative and progress rooted, here reverence and homeliness; parts of the middle class might be endangered, but not the whole. Idyllic values could be depended upon to survive in one form or another here, like a universe within a universe. The Biedermeier, it was often said, is middle-class mentality itself—smug, timorous, quaint, wishful, and selfish.[46] The least one should add is that beauty and education also figured largely in this alternative order. The many aristocratic writers who chose bourgeois aliases testify to the confidence in the bourgeois order (Lenau, Anastasius Grün, Friedrich Halm, and others). Dignified courtesy, philosophical reserve, moral earnestness, humility toward the real, and cautious political reformism were all part of the attractiveness of this type of order.

The fourth is empiricism and specialization. Although the rationalism of the Enlightenment came to fruition in metaphysical idealism, the empirical strain seems to have lost its cultural significance; even in the exact sciences the speculation on magnetism and electricity, the work of Franz von Baader, Lorenz Oken, F. A. Mesmer, and P. J. G. Cabanis, was in the foreground. Serious investigators, such as Count Berthollet, Marquis Laplace, and Luigi Galvani were much given to speculation on affinity and analogy. After 1815 there was a clear return to the specialized and exact kind of knowledge needed not only in the technical fields but also in historical and philological areas.[47] Diversity and precision: in them the present seemed to be able to ignore the past and the future. Gathering and sheltering (*sammeln und hegen*) have been proclaimed by many as the quintessential activities of the Biedermeier.[48] Although these may be associated with the middle-class ethos, it is even more appropriate to regard them as part of the empiricist impulse. In literature as in life, flowerbeds, green houses, rock collections, gardens and tillages, libraries and museums expose the urge toward objective knowledge, factual precision, and pragmatism.

Finally, the fifth heading expresses better than the others a key concern of the age: the dialectic of the individual. The forms of community begin to include, oddly, individuals as the arena of diverse and conflicting emotions and ideas. There is no question that in the Biedermeier age human personality in all its privacy, idiosyncrasy, and melancholy specialization (rebellious, hypochondriac, introspective) figured at least as prominently as in the comprehensive subjectivity of the romantic writers. But there was a much more painful awareness of the manner in which human personality functioned, and there was much doubt as to its connections with the outer world (real or desired). The titans, the overwhelming personalities, disappeared and were replaced by the crotchety and the assertive. The cult of the oversized individual and the hope of salvation in the individual mind (in Vigny, for instance) were connected with the shrinking role of the imagination.

The consciousness of Wordsworth's *Prelude* could well represent the world mind; not so the arrogant and sickly individuals who populate the pages written in the 1830s. The individual could be the place of ultimate retreat and security or the place for revolt and conquest. The individual mind became the widest framework for the possible and the desirable. It was the source of irony, parody, and the grotesque.

And it was in the individual that the deepest underlying polarity of the age rested: reality versus the ideal. The "Hamletian" inability to act, if indeed it characterized the age, was based mostly on the rich variety of "actors" inside the individual soul: a community in disarray. Perhaps this was an inability to decide rather than an inability to act; explosive, arbitrary action occurred with no firm connection to previous judgments, rationalizations, or even feelings. Fitful, impulsive, capricious heroes were frequent; they brooded a lot over the right way, weighed carefully the strengths and the weaknesses of a moral position and then, on the spur of the moment, decided to act in an almost casual manner, like autonomous agents entirely at liberty. The explanation is the duality between nature and the imagination, the kind of duality that the whole-oriented high romantics had fought so hard to unmake. But a word of caution here: the full results of the break are seen much later. For those living and writing during the Biedermeier age, the impression that a tenuous unity still held was important and quite effective in counterbalancing the conflict between action and imagination.

SENGLE and his predecessors constructed a model that reflects quite adequately the cultural-historical realities of the period. Nevertheless, a number of important questions are raised rather than answered by their work. Are the different features or "systems of order" mentioned above connected to one another? And if they are, where can this system be placed? How much reality does it have? Briefly, on what is the Biedermeier founded? Equally important, especially from a comparatist point of view, is whether there is an equivalent of this German (or Central European) period structure to be found elsewhere in Europe. Can it be thus validated by historical and cultural events occurring simultaneously in other parts of the continent? Are there similarities to the literary Biedermeier in the rest of European literature?

This book is devoted to the investigation of these and related topics.

Are there specific genres, tropes, themes, or intellectual motifs that cut across national literatures and that can be shown to have a specific connection with the configuration of the Biedermeier? Can we pull together the strands of the peculiarly neglected English literature of the 1820s and 1830s so that a coherent and significant *figura* results? Does an understanding of the German Biedermeier help? Why does French romanticism start twice? How can we explain the fact that a literature that was leading Europe in ideas and literary experiment throughout the later eighteenth century suddenly seems to stop short in its tracks and resort to Mme. de Staël actually to *import* its post-1815 romanticism? When talking about Eastern and Southern European literatures, is the concept of "telescoping" of any service? In other words, do we witness in some of these literatures a hastened development and even a chronological coincidence of phases which are slow and successive in (North-) Western Europe?

Some of these questions will be answered in the following chapters, but the first two must be approached immediately. To do so, I would like to put the subject in historical perspective. Some basic facts about romanticism, as well as the scholarly debate that has gradually delineated them, have to be recalled.

THE MODERN critical view of romanticism is founded on the articles of René Wellek. The severe and moralistic rejection of romanticism by Irving Babbitt and nineteenth-century French critics who were his mentors is no longer taken into consideration, although many of their fulminations still affect us, and his influence on the New Critics' original distaste for romanticism is still visible. (It took a while for John Crowe Ransom, Allen Tate, W. K. Wimsatt, and Cleanth Brooks to change their opinions, and they never did completely. In England F. R. Leavis and his school and in France a long line of neoclassic critics were reserved toward romanticism.) Fritz Strich's ideal typological construction of romanticism, though sympathetic, is also forgotten now; similarly Paul van Tieghem's impressive synthesis ceased to be influential, even though his three bookish categories ("les éléments intérieurs," "les éléments extérieurs," and "l'art littéraire") may be said to reappear, transfigured, in Wellek's three chief romantic features: nature, imagination, and symbol. The German tradition of *Geistesgeschichte* and the French tradition of historical positivism had themselves become unproductive. The venerable speculative line of "permanent" romanticism alternating with a "permanent" classicism seemed even more compromised. With the exception of Albert Béguin, Mario Praz alone among comparatist scholars appears to have survived intact the wholesale dismissal of the older theories of romanticism, at least in his *motif* analyses: Medusan beauty, satanic glory, vampirism, and femmes fatales.[49]

Wellek's founding gesture was the refutation of Arthur Lovejoy's nominalist theory, which had rejected the possibility of a unified romanticism. Wellek chose a small number of key features, showed how they recur in a large number of authors, and explained how other features could be subordinated to them. In the thirty years that have passed since, comparative and general theories of romanticism have refined and enriched Wellek's views rather than disproved them. Henry Remak and Geoffrey Hartman, Northrop Frye and Harold Bloom all accepted Wellek's basic insight and strove mostly to add to the features, clarify the priorities, and describe the organization of the system.[50] Even the impulses coming from Geneva and New Haven aspired first to explain romanticism as a closely knit bundle of features, an individual organism with a will of its own. However, they also energetically emphasized the interplay of the conscious and the subconscious and examined the psychological and logical mechanisms of romanticism. The process of romanticism was thus internalized.

The most comprehensive statement offered in this phase of the critical debate is found in M. H. Abrams's *Natural Supernaturalism*. Better than other critics, Abrams summarized romanticism as *plot*, thus taking a great step forward in the organization of our knowledge of romanticism. Abrams's central thesis was that romanticism was engendered by the secularization of certain theological concepts: primarily, the biblical pattern of Eden-Fall-Redemption is conceptualized as the secular dialectic of subject-object and ego-non-ego.[51] He also underscored the explosive visionary force of romantic philosophy and literature, based on eschatological millenarian traditions and the immediate revolutionary impact of historical change at the end of the eighteenth century. The identification between mind and outer universe is the great redeeming aim of the romantics, Abrams explains; the formal circularity (pp. 79, 193, 185) of such a prototypical work as Wordsworth's *Prelude* is the necessary consequence of the circularity of the transcendent structure of the "plot" itself. Return is progression (p. 261); vision triumphs over optics (pp. 366, 377). The growing mind of the poet not only stands for, but *is* the universal mind (p. 127). The unifying framework created by Abrams accommodates many of the English romantics, key figures of German romanticism (Novalis, Hölderlin, and others), and the most important post-Kantian philosophers (pp. 228, 229, 251). It fits Friedrich Schlegel's dictum that the revolutionary wish to achieve the divine realm on earth is the key to any progress.

It is interesting to note that a number of subsequent investigations seem to confirm and complete the Abramsian theory, not so much by design, I believe, as by the inherent logic of their argument. Michael Cooke, approaching the romantic experience from different directions, discovered that the romantic text is always instituted by an "act of inclusion": feminine and masculine, elegy, prophecy and satire, spontaneity and form, each and all tend toward a higher level of inclusiveness. "Feminine" for instance turns out to mean unity or integrity—not abandonment of "male values," as Babbitt had suspected uneasily, but genuine integration—hence the lofty impossibility of this aspiration.[52] Cooke removed to a higher, almost ineffable level, that regenerative wholeness which other scholars had sought to find in things more accessible to the immediate vision. Marshall Brown seemed dissatisfied with simple circularity as an emblem for the German romantics and proposed the search for the center, and later parabolic and elliptic shapes as more suitable representative images. The ellipse is important because it has two centers and yet is unified in a single curve, thus expressing the romantic's recognition of the antithetical nature of reality. Brown himself quoted Baader and others to the effect that circular centrality is merely the token of the profoundly irrational organicism of nature.[53] I tend to see these descriptions as refined and more subtle definitions of that all-embracing unity recognized by Abrams and his predecessors as the summit of romantic experience. When Paul de Man compared texts by Rousseau, Hölderlin, and Wordsworth, he observed: "Each of these texts describes the passage from a certain type of nature, earthly and material, to another nature which could be called mental and celestial, although the 'Heaven' referred to is devoid of specific theological connotations."[54] De Man's essays on romanticism are imposing when they are read in conjunction with the prevailing romantic paradigm. Even Thomas MacFarland's theory of fragmentation and ruin ("disaparaction") as the core of romanticism—which has perhaps more chances than all others to develop, in time, a new momentum for romantic studies—can be connected to that paradigm.[55] MacFarland is perfectly aware of the philosophical debate on part and whole (in our century revived by Husserl and his followers), and he admits that the intense sense of incompleteness in Wordsworth and Coleridge follows directly from the intensity of their vision of universal wholeness and oneness. MacFarland's originality in this respect lies chiefly in his choice of access to the basic "paradigmatic" truth.

It is therefore quite fair to choose Abrams's view as the focus of present-day research and as representing a kind of consensus. This choice is due to Abrams's comprehensiveness and balance, not necessarily to precedence. As far back as 1962 Geoffrey Hartman, for instance, admirably defined the *Ancient Mariner* as "the soul's birth to the sense of separate (and segregated being)" and said: "Coleridge evokes the travail of passing through self-consciousness to imagination"; in the same article the dialectics of innocence and self-consciousness is fully delineated.[56] E. D. Hirsch had published a book-length study on parallels between Wordsworth and Schelling in 1960[57]—indeed even Béguin, if read closely, will reveal sentences such as: "Les penseurs romantiques . . . chercheront à expliquer le processus même du devenir cosmique comme la voie du retour à l'unité perdue, et recourront, pour y parvenir, à des mythes qui tous s'inspirent de l'idée de la chute," or "La réintegration s'opérera le jour où la langue du rêve retrouvera son intégrité première."[58] Nevertheless Abrams's theory remains the most complete and intellectually satisfying explanatory *system*. It goes without saying that, conversely, any doubts and questionings will have to be addressed not only to his theory but to all those with which it is solidary. There is no doubt that such questions must be raised.

In illustrating his theory, Abrams discusses chiefly Blake, Coleridge, Wordsworth, and Shelley, occasionally Keats, and almost never Byron and Scott. His findings, on the whole, apply well to German and English literature, but they do not seem to account for the romanticism of French, Italian, or Eastern European literatures. There is also some difficulty in connecting this close and intense world to Victorianism; the change seems abrupt, the continuity servile, not filial. What is gained in coherence is lost in amplitude. The sharper focus outlines a self-contained, intelligible, but rather limited area. In the long run we seem in danger of foregoing the gains of the reaction

against Lovejoy and (unless we want to banish from the romantic field
Pushkin, Alessandro Manzoni, Victor Hugo, Sir Walter Scott, and
Joseph von Eichendorff) being thrust back to the nominalist concep-
tion of multiple romanticisms—regional, national, and temporal.

Another important group of questions has to do with the ontological level at which romanticism is placed: We may ask *where* is romanticism before even asking *what* is romanticism. Older definitions—and
I would not entirely exclude Wellek's from these—tended to place romanticism in an area of rationally manipulated formal devices: motifs,
themes, aesthetic doctrines, and philosophical speculations. When
Swiss and American critics suggested that romanticism was located on
a deeper level, the change was seen as a progressive insight: it provided connections with the subconscious, proximity to the mainsprings
of literary creation, and emphasis on individual consciousness.
Abrams's book, not less than the writings of Bloom or Hartman,
shows how the new locus of romanticism can threaten to isolate the
movement, to turn it into a perfect mandala, a secondary reality—autonomous, intelligible, but in a sense lifeless and separated from the
pressures of history and the surrounding culture. The logical fallacy is
that patterns of the individual psyche are projected onto social processes; collective movements are treated as if they were supported by
the unity of an integrated personal mind. It is a metaphorical procedure not unlike those used by the romantics themselves, a contamination of the epistemological model by the object of research. I am not
opposed to this time-honored form of empathy, provided it is recognized for what it is and does not claim to be anything else: metaphorical procedure and adroit dialectical substitution in the hope of better
understanding.

Romantic theoreticians have to ask themselves how to preserve the
gains of Béguin, Bloom, Abrams, and the others, and at the same time
save the system from disintegrating again and from drifting into areas
inaccessible to immediate analysis or intuitive grasp. Can we devise a
machinery that will connect the delicate inner Abramsian structure
with the outer spheres of the romantic world? The answer to this
question is blended with the answer to the question on the locus of romanticism. And both answers will provide a kind of rough floor plan of
the European Biedermeier.

LET US LOOK at the cultural and historical realities. Abrams's paradigm speaks about a poetry that emerges in the mid and later 1790s.

Few would deny that this poetry represents, among other things, an attempt to come to terms with the universe in a specific way. This poetry is informed by a coherent system of values and attitudes that was brought into being by a series of reactions to the neoclassicist Enlightenment. Once set up, this system defined itself explosively as the almost symmetrical opposition to its predecessor and sire. The somewhat arbitrary figure of preromanticism can be best understood as a series of accretions, of complementary or opposing features grafted onto the predominant eighteenth-century model even while modifying it.[59] Thomas Gray, for instance, could opt for the graveyard as a topic and for melancholy as a psychological environment even while otherwise adhering to classicist stylistics and to standards of reason and morality that would be alien to any romantic. Joseph Addison lived within the world of propriety and rationalism but could allow himself to respond enthusiastically to folk ballads, could try to understand the sublime and to enjoy freer landscape gardening. Diderot's devotion to Enlightenment ideals is undoubted, but he could find more room for imagination and sensibility than the traditional classicist. Montesquieu could roam from Formosa to the land of the Incas to Malabar and be tolerant and generous in his choice of examples and in their interpretation. But not for a second was there doubt as to the firmness of the center that he held: the Roman and Greek experience remained exemplary; classical facts and laws were the standards by which to measure the spirit of all other laws, old or new, near or far. Once all these qualifying features or ingredients had emerged, the neoclassicist prop could be discarded abruptly and the claim to a new type of relationship with reality by a new kind of "human character" could ring out loud and clear.

I have introduced here the concept of "human model." I regard "human models" and "societal models" as key factors in the self-definition of human groups, such as generations and societies, or of historical epochs. Human and societal models may be said to embody values and attitudes; they are ideal human types whose presence can be ascertained empirically by their frequency in literary and other kinds of discourse. They serve as standards for the social aspirations of large or decisive segments of society and in turn shape not only the cultural manifestations (painting, music, religiosity) of a social group but, I would contend, other characteristics as well (manners, politics, mentalities, economic behavior).[60] As Raymond Williams correctly, and slightly critically, observes: " 'correspondence' and 'homology' can be seen as forms of the 'typical': crystallizations in superficially unrelated fields, of a social process which is nowhere fully represented but which is specifically present, in determinate forms, in a range of different works and activities."[61] Or, to quote Frederic Jameson (enlarging on Theodor Adorno), "the language of causality gives way to that of analogy or homology, or parallelism. Now the construction of the microcosm, of the cultural continuum—whether it be the formed history of costume or of religious movements, the fate of stylistic convention or the rise and fall of epistemology as a philosophical issue—will include the analogy with the socio-economic macrocosm or infrastructure as an implied comparison in its very structure."[62] Obviously, such comparisons always work both ways. "Human models" often function as implied heroes as well as implied readers or as the persona chosen by the author—and thus become foci in literary works and points of connection with the realities of the historical environment. As a kind of macroimage, human and societal models belong in a class with "world images" and similar condensations of mental experience. We do not know very well how these images emerge and develop, and we know only a little more about how they interact with human reality. Nevertheless, their mental reality is solid. My key contention here is that romanticism is founded in one of these images and that its development is carried by this image. Romanticism is the unfolding of the social and cultural implications and potentialities implicit in the large human model that had been gradually constituted during the eighteenth century.

If this working hypothesis is accepted, we can begin to rearrange our information about the whole period. We can easily admit the logical difference between a phase where a model is introduced and one where the model is adapted. In the first, we would expect the paradigm to be pure and clear, as well as to stand in strong and defiant opposition to the surrounding sociocultural materials, with explosive effects. Logically, again, we could expect from a subsequent phase greater variety, a bending of the model to accommodate existing situations and needs, and ultimately a deformation. We can also expect that a period of complex build-up will have preceded these two phases.

The process delineated by Abrams is thus not unitary and singular, but is better described as a bundle of convergent lines. Wilhelm Dilthey defines romanticism as: "Eine grenzlose Energie des Willens zum Ideal und zur Freude, ungeheure Forderungen an die Ordnun-

gen der Gesellschaft, ja an die der Natur selbst, Sehnsucht an unend-
liche Fernen und nach unerhörten Glückszuständen."[63] And Harold
Bloom aptly says that "the program of Romanticism ... demands
something more than a natural man to carry it through. Enlarged and
more numerous senses are necessary, an enormous virtue of Romantic
poetry clearly being that it not only demands such expansion but
begins to make it possible, or at least attempts to do so."[64] The separate but convergent lines are the different accretions mentioned above
which seem "preromantic" but do not actually disturb too seriously
the cultural system into which they are admitted. Nature is a subject of
close scrutiny by James Thomson not less than by Shelley. But in the
first the sentiment of nature is an isolated object, not solidary with the
scrutinizing mentality; in the second it is intimately fused with the
mode of experience itself and cannot be separated from it. Lessing can
resort (in *Nathan der Weise*) to figures borrowed from a remote age
and time, but the intense pathos of the pilgrim figure of René or
Childe Harold (absorbed in their own farness) is missing. There are
perhaps several reasons for this kind of difference, but the chief is that
one element is isolated, thus lacking the support of an integrated
model. Romanticism may be said to snap into existence as soon as most
of the changing strands are in place.

The common denominator of all these changes is expansion. Expansion in space: the exoticism of the Alps and of Scotland, of the remote North as well as of the Mediterranean world, of the Balkans and
the Middle East, even of North America and Polynesia are added as
poetic and narrative space to the typical areas of the Ile de France and
southern England. Expansion in time: the Middle Ages become accessible to sensibility, along with the times of the primitive past and of
early Christianity (instead of the immediate present and abstract antiquity). Expansion in learning: the canon is enriched by Shakespeare and
the ballads, by the romance epic tradition, by a fake Ossian or a real
Nibelungenlied, by Norse sagas and Eastern European folklore. Expansion in society: the psychology of old age and early childhood become poetic topics in their own right; femininity expands into pre-
viously male themes; marginal states of mind are included—morbidity,
insanity, or at least the "nocturnal sides" round off the image; poverty
and despair are no longer shunned. Expansion of the faculties: reason
and rationality have to be completed by imagination, sensibility, instinct, and dream. The sublime is an expansion of the beautiful; open

forms and experiments expand the limits of the traditional genres, without always negating them. The universal clockmaker is replaced by the wild pantheistic spirit of clouds and forests.

In a word, the human model of romanticism is consciousness as totality. For regenerated mankind, the paradisial state is one of integrality and universality. It is, to adopt McFarland's phrase, a "holocleric" state.[65] The Abramsian paradise is the romantic conscience. The romantic paradigm is wholeness recaptured in its purity. In this respect there is actually more agreement among the best critics than one would expect. Béguin, far from "reducing" romanticism to dream-life and the nocturnal half of life as is assumed by those who confuse the object of the investigation with its results, is perfectly aware of the manner in which these themes blend with the broader ones. He says, "Mais il faut se garder de voir dans les philosophes de la Nature des apologistes des côtés nocturnes de la vie, aux dépens de l'activité consciente. Le mythe de l'Unité perdue est aussi le mythe de l'Unité retrouvée."[66] Romantic concepts such as universal sympathy, magic, astrology, essential analogy, imagination, symbolism, dynamism are attempts to grasp and describe unity. Béguin thinks that J. J. Wagner's theory of the Golden Age is an expression of high romanticism, and he explains that for Wagner the epitome of development is a return to original perfection.[67] The reference to Hamann is like an epigraph: "Hamann se représente l'état de nos ancêtres aux premiers temps comme un profond sommeil alternant avec des danses 'vertigineuses'; longtemps immobiles 'dans le silence de l'étonnement et de la méditation' ils ouvraient soudain la bouche pour 'des discours ailés'."[68] Such is this totality that, for Béguin, it has to include death. The Schlegels' views on irony are based on the same concept of paradisial totality. Indeed, it is important to remind ourselves that any true unity or completeness is not "merely" fullness of Being, that void and nothingness are its necessary parts. Dieter Arendt thinks of chaotic nothingness as the mirror-image of totality. But it would probably be more accurate, from the point of view of a continuing expansion, to speak of nothingness as a necessary completion of total unity.[69] It is in fact precisely the kind of expansion that Babbitt already had noted—and deplored. It is also, I believe, what the older critics had in mind when they took "infinity" as the emblem of quintessential romanticism.[70] If nowadays we tend to shy away from the term *infinity*, it is out of disagreement but even more out of philosophical scruple; we are, as post-

Husserlians, better aware of the dialectics of wholeness and part. Most emphatic is McFarland, who breaks down infinity into the yearning for wholeness (as a kind of Platonic vision) and the fragmentary incompleteness of the results; the door is then open to a reading of "disaparactive modes" as the best possible expression of wholeness. McFarland himself provides a comment on Crabb Robinson's statement: "Most intensely did I rejoice at the Counter Revolution. I had also rejoiced when a boy at the Revolution, and I am ashamed of neither statement"[71]—the counterpart in politics of the dialectical completeness of Schlegelian irony. For this manner of thinking we can find a robust, early philosophical underpinning in Dilthey's *Das Erlebnis und die Dichtung*. Dilthey observed that the interaction or unity between poetry and *Naturanschauung* (the perception of nature) as well as the dialectics of unification between subject and object give the peculiar romantic coloring to the period and concluded: "Dieser Wechsel vermöge dessen das ganz voneinander Abstehende wie Schatten ineinander verfliesst, liegt in der Natur dieser Konzeptionen," adding: "Ganz deutlich ist nur die negative Erkenntnis, dass die Welt, wie wir sie nicht anders als nach Analogie unseres Ich aufzufassen vermögen, nicht aus der Vernunft, als dem Grundcharakter desselben erklärt werden könne, sondern aus einer gärenden Tiefe dieses Ich, welche, uns selber Geheimnis, in Wille, Gemüt oder Einbildungskraft mindestens ebenso primär hervorbreche."[72]

THIS CORE of the romantic model and purest form—the possible-impossible expansion of the self to a seamless identification with the universe—is unstable and explosive. Harold Bloom says that "the man prophesied by the Romantics is a central man," who seems always in the process of being begotten and who has not "fleshed out his prophecy."[73] The paradisial recovery of unity, the obliteration of analytical division, cannot be maintained long in purity, not even as an impression or as an aim. The brew does not age well, not because it is too weak, but because it is too strong. The almost mystical intensity of core romanticism cannot survive long. The model is too ambiticusly designed. This explains why early death becomes almost a norm.[74] Core romanticism results in suicide, misadventure, disease, drugs, madness, and the guillotine—as exemplified by Kleist and Shelley, Byron and Novalis, Keats and Hölderlin, and Saint-Just—or alternatively deterioration and silence. The maximum expansion of human potential in space, time, psychological reach, and depth proved unfeasible, at least in the sense of leading to a regenerated humanity. The transcendence of human limitations that would result in the flowering of an angelic-paradisial state simply could not last.

For those romantics who did not disappear, disappointment and attempts at accommodation went hand in hand after the great spiritual-revolutionary upsurge failed to deliver what it had promised. An adequate analogy to the consequences is provided, I believe, by Schelling—one of the heroes of the movement—when he theorized about the nature of philosophy. Schelling believed that philosophy was the substitute for, or the equivalent of, a mystical experience—a jump into Being, which is a break with "mechanical philosophizing," a grasp of (or for) the Absolute, with neither a demonstrative nor a psychological basis, but rather an experience of transcendent wholeness.[75] Schelling and others found that poetry as well as religion were based on a kind of abrupt revelation.[76] Schelling also admitted (at least by being the author of a vast philosophical *oeuvre*) that there must come a subsequent phase of explanation and rationalization of this sudden illumination. Emil Staiger explains how the melancholy of the later Schelling is based on an imaginative play with facts which try to recast reality in small intelligible shapes, but in which the visionary gleam is extinguished.[77]

By analogy we can say that the sudden romantic synthesis is "explained" and thus brought down to earth; the sheer energy of the romantic breakthrough is captured and tamed in a long phase of late romanticism that has a configuration of its own. High romanticism was a way of relating to reality, based on an expansionist human model and its changes. This model was imperfect and developed incompletely as long as its features relied on other models and were mixed with them. It briefly reached a revolutionary and mystical moment of maximum expansion when transfiguration into organic totality seemed achieved. But this moment was followed by a longer period of disappointment and domestication. The original vision having failed, the thought occurred that it might be repaired, if only it could be damaged. Some limiting handicap had to be introduced to hamper the identification with reality, which can only destroy, not build up that radiant, perfect world in which nature and conscience were supposed to fuse. Before the romantic model disappeared into the strictly polarized field of Victorian mentality (realism versus ethereal fantasy, satire versus melo-

drama, didactic utilitarianism versus cynical aestheticism, science versus religion) it passed through a phase (much like the German Biedermeier) in which it lost some of its original coherence, unity, and
intensity, but not its basic shape; the second romanticism, the tamed
romanticism, did not break its links with the revolutionary spiritual
movement of the first; it continued, expanded, diversified its core; it
became a weaker and relativized romanticism.

The map of this development was sketched by Morse Peckham,
when he distinguished between "positive" and "negative" romanticism.[78] Peckham's first theory extended unduly the boundaries of
"positive" romanticism, swallowing up the whole of the nineteenth
century; it also failed to disclose the deeper motivations of romantic
"negativism," which we certainly should not debase to the status of
whimsical pugnacity as Peckham did. In spite of some serious drawbacks (and of unsatisfactory literary illustration) Peckham's insights
into the dynamics of romanticism were sound: there is a two-step evolution; the first phase is based on strong, radical tensions, the second
on accommodation.[79] The two are closely connected. But we must go
further and examine how this later romanticism constituted itself out
of a series of departures and adaptations from the short, central, explosive events of pure romanticism.

We can say that the Biedermeier (or later romanticism) was the
secularization of a secularization. The energetic and concentrated
spurt of high romanticism, the new human model of all-embracing,
total renewal (which, according to Abrams, was the secularization of
the Christian plot), was soon lowered into the realm of the possible.
An extreme way of putting it is, that in the long run, core romanticism
could only be a process of decline and melancholy, because the pure
paradigm was unattainable. Romanticism must become silence—or accommodation. Any practical romanticism is a late romanticism. In a
sense, we recognize here an instance of the distinction between *le mys-
tique* and *le poétique,* as set up by Péguy and Simone Weil: the ideal is
always demeaned in capture and compromise. Raymond Williams, in
an intelligent but curiously tortured argument, contended that the
concept of language as creation and activity (in Vico, Herder, and
Humboldt) was somehow debased into quasi-social forms: "either the
notion, based on an abstract version of the folk mind or the (historical)
collective consciousness; or the collective spirit . . . or persuasively, the
individual."[80] But in Abrams's terms, which we have been using all

along, we might say that the fall-redemption issue is transferred from a diachronic to a synchronic level and thus turned into a practical and soluble problem. Blake and Novalis had envisaged nothing less than total cosmic revolution; Adam Mickiewicz or Sandor Petöfi or Manzoni struggled for national revival; Heine or Thomas Carlyle (in *The Signs of the Times* or *Chartism*) declared for social reform. Charles Fourier consciously advised his followers to rediscover primitive happiness but adapt it to the conditions of modernity. The harmony and inclusiveness of high-romanticism had been total, and without exception it had been a macroharmony. In the Biedermeier, smaller, sectional societies are intended—nationalism, radicalism, socialism, later racialism—microharmonies all of them, blueprints for feasible human change. If the paradigm is to be applied on a reduced scale, fitted inside human history, then very much depends on its starting point. This point could well be, and very often was, the Middle Ages (for conservatives) but it could also be Ancient Greece, or even Happy Polynesia. In all cases, however, the high-romantic paradigm is reduced to human scale: the stages are the same, but the events to which they are applied are particular, not general. The scope of the visionary plot can be further diminished from one country and one social class to one corner of the earth, perhaps to one family. As a result, the idyllic domesticity so characteristic of the Biedermeier appears. The ultimate avenue of reduction and retreat is inside the individual. The locus of order, the place of paradigmatic regeneration, the hope for redemption can only be found in the human psyche. The all-embracing conscience of Wordsworth and Hegel, of Blake and Hölderlin, now is turned into the proud and gloomy egotism of Vigny and Lenau or the amiable, self-preoccupied ratiocination of Musset and Lamb; even more often, the absolute soul is replaced by the adventurous individual, the hero of Dumas *père* and Bulwer-Lytton. Friedrich Schlegel's "ego" had been the carrier of "Transzendentalpoesie"; after 1815 the local subjectivism of Mörike or Heine replaces it.[81]

The common denominator for all these reductions is history, the divinity of later romanticism; capturing the past, it promised, would guarantee the future. The return to a regenerated and paradisial state is interpreted as the return to a specific historical moment. National revival, social reform, conservative restoration are all historical in nature. The organic society of tradition (medieval and ancien régime) and the liberal counterorder of progress are equally historical. They are equally reductive when placed against the huge epistemological harmonies of the preceding generation. Fritz Strich is right in observing that the historicism of a (high) romantic poet is one which identifies conscience with the "real intentions" of the historical spirit and sets out to implement those intentions, unhobbled, in poetry. "Diese spezifische romantische Auffassung der historischen Dichtung unterscheidet sich noch weit von jener spätern, welche den Geist der Geschichte in seiner historischen Wirklichkeit offenbar machen wollte und sich an diese gerade gebunden fühlte."[82] Both the later historicism and the later individualism are matters of a lessened harmony and of a pragmatic vision stripped of ambitions.

The second large avenue of retreat from the regenerative and totalizing vision of romanticism is separation of the parts, loosening up of the integrative unity (*Auflockerung*). In Christian Dietrich Grabbe's *Don Juan und Faust* (IV, 3) one character remarks that God has fallen into pieces and that the heavens are the shards, while love, language, religion, and melancholy are merely the memories of a lost unity. This is in fact a fair description of the Biedermeier attitude toward the lost romantic vision. The separation and loosening up can be noticed first in the attitude toward reason. For Coleridge, as for Schelling or Novalis, reason was not something to be rejected, but to be replaced by or integrated in a larger or higher whole. For the later romantics, by contrast, the oppositions reassert themselves and are often rhetorically proclaimed (for example, in Eastern European literatures): reason against intuition, reason against feeling, Victor Hugo's opposition of book and cathedral ("ceci tuera cela"—this one will slay the other—in *Notre Dame de Paris*). Similarly, and more profoundly, the function of the imagination is treated with some suspicion. The definitive fusion of imagination and nature which had been for Blake, Wordsworth, and Coleridge a supreme aim, seems now to fade into the distance. The separation into a level of natural (or social) reality opposed to a level of imagination becomes more and more obvious. Later romanticism grows under the sign of E. T. A. Hoffmann, it draws inspiration from Keats or Vigny. When efforts have to be made to secure a function for the imagination inside—and somehow auxiliary to—reality, it is obvious that the supreme synthesis has lost its chance of success. In effect, nature and culture are separated again, as they had been fifty years before, although each is now marked by the fiery memory of Shelley's Montblanc. "While Wordsworth believed that the Romantic mind and Romantic nature could interfuse and marry even at the heights, Victorian Romantics . . . seem to have been interested in a less lonely, more literal marriage" one critic observed.[83] He also noted that Scott had already decided that Waverley must live and marry in the Lowlands—society flourishes far from intensity.

These separations meet us everywhere. Socially, of course, we recognize them in the vast migrations of the age and in the awakening of class consciousness. The growth of national literary, artistic, musical, and intellectual schools is one of the consequences: from Catalan to *Plattdeutsch.* In a more specific way, the poet (who was for Shelley, the "unacknowledged legislator," and for Schiller, humane above all others as one who gathers mankind's experience) becomes the defiant leader of a minority, the leader of the opposition. For Chateaubriand, the exceptional character (René) lacks the satanic defiance that only a few years later the Byronic heroes displayed.[84] The enjoyment of both revolution and counterrevolution is replaced by an either-or, even when the alternatives have analogous deep structures. Hyperbole becomes an isolated figure, a furious proclamation—it is no longer the unifying experience of the sublime. Literary schizophrenia will make strange bedfellows: sensationalism and moral preaching go hand in hand in Gotthelf, Thomas De Quincey, Hugo, even Gogol, while in Ferdinand Raimund the most incongruous pieces are puzzled together. Friedrich Rückert is a master of technical virtuosity and of variations upon a given theme. Fragmentation itself is no longer the expression of totality but, in Lamb or Büchner, a gesture of acceptance, of disappointment, even of almost perverse enjoyment. The change from a single to a double center (ellipsis) as described by Marshall Brown is a similar fragmentation. Prophetic vision may well be replaced by psychological speculation: the Ancient Mariner reappears at the end of *Pan Tadeusz* only to have his life thoroughly explained. A frequent mechanism of disintegration is the following. The more remote areas of experience are the first to break loose from the whole to which they had been appended and claim autonomous attention. The praise of the prostitute, of which Babbitt complains, is a topos of sorts:[85] it appears almost by chance when a central area in which contrary virtues were fused loses touch with this particular and more remote exemplification of the paradisial conversion of vice into virtue. Similar effects appear in the age of Biedermeier and later in the century when morbidity seems to become important. De Quincey's *On*

Murder and Barbey's stories offer abundant examples of this effect. Similarly, romantic expansion in time incorporates nostalgia from the past; in later literary works nostalgia occurs in isolation, without the supportive justification of a general extension of consciousness to cover all temporality. Even more frequent is moralism turned loose. In their heyday, Blake and Wordsworth, as well as Coleridge, had tried earnestly to turn the ethical into the flesh and blood of a higher, all-embracing comprehension, to make morality a function as natural and immediate as breathing, to dispense with norms and prescriptions. The relaxation of the later romantics and their fragmentary mode makes them resort again to formalization and to cause and effect relationships. In his *Tales from Shakespeare* Lamb (for whom the plays are romantic texts) sees fit to introduce ethical distinctions and justifications. In fact moralizing is most generally recognized as a Biedermeier feature.

A third line of retreat is characterized by adaptation, compromise, and reappraisal. High romanticism proclaimed organicism as the supreme goal; in the Biedermeier age the related but less ambitious concept of evolution gradually replaced it as an aim that was somehow more practical. Romantic thinkers and scientists such as J. C. Lavater, Hamann, Baader, and F. H. Jacobi were almost obsessed by analogy; after 1815 or 1820 the sciences on the Continent adopted a toned-down version of it—and comparatism reigned supreme in academic endeavors (linguistics, myth study, anatomy). Absolute love had to make room for the glorification of family affections and domestic peace. The era of high romanticism and revolution had produced the intensities of Sade's totalitarian sexuality, the novelists of the Biedermeier (Hugo, Manzoni, Jules Janin) transposed them in milder tones and more realistic circumstances.[86] Scott was a master of such transpositions: the deepest symbolic structure of the *Waverley* novels is the best testimony. But he knew how to effect transpositions of linguistic discourse, for instance by retelling in indirect discourse—Augustan, neutralizing—the folk (romantic) speech of the characters (Chapter 21 of *The Antiquary* and elsewhere). Rochester in *Jane Eyre* (the action of the novel is placed in 1825–26) is a good example of literal "taming." Ten years before, he had crossed France and Italy in despair and suffering, had lost his eyesight, and is now ready for domestic peace and tranquility. The many conversions of radical high romantics to more moderate feelings and even stolid modes of expression are too frequent to bear repetition (Wordsworth, Robert Southey, Ludwig Tieck, and so on). A striking example is G. H. von Schubert, one of whose main works on nocturnal aspects of natural science appeared first in a radically romantic version and was later (1840) rewritten in a moderate, Christian tenor. The backgrounds of many of these efforts at hobbling high romanticism have in common a reassessment of empiricism, at a point when transcendent idealism was seen as the outcome of an unchecked rationalism. Hume and Kant had developed epistemology on a rationalist basis; the apparent dead end once reached, European thinking felt encouraged to embark on its spectacular, idealistic, metaphysical adventure. Reason had thus shown itself fallible and prone to fall into the metaphysical trap; a suspicion that this might happen had always lingered in English intellectual debate. The reassertion of empiricism was in some ways theoretical, but often it was a turn toward the concrete and practical, a kind of shrug of modest indifference by people like Claude Bernard and Georges Cuvier or, on another level, James Mill and Auguste Comte.

Accommodations of this type were achieved by a kind of rehabilitation of the eighteenth century. Politicians rediscovered the virtues of Montesquieu, perhaps even of Jefferson. The Congress of Vienna, in its geographical results, struck a balance between the visionary boundaries created by the Revolution and by Napoleon and the purely irrational (historically empiric) boundaries of the ancien régime. A moderately rational historicism ensued, quite similar to the revivals of historicism in Catholicism, Judaism, and even Protestantism, that soon followed. The idyllism of Cowper and Goldsmith found renewed echoes and equivalents. The vogue of neoclassicism was renewed by authors as different as Platen, Landor, Nodier, and Keats. Perhaps the most significant achievement of later romanticism was the accord between a still coherent, if impaired, high-romantic paradigm and a tradition that it did not want to discard. The harsher intensities of romanticism were moderated by nostalgia for the Enlightenment. Much as the romantics liked to define themselves as opponents of eighteenth-century neoclassicism and the Enlightenment, they were somehow—I would almost say secretly—trying to fulfill its progressive program in one bold stroke. Progress was to be achieved by an impetuous raid, not by cautious tactical moves. The later romantics preserved the objective but changed the tactics, reverting to the more cautious approaches of their preromantic grandparents.

Finally, another important avenue of retreat from the absolute claims of the high romantics appears to be preservation of high-romantic philosophical shapes in relativized and ironic form. This is not necessarily a rejection, as often believed by contemporaries or even by some of the later romantics themselves. It seems more correct to speak about a kind of translation from absolute to relative terms. Irony is almost a reinforcement of the romantic paradigm, which is now plausible to a hard-headed, realistic audience only when accompanied by a thin, deprecatory smile. Heine was a master of this tactic, rather than an adversary of romanticism. The credibility of the vision was being questioned, its literary basis undermined, its revolutionary hopes disappointed—everything contributed to the impression that romantic energy was seeping away, that perfection had been within grasp, but was now fading in the distance. Hosbawm suggests that the opposition between cosmic romanticism and idyllic romanticism (early and later phases, I would say) is sociologically based on "the contrast between a world theoretically wide open to talent and in practice, with cosmic injustice monopolized by soulless bureaucrats and pot-bellied philistines" (as illustrated by Hoffmann's *Der goldene Topf,* as well as by the opposition between Byron's early death and the Schlegels' respectable old age).[87] This is undoubtedly part of the truth. But it has to be seen against the tremendous diffusion of romantic disappointment. The aura of irony that bathes the age does not leave untouched such authors as Raimund, amiably fantastic though he may basically be. For many others the irony may become more corrosive and satirical— Gogol or Heine. For still others (Pushkin, Musset) a sadly smiling relativism remained satisfactory. The high-romantic irony (for instance Friedrich von Schlegel's) had an epistemological function: antithesis and thesis were part of a higher unity. Biedermeier irony is different—grotesque and tragicomic. It is empirical, pessimistic, debunking; it is skeptical rather than mystical and points toward nothing, rather than toward the all. In fact what the later romantics discovered with a thud was the *self-consciousness* of romanticism: the heroic innocence of Blake and the young Schelling would not be recaptured. This post-lapsarian process inside romanticism explains why so often the poetry after 1820 (Alphonse de Lamartine would be an excellent example) is concerned with declaring rather than showing or why the precise infinity of Novalis seems different from the indetermination and vagueness in *Krol Duch* or *Beniowski.* The process of loss of vision described in *Intimations of Immortality* finds a close counterpart in Hölderlin's *Mein Eigentum*. But if we compare to these Mörike's *Besuch in Urach*, instead of a dialectically coherent process, we find a zigzagging of feelings: a kind of tug of war between visionary enthusiasm and moments of depression. At no time does the poetic persona reach beyond the enthusiasm of hope to the ecstasy of communion: "(Natur) . . . bleibt, mehr als der Mensch, verwaist, / Darf nicht aus ihrem eignen Rätsel steigen" (Nature . . . will ever remain, more than the human folk, an orphan / it may not step out of its own mystery); the poem is infused with ambiguous and melancholy renunciation.[88] Even though this landscape is called "Du meiner tiefsten Kräfte stiller Herd" (thou quiet hearth of my deepest powers) the tone remains retrospective—and a hearth is not exactly a fountainhead. Another early poem by Mörike, *An einem Wintermorgen, vor Sonnenaufgang*, presents similar problems: beauty is somehow fleeting like a will o' the wisp. The conclusion is obvious: "Hinweg, mein Geist! hier gilt kein stillestehn: / Es ist ein Augenblick, und alles wird verwehn!" (Away, spirit mine! You cannot here stay: / A moment short it is, then all will float away!)[89]

DID ALL these avenues of retreat signal a breakdown into incoherence? What do they have in common? Do they add up to a unified picture? Indeed, can we speak of a late-romantic paradigm in the same way in which we can speak of an Abramsian paradigm for high romanticism?

There are two plain answers. First, the various works offer alternatives among the different modes of Biedermeier withdrawal. Conceptual kinship and even overlapping between the different kinds of retreat from the absolute can be readily noted; indeed, pure types are infrequent in literature. Second, even though these modes of retreat differ from each other, they all refer back to the same center, the explosion of romanticism. They all relate to that missing or receding center. Something, a sublime or awesome sight, had been glimpsed and could not be forgotten. This common reference built a tremendously strong bond in the epoch.[90] It provided the firm common ground for Heine and Hugo, Musset and Pushkin, Scott and Vigny, in spite of their differences. The general lassitude, the melancholy and the anxiety, as well as disappointed irony are connected with the theme of lost identity and the search for a father. The sociocultural significance of this state of affairs cannot be separated from the passing of revolutionary promises, the Napoleonic epic, the German war of liberation, or even the hopes of the eighteenth-century Enlightenment. But ultimately the loss suffered by the post-1815 romantics is that of the romantic paradigm itself. The paradigm links the post-1815 romantics with the preceding generation, and also establishes a dialectical opposition between the two groups.

High romanticism as an absence provides a unifying framework for the early nineteenth century in Europe. Later I will explain in some detail the mechanics of romantic change. Here it may be enough to say that epigonism, doubt, and empiric reduction are characteristic of the age and of its peculiar kind of greatness. It is a greatness achieved by accommodation and dialectical perspective.

The dialectical perspective is best seen in the Southern and Eastern European literatures, which had "skipped" the expansive phase of high romanticism. In Italy Giacomo Leopardi (whose most important work appeared in the 1820s and 1830s) wrote idylls and sarcastic prose, much in the manner of his Northern European contemporaries. But in his manifesto of 1819 (*Discorso di un italiano intorno alla poesia romantica*) Leopardi carefully repudiated the extremism of Northern European poets in the name of a poetry in many ways analogous to that of the Biedermeier. The chief organ of Italian romantic doctrine, brought out by Silvio Pellico and Berchet in 1818–1819, had the title of *Il Conciliatore*, hardly the herald of revolutionary daring. Manzoni, under the influence of Vincenzo Cuoco, as well as following the impulses of his own art, achieved one of the most masterful syntheses of tamed romanticism. Even Foscolo, who wrote his best work after 1800 (*I Sepolcri, Alla Sera*) seems to fall in a class with Landor or Platen, that is, he can be fully understood only as a kind of late-classical reaction to a presupposed background. For most of the writers of the 1820s and 1830s, though not for Foscolo, the absent background had been provided by Mme. de Staël's enchanted narratives of the intrinsic and absolute romanticism of Germany, which she recommended to the Italians in her famous letter of 1816.[91]

A similar situation occurred in Spanish literature. Spain, like Italy, provided Northern Europeans with symbolic landscapes for their actions. The choice was not arbitrary. In both areas the values that were to be affirmed explosively in high romanticism were already diffusely present in language, social actions, and the "poetical" extremes of existence. Thus in Italy, L. A. Muratori, G. V. Gravina, and F. S. Maffei already prefigured elements of romantic thinking.[92] Similarly in Spain the baroque tradition could substitute for many romantic intensities or approaches to cosmic unity. What therefore may appear as a kind of belated preromanticism in Spain is really a fully synchronic "later" romanticism, with many Biedermeier features. The revolutionary or Byronic pathos of José de Mariano Larra and José de Espronceda lives side by side with Donoso Cortés's absolute conservatism. If the latter is the equivalent of Joseph de Maistre, G. A. Bécquer's ironic rhymes are the counterpart of Heine's, and Gil y Carrasco or López Soler follow the lead of Scott. Nor is the example of Hugolian theater lost on Juan Eugenio Hartzenbusch's *La Jura en Santa Gadea* (1845) or even on Agustín Durán. López Soler discussed early (much in the vein of the Italians, though with more medieval gesturing) the romantic challenge in *Análisis de la cuestión agitada entre románticos y clasicos* (1823). We have to go all the way to Gotthelf or Jan Neruda to find the kind of pious and kindly sentimental Biedermeier novel that was tried with much public success by Fernán Caballero (Cecilia Böhl de Faber) in *Clemencia* and *Elia,* and later, in a broader sense by Alarcón.[93] The most significant manifestation of the Spanish Biedermeier remains the so-called *costumbrismo,* the trend toward vivid, well-focused portraits of local realities and customs, human types, and fads. The *costumbrismo* of Mesonero Romanos and Estébanez Calderón was placed at a kind of middle level of reality, at some distance from the cosmically absolute as well as from the strictly individual. The style itself shows the same broad-minded compromise: eccentricity and generalization go hand in hand, and the genre itself floats gracefully between an aesthetic style and theoretical discourse. Picturesque moments, satirical intentions, and traditionalist sensitivities are all tamed through conversation. Sociological reality and imaginative energy are fused in the service of a heightened practical culture, that is, in the service of the plausible or feasible romanticism that was taking shape at that time throughout Europe. This essayism was practiced by Hunt and Lamb in England, by Mihail Kogălniceanu and Alexandru Odobescu in Romania and Garay Janos in Hungary, and it can be encountered in Russian, German, and French literature as well. It shies away from romantic intensity, but endeavors to take advantage of romantic liberties of form.

When in 1831 the *Cartas Españoles* began publishing Calderón (after Larra and Mesonero Romanos in the 1820s had already initiated the Spanish equivalent of the conversational essay, the *cuadras* and the *articulos de costumbres*) they were looking back to some Spanish traditions. But they were chiefly turning back in order to *respond* to the high romantic surge. They were taming an absent romanticism. The *costumbristas* wanted to reply to the romantic image of Spain as the land of feverishly high-pitched existence and exotically unfettered attitudes. But beyond the objection that Spain was unsuitable as a substitute for cosmic integration, they were reacting against such a transfigured existential locus per se. The substance of romantic regeneration was replaced by an acceptance of autonomous realities. Cecilia Böhl de Faber might have spoken for the whole movement when she demanded a more practical and social romanticism, one thoroughly cleansed of fatalism and individualism and thus "secularized."[94] Soon Spanish romanticism, like the German Biedermeier, turned toward *Heimatroman* and realism (Alarcón, Perez Galdos) or toward the philologism of Menendez Pelayo.

This whole European culture of absence, of which the Spanish and Italian poetic and intellectual worlds of the 1830s are merely two examples, could only coalesce by a subtle interlocking of doubt and trust. Trust meant postulating an absent center, it meant writing as if the overwhelming event had been the great attempt to detect the path to cosmic regeneration, rather than reaching cosmic regeneration as had been the case for the visionaries and revolutionaries of the preceding decades. Doubt was the great relativizer and leveler. Doubt led to the lowering of tone, to the hushing of all romantic intensities. Thus the most impressive phenomenon after 1815 is the general resurgence of idyllism.[95]

The importance of the societal idyll as a literary framework for the eighteenth century is amply documented. After 1750 it provided a convenient literary landscape in which writers could exercise sentimentalism with moderation, confront the individual with society, curb neoclassical rigidities, reconcile nature with civilization, depict a plausible economic cooperation—in other words, the idyllic model was a reserve of sensible humanism for William Cowper and Tobias Smollett, J. H. Voss and Goethe, as it had been farther back, for Fielding and Rousseau. It had seemed that the romantic onslaught had once and for all laid to rest the popularity of this topos. In fact in its fleeting appearances in the pages of Novalis or Tieck it is usually reduced to a contrastive role. But soon thereafter a renewed revival of idyllism was noted. This revival could use idyllism in a serious and didactic vein, as the more popular literature in Germany did, all the way down to the *Gartenlaube.* Or it could take an ironic turn as it does in Carlyle's *Sartor Resartus* and in E. T. A. Hoffmann's prose.[96] But the most responsible task assigned to idyllism in Biedermeier literature was to act as a credible level of substitution for the recaptured perfection of high romanticism. Although the idyllic model may be in some ways utopian, it is certainly much more plausible for the ending of a novel by Scott or Manzoni than a full embodiment of the Hegelian "World Idea" or than Wordsworth's "spots of time" in their absolute unity of consciousness and nature. At the same time the connotations of the idyllic topos were secure and familiar for those in search of either symbolic or actual fulfillment. The cyclical return was not to the beginnings of history, but rather to an age merely two generations back.

Thus idyllism provides a conceptual and visual background for the Biedermeier as a whole, coloring all its activities, even the politically radical nationalist, democratic, or socialist trends. They all were engaged in a world of the possible, in a work of taming. The central concern of the period seems to be how to preserve the hope for a regenerative change in history while taking into account defeat and limitation. Nor should this aim be scorned as pettier than the visionary and revolutionary aims of high romanticism. It is less grandiose, but equally impossible. The task of restoring and compromising without entirely relinquishing paradise is a tremendously complicated one. It involves following the dialectics of a subjective change from simple innocence to an innocence inclusive of guilt, while the objective world undergoes a similar but not always identical evolution; it involves coordinating these changes and noting their ironies when necessary. We may want to describe this as a decadence of romanticism, if we dwell on the lowered sights and the abandonment of a clearly unified perspective in many of the writers of the period. But in doing so we are perhaps guilty of a romantic fallacy: contamination of tenor by vehicle. Perhaps a critical judgment of superiority expressed in categorical terms is itself romantic in that it proclaims the perfection of a specific historical area and of its understanding of the world.

2

SUPPORT FOR AN
ENGLISH BIEDERMEIER

OFTEN the 1820s and 1830s seem an embarrassment to the historian of English literature. The Victorian age cannot be said to begin earlier than the late 1830s or early 1840s, while romanticism proper is never stretched beyond the early 1820s. Nobody knows exactly how to categorize those years, during which romantic influence seemed to fade and a kind of reaction set in. The twenty years after 1800 teem with writers who seemed to oppose their romantic contemporaries and to harmonize more with the writers of the late eighteenth or mid-nineteenth century. Ian Jack's prestigious volume of the *Oxford History of English Literature* is devoted to the period between 1815 and 1832, but its author never tries to provide a coherent image of the epoch, to distinguish a *morphé* or even to explain why this particular period should be treated as a unit—other than for reasons of political chronology. To obtain a more coherent image of those decades an expanded concept of the Biedermeier may prove helpful.

A few half-hearted attempts have already been made to suggest such a relationship. For example, Norbert Fuerst applied the categories of Victorianism to nineteenth-century German literature and in the process found parallels for German periodizations in English literature.[1] Friedrich Brie maintained that an English Biedermeier started with Wordsworth's *Ode to Duty* and included almost all of Tennyson, most of Dickens, Thackeray, and many minor writers like Felicia Hemans, Charlotte Yonge, Charles Reade, Eliza Cook, and others.[2] Although Carl Dawson briefly considered the usefulness of the term then dismissed it, some individual parallels are more useful. Dawson himself compared the abortive Pre-Raphaelite *The Germ* with Dickens's *Household Words*. Dickens was in the rearguard—his Biedermeier values (sentimentality, practicality, populism) were widely accepted by a broad and low readership, and in consequence his journal was hostile to the pale subtleties of the Rosettis.[3] L. H. C. Thomas expatiated on the parallels between Thackeray's *Pendennis* and *Wilhelm Meisters Lehrjahre*: Blanche-Philine, Emily-Marianne, Laura-Natalie, Meister-Pendennis.[4] Ilse Hecht and Pius Wolters were among the many who focused on Dickens. The latter found that the naive, stingless drollery of Mr. Pickwick and his associates (but also of a Mr. Micawber or a Mr. Swiveller) is typically Biedermeier; children, animals, dwarves, and retarded creatures often provide the sentimental and purposeless comic relief of Dickens' novels; the parody of the supernatural is handled in the *Pickwick* inserts (as well as by contemporaries like Thomas Hood and R. H. Barham) as deftly as by Raimund, Johann Nestroy, and the later Hoffmann.[5]

Mario Praz provided the best overview, concentrating on the portrayal of characters rather than on literary structure. Like others, he made extraordinary claims for the scope of the Biedermeier in English literature. According to him, Dutch genre painting was a basic influence, verses of Wordsworth and Coleridge on homely and intimate themes provided early examples of English Biedermeier, and thence—through Scott, Lamb, and De Quincey—it continued to flourish practically to the end of the century and included George Eliot, Anthony Trollope, and Thomas Hardy.[6] One wonders what is *not* Biedermeier in Victorian literature. Moreover, Praz's analyses were cramped because he clung to the old, limiting view of the Biedermeier, discussed earlier. Nevertheless many of his insights were valuable and will be referred to more than once hereafter.

If any valid period structure can be set up using the Biedermeier as an auxiliary it must resort to some help from the structures worked out for German literature. Besides the pleasure of tinkering with literary periods, we may hope thus to obtain a better explanation of what went on in the 1820s and 1830s and of how the Victorian age was linked to the romantic period. I will therefore provide a very rough sketch of contemporary German developments for reference.

German romanticism started in the 1770s and 1780s and flourished in the 1790s and in the first two decades of the nineteenth century. By 1810 or 1815 most of its greatest works had been conceived, even though some key masterpieces such as Goethe's *Faust* or Hegel's *Philosophy of History* were published a little later. German romanticism may rightly claim not only the Jena group (the Schlegel brothers, Tieck, Novalis) but also Hölderlin and most of the early work of

Goethe and Schiller (*Werther, Götz, Die Räuber,* and so on); seen from a European perspective, it should also include most of Jean Paul's novels, the whole of Heinrich von Kleist, the writings of Brentano, Arnim, Wilhelm Hauff, and E. M. Arndt, as well as many of the writers and thinkers of the *Sturm und Drang* (Herder and Hamann, F. M. Klinger, K. P. Moritz and G. A. Bürger). It is widely accepted that Schelling, Hegel, and Fichte were thinkers belonging to romanticism. There had also been a contemporary reaction to high romanticism, provided primarily by some "classicist" works of Goethe and Schiller: *Tasso, Iphigenie, Römische Elegien, Das Ideal und das Leben,* as well as by the writings of Voss or Friedrich Nicolai.

Around 1815 three important things happened. First, some central figures of German romanticism changed markedly in attitude: Friedrich Schlegel, Ludwig Tieck, and Schelling come easily to mind. They became more conservative in politics and more moderate and sceptical in their writing. Second, a number of new figures rose to prominence, and they may be said to have placed themselves halfway between romanticism and the Biedermeier. For example, E. T. A. Hoffmann and Eichendorff.[7] Third, the Biedermeier proper emerged, to be soon followed by its complement and symmetrical opposite: the rebellious Jung Deutschland, Jung Hegelianer, *Vormärz,* and loosely related writers. Together these dominated the literary scene for three decades or so. German realism emerged in the 1840s and prevailed in doctrine as well as in literary practice after 1848 or 1850. Theodor Fontane, Gottfried Keller, and Theodor Storm, although rooted in the experience of the first half of the century, blossomed fully only with the academic realism of the second.

Can we identify a similar scheme in English literature? There is hardly any dispute about the early part. English romanticism flourished in the 1790s when the manifesto of the *Lyrical Ballads* appeared, when Wordsworth and Coleridge conceived some of their key works, and when Blake's work changed decisively after *The Marriage of Heaven and Hell* (1793). Other works can be attached, by general agreement, to these developments: many of the Gothic novels (and chiefly Beckford's *Vathek,* 1784), some of William Godwin's and Thomas Paine's theorizing, many of Robert Southey's ballads and short epics. This trend continued in practically the whole of Shelley's work, in Scott's early collections, translations, and perhaps his balladry, most likely in Byron's *Childe Harold's Pilgrimage, Manfred,* and

Cain, and also in Keats's *Endymion.* Like their German counterparts, these works fit the paradigm developed by Abrams and share other features (forms of expansion) that I attributed in the first chapter to the core romantic model. I will try to show that the three developments that mark German literature after 1815 or 1820 can be observed in English literature also, that the "classicist" counterpoint may also be noticed (though differently), and that in the transition to Victorian realism there are many similarities to the German transition. Needless to say, none of these similarities of structure or period should be taken as indicative of a value judgment: the same process may be expressed by a superlative achievement or by a rather insignificant production. Nor are they tokens of influence in one direction or the other—I see them as symptoms of a common process.

A CHANGE of heart in the early English romantics has always been acknowledged and recognized as significant, even though many critics have tended to explain it away as either a psychological reaction to the French Revolution or a mere whittling down of the creative impulse in Wordsworth and Coleridge.[8] This type of change is widely spread throughout Europe and cannot be explained away as a multitude of individual cases which happen to converge. Lamartine, speaking in a tired voice about returning to home and peaceful resignation after the sublime eagle's flight to high adventure and divine challenges, certainly was not describing his own adventure. Musset's long and tortuous explanation in the introduction to *La Confession* was essentially correct in claiming a continuity of sensibility between the postwar generation (with its pessimistic discouragement) and its predecessors. Goethe, who more than anyone else had the right to claim a personal rhythm of development, can also be said to slow down as the nineteenth century progressed. Friedrich Schlegel and Ludwig Tieck are additional examples of adaptation to established values, quite similar to those of Coleridge and Wordsworth. Ideological compromise was even a route to physical salvation. Coleridge became a conservative in his old age not because of his illness, but in order to escape it.[9] Could Lamb have eluded insanity if his writing had not been in the soothingly idyllic Biedermeier mode? Was not Lamb's mental disposition somehow dictated by his will to be healed and survive? The incidence of mental breakdowns and violent deaths among the romantics was high. Byron's Manfred observed:

> there is an order
> Of mortals on the earth, who do become
> Old in their youth, and die ere middle age,
> Without the violence of warlike death;
> Some perishing of pleasure, some of study,
> Some worn with toil, some of mere weariness,
> Some of diseases, and some insanity,
> And some of withered or of broken hearts.[10]

It had something to do with the volatile and dangerous nature of the absolutist romantic paradigm. Close personal and axiological identifications with it led either to traumatic shocks or to withdrawal into more peaceful zones of intellectual activity. The model itself was unstable, and psychological involvement with it made for instability: perfectly good reasons for change and compromise.[11]

The political sympathies of the Lake Poets had been close to the most radical political movements of the time. Wordsworth's *Girondin* friends were ardently republican and democratic, the pantisocracy scheme of Southey and Coleridge was not far from communism, and Godwin may have influenced Wordsworth. By contrast in the 1820s both Coleridge and Wordsworth had become defenders of the Church of England, of order, and of the social hierarchy. Southey, the author of *Wat Tyler*, became the hated symbol of conformity as poet laureate and outspoken defender of conservatism; for the last century and a half he has been paying the price by being underrated as a writer.

The changes in the substance of their poetry are even more significant. The Wordsworth of the poetic sublime and of the search for the unadulterated vision, the Wordsworth of the early *Prelude* and of *Tintern Abbey,* the Wordsworth who constantly used the language of explosion, fireworks, and projections of light to depict even the ordinary situations of the mind's interaction with nature did not last long.[12] The poetic decline in Wordsworth's life is set by some at 1810, by others at 1808, 1804 or even 1802.[13] Softening, relaxation, and serene acceptance prevail thereafter. The changes in *The Prelude* are all too well known.[14] Vincent De Luca analyzed the treatment of Mount Snowdon by De Quincey in the *Confessions* and by Wordsworth in the two versions of *The Prelude.* His conclusion—that whereas "Wordsworth's vision . . . emphasizes a more dynamic conception of mind," in De Quincey "the dominant emphasis seems to fall upon the attainment of an ineffable rest"—throws into sharp relief the changing makeup of the two successive phases of romanticism. De Luca shows how, owing to De Quincey's influence, the late version of the famous episode loses the dynamic force of the early one, moves from iconic fusion to allegorical typology and, as a result, "the poetry itself seems to imply a wider separation between the observer and Nature."[15] But he also admits that these alterations cannot be attributed merely to De Quincey since "the emphasis on the moral consequences of mental sublimity" is part of Wordsworth's own development.

If these consequences are moral, they are also practical or applicable. Measured against the immense realities of sublime fantasy, they appear shriveled or defective, but the opposition between the two is structural rather than substantive. The philosophical conservatism of Coleridge's later years—the peer of any high point of European Biedermeier thinking—is actually compatible with the tenets implicit in his early writing. *Biographia Literaria*'s distinction between fancy and imagination, or between reason and understanding, not less than the distinction between allegory and symbol can be easily organized into a distinction between a rationalistic-egalitarian order and the highly diversified and hierarchic project of the *Constitution of Church and State* (1829). It would not have been impossible to draw a different conclusion from the same type of opposition and to clamor for the revolution of imaginative synthesis and creative brotherhood against the old mechanical order of addition and combination. Indeed, Shelley and Hazlitt were doing precisely that. But for them, as well as for Wordsworth and Coleridge, the important point was that the visionary world crossed over into a political-moral (applicative) one at all; the *kind* of application chosen was slightly less important.

OTHER KINDS of dynamics are less readily observed, but they are present nonetheless. The careers of Byron and Keats may be considered too short to warrant a search for internal changes. Yet their careers contained transitions even though their work as a whole was transitional. Thus, the earlier Byronic heroes themselves (Childe Harold, Manfred, Lara, perhaps even Cain) were designed as departures from the dialectics of high romanticism in so far as they lack a fulfillment, a final redemption, a transfigured reconciliation of essential contradictions; the basic situation was already one of defeat and hopelessness. In addition most of the heroes (from Childe Harold to Conrad, Lara, or the Giaour) seem too individual to be classed with the abstract, mythical, or philosophical figures created by Wordsworth, Blake, or Coleridge. In Abramsian terms, the circuitous journey was not quite closed, the alienation was not entirely overcome, the early poems of Byron presented incomplete forms of romantic secularization. The moments of transfiguration or of achieved totality seem sporadic, unless we resort to the convoluted argument that Byron (like Kierkegaard and some twentieth-century existentialists) regarded despair and defeat as redemption or as the moment when authentic contact with the wellsprings of Being was resumed.

The Byron of *Beppo* and *Don Juan* in turn offered a relativized, ironic version of romantic ideals and motifs; at this point, Byron was plainly the contemporary of Heine, not of Blake. The transitional early Byron was replaced by a poet whose opposition to the high-romantic paradigm has often been observed. Jerome McGann emphasized the deep-seated difference between the "teleological sense of order" inherent in "the Romantic sense of quest and pilgrimage" and Byron's indebtedness to Hume, empiricism, and the Enlightenment *philosophes*, an indebtedness that has as a correlative, I hasten to add, an aesthetic vision.[16] In fact in *Don Juan* "Byron makes a great virtue of not comprehending the world in a unified, integrative, or closed system" (p. 103). The Coleridgean (high-romantic) *Weltanschauung* of closeness is opposed to the Byronian desire to convert wholeness into episodes (pp. 107–114), and yet the latter derives from the former. Byron's allegiance to a Humean formalization of the world was a deliberate choice, consequent upon a desire to respond to the high-romantic view, to which the view no less than the author were dialectically tied. His episodic world cannot even be imagined as a mere continuation of Smollett's, without the foil of Coleridgean holism; his vision of the "second fall" (pp. 146–148) was possible because the scheme of first fall and redemption had been so forcefully declared. Byron resembled the Biedermeier authors in that he tried to found a new verbal state by synthesizing eighteenth-century values and romantic explosions. He borrowed from the Enlightenment because in fact he wanted to keep romanticism alive and to turn it to good use in a moral, political, and psychological way. To do so he had first to contend with imperfection through despair and defeat or irony and empiricism.

The development of Keats was fairly similar, even though his choice of tools was different. *Endymion* can perhaps be described as a work of high romanticism. But for the Keats of the *annus mirabilis* beauty and security went hand in hand; dream was a soft halo around a starker reality; abyss and heights were horrifying and insufferable; happiness was as often as not in rest and stasis. In the odes Keats was clearly less concerned with the pilgrimage to redemption than with what happens once you are there. He did sketch his own version of paradise regained in the "negative capability," as well as in the (almost) reunited faculties of *Ode on Melancholy,* or of time and eternity, beauty and truth, progress and being in *Ode to a Grecian Urn;* he did show himself aware of the need for an integrated vision of life and death, delight and suffering, growth and decay (*To Autumn, Ode to a Nightingale*).[17] But this kind of paradise of wholeness seems never fully palpable, always slightly improbable. The energy that had allowed Blake to transcend the dilemma of real versus ideal solutions and to set up the visionary final society on a plateau from which such a concern seemed tiny and peevish was conspicuously lacking in Keats. The polarization of fantasy and locality was not yet painful and harrowing, as it would become later in the century, but we perceive its delicate outline as through a golden mist: "Fled is that music . . . Do I wake or sleep?" His doubts about the capabilities of imagination grew rapidly from *Endymion* to *The Fall of Hyperion.* In this interval, when he wanted to correlate the dream and the cruder facts of life, Keats used a kind of soft dialectics, for instance in *The Eve of St. Agnes.* This is, I believe, one of the keys to Keats's reputation in later years: the impression that he could master the opposition, without ignoring it. From this vantage point we can also understand the troublesome question of Keats's "classicist" bent, the true meaning of which is merely the toning down of high-romantic impulses.[18] The poet reached back for eighteenth-century reassurance: he picked up shapes, not shaping principles. Keats was perhaps the perfect case of a "transitional" poet within romanticism, whose discourse encompassed the truths of both the chief moments.

KEATS and Byron appear to be acted upon by an interior dynamic and become transitional figures particularly when they are viewed against the background of a mass of writing that reveals a powerful consistency of symptoms. After 1815 the English literary scene was dominated by precisely those writers who made it their business to turn romanticism into something both social and intimate, both practical and domestic, while preserving—to whatever extent—the original vision. At least some of these writers were making a deliberate effort to organize the change. They had been in close touch with the early figures of romanticism and were trying to make their views and works more palatable and accessible while playing down the "scandalous" or "frightening" sides. This was particularly true of Charles Lamb, who was close in age to Wordsworth and Coleridge and had developed an early intimacy with them; it was also true of De Quincey, who was somewhat younger and got to know Wordsworth and Southey personally a little later, although he had known and been devoted to their work for a long time.[19]

Wordsworth insisted in 1814 that Lamb should be the reviewer of *Excursion* in the *Quarterly Review*. Soon Lamb was quoting respectfully from the poems of Wordsworth and Coleridge as if they were classic authorities (in "Witches, and Other Night Fears" and elsewhere), and he became their privileged spokesman. Yet he knew perfectly well, as early as the 1790s, how to criticize the "excesses" of his betters and how to rebuke their departure from religious orthodoxy: "high as the human intellect comparatively will soar, and wide as its influence, malign or salutary, can extend, is there not, Coleridge, a distance between the Divine Mind and it, which makes such language blasphemy?" he wrote as early as October 24, 1796. Lamb's question measured the distance between the two phases of English romanticism.

Lamb's true critique of the high-romantic paradigm and his manner of qualifying it are revealed by the very texture of his *Essays*. Lamb became a productive writer at the time when his best friends had ceased writing. Fred Randel has described in detail how many of the whimsical prose pieces with quaint titles such as "Old China," "A Dissertation upon Roast Pig," and so on, embody powerful conflicts between the self and infinitude, attempts to cope with the absurd, endeavors to structure space into intelligible shapes, or clashes between Will and Matter. However, the issues were deliberately miniaturized in an effort that does have some biographical reasons, but is largely a conscious literary-philosophical strategy and not unique at the time, since it can be encountered as well in Leigh Hunt and others.[20] Part of the domestication process was Lamb's renewed interest in the idyllic society that had been such a central topic for Goldsmith and Cowper and that the high romantics had so decisively rejected. Elia, the harmless and learned eccentric, pieced together the idyllic world in an ironic and playful manner; he made even London (for example, in "The Old Benchers of the Inner Temple") seem a small town, quaint and delicate, familiar and peaceful, and not entirely unlike Mrs. Gaskell's Cranford.[21] This technique applies to a social and physical place the procedure used in another essay to prove that true genius is essentially sane and normal, not sublime and awesome. His accents are those of a "languid, intimate, bourgeois Romanticism: family affections contemplated with nostalgia and with a gentle pain that is not devoid of a certain pleasure."[22]

In general the writers of this lower romanticism tended to rely on other sources and on rewriting. They were in fact lured by the secondary: whether it was secondary subjects or the rewriting of others' material or reliance on greater figures. The typical case was De Quincey with his continuous *rifacimenti,* as one critic called them, with his parasitical existence around and in the service of great figures, his commentaries and his huge dilettantish learning, which seems both genuine and phony at the same time. Critics have often vented anger and indignation at Coleridge's borrowings and at his reliance on other persons and sources. But, looking more closely, we see these as strikingly different from those of De Quincey. Coleridge was finding material for what was already in him; he was dominated by an awe of their resonance, a kind of sacred surprise at finding himself in Schelling seized him. He acts as one who is stunned and does not know what he does; whatever it is, it is in total good faith. De Quincey's good faith is in a different key: he counts himself so small and insignificant as to be entitled to borrow and adapt. And he did it with a vengeance. Alexis De Valon's translation of Bergmann's voyage to central Asia served him as well as M. de Ferer's edition of a seventeenth-century Spanish manuscript (for *The Spanish Military Nun*), newspaper articles for *On Murder,* Willibald Alexis's hoax (a pretended adaptation after Scott) for *Walladmor*.[23] His polyhistoric works were fanciful. He pretended to abridge a study of Hebrew fashion and manners, but merely translated part of it; he spiced up reminiscences of Kant's intimates into a vivid historical tableau; he whipped up an imaginary "philosophy of Herodotus" out of genuinely learned sources. This manner of writing was not much different from the ideological calligraphy of his contemporary historians, but he took it one step further: he was more literary because he felt less responsible toward his sources, and he was more reliant on them because his original contribution was so negligible.

The same dependency was at work less specifically in De Quincey's most literary works. He imitated not an individual work but the high-romantic paradigm as a whole. Praz noticed that the "Society for the Encouragement of Murder" was an ironically dampened version of Sade's "Société des Amis du Crime" (*Juliette*).[24] In a broader sense De Quincey's aim seems to have been to ensconce dream, crime, and vision in a bourgeois setting, thus multiplying ambiguities and relativizing the romantic explosion. Opium was linked with tea and coziness; it was no longer alien and dangerous. Murder became—to the lecturer and to the audience—sterile, impactless, terrorless; it was transposed into a Grecian urn, as it were.[25] The dreams became beautiful objects to be put on shelves, losing thereby their immediate existential force and their connection with the inner motors of being. The experience of the mail coach was no genuine transfiguration. Praz analyzed *The English Mail-coach* in some detail and found that many episodes were vignettes of a bourgeois and intimate character, carefully drawn genre pictures. When a collision was threatened between the huge, rapid vehicle and a "frail reedy gig" with two lovers in it, "The idyllic picture changes to a nightmare; the two planes upon which the spirit of De Quincey moves . . . cross . . . the funeral march is succeeded by a hymn of victory."[26] Philistinism and nightmare went hand in hand, as in Hoffmann or in Gogol. The romantic revolution was demoted to mere sensationalism and titillation, sin was turned into vice, cosmic alienation into social malfunction. Perhaps nobody understood the great romantics better than De Quincey, but nobody worked harder than De Quincey at defusing their message.

Carlyle's *Sartor Resartus,* a work traditionally difficult to place, is another example of borrowing, blending, and diluting. It was not a valid expression of romantic vision,[27] but a typical Biedermeier work, based on the dualism of creative power and everyday life, as well as on relativism: each half resulting from the break is mirrored ironically in the other. The pattern of romantic philosophy was faithfully preserved in Teufelsdröckh's opinions and destiny, but its body was blown up and twisted in grotesque postures. Teufelsdröckh, judging from his rural origins and his ultimate residence, was the product of an idyllic society and its ambassador in a world of spiritual energy and cosmic vision. We are obviously far from the transfigurations of core romanticism when the two opposing worlds so obviously *need* a connecting element, and when imagination has to stoop to an instrumental role.

These writers, who are sometimes labeled "half-romantics," and whose place was wittily defined by Chesterton ("that which in Rousseau was a creed, became in Hazlitt a taste and in Lamb little more than a whim"[28]), were provided with a theoretical platform of sorts in the critical writings of Hazlitt. Like Lamb and De Quincey, Hazlitt was deeply influenced by the Lake Poets. His later career was an attempt to live down this experience. His acerbic attacks on Wordsworth for having betrayed his early political views were designed to conceal Hazlitt's own and more profound betrayal of the integrative vision of which he had partaken. He knew perfectly well what he was doing. When he was giving his *Lectures on the English Poets* (1818) he concluded with a succinct and just definition of the Lake Poets, whose aim toward general regeneration he understood: "The change in the belles lettres was as complete, and to many persons as startling, as the change in politics, with which it went hand in hand . . . all was to be natural and new. Nothing that was established was to be tolerated . . . The object was to reduce all things to an absolute level."[29] He also understood their structural ties with the French Revolution and German romanticism. He rose quite consciously against the "inequality and injustice" (that is, arbitrary creativity) that he sensed were innate in the principle of imagination (VIII, 115). When he criticized Wordsworth and Coleridge for what he took to be political failings, he repeatedly used the imagery of extremes, the swerving or tottering from one extreme to the other, or of Coleridge's going up in a balloon from which Hazlitt is then thrown down (VII, 129).[30] Behind the liberal criticism, the moderate would like to make himself heard, and indeed Hazlitt was consistent enough to demur against the poetic manner of the politically compatible Shelley (XII, 245–246), on grounds similar to those used against *Christabel* and *Kubla Khan.* Patently, Hazlitt was undertaking a systematic and intellectually respectable process of miniaturization: romanticism to Biedermeier. "The golden mean" he wrote toward the end of his life "is, indeed, an exact description of the mode of life I should like to lead—of the style I should like to write" (X, 297). His complaint that in this he would never succeed is justified only in small part.

Hazlitt tried hard and successfully to temper the explosive romanticism of his early mentors, which he never totally abandoned, with his extensive readings in eighteenth century thinkers and writers,[31] in other words to circumscribe an area halfway between Reynolds's *Dis-*

courses and Coleridge's *Biographia.* A comparison with Coleridge shows a continuous toning down, a transcription in a minor key, as it were.[32] Hazlitt substituted for the absolute imagination the more mundane values of "gusto" and "intensity of power," and he tried to reconcile romantic ideals with empiricism and common sense (IV, 77–80).[33] The definition of "gusto" is most notable for that which it does not contain, namely the element of transfiguration. Hazlitt defended "genius" against Reynolds and against the idealized nature of the classics, but almost like Lamb he spoke about genius as quantitative and methodic, that is, as not as totally irrational, mysterious, and divine as it was often believed to be (XII, 60). Actually, the critique of Reynolds's concepts of genius and originality was a critique of exaggeration and half-truths rather than a radical negation; he intended to disprove "a set of half principles, which are true only as far as they imply a negation of the opposite errors" (XVIII, 62). The sympathetic imagination and an approach both empirical and tender toward the individual object were supposed to correct both Reynolds and Coleridge. And where Coleridge (or even Lamb) tried to establish a countertradition against the neoclassicists for the use of romantic writers, Hazlitt simply worked in favor of pluralism in literary studies (*Lectures on the English Poets, The English Comic Writers, Dramatic Literature of the Age of Elizabeth*).

In the last analysis Hazlitt was a careful, liberal, socially aware *littérateur* whose Biedermeier shading and outlook can hardly be overlooked. The seeds that would grow into full Victorian dilemmas were already sown: the sneaky admiration for the strong arm of Napoleon; the cultural pessimism (circular repetitive fate replaced the high-romantic fireworks); the determinism of character, sex, race, and ethnicity; the split between the principle of reality and imagination (XII, 230–236). But the sublimities of romantic integralism were still close enough, and so these growing dilemmas and splits could not fully blossom.

Hazlitt's counterpart in prose was Thomas Love Peacock who, like Hazlitt, was connected to some of the romantics, like him saw fit to do battle with them, and also like him did not actually place himself outside the romantic framework. Even in *The Four Ages of Poetry* he was joking and, one may assume, inclined to modify rather than to demolish. Also like Hazlitt he was devoted to the concept of the "spirit of the age," which can well be taken as an acknowledgement of the paradigm of core-romanticism that he felt should be qualified and reduced to scale. The general tone of his prose can best be understood by analogy with Heine and Pushkin in general, and specifically with Grabbe's *Jest, Satire, Irony and Deeper Significance* with which he has in common particularly the rough-and-ready treatment of character, the jocular choice of names, and the absurd fantasy popping up with sudden exasperation at different points in the narration.

Crotchet Castle provides a convenient vantage point for observing Peacock because, as Marilyn Butler correctly noted, "it is a quintessential book, with something in it of all the others," that is to say it combines the manner of the earlier satires with that of the later historical romances.[34] *Crotchet Castle* developed variations on at least two main themes of high romanticism. One was the regeneration of mankind. Lady Clarinda gave in Chapter 5 a spirited and sarcastic speech (occasionally interrupted), in which she characterized Mr. Skionar ("a sort of poetical philospher, a curious compound of the intense and the mystical"), Mr. Chainmail ("holds that the best state of society was that of the twelfth century"), Mr. Togood, Mr. Trillo, Dr. Morbific and so forth—all shards of the large broken vessel of high romanticism. These are also pieces left over from the universal projects and statements that abound in *Nightmare Abbey* (Scythrop Glowry is the author of "Philosophical Gas; or a Project for a General Illumination of the Human Mind"—Chapter 10). As a critic remarked, Peacock knew how to distinguish the different levels on which a common spirit of the age existed.[35] After some further debating and even a lyrical escalation, Peacock provided an aptly dry epitaph for the episode: "The schemes of the world's regeneration evaporated in a tumult of voices" (end of Chapter 5). I believe he refers not only to what happens at the end of the scene, but to the "spirit of the age," to the "tumult of voices" into which the organic unity had been fragmented, as described by Lady Clarinda.

The second theme is embodied in the adventure of Mr. Chainmail, "a good-looking young gentleman" enamored of the Middle Ages and resentful of the dawning industrial and technological age. In the mountains of North Wales he was confident to find a romantic peasant girl, a spirit of the place: actually what he found was Susannah Touchandgo, the thoroughly urban daughter of a sharp-dealing businessman, disguised in rustic attire. He would marry not the innocence of nature, but its substitute. Narcissus-like, he loved best his own mir-

ror-image: disguise seeking disguise. This may well be Peacock's supreme irony.

Peacock, like Hazlitt, had a good feel (similar to that of Herder
whose work he did not know) for the spirit of the age. His adversities
and mockeries were not induced by politics. He was rather evenhanded in caricaturing Coleridge, Shelley, and Byron (the Byron of
Childe Harold's Pilgrimage, not the one of *Don Juan*).[36] With ease and
equanimity he changed the direction of his political satire: against the
conservatives in the earlier, against the radicals in the later part of his
career. He was sincere each time, for political concerns were always
overshadowed by the opposition to universal claims.[37] In *Maid Marian*
where he tackled Scott, to whom he is related in so many ways, Peacock's satire was light and playful. His voice hardened when he came
against utopianism, generalization, perfectionist claims of all kinds and
against sins toward empirical common sense. Mr. Hilary admonished
Mr. Cypress in a passage that was later often singled out for comment:
"You talk like a Rosicrucian, who will love nothing but a sylph, who
does not believe in the existence of a sylph, and who yet quarrels with
the whole universe for not containing a sylph" (*Nightmare Abbey,*
Chapter 11).

Like Jane Austen and Byron, like Hazlitt, and indeed like Pushkin
or Musset or Grillparzer, Peacock turned for support to the eighteenth century. However, he never forgot that his writing was
founded on the romantic "spirit of the age," on which it relied for a
level of reference. This neo-Enlightenment was qualified by an awareness that romanticism was a reality that could not be simply wished
away. He was a progressive of the past, who loftily assumed that the
world should pick up where it left off in 1788. This progressivism,
widespread after 1815 was, needless to say, a kind of civilized conservatism. Peacock's strategy was that of Heine and Grabbe, namely the
leveling and undermining of the alternative historical and intellectual
route through irony: since romanticism was a rationally unlikely occurrence, it could be reduced in the reader's eyes to an imaginative ex-
crescence. Jane Austen's *Northanger Abbey* had used a similar
procedure: not denial and opposition but reduction and assimilation.[38]

SOME MAY object that all the writers discussed above are not the
major literary figures of the time and that they inevitably adopt a reductive and prettifying manner, not for historical reasons, but simply

because they are less talented and thus less able to do full justice to the romantic vision. This is the argument made by most of the chief English literary historians. But consideration of two writers who are major by any standards and whose aesthetic and intellectual strategies are analogous to those of the "half-romantics" will prove this argument invalid. Jane Austen and Sir Walter Scott fit into the framework of the English Biedermeier, whose greatest representatives they are.

Jane Austen is certainly in need of a historical niche. It is no longer possible to act as if any critical analysis of Austen should be placed under a bell jar, as was the rule for a while. Nor can we be content to treat her as a remote ancestor of Conrad and James, as was done in the wake of F. R. and Q. D. Leavis's judgments. And surely the view that Austen was a belated eighteenth-century novelist is no longer tenable. Jane Austen was not cut off from contemporary literary life; she was well aware of romanticism and revolution, as Lionel Trilling observed in the 1950s. Alistair Duckworth and Avrom Fleishman have analyzed her underlying conservatism and organicism, and Marilyn Butler and Warren Roberts have pointed out in remarkable detail that the author of *Emma* was fully integrated into the novelistic trends of the time and that her own work promptly responded to the challenges of the period.[39] The conclusions of this research are important breakthroughs in our understanding of Jane Austen, but they fail to acknowledge "the spirit of the age" as the ambiance of sentiments, impressions, prejudices, and prospections which absorbs and diffuses the impact of contemporaneity on the individual author. It was to this thick intermediary atmosphere that Jane Austen related rather than (mechanically) to the raw events to which, the new Austen criticism almost leads us to believe, she then allegorized her responses. In fact when Jane Austen engaged in battle it was against "the spirit of the age," against what appeared to her as the exorbitant vision of high-romanticism. The targets of her criticism—whether revolutionary impulses, theatrical experiments, evangelical excess, Gothic mania— were just different ways in which extravagance revealed itself. These targets were different and yet related, somewhat in the manner in which Peacock's characters in *Nightmare Abbey* or *Crotchet Castle* are related.

Austen's first important critic, Sir Walter Scott, understood perfectly well what she was trying to do, perhaps because he felt that he was doing something similar himself. Scott maintained nothing less than the victory of the ordinary over the extraordinary in a kind of English *nouveau roman,* which dealt with "the middling classes of society," with the subtleties of everyday life, and with the great principles of ethics and the imagination as they functioned under normal circumstances. Jane Austen, Scott suggested, restrained adventure within the limits of the socially possible.[40]

It is interesting that his fundamental statement came well before the appearance of *Northanger Abbey* (1818), the novel in which Austen's strategy is most strikingly evident. However, all her novels have an underlying romantic potential (plots, situations, characters) which, each time, is suppressed and thwarted with cool deliberation by both the characters and the author. The fundamental thing to understand about Jane Austen is that the nature of her thinking was not preromantic or not-yet-romantic or incompletely romantic, but rather late romantic in her reaction against the comprehensive paradigm of high romanticism. She was well aware of what Wordsworth (Fanny Price had a transparency of *Tintern Abbey* in her room), Southey, Scott, and Byron were doing. In Ann Radcliffe she had a mine of romantic material. We may be allowed to speculate whether even Dr. Johnson or Cowper or George Crabbe, her great favorites, did not strike her as somehow like Goethe—that is, as those who had succeeded in holding back or neutralizing romantic impulses. Her task was analogous to theirs: to battle the romances, those stand-ins for Jacobins and heaven-storming bards. Like Cervantes in his age (to quote Q. D. Leavis's apt parallel) she felt she could battle the general Gothic spirit and still preserve or assimilate it.

In *Northanger Abbey* this program was fully and masterfully achieved. The novel begins as a Gothic story of horror and destruction, but from the outset there is an important difference: the Gothicism is willed and deliberately contrived by the imagination of Catherine Morland, by her selection of reading material, and by the projection of a mysterious halo upon Isabella and John Thorpe. The intensities of a romantic plot are thereafter eased, first by the fact that, as Marvin Mudrick has pointed out, the main characters are reversals of the usual Gothic types (Henry Tilney, Mrs. Allen), then by the action itself.[41] Catherine eventually discovers that the romantic plot of intense pain and danger followed by miraculous salvation is possible only in an impure fashion, and only on a reduced scale. Catherine muses: "Among the Alps and Pyrenees, perhaps, there were no mixed characters. There, such as were not as spotless as an angel, might have the dispositions of a fiend. But in England it was not so; among the English, she believed, in their hearts and habits, there was a general though unequal mixture of good and bad" (Chapter 25). But there is villainy in the general mix and the heroine *is* saved and improved toward the end. Core romanticism is both rejected and accepted in *Northanger Abbey.* Ultimately this procedure was no different from the miniaturization of Lamb or De Quincey. The huge Gothic theme with its connotations (emotional depth, persistent mystery, grasp of the sublime) was delineated as a brittle and imperfect construct. Indeed it has been argued that Austen related to the Sadian plot (elsewhere in this book I argue that the Marquis should be seen as one of the masters of core romanticism in France) in the same reductive ratio.[42]

Only in her actual narrative techniques did Austen differ from the essayists. Irony was one of these techniques. It has always been recognized as central to Jane Austen and need not be further discussed. Robert Kiely pointed correctly to another technique, which was in fact the presupposition of irony: "Jane Austen's crucial method is to introduce one 'romantic' character into the non-romantic world of marriage and money. Talk is difficult, but necessary. The romantic figure is not permitted the luxury of addressing a mute and spellbound stranger who cannot 'choose but hear.' In the world of Jane Austen, nearly everyone talks back, even to heroes and heroines."[43] Alistair Duckworth has drawn attention to the reconcretization going on in Austen's novels; her basic strategic move, he said, was to translate values and emotions into the firm physicalness of manor and estate.[44] The flittering mutability of theatrical innovations were disliked no less than "the rise of the economically motivated landed gentry," because they threatened a deeper harmony between natural and moral values. We hear the voice of Adalbert Stifter in the plans for improving Thornton Lacey (*Mansfield Park,* Chapter 25): "the farmyard must be cleared away entirely, and planted up to shut out the blacksmith's shop. The house must be turned to front the east instead of the north. The entrance and principal rooms must be on that side . . . You must make a new garden at what is now the back of the house . . . The meadows beyond that *will be* the garden, as well as what now *is*, sweeping round from the lane I stood in to the north-east, that is to the principal road through the village."[45] It is the voice of practicality as the expression of aesthetic vision.

Finally buried in the text and absorbed into it is the ultimate reduction: the attempt to tame the new ideology (romantic and revolutionary) with its open historical (social-political) implications and to shape it into manageable objects and units. This was another strategy, one that brought Jane Austen in line with Hazlitt or Hunt, although they believed that reductive efforts should ultimately result in liberalism, while the author of *Emma* assumed that the true answer was a stable traditional and organic system in which new ideas served chiefly as ephemeral challenges and vivifying but secondary goadings. The process of ideological and historical reduction can be observed in all her novels, but particularly and symphonically in *Mansfield Park*.

In this novel the important thing to note is the distinction between Sir Thomas and Lady Bertram on the one hand and Edward and Fanny on the other. It is true that the latter strenuously object to the idea of a family gathering to which the absence of an important ingredient, actually of the family's center, would give an air of insubstantiality (Chapter 9). Their common opposition to the theatrical exercises has often been discussed. It is equally true that Fanny is intensely aware of the dignified fullness of Lady Bertram, as the "picture of health, wealth, ease and tranquility" (Chapter 13). She loves Mansfield because there "no sounds of contention, no raised voice, no abrupt bursts, no threat of violence was ever heard; all proceeded in a regular course of cheerful orderliness; everybody had their due importance; everybody's feelings were consulted" (Chapter 39).

But the differences are equally significant. Edmund and Fanny, unlike the elder Bertrams, are romantics.[46] In addition, Fanny comes from a modest family background, from outside the traditions of Mansfield Park; Edmund himself is, as a younger son, somewhat on the periphery of these traditions. Fanny forcefully proclaims her views in talking to Miss Crawford. The material and social implications of the Bertram estate are of no interest to her; indeed they carry some connotations of hostile coldness and emptiness: "But there is nobleness in the name of Edmund. It is a name of heroism and renown; of kings, princes, and knights; and seems to breathe the spirit of chivalry and warm affections" (p. 190). Fanny "saves" Mansfield through her calm confidence, through the "quiet thing," a phrase that reminds us of Stifter's concern for "die Stillen im Lande" and "das sanfte Gesetz." Tony Tanner observed correctly that "it is only Fanny's stubborn tenacity that prevents their complete usurpation and demolition of that

world."[47] But it is equally important to note that she and Edmund
were not its inheritors, nor did they take it over. What they tried to do
at Thornton Lacey (and thereafter at the Mansfield living) was to
apply the values that they cherished. In *Mansfield Park* we witness the
severing of conservative values from their crumbling support and their
grafting on other, more adequate stems. The latter are, significantly,
much smaller in size. To survive, the harmony and gentility of Mansfield Park must be tranferred into another sphere. The romantic excess and the Jacobin adumbrations of the outside world are neutralized
in the novel by change, reduction, and assimilation.

We know now that through her family and friends Jane Austen was
aware in a very personal way of the French Revolution as well as of
the ensuing Reign of Terror and Napoleonic wars of conquest, to
which she was naturally opposed. She was by instinct uneasy with the
Evangelical revival.[48] Her opposition to the prose of Gothic romance
is plain. Of feminist affirmation she was suspicious. Individualism, subjectivism, and worship of the self were her most consistent adversaries.[49] To subsume all these features under the metaphor of Burkean
ideology—because, lest we forget, that is not and cannot be anything
else but a critical metaphor—is not wrong, but it pays attention to
only part of the picture. Jane Austen was, as Irvin Ehrenpreis showed,
equally eager to domesticate the Christian hero: "When Mr. Knight-
ley in *Emma* dances with Harriet Smith to rescue her from Mr.
Elton's scorn, he shows the courage that Austen meant to celebrate.
When Tilney in *Northanger Abbey* defies his father and goes forth to
find Catherine Morland, he is acting out Austen's response to the
manners of the Giaour."[50] The domestication, to elaborate for a moment, was not ideologically distorted. The exclusion of the higher social levels from the novels carried a message of its own, one not less
clear than the much-vaunted discretion in avoiding direct references to
the political-military events of the day. Like many Biedermeier writers, Jane Austen resorted to the idyllic model and superimposed it
upon romantic aspirations. In playing out "the gentry against the
peerage, the lower clergy against bishops, the tradesmen of the provincial towns against the great merchants and bankers in London,"
she came much closer to Cobbett than critics will admit.[51] In any case
her purposes were fully achieved: absorbing feminism into the family,
toning down the upsurge of visionariness, transforming wealth into
manners, neutralizing political revolt, conferring the gift of proportion

on the body social, and taming high romanticism into a mode analogous to that of the Biedermeier.

SIR WALTER SCOTT was perhaps even more than Jane Austen a central figure of the English Biedermeier. The relative aesthetic insignifi-
cance of his early work made it easier for us to think of him as
somebody who emerged on the literary scene after 1815. Even his resort to the historical novel as a literary vehicle showed that he had
been somewhat uncomfortable with the forms of early high romanticism. Throughout the nineteenth century he was thought of as a
writer who investigated the opposition between the past and the present and reveled in violent conflicts and the luxuriance of local color.[52]
This distorted perception is meaningful. Readers knew intuitively that
Scott was adapting the forbidding patterns of romanticism to more
practical and domestic uses and, like Austen, was bringing Romanticism into the parlor and showing its compatibility with bourgeois
amenities and sedate comportment.[53] In another chapter I will discuss
Scott in some detail. Here I want to mention the relationship between
Scott and the paradigm of core romanticism, as well as the problem of
value transfer which, as I indicated above, provides the key to the sociopolitical overtones of *Mansfield Park.*

The importance of the epic tradition for the historical novel has
often been emphasized and rightly so. But other sources were perhaps
even more important since they expressed the dynamics of romanticism and Scott's part in it. In a sense the historical novel responded to
the Gothic novel; the historical novel tried to preserve the shock value
and strong colors of the Gothic novel while using plausible locales and
actors, thus landing half-way between the supernatural and the trite.
The historical novel was a device for moderate estrangement.

The long philosophical-lyrical poems of early romanticism, for instance those of Coleridge, Wordsworth, and even Blake, were an
equally important complementary source of the historical novel. As in
the case of Gothic fiction, and indeed, as in the case of the old epics,
we cannot speak here of an immediate filiation, but rather of a series of
structural relations (analogies, oppositions) to such gestures and intentions as seem basic to the core romantic system. Scott, particularly in
the *Waverley* novels, used a procedure borrowed from the high-romantic writers. The underlying "deep structure" of his novels was
identical with that of high romanticism. The specific differences indi-

cate precisely the nature of the historical novel, as well as of the literary period when the new genre was developed.

How did this adaptation work? The *Waverley* hero has been said by several critics, correctly I would contend, to be similar in many ways to some prototypical figures of romantic lyricism, such as Keats's "sleepers" and Wordsworth's "wanderers," and, I think, the dreaming lyrical personas of some Blake and Novalis works. The passivity of the typical hero of the *Waverley* novels and his trance-like state were close to romantic ecstasy; they were necessarily transitional, leading to an improved and higher state. Far from being demeaning, passivity was a sign of election; it prepared the hero and turned him into a solution maker. The disposition of the novels' adventures and the organization of the plot had the shape of the paradigmatic high-romantic story.

Usually Scott's heroes did not have an Eden from which they started, they just dreamt of one. That was the case with most of their high-romantic counterparts also. Heinrich von Ofterdingen did not start from any paradisial state, he just knew he must seek one. For Shelley's Prometheus the perfection of freedom was a dim memory (or a visionary hope), for the Hegel of the *Phenomenology of the Spirit* it could be nothing but an intuition or reconstitution through documentary deduction. Similarly Wordsworth's *Prelude* was a search for reintegration, for a primary full accord of the mind with nature. The convention chosen was that of a point in time consequent to Edenic infancy, which by its very nature did not allow much logical and psychological space for self-contemplation, self-reflection, judgment, and comparison.

Therefore it should not be surprising that Edward Waverley, Frank Osbaldistone, or Darsie Latimer were, even at the beginning of their adventures, deeply split characters. On the one hand they had a red-hot imagination, intense sentimentality, and a bias in favor of the past; on the other they were structurally linked to the modern world around them. Edward Waverley is shaped (we are told in Chapters 3 and 4) by his whimsical and self-indulgent adventures in reading in the "Library at Waverley-Honour, a large Gothic room, with double arches and a gallery": Shakespeare and Milton, Spenser and Drayton, Pulci and Boccaccio, Froissart and Brantôme, the *Adventures of Don Quixote* and the writings of his corrupting mentors.[54] Family history, folk legends, and personal imagination rounded off his early education, which is essentially an initiation into the world of Edenic integrity.

The direction of his career and his attraction toward the archaic social wilderness and the unfettered natural sublimities of the Highlands must be understood as attempts to actualize this imaginary world. On the other hand Waverley comes from parents who have accepted the Hanoverian compromise, he feels impelled to save Colonel Talbot's life, feels more at home with the Bradwardines than with the Mac-Ivors, and breaks with the Pretender. The split in Frank Osbaldistone is quite similar. He is on his way to a business and accounting career in his father's firm, and there is no indication that he is objectively un-suited for it. However he much prefers the leisurely world of senti-mental poetry, travel, and indulgence in natural feelings. These inclinations are gratified by his father's decision to send him north: "to pay your uncle a visit, and see the state of his family."[55] It is not clear to what extent this was vengeful punishment and to what extent it was based on ulterior educational motives. In effect it means that Frank, like Edward, will have the chance to confront the realities of the ro-mantic system of values he had wanted to identify with and to acquire a better knowledge thereof. This procedure is further verified in the case of Darsie Latimer who sets out deliberately in search of what he takes to be his original state of perfection. He had obviously been shaped by the Fairfords and their associates, by their stern classicism and pragmatic rationalism. But he considered himself analytically rent and sought the fulfillment of fantasy, sentiment, and desire. He is soon confronted with the geological eruption of those original strata he is looking for, in the person of his formidable Uncle Herries of Birrens-work.

These and other similar young people in the Waverley cycle emerge as regenerated individuals. Part of their change is normal growth and maturation. (There is a strong streak of the *Bildungsroman* in Scott, which most of us overlook.) But this change also signals the birth of a "new race," intelligent and practical on the one hand, with an internalized sensibility on the other. Thus Bloom's felicitous phrase the "internalization of quest" can be fully applied to Scott, also. Ed-ward Waverley chooses Rose Bradwardine over Flora MacIvor. The Tully Veolan of which he becomes the laird is itself a realm of unifica-tion, synthesizing the modernity of England and the sublime wilder-ness of the remote north. Edward is of course symbolically the son of both the opportunistic and adaptive Richard and the crusty recalcitrant Sir Everard; he had acquired a very useful further father in the loyal, forthright, and progressive Colonel Talbot and finally endowed himself for good measure and wise balance with Cosmo Bradwardine, himself the emblem, as it were, of Edward's months of Highland experience and years of romantic revery. When they marry, Edward and Rose gather and embody the past and adumbrate the future. Somehow paradise is regained, or so we are encouraged to believe. Frank Osbaldistone's union with Di Vernon likewise establishes itself in a geographical area separate from the martial anarchy of the Campbells and the Scottish Osbaldistones no less than from the dry commercialism of the family's southern branch. Frank accepts as guide and political model the adaptive Bailie Jarvie who could function in both areas.

Another set of changes prominent in the Waverley novels also suggest a restoration of integrity and the recapturing of a last, remote image of perfection. When Edward Waverley returns to Tully Veolan during his search for his loved ones after the debacle of the 1745 rebellion and campaign, he finds total desolation: "The battlements above the gate were broken and thrown down—The avenue was cruelly wasted. Several large trees were felled and left lying across the path; and the cattle of the villages, and the more rude hoofs of dragon horses, had poached into black mud the verdant turf which Waverley had so much admired" (p. 392). As he walks around, the signs multiply. Only the structure itself ("the thickness of the walls") had survived malicious attempts at arson. Otherwise everything had suffered direly: "The towers and pinnacles of the main building were scorched and blackened; the pavement of the court broken and shattered; the doors torn down entirely, or hanging by a single hinge; the windows dashed in and demolished, and the court strewed with articles of furniture broken into fragments . . . The balustrade was broken down, the walls destroyed, the borders overgrown with weeds, and the fruit-trees cut down or grubbed up" (p. 392).

The scene is frightening and repulsive in itself, but also because the observer had known its previous aspect well and is thus continuously drawing comparisons. In this he resembles the lyrical persona of "The Deserted Village," one who knew masterfully how to juxtapose the violence wrought by time and man on the complicated, unstable unities of nature and civilization. There is throughout this descriptive episode of Chapter 63 an undercurrent of symmetrical opposition which reminds us of Goldsmith, as well as of the outraged Matthew Bramble of the letter of June 8, in which he enumerated the ways in which the air, food, and sounds of London were inferior to those of his native Wales. But of course what Waverley inspects is more specific. It is a "great good place," a baronial residence, a park and castle, a residence for many generations, an embodiment of history. What he observes is an object shaped by history, one in which history had nested, and in an empirical sense one which *is* history, or what we can know of history. Like Volney gloating over the melancholy passing of the Eastern Mediterranean empires, Waverley is conscious of watching history in action and surveying the march of time. He is very sensitive to the fact that those concentrated carriers of axiological significance (the Bears of Bradwardine, the family pictures, the plates, the horse-chestnut trees) were singled out for precise mutilation and obliteration, more than others. Like Werther, who before his suicide, scrutinized from a changed point of view the haunts of his once glad idyllic hopes, Waverley muses on places which had been invested with emotional attachments: Rose's little balcony on the fifth floor, the fountain, and the stone-basin. The tears flooding his inner soul are seen in the flooded courtyard, much as Werther's desperate inner crying had filled the landscape of his mind when masses of water swamped Wahlheim (December 12) and all the valleys Werther had walked a year ago. And as Renzo in Manzoni's *I Promessi Sposi* (Chapter 33) returns to stare sadly at his vineyard turned into inextricable wilderness—calling to mind early seventeenth-century Italy no less than the hero's own complicated and desperate life—so Waverley sees in the ruin of Bradwardine the destruction of a social system and the destruction of his own hopes of being integrated in a romantic whole. Waverley is a hero who, like the Ancient Mariner, owes his salvation, practical and perhaps moral, to a spontaneous act of goodness and generosity (he opens himself fully and defenselessly to the universe by sparing and rescuing Colonel Talbot). But as he steps slowly, broken-heartedly among shattered memories, he is certainly not a Coleridgean hero; he is in fact exactly like a Wordsworthian lyrical persona, "with feelings and sentiments—how different from those which attended his first entrance! Then, life was so new to him . . . Now, how changed! how saddened . . . was his character" (p. 392). Like Goldsmith and Volney, Waverley knows that objects change and palaces fall into ruin, but like Wordsworth near Tintern Abbey he knows that the observing conscience has also changed.

The first significant feature of this scene in Chapter 63 of *Waverley* is the coincidence of the two kinds of changes (that of the observer and the observed, of the subject and the object, as it were). The second feature, also explicitly mentioned, is the quickness of the change. Volney needed centuries, Goldsmith a generation, Wordsworth five years (or, elsewhere, the passing from childhood to maturity); for Waverley, less than a year suffices. The passage quoted above continues: "yet how elevated was his character, within the course of a very few months. Danger and misfortune are rapid, though severe teachers. 'A sadder and wiser man' he felt, in internal confidence and mental dignity, a compensation for the gay dreams which, in his case, experience had so rapidly dissolved" (p. 392). (The actual quotation from a lyrical work must be seen as highly significant.) There is, the reader cannot help but suspect, something a little strange here, some kind of manipulation, an impatience or a demonstrative streak to which the high romantics had not really accustomed him.

These suspicions are both confirmed and allayed by the third important feature. There is in this novel—as there certainly does not *have* to be—a solution, a happy ending. Only a few months later, as Baron Bradwardine traveled through Scotland with his daughter and his son-in-law, he found that everything was being returned to him in good condition, and that, like Dr. Primrose, he was now restored to his former happy state. The circumstances that had led to this follow: The peasants had disliked the new owner, a collateral kinsman. The kinsman had decided to sell. The buyer was not Colonel Talbot as widely believed—and as poetic justice might possibly have dictated— but rather wealthy Edward Waverley himself, who decided to offer it (as an inverse dowry, we might say) to his father-in-law, after lovingly restoring everything, including, miraculously, "the celebrated cup of Saint Duthac, the Blessed Bear of Bradwardine!" Miraculously? Perhaps not: Colonel Talbot hastened to explain how it was traced through the good offices of the orderly Spontoon from Mrs. Nosebag, "originally the helpmate of a pawnbroker" and as a result of the enthusiasm of Frank Stanley for Scottish antiquities and manners. Miraculously? Perhaps so: after all the cup does function as the Holy Grail of the Arthurian empire of Bradwardine. (Scott, in *The Bridal of Triermain* let us remember, was the first of a host of nineteenth-century writers to adapt an Arthurian theme.) A mystical allusion is embedded here. And so everything is set right again.

Or is it? We notice several little signs of a changed situation in

Chapter 71. Cosmo Comyne had been utterly subdued by his defeat and by his plunge (much like that of King Lear) into the depths of human misery and moral suffering. He accepts his restoration with a kind of resigned happiness. His freedom will be effectively checked in the future by the financial burden of a mortgage (gentle and familial as that may be). He surrenders the head of the table to Lady Emily and concedes the right of benediction to Reverend Morton, the outside visitor. Even more important, the closing words of the chapter express the author's confidence in the glad fusion of the houses of Bradwardine and Waverley. In this symbiotic relationship, substance as well as appearance are provided by the Bradwardines, but (male) leadership and initiative are contributed by Edward. In spite of everything, he is the general inheritor.

Both observer and scene change twice. They change so rapidly that we are impelled to see the change as a signal for something else. And the restoration of the scene, we may assume, is due to the fact that the observing conscience has itself changed and is now ready and entitled to assume the inheritance. Many examples confirm this assumption. *Rob Roy* is largely a story about an inheritance. Rashleigh tries to turn himself into the inheritor and synthesizer of the trading and landowning branches of the family; he tries to use the dynamics of progress to further his reactionary aims. Frank Osbaldistone grows like any young man in a *Bildungsroman.* The point of the novel is to prove that he is capable of the right kind of change, synthesis, and compromise. He has to be able to prove that he deserves to be the restorer. *Redgauntlet,* of course, also circles around the concept of inheritance. Its subject is, at least in part, as it had been throughout the *Waverley* cycle, a matter of the legitimacy of the dynasty—England and Scotland themselves as contested inheritances. (The plots of *The Antiquary, Old Mortality,* and *Ivanhoe* have a similar structure.)

How does this kind of problematic fit the new literary species and the thinking of the laird of Abbotsford in the general period dynamic of romanticism? Is there a typological relationship between this emergent historical novel and *The Prelude,* even if we dismiss a direct historical connection? *The Prelude* exemplified some of the highest ambitions of romanticism in a pure form. It attempted to capture the formation of the spirit in its entirety, and it attempted at the same time to show the formation of a spirit whose inevitable purpose was to recapture its original purity and integrity. The lyrical persona who reached the top of Mount Snowdon or whose prophet-like calling was suddenly revealed was human conscience pushed to some outer limits and thus transfigured. It has been rightly likened to Hegel's universal spirit.[56] This lyrical persona has overcome, at least for a while, the oppositions between individual and society, between reason and emotion, between mind and nature. Is such a transfiguration real? Is it something that actually happens or is it just imagined? Is it something that can happen now or merely something that will happen in some indefinitely remote future? Is it something that happens for a short moment, a flash of insight as it were, or is it a durable change? Does it or will it happen to everybody or is it limited to a few chosen ones—visionaries, poets, and rebels? These were the questions against which high romanticism broke; they explain why it was so short-lived and why it was received with such general hostility and scorn when not ignored.

The dialectics of restoration in *Waverley* were meant to indicate a solution to the divisions of the present as set against the lyrical integrity of an assumed past or of some privileged moment of transfiguration. The individuals who represented hope achieved in their own way the integration of faculties that the past (individual or sociocultural) had provided. They were a regenerated race; in a sense they brought back the paradisial unity.

In comparing the *Waverley* novels with *The Prelude* we notice two important differences. One is precisely the character of this third, "synthetic" stage. In the Mount Snowdon episode this stage had been a quasi-mystical experience, truly unique, a tremendously intense identification with the cosmos, but—if we can apply time measurements at all—of short duration. Alan Fairford and Greenmantle, or Waverley and Rose embark on a different life. Their integration of values is much less ambitious; it can claim no mystical or cosmic dimension—in fact they are probably still beset by imperfections and questions. Yet theirs is a durable and above all *practical* solution. There is some similarity between the framework of the way of life adumbrated in these historical novels and some actual and possible social situation. The integration is imperfect but efficient.

The second is the attitude implicit in all the *Waverley* novels toward the "original" state of the mind or of mankind, and this attitude was not one of uncontaminated trust. Unlike Wordsworth, Scott had learned to suspect the primal state. He tended to identify an aggressive, future-oriented revolution with a past that had not been exactly paradisial. In turn, the Fall, the state of modified growth, of separation and secularization, was not necessarily all evil or hateful. Or, to put it in different words, the moral separation and the historical separation no longer seemed to coincide. Although the Scottish past of the Mac-Ivors in *Waverley* or the MacGregors in *Rob Roy* may have been awesome and sublime, it was also dangerous, destructive, and anarchic (something the passive heroes did not recognize at first). It was in many ways similar to the revolutions of Scott's day. (In fact it would seem that in opposing the Scottish past to the English present, Scott used the first term as a metaphor for a threatening revolutionary future.) Therefore Scott's *Waverley* cycle can be read as a deliberate attempt to qualify the inherited romantic paradigm, to soften its starkness. Above all, the future must be a compromise and not a return—a genuine synthesis of previous elements, rather than a leap into an unknown regeneration.

THE TOWERING figures of Scott and Austen, the consistent direction of change of most of the great romantics (Wordsworth, Coleridge, Byron, Keats), the coherent movement of the conversational essayists (Lamb, De Quincey, Hazlitt) were not events that occurred in a vacuum. They were supported by many phenomena in the social sphere as well as by facts of an intellectual order, and they were homologous with the great patterns of society at that time. The Biedermeier model can help arrange and explain many social-intellectual occurrences of the 1820s and 1830s that seem somewhat puzzling in isolation. These occurrences logically became parts of the more relaxed romanticism of the post-Napoleonic period and indeed fleshed out the modified paradigms of the 1820s. I want to cull a few scattered facts to illustrate these statements.

The somewhat incoherent editorial policies of the reviews, with their contradictions between ideology, taste, and critical principles, make more sense when seen as the deliberate search for the best formula of a national Biedermeier: the *Edinburgh Review* was Whig and rather antiromantic; the *London Magazine* liberal and proromantic; the *Quarterly Review* and *Blackwood's* Tory and proromantic in a qualified fashion. If we go beyond personal skirmishes and analyze the serious orientations and intellectual visions that informed their cultural policies, we find that they share the conviction that the total transformation enjoined by high romanticism was unfeasible and that something had to give. Differences arose simply from the manner and place in which the adjustments were supposed to be made, but they all had in common a certain spirit of compromise. Francis Jeffrey for instance believed that the Whigs were walking the middle road between Tories and Democrats. The intellectuals of his stamp were directly connected with the great Whig power centers, such as Holland House, and with the academic liberals of the Speculative Society. Tories naturally enough thought that *they* were the voice for moderation and for the organic collaboration between the parts of society. But even a socialist like Hodgskin concluded that "Productive capital and skilled labour are . . . one."[57] I believe William Cobbett can be said to be a social ideologist in the populist Biedermeier vein in England, equally opposed to the relentless growth of capitalism and to the messianic notes of radicalism. *Rural Rides* appeared between 1821 and 1834 and *Advice to Young Men* in 1829—both operated in the frame of the idyllic societal model, both opposed empiricism to rationalism, common sense to theory, cultivated nature to the extremes of primitivism and sophistication, authentic labor to alienation and exploitation. Like Paul-Louis Courier in France, Cobbett knew how to elude the usual blandness of synthesis by alienating all sides at the same time. The common feature of all these ideological lines, different from each other as they may be, is the search for compromise: a reflection of the age's combination of ideal totality with practical realities.

Compromise in social and ideological matters was reinforced by the utilitarian tenor of the age. The Benthamite level of reference was always there—for those who adhered to it as much as for those who did not. Happiness and practicality were understood to go hand in hand by almost all the politicians and intellectuals. Significantly, the Sunday school system and the Lancastrian monitorial system spread out at about the same time, as attempts by religious and secular educators to enlighten the children in a practical way.[58] In fact what the Evangelicals were doing in religion was somewhat similar to what utilitarians were doing in social politics—searching for practical happiness. From the later 1820s and 1830s on even the rise of the "shilling shockers" (paperbound abridgments of Gothic novels), cheap reprints, and serializations served purposes other than the purely commercial, in that they began to build a new and very broad readership. It was an enlightenment of sorts, a utilitarian diffusion of reading habits and literary patterns.[59]

Other reductive (Biedermeier) features besides compromise and utilitarianism can be recognized in the attitude toward travel in post-Napoleonic Britain. This was of course the age in which railways and steamships were becoming part of the social fabric, as well as the age of the fast mail coach, the age of Thomas Telford and John Mc-Adam's new road system. But it was also typically an age of armchair traveling. The boom in travel books and geographic descriptions shows that the desire for expansion can find its own substitutions and reductions.[60] Similarly "the golden age of pugilism" represents a kind of substitute warfare in which all parts of society took part and which produced its own prominent chroniclers such as Pierce Egan.[61] This kind of reductive adjustment of broader aims to social needs and possibilities resembles what Austen was doing in her novels. Analogously what the architects and the furniture designers of the day were doing might be compared to the historicism of Walter Scott, if we think of their allusions and references to Egyptian, Far Eastern, neoclassical, and Gothic styles. The great caricaturists of the age, Rowlandson, Cruikshank, and many others combined the satirical traditions of the eighteenth century with a newfound cranky coziness in a Biedermeier-type combination that was soon to bear fruit in the work of Surtees, Dickens, and their illustrators, and which has many German counterparts.

Perhaps the most striking sociocultural phenomenon was dandyism. The dandies and eccentrics of the day ranged from somewhat respectable and literary types, such as Byron's friend Scrope Davies to Jack Mytton (1796–1834) a kind of Evel Knievel of the day, who was said to own seven hundred pairs of boots and slippers, three thousand shirts, and one thousand hats—to have spent half a million pounds on liquor, and who once set himself on fire to cure his hiccups.[62] Beau Brummell remains the textbook example of a dandy. He, as well as those who imitated him, may be said to have bent the revolutionary impulse into mere playfulness and gratuitous provocation. (A short two decades before Brummell's heyday, the Directory fops of Paris, the *incroyables,* were using a similar strategy in their way of dressing and behaving.) The minor refinement and wit of Beau Brummell could be described as a romanticism with the materials of the ancien régime; not a blowing up of forms, not a destruction, but a rearrangement. At Calais, after his flight from pursuing debtors, his quarters and his mode of life were Stifterian and "altwienerisch." But even in his prime, Beau Brummell's insistence that elegance lay in detail and craftsmanship, as well as his basic tenet that the acme of elegance was lack of stridency—revealed the moderate soul of the Biedermeier burgher.[63] Nor was this an isolated instance. We have only to think of Leigh Hunt transforming his prison cell into an elegantly cozy little nest with a pianoforte, wallpaper forming a bower of roses under a Florentine heaven, and a lute and busts of great poets among the bookcases.[64]

The unifying patterns emerge in poetry also and go some way toward explaining the apparent ferment and disorder of the literary scene. The discrepancy between a contemporary romantic elite and a vast anticlassic foundation of popular poetry is in some ways misleading, although some of the latter does function as a kind of counterpoint to the romantic revolution. In such marginal works as those written by George Darley or massively represented in *The Annuals*, traces of the same hybrid combinations of tame romanticism observed in the chief quarterlies can be noted. (*Forget-me-Not, The Literary Souvenir, Friendship's Offering, The Anniversary*, and others all appeared in the 1820s, apparently under the influence of German models; they are a typical example of Biedermeier popular diffusion of lyricism.)[65] But, more to the point, W. M. Praed tones down Byron, Thomas Beddoes tones down the Gothic impulse, W. S. Landor fully builds up the romantic version of classicism. (Along with Platen in Germany and Nodier in France, Landor belongs to the makers of the typical nineteenth-century blend of neoclassicism—a sophisticated, complex, and ultimately decadent juggling of all previous kinds of neoclassicism, that is, of all the successive assimilations and revivals of the classical tradition.)[66] Thomas Moore, Samuel Rogers, and Thomas Campbell all further exemplify the determined attempt to bring romantic sublimity and visionariness under control. A close look at this abundant body of minor work can qualify the generalizations regarding a national English sublimity versus the sedate verbalism of Victor Hugo.[67] Hugo was a much greater artist, but his domesticating impulse directed him in the same channels as his English poetic contemporaries of the 1820s and 1830s. The explanations of "epic tradition" in romantic poetry, useful as they may be, similarly translate into generic categories (lyrical-epic) the historical realities of internal romantic dynamics.

The two most interesting poets (aside from Landor) were Crabbe and John Clare. Crabbe foreshadowed the later antiromantic responses. He did not *continue* the eighteenth-century tradition, he *resumed* it. "From Pope's death until the appearance of Churchill in the early 1760's there was no major satirist in England except Johnson of the Juvenalian imitations; from Churchill's death in 1764 until the publication of "The Village" in 1783, there was no major verse satire published in England," said one critic.[68] So in a peculiar way Crabbe reacted against eighteenth-century poetry, but he came too early, before a full change was upon English literature. The leading figures of the English Biedermeier recognized him as one of theirs and celebrated him, first for his artistry in the depiction of details (Crabbe was a "Dutchifier" of the first order), but more generally for his apt combination of the classic and the romantic. Lamb adapted *The Confidant* into a drama. Byron considered him one of the few contemporary poets "not on a wrong track" (letter to Thomas Moore, February 2, 1818). Campbell had "filial" feelings toward him, Ebenezer Elliott thought of himself as a disciple, Tennyson and Browning in their youth were influenced by him. He was an intimate of Samuel Rogers's. On Scott's list of preferences he ranked high and may have been an example for his early writing. Crabbe's latter-day reputation effectively integrated him into the literary life of the English Biedermeier.

John Clare was even more firmly ensconced in the poetic processes of later romanticism. The volumes published in his lifetime (in the 1820s) were quickly recognized by Lamb, De Quincey, and others as germane to their own preoccupations. I would venture to say that they appreciated in Clare a kind of relocalization, a precise placing in time and in physical reality of some general sentimentalist and naturalist feelings whose expression in poetry had been pioneered by James Thomson and Cowper.[69] For my purposes here it is more interesting to observe how Clare used the wording and the sentimental connotations of Goldsmith's *Deserted Village* to simplify Wordsworth's dialectical anamnesis and to pin it down in a concrete framework. In *Helpstone Green*, one stanza incorporating Wordsworthian sentiments such as "O'er its green hills I've often stray'd / In childhood's happy hour . . . But now increasing years have coin'd / Those children into man" (lines 26–27, 31–32) is preceded by more precisely descriptive lines on "The well-known brook, the favourite tree" (1. 21), or "hawthorn bowers" and "Long waving rows of willow." Moreover,

the Wordsworthian "loss of vision" is given a precise social and historical explanation (the process of agricultural enclosure). The broad philosophical pattern of high romanticism thereby acquires a focus and is
applied to a limited and particularized situation in the Biedermeier
manner. At the same time that grand Wordsworthian achievement,
the synthesis of simplicity and transfiguration, is broken down into its
component elements.

The minor prose of the 1820s and 1830s in England took on forms
of expressions and moved in channels that appear to be analogous to
those on the Continent, and particularly in Biedermeier Germany.
The sentimental coziness, smiling moderation, home-and-hearth atmosphere was rendered by Mary Russell Mitford, as well as slightly later
by Elizabeth Gaskell in *Cranford.* R. H. Barham in *Ingoldsby Legends,*
shrewdly preserved an array of romantic-fantastic elements while establishing a reassuring framework of humor around them. Robert Smith
Surtees was typical[70] of the minor writers of the day in his accent
on the harmlessly droll and on contented jollity. John Galt in a more
serious vein represented the revival of a Goldsmith tradition in prose.
At the other end of the literary spectrum, the pure exoticism of J. J.
Morier and the sensationalism of C. R. Maturin can be contrasted
with the richly symbolic texture of the high romantic William Beckford. Barry Cornwall and particularly Landor were superlative practitioners of the *tableau vivant*—a quintessential Biedermeier genre that
aimed to transcend both historiographic discourse and literature. The
"imaginary conversation" proposed to recapture the past and invent it
at the same time, applying, as it were, the technique of Wordsworth's
recollection outside poetry. The circular pilgrimage was expressed in a
specifically modified event: what was captured was not the original
unity of paradise, but merely a particular and well-delineated historical
event. In the process, inevitably, imagination became an instrument; in
a sense it had a utilitarian use. Tibullus and Messala, Cromwell and
Walter Nobel, teenage Shakespeare and Sir Thomas Lucy, Petrarch,
and Boccaccio, Louis XIV and Father La Chaise are among the many
characters evoked with varying success, but with firm elegance by
Landor. (The similarities between Landor and Scott should not be
overlooked; their purposes were the same, only their procedures differed.) Like some of Musset's armchair dramas and illustrations of
proverbs, the writings of Barry Cornwall (Bryan Walter Procter) were
illustrations of given models: "The Rape of Proserpina," "Julian the

Apostate," "The Return of Mark Antony," "Mirandola," and so forth.

The prose of the day was prey to massive anxieties and crises of identity. History and sociology were the most serious temptations and were used to justify the writing of fiction. But of course essay writing was always there as a combinatory exercise: Leigh Hunt and Charles Lamb were prime examples.[71] Even the renewal of the novel by Dickens, Eliot, and the Brontës—when compared with eighteenth-century novels, was due, according to one critic, to their absorption of the poetic substance of romanticism, that is, to a hybrid and compromising impulse.[72] The 1820s and 1830s were the indispensable transitional period when the romantic vision was being processed and assimilated or bent and melted in dozens of little forges, as well as in some large and masterful ones.

CAN WE THEN assert with confidence that there is an English Biedermeier? Let us say, guardedly, that it seems difficult to write on the history of English literature in the first half of the nineteenth century without postulating one, because otherwise too many writers remain unaccounted for. Besides, a dynamic understanding of the period can explain much better the complex relations between succeeding generations and the literary interaction with historical realities in general. The correspondences with the evolution of German romanticism are quite clear if looked at from the angle I have discussed. The generation of Novalis, Hölderlin, Tieck, and the Schlegels corresponds to Blake, Wordsworth, and Coleridge in time as well as in ideas and style. Tieck and Friedrich Schlegel changed after 1815 much like Wordsworth and Coleridge. (Schelling changed also, but in a different way.) There are some transitional figures such as Eichendorff and E. T. A. Hoffmann whose literary position can be said to correspond to that of Keats. The common articulations of the Biedermeierzeit can be observed. *The Examiner, The Liberal,* Leigh Hunt and his friends resemble in many ways Jung Deutschland, even though they confronted less formidable forces. An analysis of their positions on external affairs (Italy, Poland, slavery, the Spanish colonies) shows close analogies in the way they looked at the world. Heine has often been compared to Byron, and no further elaboration is necessary. Southey's ballads of heart-warming goodness, rousing heroism, and strapping humor (as well as occasionally Moore's or Hood's) are the equivalent of those that Swabian writers (Uhland, Kerner, Schwab) would be writing a very few years later. Keats and Brown's *Otho the Great* is the counterpart of Grillparzer's Biedermeier tragedies. (Grillparzer in turn exerted some influence on Byron.)[73] German literature was thoroughly familiar to some of the great figures (Coleridge, Scott, Carlyle, De Quincey), but not only to them. Shelley had read some of the Germans; Byron, Wordsworth, Keats, and Hazlitt were all touched by German literature to some degree; and Beddoes, Darley, John Gibson, Lockhart, and Henry Crabb Robinson had a specialized knowledge of German. August von Kotzebue and others were well known to a broad English public. Cozy sentimentality, harmless drollery, historicism, and exotic sensationalism abound in the popular literature of both countries. An awareness of such connections and equivalences can help us define the period between 1815 and 1848 as one with a paradigm of its own, distinct from romanticism, yet continuing it, much as was the case in Germany. A classicist counterpoint to the romantic offensive can be observed in both literatures.

The other important need that may be fulfilled by using the category of Biedermeier in English literary history is the effective closing of the gap between Victorianism and romanticism. Some of the greatest Victorians—Dickens, Thackeray, Tennyson, Browning, Carlyle—did not have a direct relation to romanticism, but rather one mediated through the later romantics. Bulwer Lytton and, to some extent, Charles Reade (*The Cloister and the Hearth*) were deeply indebted to the work of Scott and were rooted in the literary environment of the 1830s. Browning's early works (*Paracelsus, Dramatic Lyrics*) perhaps come closer to being historical tableaux in the manner of Landor than works of the more psychological and argumentative type he later produced when he tended to play down the mere historical aspects. Tennyson's classicized, tempered, and more realistic romanticism may well be understood as the answer to the needs of a Biedermeier age that never quite succeeded in producing a great poet; he continued Keats by divesting him of all visionary grandeur, but preserving the magic, the nostalgia, and the doubts. The first works of Dickens owe virtually nothing to core romanticism, but they are impossible to imagine without Lamb and his colleagues, without Surtees and the caricaturists. Thackeray, before developing fully into a psychological realist and aesthetic sentimentalist was something else: a writer of burlesques, sketches, humourous essays, travelogues. In fact at least one critic maintains that Thackeray's best work was written in his youth, when he transposed the manner of Cruikshank and Rowlandson in prose.[74] As a "high popularizer" and parodist he brought lofty, abstract categories down to earth. The continuity between the early and later part of his work is plain, and *Pendennis* may indeed be said to be a belated example of Biedermeier prose.[75] In a word, while the great romantics may have been inspiring examples, they were not the direct predecessors of Victorianism; only through the filter of the English equivalent of the Biedermeier could Victorianism emerge.

The Victorians themselves were aware of the passing of an age. The tensions that in the 1820s and 1830s had been suspended in a light precarious balance were gone. There was in England no strong voice such as that of Burckhardt or Renan to deplore the loss of one of the sweetest and most civilized ages in European history. But there was awareness. Charlotte Brontë's Rochester was an aging Byron who was being domesticated willy-nilly, taken over into the structures of society; some of the wildness of an earlier age was still in him. George Eliot's *Middlemarch* was full of the nostalgia for the simpler life of several decades past. In *Adam Bede* Eliot described and compared "old leisure" to the Victorian world. Tennyson's poem *The Lotus Eaters* (ll. 75–85) related to Keats's *To Autumn* and perhaps to Wordsworth's *Nutting* as a conscious step forward in the exploration of ripeness. "Lo! sweetened with the summer light, / the full juiced apple, waxing over-mellow, / Drops in a silent autumn night. All its allotted length of days / The flower ripens in its place, / Ripens and fades, and falls," said Tennyson's choir.[76] Ripeness was no longer all, it was a passing moment in a cycle. The rich, overflowing, tantalizing ambiguity of Keats's *To Autumn* was for the great Victorian a thing of the past.

3

FRENCH ROMANTICISM:
TWO BEGINNINGS?

WHY does French romanticism begin in the eighteenth and again in the nineteenth century? The French romantics are, schoolbooks tell us, Hugo, Lamartine, Vigny, and their cohorts; the legendary battle of *Hernani* and the preface to *Cromwell* are still remembered; *La Confession d'un enfant du siècle* summarized for many the dilemmas and sensitivities of the typical French romantic. And every reader knows that the grande dame of the movement, its inspirer and teacher, was Mme. de Staël, that she was the one who brought to the attention of French readers the cool, mossy delights of dreamy German philosophy, thus unleashing the generation of the 1820s.

Did French literature really deserve a romanticism imported from abroad? Why was French literature the rearguard of this Europe-wide movement, sending out its troops into battles that had already been fought and won twenty-five years before? Moreover, the reader can point with a slight embarrassment to the hybrid character of this romanticism. These romantics are, as romantics, rather unsatisfactory. The great scholar Pierre Moreau devoted a whole book to their "classicism."[1] To be blunt, they seem wooden in tone, timid and half-hearted in setting their goals; there is an unmistakable air of defeat and mourning about them. But then, if Vigny and Musset do not quite measure up to the standards proposed by Bloom, Abrams, or even Béguin, they do not measure up to some intuitive standards of "Frenchness" either. They have always been suspected of being outside the mainstream of French literature. Their romanticism is perceived as an inability to be fully classic. For quite a few readers the French romantics are not much more than limping poor relations. When Béguin needed a fuller French romanticism, he desperately reached out to Rimbaud and Proust. A recent collection of French literary history decided that three volumes had to be devoted to romanticism, covering the whole of the nineteenth century.[2]

Why must Van Tieghem bill 1760–1820 as preromanticism—a prologue twice as long as the main piece?[3] Why do others, Marxist or not, feel obliged to throw away literary periodization and cling to the reassuring certainty of historical cornerstones (1789–1815: La Révolution et l'Empire; 1815–1848: La Restauration, and so on)?[4] Why this need, when in the eighteenth century France had been in the vanguard of literary and intellectual progress as much as England and certainly much more than Germany? Daniel Mornet, as far back as 1912, spoke eloquently of romantic passions and feelings in the eighteenth century.[5] Without Rousseau it would be difficult to talk about a European preromanticism at all, and certainly a large section of romanticism (particularly German romanticism) would have been ideologically disarmed without *La Nouvelle Héloïse* or *Discours sur l'origine de l'inégalité,* and the *Rêveries* offer to French literature what Gray and Young, Goldsmith and Cowper gradually brought to English literature. Diderot was a typical example of Enlightenment modeling with substantial opposite reactions built in (his enthusiasms, his tears, his feeling for the sublime). Numerous other currents and names could be mentioned: Beaumarchais was "in advance of his time," the Florians and the Berquins provided rich sentimentalism, Gothic terror and garden-variety idyllism freely flourished; even Marivaux or the Abbé Prévost (particularly with *Manon Lescaut*) can be summoned as witnesses.

But is there at least a strong connection between the self-proclaimed young romantics of the 1820s and 1830s and this powerful, diverse preparatory movement? If there is, it has been strangely ignored by historians, as well as by the actors themselves. And, after all, why *should* there have been a sense of continuity over fifty or sixty years? Why should Musset have felt himself the heir of Rousseau, or Vigny of Prévost? In literary history how many cases of connections that skip a generation do we really know? The much-praised continuity of French literature would seem to show a crack, and the following sequence would show the progression of romanticism in its simplest form: Rousseau—English and German romantics—Scott, Byron, Staël—Hugo and Lamartine.[6] This, incidentally, is the trajectory of the French aristocracy from progressive posturing to emigration to disgruntled, pessimistic return. Henri Peyre perceived the problem

and struggled with it. He balked at the idea of a double French romanticism, but ultimately did not offer an explanation. To explain
those empty pages, he spoke about the lure of the army, administration, and science for young talents; he called to mind many meritorious
émigrés; he mentioned consolingly other sterile decades. More important, Peyre spoke of the romantic sensibility and style of the young political leaders of the 1790s. Still, his outline did not depart from the
traditional scheme, which suggested a detour through the rest of Europe in the development of French romanticism.[7]

The situation seems strange, and the chief explanations available
seem contrived and full of coy little hypocrisies, as if they wanted to
hide a blot on the family escutcheon: the lack of literary excellence
during the French Revolution. The Bourbons had to come back before good literature could appear again, but let us not spread the
shameful little secret.

Perhaps a different view can be put forward by first making a few
simple changes in terminology and then reorganizing the period structure from 1780 to 1850 with an eye to the European scene. The
French romantics between 1815 (or 1820) and 1848 are not innocent
babes; they have an intense historical conscience. They did not forget
the recent past or the eighteenth century; how could they, when the
very chemistry of their sociopolitical situation was a combination of
revolutionary, imperial, and ancien régime elements? They were for-
cibly pushed toward awareness and reflection on historical and cultural
evolution. They were equally attentive to current developments in the
rest of Europe; never before (and perhaps never after) was French literature so hospitable to external influences. It is therefore quite reasonable to judge a literature so intensely historical by strict historical
standards. It is quite reasonable to place it synchronically in a system
and in a proper context: that of European literature of the 1820s and
1830s as a whole, of a period which already had the great achievements of Hölderlin and Novalis, of Blake and Wordsworth behind it.
This literature was now busy accommodating and whittling down the
high-romantic constructs: it was, or was becoming, Biedermeier. It is
quite normal that Vigny, Musset, and so many others should not fit
the mold of high-romantic definitions, since they belong to a rather
different company: Pushkin and Heine, Byron and Lenau, Mörike and
Lamb, Grillparzer, Manzoni, and Mickiewicz. The French writers
after 1820 are, like their contemporaries, late-romantics, continuators,

not initiators. They are, not less than their European colleagues, Biedermeier writers.

A cursory list of examples drawn from some of the leading figures
of the age will perhaps illustrate what I mean and will help answer the
original question and explain both the correspondence to and the deviations from the "general European" development. We can then return to French literature better armed, explain some of the apparent
incoherences mentioned above, and propose a periodization in keeping
with the literary realities as well as with the cultural-historical development. Surprisingly, the comparative approach may throw more light
on national literary patterns than an analysis confined to strictly internal developments.

WHEN Alphonse de Lamartine inaugurated the romanticism of the
Restoration, his themes and his tone were both original and devoid of
originality. He seemed in many ways related to Young, Gray, or Goldsmith when he gracefully integrated the tones of Rousseauian sensibility in his *harmonies* and *méditations,* and when he turned time and again
to the idyllic model. It is tempting to draw the erroneous conclusion
that Lamartine was a belated preromantic, lolling in reluctant melancholy by the banks of the torrent and, once in a while, elegantly dip-
ping his toes in the waves.

But even the most intensely and completely idyllic of the *Harmonies
poétiques et réligieuses* (Number 5 of the first series, *Bénédiction de Dieu
dans la solitude*), with its painstaking inventory of tranquilizing techniques, can show us what Lamartine truly pursued. The peaceful harmony of modest work and protective nature was not a primary goal,
but rather a line of retreat; he sought quiet not because it was desirable, but because it was helpful to a bruised soul. The lyric persona of
Bénédiction is tired and defeated, can no longer endure being "incer-
tain, agité, / Et sur les flots du doute à tout vent balloté," can no
longer communicate with "des coeurs retentissant d'orages," and re-
joices that man's soul, like the surface of the water,"dès qu'un moment
le vent s'est endormi, / Repolit la surface où le ciel a frémi."[8]

Here and elsewhere Lamartine's central lyrical strategy was to preserve the emotional intensity of some major superhuman adventure,
while avoiding the consequences of that adventure or the commitment
of an actual transformation. His poems illustrate an admission of painful and sweet defeat; the challenge of total human expansion and the

reconquest of paradise was left behind, though not entirely forgotten; even the pleasures of unbridled intensity, of the ruthless exertion of human potential were now present merely as sadly smiling memory.

Lamartine's *Prelude*, his *Faust*, his *Juliette*, was called *Jocelyn*—the most comprehensive statement of his poetic philosophy. The historical and geographic placement of the plot—somewhere on the outskirts of the central events, at the periphery of the century's spiritual and social battles, in the later 1790s, in southeastern France—is of the first significance. The curve of Jocelyn's development is equally eloquent. Its shape was not determined by some titanic effort at reintegration; the conflict was not controlled by some tragic awareness of alienation, analytical breakdown of faculties, or catastrophic Fall. Jocelyn ascends from happiness to paradise without passing through the Fall: he is the passive object of external forces, and, unlike the Ancient Mariner, he is never involved in powerful, shattering, personal decisions. The Jocelyn of the "Première epoque" is unquestionably happy in the midst of young girls who, "baignés du matin," gather lilacs and carnations while the smoke rises gently from the cottages and the trees are vivified by the melodious trills of the birds.[9] But he is equally happy in the pious loneliness of the convent and even happier upon arrival at the Grotte des Aigles ("Troisième époque"). The Revolution pushes Jocelyn away from society and its gratifying routines, but this is neither a break nor a fall, since the sufferings it produces are "normal" (family anxiety, an interrupted education, government change, loss of property). In fact, unwittingly, this ephemeral fall leads to a much more glorious, paradisial state. His stay in the seminary had been a mere preparation for the true priesthood, communing with nature in the Grotte des Aigles. The ontological caves of Novalis are turned into the retreat of Platonic love. Paradise has been achieved in this world of suspended opposites: loneliness and society are fused there, communication with the self and communication with the other overlap (since Laurence is, in the beginning at least, the echo and equivalent of Jocelyn), innocence and voluptuousness are united, sexuality and purity are not yet separated, male and female are (as in the Platonic myth) still an original unity; nature and civilization are finely tuned to each other. This is the mirror-image of the tillers led by Father Aubry in Chateaubriand's *Atala* and, like the happiness of Chactas, the happiness of Jocelyn breaks down when "le cuit" of religious obedience and moral duty takes precedence over "le cru" of emotional ties. Paradise regained, paradise relost: Jocelyn melts in the quiet flow of comforting tears. Jocelyn accepts the call to priesthood under the gentle pressure of his superiors, Laurence disappears in the face of what she regards as the betrayal of prior and more sacred vows. Jocelyn again loses consciousness: throughout the poem we see him repeatedly in hospital or swooning or in states of unconsciousness. But, significantly, these are not the powerful half-oneiric and visionary states described by a Novalis, Wordsworth, or even Keats, but, as for Scott's Darsie Latimer, states of lassitude, passivity, helpless self-abandonment into the hands of strangers. If for Wordsworth "recollection in tranquility" was a genuine embrace of reality and a substitution which vigorously competed with the original experience, for Lamartine, a visionary closer to the Biedermeier than to the romantic mode, it was a long series of softly blurred and ever diminishing pictures. Jocelyn is a teacher, Jocelyn fights against the plague, Jocelyn offers the last sacraments to Laurence, Jocelyn weeps. Almost half the poem is complaint for loss and consolation in a rural simplicity which is itself only a copy of the larger synthesis of the Grotte des Aigles.[10] Regeneration is turned into mere memory, the contours of experience are precious because they are ever more vague. Whether we choose to look at *Jocelyn* alone or as part of a huge uncompleted cycle (that is, together with *La Chute d'un ange*) we would still have to conclude that no blazing image of renewal is posited at the end of the cycle, no true redemption, merely a gentle, sad copy—a consolation which deliberately defines itself as a second-best state.

Lamartine's *Méditations* can be better understood if seen in the light of *Jocelyn,* as autonomous illustrations of a consistent poetic approach. *La Retraite* in the first series of *Méditations* explicitly referred to the romantic expansions of identity: geographical ("aux bords du Tibre, et du Nil et du Gange"), historical ("empire, gloire, liberté"), emotional ("par la jeunesse et l'espoir emporté, / Je vais tenter encore et les flots et l'orage").[11] These are rejected with firm finality as pointless in reality, but useful for contemplation ("Mais ton esprit plus vaste étend son horizon; / Et, du monde embrassant la scène, / Le flambeau de l'étude éclaire ta raison").[12] The idyllic framework of *La Retraite* is just that: a convenient fallback for a defeated romanticism to return home to. The same *démarche* can be recognized, in a philosophically more explicit idiom, in *Philosophie.*[13] The poetic persona proclaims himself: "âme erranté," youth mellowed by the rays of misfortune, a

seeker to the very confines of the cosmos, "aigle souvent trompé."
This vast soul seeks, and ultimately rediscovers, limitation, small joys,
and finds the way back to some unproblematic God, some peaceful
hut, and occasional poetry. Therefore, the whole quest was probably
useless, or at best provided just a backdrop for the true pleasures of
limitation. Here it is no longer the idyllic limitation which provides the
contrast, but in an ironic reversal, the wide world. The main point
hinges on the *return* to the "rustique enclos, par mes pères planté."[14] I
do not wish to ignore the large number of poems of departure written
by Lamartine, but it would seem that in most of these the departure is
deplored, and some new return is hoped for.[15]

Lamartine's poetry frequently contains cosmic pictures and confrontations with nature, but a closer look reveals important differences
from Wordsworth or Hölderlin. Poetic conscience has abandoned its
integrative ambition and now adopts a spectator's stance.[16] In *Les
Étoiles* the galactic vista is an impressive picture, aesthetically moving,
but existentially bland and calming; its otherness is undoubted by the
contemplating eye. In fact, we are told that only God can know the
number, age, and remoteness of this sublime production ("ouvrage").
Man merely salutes the stars and bestows arbitrary names upon them:
that of a beloved mistress, of a brilliant bird, of a racing steed. The gal-
axies are a pretext for metaphorical exercise. The soul can envision in
some remote future the identification with a modest part of the majes-
tic wholeness: "J'ai murmuré tout bas: Que ne suis-je un de vous!"
The hope is merely "briller sur le front de la beauté
suprême, / Comme un pâle fleuron de son saint diadème!"[17] This
leads to the ironic conclusion of the transfigured soul plunging from its
astral heights to console a kindred melancholy individual. The high-
romantic fusion of conscience and universe is turned into a partial and
reversible fusion of two *local* and precise elements of the whole. Similar sentiments are expressed in *La Solitude,* where the high mountains
preserve full autonomy and the ego its detachment, and where the poetic reaction is one of enjoyment, not of ecstasy. What is more, the
framework is not one of terror or exaltation in facing the sublime, but
of security and serenity; the individual not only delights in the solitude
obtained, but dwells on the protection offered by the durability of objects that have never "changé de forme et de contour," in escape from
chaos and mutability: "Oui, dans cet air du ciel, les soins lourds de la
vie, / Le mépris des mortels, leur haine ou leur envie, / N'accompag-
nent plus l'homme."[18]

In fact in Lamartine individualism no longer relies on its exchange value with the universe; the individual reverts to his stark uniqueness and thus to a local basis. *Consolation, Les Préludes, Chant d'amour* are possible illustrations of the consoling (not healing) power of love and of the limiting or focusing power of sadness.[19] In so saying we can qualify, I think, some of the conclusions of George Poulet and Jean-Pierre Richard.[20] There is no reason to question the value of their truly subtle and profound observations on the dialectics of infinity and narrow closeness in Lamartine's poems; any reader who is sensitive to Lamartine must concede that the interaction of intimacy and free wandering creates spaces of vague mists and diffuse shining that seem to nourish the Burgundian poet's lyricism. But these relationships do not function entirely in a vacuum. We have to insist on noticing a diachronic relationship: the retrenchment of infinity. True, "Le moi, bien protégé dans sa retraite, ou bien attaché à son support, n'y craint plus de se jeter—imaginairement ou visuellement—dans ce lointain qui lui apparaît alors vidé de maléfices. La sécurité de son site d'observation écarte en effet de lui tout risque d'éparpillement."[21] But in order to reach this vantage point, this recurring "vallon," consciousness must first divest itself sincerely of pretensions to universality and confine itself to a merely symbolic roaming, as well as to a vision that is itself "brumeuse" and "ennuagé." In terms of Lamartine's *Weltanschauung* the same failure to operate with a crucial distinction will be noted. Lamartine declaims his love for organic pantheism because he is cut off from it; his liking is a retreat from the pointed and challenging "literal" organicism of the high-romantics and from their attempt to identify language with nature. His exercises in limitation and vagueness are very similar to those of the Biedermeier.

FRENCH LITERATURE in the 1820s and 1830s does not lack poets who could be described as Biedermeier in the old and limited sense of the word—from Nicolas Martin, who seems to have been influenced by the Germans, to Jules de Rességuier and Edouard Turquéty.[22] Of these strictly Biedermeier poets, Sainte-Beuve is perhaps the most distinguished. The older clues, such as "Il ne m'aurait fallu sur un coin de la terre, / qu'un loisir innocent, un chaume solitaire,"[23] are not absent, but this "bonheur champêtre" proves either illusory or downright unsatisfactory: "Tout cela, pour un jour, c'est enivrant; mais vienne, / Vienne le lendemain!"[24] As compensation we are much more frequently offered alternative environments for retreat. Thus, for the ultimate withdrawal, suicide, Sainte-Beuve suggests a long and narrow valley which should be "Loin des sentiers battus; à peine du chasseur / connue, . . ." but in which, on the other hand, the grass does not hide "sous vos pas couleuvre ni vipère."[25] Should the withdrawal be less radical, then frivolous light leisure can gently rock the boat of the lazy dreamer on the blue lake of life.[26] Farming scenes and cultivated parks occupy an equally important place:

> et les moissons fécondes,
> Et les pommiers sans nombre avec leurs touffes rondes,
> Pareil, aux cerisiers tout rouges de leurs fruits;
> Les fermes d'alentour dont j'aimais tant les bruits;
>
> l'enceinte bordée
> De mélèzes en pleurs et d'arbres de Judée
> Et de faux-ébéniers;
> Bosquets voilés au jour, secrètes avenues,[27]

as well as

> ces gazons qu'elle arrose,
> Ces courbes des sentiers dont à son gré dispose
> Un caprice adoré;[28]

But urban and quasi-urban frameworks play an even more notable part. Some of these may sound odd:

> Oh! j'ai rêvé toujours de vivre solitaire
> En quelque obscur débris d'antique monastère,
> D'avoir ma chambre sombre, et, sous d'épais barreaux,
> Une fenêtre étroite et taillée à vitraux,[29]

but others are merely quaint in a Lambian sense, such as the admired "portails, clochers et tours, / Et les vieilles maisons dans les arrière-cours,"[30] and specifically the barbershop in the back alley in which some Renaissance splendors are hidden. Quite frequently *Mes livres* (enumerated in loving detail) may suffice as providers of gentle security.[31] In a more complex vein, "Les Rayons jaunes" creates the bourgeois interior coziness of color, sound, furniture, and nostalgia.[32]

But Sainte-Beuve's Biedermeier attitudes are not confined to backgrounds and retreats. He deftly turns erotic passion into mere sheltered intimacy,[33] while a Wordsworthian call to duty is proclaimed with loud resignation: "et c'est ainsi qu'il faut, au ciel avant le soir, / À son coeur demander *un malheur, un devoir!*"[34] An amusing low romantic variant of Shelley's *Ode to the West Wind* has Sainte-Beuve turning spring into death, so that the pleasures of early sun in February are still partly rejoiced in, but with a cautionary note:

> Fleurs, ne vous pressez pas d'éclore;
> Février a des jours encore,
> Oh! non, l'hiver n'est pas fini.[35]

A similar type of defusion occurs when an experience similar to Wordsworth's daffodil illumination is recorded "du côté de Saint-Leu"—the poet's reaction is merely: "Et moi, dont l'oeil se mouille et dont le front s'allume, / Tête nue, adorant, je récitai l'Ave."[36] One more example of the taming strategy is provided by the manner in which Sainte-Beuve applies the Werther schema to his triangle with the Hugos (in the real life variant, as we know, this new Werther was not quite as hapless as his literary prototype in the wooing of his Lotte-Adèle): the young wife in piquant and snug tête-à-tête with the humbly scheming visitor is directed to slake her Bovaryian longings with contemplation of gracious divinity, and when the solitary friend has to abandon temporarily the "couple heureux et brilliant," he restricts himself to groans and adoring envy.[37]

Sainte-Beuve's later and longer poems are starkly Biedermeier. Stifter often comes to mind when we read *Monsieur Jean, Maître d'école,* or *A Madame la C. de T . . .* (in which the tones of Mérimée can also be noted, as well as similarities to Mörike's *Mozart auf der Reise nach Prag*).[38] One poem, *À Boulanger,* can in fact be read as a description of the birth of the Biedermeier period.[39] It concentrates on the importance of concrete details, in the manipulation of which Sainte-Beuve often proved his mastery. The opposition established between two types of poets (extrovert and introvert) is only apparent; the essential thing is the "Goutte à goutte à genoux suant ton agonie," that is, distilling into small and precious objects the flight of the mind and of the body.[40] The art of the poet is miniaturization.

ALFRED DE VIGNY, because he wrote less than his colleagues and because his main work was not spread over a long period, was in his own way an equally good example of the transformational formula that united the French writers of the 1820s and 1830s with their European contemporaries on the one hand and with their romantic predecessors on the other.

The pessimism and the stoic, somewhat stiff gravity of the man and the poet might make us forget that he was by no means an outsider.[41] His own contemporaries perceived him as a principal actor in the literary or ideological affairs of the day. His awareness of idyllism was indubitable. After 1848 he lived on his estate, very much in the fashion of P. L. Courier: "Nos blés sont tous dans les granges; je fais établir et perfectionner une distillerie d'eau-de-vie puisque nos raisins produisent le *cognac* le plus pur."[42] Although such a way of life is partly a matter of personal choice and social need, it also makes a cultural statement, which grows in importance when it is part of a recurring pattern. We can place Vigny's housing and way of life in the stylistic vicinity of Leigh Hunt or of Lamartine, who had so much impressed Sainte-Beuve with his idyllic coziness. For example, in *La Dryade* Vigny offered quite openly, without Lamartine's cunning lyrical evasions, a sample of poetic synthesis which pulled together the strains of a whole genre, from Theocritus to Gessner and André Chénier.[43]

Most significantly, "La Maison du berger" is the symbolic title for what is perhaps Vigny's most articulate philosophical poem, one in which he hurled angry and energetic accusations at the modern age in the name of nature. The poem became famous for its denunciation of railroads as the hostile agent threatening freedom and sweet diversity and as the adjunct of soulless capitalism and of uniform social leveling: "Les merchands sont jaloux. / L'or pleut sous les charbons de la vapeur qui passe" (ll. 86–87), and "Chacun glissera sur sa ligne, / Immobile au seul rang que le départ assigne, / Plongé dans un calcul silencieux et froid" (ll. 124–126).[44] Although he passionately rejects Saint-Simonism, the poet's confidence in the solidarity of Nature (or even Poetry and Love) with human functioning and hope is rather shaky and does not seem to offer a full substitute.[45] Nor does it entirely blot out the nervously reluctant acceptance of industrial civilization, almost unique in Vigny's writings: "Mais il faut triompher du temps et de l'espace" (l. 85) or "Eh bien! que tout circule" (l. 92) or even "Sur le taureau de fer qui fume, souffle et beugle, / L'homme a monté trop tôt" (ll. 78–79).[46]

Given these ambiguities, a purely idyllic reading of the poem seems unsatisfactory. First, "la maison du berger" seems an ironic choice; it

suggests the humble contented cottage, but it is really a movable con-
traption that brings to mind the wagons of theatrical itinerant groups,
circus people, or even gypsies (hence the parallel to railroad cars). Second, the opposition between town and country is no longer the relatively placid one of Cowper and his eighteenth-century forerunners
but is rather harsh and morose, with an occasional tone of despair.
Cities are "rocs fatals de l'esclavage humain" (l. 25), and the countryside provides not merely the traditional retreat, but a necessary asylum, "vastes asiles" (l. 26). Cities are somber, imprisoning islands in
the universal sea. Since, however, the universal sea itself (Nature) may
be indifferent and haughty, and since "la maison du berger" is, if not
incarcerating, at least confining (in order to be sheltering), we have to
conclude that Vigny, the most radical pessimist of his age, actually
confronts two ambiguous and unsatisfactory goods. We can also speculate on the subterranean connection of the title with "Poésie! ô
trésor! perle de la pensée!" (l. 134).[47] Is the "maison du berger" similar to Mörike's Orplid—a surviving island in a ruined and fallen
world? Or should we rather conclude that as the mind produces the
pearl of poetry by illness and reduction, so the production of a streamlined, simplified, denaturalized humanity follows the analogous productive impulses of industry? "La Maison du berger" shows mainly
that Vigny was disturbed by and doubtful about oppositions that
seemed to have lost their validity. The response to this anguish is the
projection of sheer, arbitrary will to cut through the maze of dilemmas. Hence the gallery of dark, powerful, illusionless figures in
Vigny's work.

The use of Old Testament figures is weightier and graver, they
carry more awe and power, than in a Protestant framework where
they would be more familiar or even worn by use.[48] The ring is louder
and deeper: Moïse behaves in effect like the equal of God. He is a
Promethean late-romantic man, "puissant et solitaire" (four times repeated), much in the manner of a Byronic hero. After many achievements he is now aimless. But even from the beginning, power and
purpose were accompanied by solitude and sadness. Death, in Moïse's
case, is the ultimate desire of fulfilled energy. Such a staging of titanism illustrates pure, meaning-free will with no less eloquence than any
page of Vigny's close contemporary, Schopenhauer. Nor is it isolated
in the spare work of the squire of Maine-Giraud. La Mort du loup kept
the idea and merely changed the environment and the circumstances:

Fais énergiquement ta longue et lourde tâche
Dans la voie où le Sort a voulu t'appeler,
Puis, après, comme moi, souffre et meurs sans parler.[49]

Savagery, honor, silence, unreflexive certainty, and directness are the
key principles of a mind that has lost the hope of fusing reason and
imagination. The great prophet and the noble beast of Vigny both
substitute authority and will for the integrity of natural developments.
The high-romantic harmonizing enterprise had been driven by the
hope that voluntarism would disappear, that it would be absorbed organically into a new synthesis. Vigny's is a renewed voluntarism,
which emphasizes the opposition between consciousness and natural-
ness. Exceptional titans were not the "correct" answer. But the Satan
in *Eloa* is identical with them with the exception of a different mathematical sign before his name, through which he becomes theologically
loathsome. Satan endows himself with a purpose that is negative and
thus, we are given to understand, similar to a lack of purpose.[50] The
story of Eloa herself is not really a story of fall and redemption, sin and
salvation, but rather one of failure of communication, of disintegration. Satan *almost* enters a new type of whole; Eloa *almost* succeeds in
constructing a new unity; but they finally prove irreducible and separate.

Vigny knew—like Uhland, like Scott and Southey—the delights of
historical rummaging: *Madame de Soubise* or *La Neige* strikes the right
ballad tone—adventurous and erotic narration made compact to substitute for a lyrical effect.[51] But in *Cinq-Mars*, historical play and grave
transhistorical concerns coincide. With admirable frankness Vigny
admits in the theoretical introduction preceding the volume that "Il
faut le dire, ce qu'il y a de VRAI n'est que sécondaire; c'est seulement
une illusion de plus dont il s'embellit, un de nos penchants qu'il
caresse."[52] Art, we are told, uses reality as an ornament. By art,
Vigny, no less than Shelley or Hölderlin, understood the very morphology of Being, the identical deep structures of the mind and of existence. Naturally enough, mimetic detail could be only a corollary or
embellishment of art. Therefore design was more important than dimension, and the episode (*Cinq-Mars*) could stand for the unfinished
longer piece—the description of the decline and fall of the French aristocracy ("Histoire de la grandeur et du martyre de la noblesse de
France"). Of course, the point is that Vigny (much in the fashion of

the Biedermeier) reached for "le Vrai," for lack of "Art," one assumes.

The story, like that of so many Biedermeier historical novels, is strongly allegorical. The nobility opposing Richelieu's plans of centralization is the author's cipher for liberty and dignity endangered by the anomie of a totalitarian technology (like the railways in the above-mentioned poem). In the keynote discussion at the dinner-table in the first chapter, the old maréchal de Bassompierre telescopes the shipwreck of a class and the shipwreck of the individual in a prophetic manner.[53] In counterpoint young Cinq-Mars, ready to embark upon the business of living, sees the beginning of life as the end of life: "Heureux celui qui ne survit pas à sa jeunesse, à ses illusions, et qui emporte dans la tombe tout son trésor!"[54] Actuality is death; potentiality alone is life; unfolding of the potential is tantamount to its wasting. Thus, when (by the end of Chapter 20) it becomes clear that the conspiracy has been betrayed, the reaction of M. le Grand and of his allies is not so much courage as indifference: "Les jeunes gens applaudirent en riant, et tous remontèrent vers la salle de danse comme ils auraient été se battre."[55] Louis XIII is empty and pitiable; he represents the death of the monarchy, but also the death of the human being, since he is unable to establish an equilibrium between centrifugal and centripetal forces, between diversity and control.[56] His is the ultimate victory: neither Richelieu nor his aristocratic opponents achieve their aims. "Le Parlement est mort, disait l'un des hommes, les seigneurs sont morts: dansons, nous sommes les maîtres; le vieux cardinal s'en va, il n'y a plus que le Roi et nous." And Milton's rejoinder a little later is that Richelieu will create the republics of the future by undercutting the present monarchy.[57]

Thus Vigny, like so many other writers of his generation, bases his narrative on the scheme Fall–Redemption–Fall. The only ideal redemptive action is the hopeless surge of the young male company led by de Thou and le Grand. The Fall is, however, inevitable; it is represented by the breakdown of the integrative capacity of the body politic and, as well, by a strong disbelief in reality: de Thou chooses from Descartes' *Méditations métaphysiques* those passages that deal with sleep and illusion.

VICTOR HUGO'S early poetry differs considerably from his later works, such as *Les Châtiments, La Légende des siècles,* or even *Les Con-*

templations, which are typically Victorian. His theatrical work was concluded by 1843. It may even be argued, though perhaps with slightly less conviction, that *Les Misérables* and *Les Travailleurs de la mer* differ from the series from *Han d'Islande* to *Notre-Dame de Paris,* because they point toward the naturalism and sentimentalism of the Victorians and are concerned with working-class problems in a manner in which the earlier works are not. Perhaps it is equally important to observe that many critics separate Hugo's early philosophy from that during and after the exile.[58] For all these reasons it seems permissible to conduct a separate study of the early Hugo, up to 1843. Such a separation shows much more clearly that the young Victor Hugo is indeed related to the Biedermeier writers.

The first and most obvious signs of Hugo's allegiance can be found in his poems. In a recent book Claude Gély argued forcefully that Victor Hugo persistently used "le nid," "la maison," and "le jardin" as reference points and that this imagery was closely woven into the texture of his early psychological experiences. Gély claimed that a combination of the bucolic tradition and Rousseau's sentimental idyllism was decisive in Hugo's literary growth, and that his poetry up to 1843 was a search for or an anxious struggle to preserve the *style intime.*[59] Obviously not all of Hugo's early poetry will fit the categories set up by Gély; however it is difficult to find even in *Feuilles d'automne* or *Les Rayons et les ombres* larger sketches of the kind of prefigured symbolism which characterized many of Hugo's foreign contemporaries. The mass of verbose and prosaic versification in these two volumes is amazing: memories from childhood, melodramatic evocations of Napoleon, praise of different arts, pseudo-philosophical lamentations. Hugo's best poetry was often influenced by Lamartine and by idyllic elements ("Oui, c'est bien le vallon! le vallon calme et sombre! / Ici l'été plus frais s'épanouit à l'ombre"), some of which seems to be taken directly from Sainte-Beuve:

> j'aime le chêne altier moins que le nid de mousse;
> J'aime le vent des prés plus que l'âpre ouragan;

and later

> . . . à travers une claire feuillée
> Sa fenêtre petite et comme émerveillée
> S'épanouit auprès du gothique portail.[60]

Even glimpses of impressionistic audiovisual blur can be noted:

> Ce fut d'abord un bruit large, immense, confus,
> Plus vague que le vent dans les arbres touffus,
> Plein d'accords éclatants, de suaves murmures.

Occasional Turnerian shadings:

> Le soleil, à travers leurs ombres, brille encor;
> . . .
> On dispute aux brouillards les vagues horizons;
> On découpe, en tombant sur les sombres gazons,
> Comme de grands lacs de lumière)[61]

pass from perceptual confusion to visions of universal chaos (*La Pente de la rêverie*).[62]

Still, on the whole, Hugo seems almost as obstinately conservative and Biedermeier as Mörike, for instance. What one does find—particularly in the *Odes et ballades* (the fifteen ballads) and many of the *Orientales,* but also in *Les Rayons et les ombres*—is an intense sensitivity to color and the picturesque and a commitment to the dramatic episode even when it lacks resonance. Hugo's ballads are without the moral or psychological intensity of Schiller's, Goethe's, or Coleridge's. His writing resembles more that of Scott, Southey, or Schwab; it is often dedicated to rhythm and sound exercises (*La Chasse du burgrave, Le Pas d'armes du Roi Jean*) or devoted to spectacular pageantry (*La Fiancée du timbalier*).[63] And although Hugo often slides into purely atmospheric evocations, he seems to differ little from the large army of late romantic balladeers. This should not be surprising in a man who was more than once seen as the voice of Germany in France; Heine said that he offered the French "les desserts de la cuisine allemande" and the influence of Grillparzer and Zacharias Werner on *Les Burgraves* has been insistently pointed out.[64] (Walter Scott and others were of course equally influential.) But influences do not explain everything. Hugo's ballad-writing impulse, his gift for the spectacular and episodic scene, was very strong. I believe that even some early novels such as *Han d'Islande* and *Bug Jargal* or a good many of his plays (not least *Ruy Blas*) should be seen as expanded ballads.[65]

In discussing the outlines of Hugo's early work, a look at his philosophy may be of some help. The opposition between the increasingly radical and pananimist position of the 1840s (and later) and the early conservatism (and even religious fervors) of the 1820s has often been noted.[66] Awareness of this opposition can lend a sharper contour to the young Hugo and his Biedermeier-like activity, particularly if we consider that this conservatism is qualified, much like Chateaubriand's, and can thus accommodate genuinely democratic feelings in a nostalgic-ideal framework. Hugo's peculiar combinations differ little in their general thrust from those of contemporary moderate conservatives such as Guizot, Tocqueville, Thiers, or even (later) Taine. The various ingredients seem smoothly blended in these thinkers, but unstably combined in Hugo. A consistent philosophy is secondary in a writer who was chiefly an imaginative writer. The early Hugo did not feel that political reaction excluded social compassion or even progress. Furthermore, strongly restorationist feelings could purify, in retrospect, the relation between social classes. Hugo thought of his earliest formation as being under the sign of "Voltairian royalism."[67] Feudal yearnings, eighteenth-century nostalgia, and social sensitivity were part of the makeup of the age, and Hugo's gargantuan cultural appetite did not want to miss any of them. But perhaps Hugo also realized intuitively what it took us over a century to note: that the modified romantic paradigm was equally the foundation of entirely conflicting positions, not only those of the Vicomte Bonald, Auguste Comte, Henri de Saint-Simon, and Felicité Lamennais but even, a little later, of Karl Marx and Sören Kierkegaard, and that there was no reason not to skip from one to another or to mix them.[68] A look at *Notre-Dame de Paris*, Hugo's broadest and most complex statement in the 1815-1843 period, will reveal ideological, stylistic, and cultural elements organized along Biedermeier lines.

WE NO LONGER want to read *Notre-Dame de Paris* as a triangle—soul (Quasimodo), intelligence (Claude Frollo), beauty (Phoebus)—as Eugène Sue had at first suggested.[69] Rather, we tend to underline some binary oppositions and their multiple configurations.

Frollo, a Faust-figure,[70] stands indeed for pure intellect and culture, while in their different ways Quasimodo and Esmeralda stand for pure nature, for the innocence of simple matter. The dynamics of these relationships show that Hugo follows by and large a narrative strategy best represented by E. T. A. Hoffmann. But whereas the latter posits the dichotomy of reality versus fantasy, simply and as a matter of fact, Hugo's oppositions are multilateral, broader, and more ponderous.

Frollo is abnormal because he is incomplete, reduced to one set of faculties. His movement toward completeness as a human being leads to disaster; he becomes a demonic figure (in the scene with Esmeralda in prison).[71] In the end he is not more complete; he has merely succeeded in standing his spiritual-intellectual deformity on its head, not in changing it. In a key passage, Claude Frollo in fact admits that his happiness had been the purity preceding the contact with Esmeralda and love.[72] Conversely, Quasimodo tries to open himself to the spirituality of love. His movement beyond the state of agile, mute, cyclopean goat, climbing the stone mountains of the cathedral, results in a disaster no less than Frollo's attempt to change. Quasimodo perishes in the absurd knightly heroism of single-handed combat.

He is destroyed by the denizens of the Cour de Miracles—the gargoyles and monsters of Notre Dame, walking freely around, the natural allies or even siblings of Quasimodo, who had elected him king for a day, the counterparts of the figures among which alone Quasimodo had found peace and understanding. They stand for the vitality, diversity, and unshapeliness of free nature. They are in turn the innate enemies of Louis XI (the great streamliner, logicizer, and scheming centralizer), inevitably of Claude Frollo, too, as well as of the rising analytical world of books. When Claude Frollo says "ceci tuera cela"[73] he is not making a statement of sociocultural history (typography over architecture), but an immediately physical statement—some creatures will be obliterated. Thus, in battling the Cour des Miracles, Quasimodo has turned against himself. The world of matter or of physical immediacy self-devours.[74] Even at this point we notice how the binary oppositions subdivide and multiply. Ironic internal conflicts are thrown in for good measure.

Needless to say, Esmeralda, the center of the struggle, is more thoroughly ravaged than any of the others. Esmeralda, the unattainable and pure "axis of the world," stands for authenticity and integral lack of alienation; Djali, the goat, is her alter ego, an emblem for the blending of kind sexuality and of sacrifice.[75] Only a combination of the faculties separated in Frollo and Quasimodo (or Phoebus and Gringoire) would have deserved marriage with Esmeralda (that is, merging with the center of authenticity). As it happens, Pierre Gringoire, the irremediable formalist, whose sins toward reality (authorship of a mannerist play) were to have been expiated by his slide down from official recognition to the Cour de Miracles, is ready to overlook the unconsummated marriage and contents himself at the end of the novel with the caprine emblem Djali, the verbal artifact, imagination as reproduction, the second-best choice.

What Hugo suggests through the destiny of the main characters is that the separation of faculties is not "natural," but not avoidable either: unification leads to catastrophe. The best we can hope for is the uneasy and unequal alliance signaled by the association between Claude Frollo and Quasimodo in the earlier part of the novel. The irremediable split between the human faculties, and inside the universe itself, is confirmed by the images of normal, typical, or average people. These are either, like Gringoire, totally passive (along the lines of Waverley or Darsie Latimer), incapable of initiating epic momentum or of functioning as a unifying center,[76] or even worse they are like Phoebus (a creature purely of the day, as the name suggests: most other characters are beings of the night), the average male—banal, insensitive, ultimately cruel and evil. Thus Hugo seems to agree, in this respect, with Gogol or Hoffmann, as to the evil of banality—mediocrity always carries within it a demonic potential.

The breakdown of integration and the pessimistic view of its chances (of which a secondary and aesthetically unpleasing consequence is the multitude of sensationalist and melodramatic scenes) is probably reflected in the main narrative strategy of Hugo in *Notre-Dame de Paris.*[77] He uses this strategy in other novels, too; it is also shared by such novelists as Scott, Manzoni, Stifter, and others. Roger Ikor wittily summarized the method: " 'Au coeur de la grotte sous-marine, soudain happé par une lanière froide et visqueuse, Gilliat reconnut la pieuvre!' Point, à la ligne, changement de chapitre: 'La pieuvre est un octopode qui . . .' Suivent dix ou vingt pages dans l'esprit le plus didactique de Buffon, avec le jaillissement habituel, çà et là, d'images antithétiques qui se gonflent comme des bulles et pètent en vain."[78] This is very far from being the romantic self-parody Ikor intended.

Hugo integrates in a spectacular manner theoretical and literary discourse; it is the procedure of Augustin Thierry, Jules Michelet, and Edgar Quinet, though naturally with a different emphasis. High romanticism (in France or elsewhere) had felt free to substitute reciprocally literary and theoretical discourse; Biedermeier writers usually contented themselves with mixing them. Thus, developing a theory of architecture seemed normal to Hugo, as it was for Stifter to bring in geology and botany. But there is a second aspect to consider. High romanticism was notoriously given to playing down causal elements of the narrative. The insecure state of the romantic impulse is easily recognized in the rhythms of *Notre-Dame de Paris* (and in other novels of the same period). Leisurely beginnings and spacious explanations create a vast causal framework; this is carefully integrated in the action and will lead immediately to a narrow, precise effect of explosive force. The military scuffle in front of Notre-Dame between the king's men and the rioting populace is described in a couple of paragraphs (X, 7), but prepared for by an interminable description (X, 5) of King Louis at work on affairs of state. This description is only partly justified by Hugo's pleasure in the picturesque and by his ambition of historical reconstitution. It is much more decisively an outcome of Hugo's explanatory obsession: order versus disorder, rationality versus magic, books versus architecture, organization versus impulse. A remote and broad cause produces a precise result; without the explanation, the event would be absurd and arbitrary. Similarly Books I through III (the debacle of Gringoire's premiere, his ensuing marriage, and the theory of medieval Paris) are merely vast explanatory frameworks. Other examples are provided by the learned disquisition on asylum in medieval churches or the lurid psychological motivations of Claude Frollo and many others.[79] The order of cause and effect in the presentation is secondary compared to the presentation per se and to the opposition between calm, quasi-scientific description and scenes of intense horror or melodrama. This procedure, incidentally, provides an excellent opportunity for the practice of the *tableau vivant,* the focused, intense scene with sharp contours: Esmeralda with the goat, the dark brows of Frollo, Phoebus indifferent, surrounded by many ornamental figures—in all respects like a mock-medieval tapestry.[80]

Other features suggestive of the Biedermeier are the treatment of architecture, politics, and sexual coercion in the novel. This is not the place to go into the details of Hugo's architectural theories. Jean Mallion has suggested that architecture played a central part in Hugo's thinking, because more than any other art it intimately fuses form and idea.[81] It might be added that Hugo took obvious delight in the hybrid and collective nature of architecture, in its capacity to be totally and generously universal, that is to accommodate variety.[82] Architecture represents a kind of community, unified and differentiated, that can no longer be encountered in social reality. Hence there is a great stress on the live character of architecture and distrust of neoclassical revivals, which are too logical. A key passage opposes book to edifice (in a witty variation on Lessing's distinction) as a flock of birds to a towering static mountain, as analytical order to organic creation.[83] (Much like Borges, Hugo fantasized the sum of printed books into a new tower of Babel.[84]) Holdheim offered an even more general theoretical framework for reading *Notre-Dame de Paris,* starting from architecture. He maintained that the architecture and the statuary in the novel and in particular the cathedral itself, are forms of petrified time. The chief underlying philosophical opposition is between the epic (or dynamic) and the architectural (or static). Narratively this results in the contradiction between assimilation and alienation of the different characters. The abundant digressions do not belong, in his opinion, to the realm of cause, but rather are attempts to hold back the action, to dam up the epic flow. The transfer of progression (even circular progression) into descriptive expansion is one of the features of Biedermeier writing.[85]

The sexual scenes of the novel were clearly inspired by the high-romantic intrepidity of Matthew Gregory Lewis and the Marquis de Sade. The female sexual victim is part of a situational system identical to those devised by the writers mentioned: the difference is that the system does not work. The victim proves as powerful as the torturer, who is seen defeated, humiliated, and suffering—and thus Sade is inverted, Justine and Antonia are redeemed and avenged.[86] Such a reversal becomes possible mainly because Hugo withdraws from the absolute situation to a relative one, which is historically plausible; under such circumstances hope cannot be entirely dismissed.

This brings us back to the political meaning ensconced in the flesh and brick of *Notre-Dame de Paris.* Explicitly Hugo professes a Tocquevillean faith: he sees an uninterrupted growth of centralization from Louis XI to Mirabeau with a certain equanimity,[87] unlike Vigny, whose gloomy view of the same process I noted above. Hugo is not stingy with his democratic enthusiasm. He admires the good burghers of Ghent, heavily condemns the hysterical and mad racism of Esmeralda's mother, and sympathizes at many points with the Parisian revolt, as well as with the boisterous student revolts and pranks.[88] If there is any conclusion to be drawn from this apparent contradiction, it is only that for Hugo the foremost value was "localism," by which he meant the right to logical, aesthetic, and moral preferences and judgments in terms of empirical premises, of present and individual situations. This is plainly similar to the minimal Biedermeier response to the conjunction of romantic and eighteenth-century elements, and it reinforces our understanding of the early Hugo's place in European literature.

* * *

ARE THESE brief analyses of some leading literary figures of the period between 1815 and 1848 confirmed by the atmosphere and the general supporting background, with its more or less talented writers? About Musset's tragicomic efforts and the way in which they signify Biedermeier reactions I speak elsewhere. Alexandre Dumas *père* and Eugène Sue wrote their major works in the 1840s; their sensationalism and commercialized historicism, their cheaper visions and handier unifying insights make them outstanding corroborating witnesses in the trial of later French romanticism. If we really want to explore the recesses of the age's literary production, we may extend our sampling to include such figures as Marceline Desbordes-Valmore and other sentimentalists of the time, as well as a number of "poètes du terroir" (J. A. P. Brizeux, Napoléon Peyrat, J. P. Veyrat, and Hyppolite de La Morvonnais among those so described by Van Tieghem).[89] The later phenomenon is worth mentioning, because it is usually thought of as typical only of the German-language Biedermeier. In fact it can be identified not only in French, but in Italian and English literature (John Clare), also. Ultimately, it is part of a larger historical trend that manifested itself in the resurgence of smaller European literatures (Romanian, Bulgarian, Catalan) as well as in the decision to publish literature in dialect. But it is equally interesting to take into account other signals such as the wealth of references in the French literature of the early nineteenth century to the painting of Holland and Flanders, which reveals the attraction toward realistic minuteness.[90]

Perhaps the broadest "literary" framework defining the "French Biedermeier" and differentiating it from the preceding periods is the dramatic expansion of political, literary, and intellectual media of information and discussion. The French press system was shaped after 1815 and was to remain unchanged in its structure for almost a century and a half. It was an accommodating system of abundant variety, growing circulation, and ideological flexibility, which differed sharply from the heroic and individualistic productions of a J. R. Hébert, Antoine Rivarol, Jean-Paul Marat, or Camille Desmoulins. (The distance is the one from initiative to application.) This growth was enhanced by book production, book trade, and the dramatic expansion of the *cabinets de lecture,* which reveal decisive changes in the size and composition of the reading public.[91]

But even at the level of aesthetically more significant literature, there is no dearth of examples. Thus, Prosper Merimée, who published his most important works between 1828 and 1845, could be a good French example of what in German literature is still sometimes called "poetischer Realismus." The purpose of such writing is ostensibly a complete high-romantic endeavor, yet the full unfolding of potential romantic processes was replaced in it by positivistic or empirical endeavors. Thus Merimée showed himself in the praxis of his literary work obsessed by psychological and contextual probability; picturesqueness or exoticism, originally just auxiliary embellishments or parts firmly held in rein, became autonomous and emphatic, while their aim shriveled.

A parallel failure is seen in Maurice de Guérin's *Céntaure*. Even leaving aside the Vignyian pessimism of this piece, how is the reader to accept the complaint about the split human race, coming as it does from an obviously split observer? How can a successful pantheistic embrace of the *Seinsgrund* succeed, when even the intentionally absconding divinities, our convenient everyday deities, are out of reach? In other words, we find in Guérin, too, the "out-of-reach" syndrome of a later romantic who does not quite fulfill his ambitions. Was this not the tragedy of Aloysius Bertrand also? Some readers claim for him the status of a full romantic, indeed of a privileged romantic, but is not his fragmentation that of a late romantic? Is he not closer to the aestheticism of a later period, to Barbey d'Aurevilly, for instance? Is he not the calligrapher of morbidity and the picturesque? Stooping a little lower we can distinguish, around Bertrand and Petrus Borel, an army of smaller or would-be romantics, who revel in the vistas of fantasy and the unfettered narrative or lyric liberties provided by romanticism. "L'extase retombe sur l'angoisse . . . La condition propre de l'homme ne lui a pas permis de soutenir son assaut. Passage du ravissement à la langueur, de l'extase au temps, de l'innocence à la culpabilité," said a particularly lucid observer, who added that Philothée O'Neddy, Petrus Borel, H. F. A. Esquiros, and Xavier Forneret dealt not in despair but in "espoir satanique traversé d'angoisses intermittentes."[92] Meanwhile Victor Brombert's apt thesis regarding incarceration (demonstrated particularly well on texts by Borel) showed how a whole poetic age could remain under the influence of limitation and reduction: the reduction indeed of the high-romantic paradigm.[93]

Honoré de Balzac and George Sand must also be mentioned in this context. Like Dickens and Thackeray (or Tennyson and Browning, or

Keller and Fontane, or Turgenev and Nekrasov), they were already Victorian writers; that is, they were largely realists or at least subject to types of tension different from those of Vigny and Hugo. However, they were shaped by the period of later romanticism in which they grew. Balzac became by and large more "scientific" and sociological after 1839; George Sand hovered uncertainly between realism and Biedermeier romanticism.[94] Besides, not only Balzac's early, terror-filled productions but even, for example, the organization of his novels along large-scale, systematic lines seem to me rather Biedermeier in nature, not less so than the narrative and literary *écriture* of Thierry and Michelet.

The whole of the period 1815–1848 can be correctly and fully understood only if French literature is placed in the wider and illuminating context of European literature. It then becomes clear that French romanticism in those years was dominated and obsessed by the achievements and ideals of the preceding generation. Relating to this standard, its main writers were beset by doubt and anguish, or they sought shelter in irony, in sensationalism, in idyllic retreats, or even in cruel voluntarism. They expressed at bottom disappointment and pessimism even when on the surface we see militant agitation and passionate energy. These attitudes and literary phenomena can be understood to a large extent as transformations of a missing central *figura*, the high-romantic paradigmatic human model. It explains a good deal of the literary epoch, even though inevitably some authors or aspects will not fit the picture.

THE MAIN difficulty with the model proposed here is specifying time spans. If indeed what is described as French romanticism is the equivalent of later romanticism in England and Germany and of similar developments in Southern and Eastern Europe, and thus at least analogous to the Biedermeier, when did it actually begin? Quite a few of the writers whose main works were written before 1815 differ little or not at all from the main writers of 1815–1848. For example, Paul-Louis Courier could undoubtedly be claimed for representation of the Biedermeier mentality in France, an equivalent to Leigh Hunt and Cobbett—a rebellious liberal who fought as much for tradition as for progress. He supported the values of home and rootedness, protested against banning dances on Sunday, praised the decency, wisdom, and sweetness of country people, and generally supported individuals and small communities against the regulations of centralized power.[95] He delighted in quaint, small, precise things. How different was Xavier de Maistre's *Voyage autour de ma chambre*, written about a quarter of a century earlier? There are differences in subject matter but little difference of tone: the same elegant precision, the same feigned frivolity and humorous indifference, the same politeness, the same concentration on small processes as the best carriers of vast meanings.

Historians have viewed Benjamin Constant as an outsider, somewhat like Jane Austen in English histories of literature, an isolated psychologist untouched by Rousseau or Chateaubriand. But if the dominant note of French literature in the early nineteenth century was a deliberate withdrawal from romanticism, then the author of *Adolphe* was not such an oddity. His main novel (1816) at least could be seen as something more than a late descendant of *La Princesse de Clèves*, namely, as an attempt to offer an articulate, rational, and controlled translation of feelings and relations that might otherwise have been treated in a purely romantic fashion. He may be seen as reacting against a romanticism that had peaked and thus as on the same side of the barricade as Lamartine and Sainte-Beuve.

Another example of apparent period alienation is André Chénier: a revolutionary persecuted by the revolution, a classicist loved, published, and read by the romantics (only after 1819). His poems written in the late 1780s and early 1790s seem to fit perfectly with those of Lamartine and his younger brothers.

Nodier was also in many ways closer to high romanticism than his younger colleagues after 1815. *Smarra* established very early the pattern of an artificial Biedermeier neoclassicism (Platen and Landor would later provide even better and more complete treatments), and in France this "fantastic" classicism was destined for a solid career. *Jean Sbogar* is an energetic story that resembles Merimée's works. But *Trilby* and *La Fée aux miettes* suggest Hoffmann's distinction between a degraded reality and a farfetched, imaginary state. He developed the thesis that *le féerique* and *le fantastique* should be used as vehicles of romanticism rather than *le frénétique*—that is, he urged (around 1820) a domestication of romanticism. In a word, Nodier seems to be one of those transitional figures, like Byron, Keats, Hoffmann, and Eichendorff, who belonged at once to the early and to the later forms of romanticism.

One more Biedermeier symptom of the same type may be found in the history of French intellectual debate. Destutt de Tracy and other ideologues of the 1790s provide a remarkable continuity from Turgot and Condorcet to the thinkers and poets of the 1820s (for example, J. C. L. S. de Sismondi). Nor are they incompatible with Guizot and Tocqueville, whose historical theory helps explain the reasons for this compatibility. Turgot's practical program among other things had been achieved by the Revolution. It was the systemic (that is, romantic) intensity of the Revolution that came to be rejected by late romanticism, not the separate, specific points of the program as they had existed before their romantic apotheosis.

Although there may be some historical or literary advantage in definitively placing these writers and thinkers within a cultural movement, the problem of periodization is thereby further complicated and obscured. Why should Biedermeier or late-romantic writers, if that is what they are, be spread out over so many decades? And if Nodier is indeed a transitional figure, from *what* to *what* did he establish a transition? To answer these questions we have to look a little at the sociocultural and intellectual developments which are solidary with the literary evolution of Europe from 1780 to 1820 and reiterate some of the postulates of the first chapter.

Romanticism was the outcome of a series of systemic changes that occurred in the human and social model of Enlightenment classicism. When such radical and explosive changes fulfill their potential and reach a point of maximum impact, decline will follow, usually in the form of fragmentation or reduction of scope. The eagerly expected regenerations of humanity either fail to take place or fall far short of expectations. In England the high point reached by Blake, Coleridge, and Wordsworth was followed by a gradual and orderly withdrawal. There is no reason to expect a different, longer, or more spectacular development in French literature. Nor should an early and long withdrawal from an explosive high romanticism be more surprising in France than anywhere else. The problem is to locate this elusive French high romanticism.

In a brilliant analysis, Eric Voegelin has shown that, after the Revolution, French Restoration took place in six phases from 1794 to 1815 and that in their turn these changes corresponded to the rapid developments between 1789 and 1793, with their four or five successively more radical courses of action.[96] François Furet and Denis Richet confirmed Voegelin's phase theory by stating that the Diréctoire launched the Restoration: "on souhaite Louis-Philippe ..." when Bonaparte takes power.[97] It is quite appropriate that French literary developments should display a solidarity with the general curves of social development: to quote Howard Mumford Jones, Danton, Marat, and Robespierre were romantic heroes whereas the great figures of the American Revolution were classical and Enlightenment heroes.[98] If in France the Restoration began earlier than in the rest of Europe (than in German-speaking areas for instance), is it not natural that late romanticism, the "French Biedermeier," should also have begun much earlier? Moreover the relationship between political history and literary production is never chiefly one of cause to effect, but rather one of fusion and at least partial identification. Howard Mumford Jones's quip, exaggerated as it may seem, points to an important truth: in the 1780s and 1790s literary production was submerged in a mass of "texts," many of which were political, mystical, philosophical, scientific, and polemical. It is in these writings or texts that we must look for the short but powerful high romanticism of France.

Any literary piece is also a text, but not all texts can be considered literary. An aesthetic component is, as Mukařovsky has pointed out, a necessary part of any human product;[99] in some products the aesthetic component becomes more important than the utilitarian one. Between approximately 1780 and 1800 French culture passed through a phase in which texts prevailed over literary productions. By 1800 a worried Napoleon had to take active measures to "get literature moving again"; he had to assign to quasi-political bureaucrats like Fontanes and Joubert the task of encouraging young people to write actual literature again.

The problems of literary investigation when applied to "mere" texts are formidable in spite of recent critical developments that seem to offer some guidelines. The first problem is to select the relevant text from a mass of critically unprocessed material. As long as a corpus of such texts has not been established, there will be inevitably some groping and guessing between for example Linguet and Turgot, Marat and Robespierre, Chamfort and Rivarol, Mirabeau and Camille Desmoulins. The second problem is to apply literary categories to such texts. In my opinion the main features of any high-romantic writing can be recognized in many of these texts, though in a somewhat different shape: intensity of feeling and situations, reaching out for integration, joy in the absolute, the paradigm of regeneration. The

French core romanticism, the French literary equivalent of Blake and Hölderlin, is represented by such authors as Saint-Just, Sade, Ballanche, Saint-Martin, and many other minor figures.

EVIDENCE supporting Saint-Just as a representative of the high-romantic period in France comes chiefly[100] from the posthumous "Fragments sur les institutions républicaines" and the constitutional project presented on April 24, 1793, to the Convention.[101] These texts differ from an ordinary constitution or legal text in that they are less technical. They are not systems of abstract propositions and logical units forming an arena inside which a real event can take place; rather, they offer the event itself as a representation of future and similar events. Saint-Just's texts function as they were designed to do, but they also display the use of imagination in a specific manner, which in fact may be aesthetically valid. Both of Saint-Just's texts are world-descriptions achieved by projection and the search for a kind of transcendence.

Saint-Just set the stage by imposing external patterns on the sequence of sentences and on the word picture of the structure being erected before us:

> "La division de la France en départements est maintenue: chaque département a un chef-lieu central . . . La population de chaque département est divisée en trois arrondissements; chaque arrondissement a un chef-lieu central . . . La population des villes et des campagnes que renferme un arrondissement est divisée en communes de 6 à 800 votants; chaque commune a un chef-lieu central"

or

> "Chaque citoyen prononce son voeu par oui et par non . . . Le voeu de la majorité est celui de la commune . . . Le président fait passer aux diréctoires le voeu de la commune. Le diréctoire rend sur-le-champ public le voeu des communes de l'arrondissement . . . Les diréctoires font passer les voeux des communes au ministre des Suffrages . . . Le ministre des Suffrages en rend compte à l'Assemblée nationale, à mesure qu'ils lui parviennent" (pp. 125–6, 138).[102]

This symmetry derives from an arbitrary positing of order, expressive of an absolute and superior kind of freedom. No one in that age more literally fits Shelley's definition of the poet as the "unacknowledged legislator of the world" than Saint-Just. The severity of the tone is misleading—it is merely the natural proclamation of the Goddess-

Revolution's herald. Everything is definitive, clear, victoriously care-free: "La force publique est le peuple en corps, armé pour faire exé-cuter les lois . . . Les armées font partie de la nation . . . Il n'y a point de généralissime . . . Dans les triomphes, les géneraux marchent après leur armée . . . Une armée française ne peut point se rendre sans infa-mie" (p. 148).[103] The speaker disposes, punishes, and protects; he is serenely omnipotent and can therefore touch the chords of the sublime without any self-consciousness:

> "Le peuple français se déclare l'ami de tous les peuples; il respectera religieusement les traités et les pavillons; il offre asile dans ses ports à tous les vaisseaux du monde; il offre un asile aux grands hommes, aux vertus malheureuses de tous les pays; ses vaisseaux protégeront en mer les vaisseaux étrangers contre les tempêtes . . . La République . . . re-fuse asile aux homicides et aux tyrans . . . La République française ne prendra point les armes pour asservir un peuple et l'opprimer . . . Elle ne fait point la paix avec un ennemi qui occupe son territoire . . . Elle ne conclura pas de traités que n'aient pour l'objet la paix et le bonheur des nations . . . Le peuple français vote la liberté du monde" (pp. 148–149).[104]

The reader is, even nowadays, sensitive to this apotheosis—Saint-Just's words vibrate like so many huge gongs in the vernal air.

But on a less general level the visionariness of Saint-Just's constitu-tional project is not vague and expressionistic; it is rich in characters and concrete scenes. The figures that we perceive have regular fea-tures and muscular bodies, they are dignified and well-proportioned; in their behavior they have much of the imposing simplicity of the noble savage, but of one who has been or is in the process of being redeemed or reborn out of the material of an imperfect civil society.

Here are the children: "On élève les enfants dans l'amour du silence et le mépris des rhéteurs . . . On doit leur interdire les jeux où ils déclament et les accoutumer à la verité simple." And, straight out of Xenophon's *Cyropedia:* "Les enfants, depuis cinq ans jusqu'à dix, ap-prennent à lire, à écrire, à nager" or "Les enfants sont vêtus de toile dans toutes les saisons. Ils couchent sur les nattes et dorment huit heures. Ils sont nourris en commun et ne vivent que de racines, de fruits, de légumes, de laitage, de pain et d'eau." Their rites of passage are similarly conceived: "Ils ne peuvent prendre le costume des arts, qu'après avoir traversé, aux yeux du peuple, un fleuve à la nage, le jour de la fête de la jeunesse" (pp. 342–343).[105]

And here we see them near the end of their lives: "six vieillards rec-
ommendables par leurs vertus, dont les fonctions seront d'apaiser les
séditions . . . Les vieillards sont décorés d'une écharpe tricolore et d'un
panache blanc; lorsqu'ils paraissent revêtus de leurs attributs, le peuple
garde la silence et arrête quiconque poursuivrait le tumulte." They do
not resort to force, but can decree "le deuil de la loi" and "Si un vieil-
lard est assassiné, la République est en deuil un jour et tous les travaux
cesseront" (pp. 142–143). The end of all endeavor is described in this
little vignette: "Il y a un petit champ donné à chaque famille pour les
sépultures. Les cimitières sont des riants paysages: les tombes sont
couvertes de fleurs, semées tous les ans par l'enfance. Les enfants sans
reproche placent au-dessus de la porte de leur maison l'image de leur
père et de leur mère" (p. 354).[106]

Unpredictable sequences of objects enhance the concreteness of
Saint-Just's visionary writing. Like Borges, he did not avoid purely poetic enumeration: "Le conseil protège l'agriculture, il entretient
l'abondance, il repartit les contributions directes, il présente à l'As-
semblée nationale les vues d'amélioration, les récompenses et indem-
nités à accorder . . . Il veille à l'entretien des routes, des postes, des
fortifications, de la navigation intérieure, des mines, des forêts, des
propriétés nationales; il surveille la fabrication des armes, des poudres
. . . Il dispose le triomphe des armées, il protège les arts, les talents, les
institutions publiques" (pp. 134–135). But the sentence sequence
shows the tight connection of each object enumerated to the overall
vision. One article painstakingly pinpoints which categories of magis-
trates are elected for how long and when. The one immediately following breathtakingly opens up the horizon: "Les tribunaux sont gardiens
des moeurs et dépositaires des lois: ils sont inflexibles" (p. 146).[107]

A few remaining questions about Saint-Just's work will not change
the high-romantic nature of his vision. Was there a neoclassic influence? The denizens of the regenerated world may indeed resemble
Poussin's toga-clad Arcadians, but not more so than the figures popu-
lating *Prometheus Unbound* or Hölderlin's Elysian glimpses. Like Shelley and his other colleagues, the French revolutionary used ancient
Mediterranean forms with perfect ease and indifference. Classical elements were for him a mere backdrop, and they often appeared with
other, for example, Gothic, elements: "Les meurtriers seront vêtus de
noir toute leur vie, et seront mis à mort s'ils quittent ce habit" (p.
350). "Nul ne mangera de chair le troisième, le sixième, le neuvième
jour des décades" (p. 355). Classical brevity can serve the vehe-

mently revolutionary discourse: "Strasbourg, le 11e jour du 2e mois de l'an II. La République Française ne reçoit de ses ennemis et ne leur envoie que du plomb. Saint-Just, Le Bas" (p. 288). And of course there are the intensely personal touches which slip into even the most sober texts: "Je méprise la poussière qui me compose et qui vous parle" (p. 310) or "Les amis sont placés les uns près des autres dans les combats. Ceux qui sont restés unis toute leur vie sont renfermés dans le même tombeau. Les amis porteront le deuil l'un de l'autre" (p. 344).[108]

Nor should it trouble us that Saint-Just suggested that ruling innocently is impossible (p. 316). Seen against the background of the perfect society just described, it is clear that the rule in question refers to how to progress toward that perfect society and how to manipulate the nation in a certain direction. The ultimate aim is innocent, even if the means are not. And this is, I believe, the secret of Saint-Just's amazing purity: his conviction that at any point he can crystallize an action back into its original substance—unsullied, pure reason. Establishing the "institutions" is showing people the redeemed society in which nature and culture are reconciled. In this society reason is not used analytically but is inherent in the fabric of society and in the patterns of human behavior. Saint-Just admits openly: "S'il y avait des moeurs, tout irait bien; il faut des institutions pour les épurer . . . tout le reste s'ensuivra" and "qui nous délivrera de la corruption? . . . Des institutions."[109] In other words a perfect state is one with perfect *moeurs* (spontaneous impulses and patterns of behavior); to achieve these, terror and correcting institutions are required (p. 319). The historical imagination in post-Scottian Europe functioned in a similar manner: by producing unusual and provocative symbols of values, by renewing values through "defamiliarized" settings, and even by experimenting with versions of an ideal society. But the difference is obvious: Saint-Just was not a historicist, not a relativist trying on for size this and that type of world—he was ready to assume the risk of setting up the definitive historical-transhistorical world.[110]

THE DIFFERENCE between literature and text, mentioned earlier, is purely practical, just a rule of thumb. In fact, French romanticism reached one of its heights with the writings of the Marquis de Sade, who was not as disconnected from the circuit of literary values as the later nineteenth century wanted to make us believe. Thus, Barbey d'Aurevilly's debut in 1831 was the (well-tamed) adaptation of a story by Sade, and Roland Barthes posthumously urged Hugo and Michelet to recognize their predecessor and master in things libertarian.[111] Rousseau's influence on Sade is generally recognized and accepted (examples are given hereafter).[112] Wordsworth's high-romantic paradigm is translucent in Sade's writing. What is more, Barthes shrewdly observed, "imagination is the Sadian word for language."[113] Sade exploded the perceived limits of human personality in a manner perhaps unequalled to this day. Although the world thus created may well be "kakotopian" rather than utopian, as Thomas Molnar contended, Sade's vision was nevertheless purely Blakean.[114]

The "destruction of God" was for a high-romantic a purely structural gesture, in no way different from co-opting the divine into nature or into some absolute consciousness. Besides, for Sade the adversary was not so much God as the irreducible identity and dignity that the individual gains through the existence of God. The individual personality, Sade seemed to suggest, was too static a concept; it must be hidden and replaced by a total and anonymous subjectivity. The obstacle of individual personality must be overcome to release subjectivity in the same way that the active body must be overcome by sleep to release dreams.[115] As Foucault correctly noted, Sade expounded the "sovereign rigor of subjectivity in the rejection of all natural liberty and all natural equality," leading finally to the "free exercise of sovereignty over and against nature."[116]

But it is much more questionable whether Sade indeed ignored the dialectics of a return to a redeemed, paradisial order, as Foucault contended. The idea that subjectivity (as total limitless liberty and disponibility of others) can swallow up, dissolve, or even negate the concepts of God, nature, or social bonds does not necessarily entail a breakdown of hope. After all, if we take at face value the sexual and blasphemous activities in *La Philosophie dans le boudoir,* we must also take at face value the attempts at human improvement theorized there by Dolmancé. What is sensational in *La Philosophie dans le boudoir* is the manner in which every theory finds its exact and immediate counterpart in the actions of the characters.[117] I believe Foucault erred in not separating the variable lyrical moods of the narrative persona from the paradigmatic structure that sustains the narrative. In a very elementary way, the same plot outline can be colored in black or in pink depending on the point of view adopted, but the story can still have an independent semantic value. Whether the mood is pessimistic or not (in *Justine* it is, in *La Philosophie* it is not), the structure may still preserve a luminous hope of its own.

The misfortunes of Justine-Thérèse result from humanity's unregenerated state and in particular from the way in which she sets herself up as a lightning rod for disasters. An attentive look at Sade's writings will reveal that the properly criminal acts are rarely gratuitous: they are acts of revolt and revenge. The only brutal activity in *La Philosophie* (which I consider the centerpiece of Sade's work) is the punishment inflicted on Mme. de Mistival for her repressive obstinacy—something in the nature of a lesson.[118] The different punishments inflicted as part of the sexual game on Eugénie, Dolmancé, Mme. de Saint-Ange, or the Chevalier de Mirvel are pleasures and initiations. Mme. de Mistival does not derive any pleasure from torture. That is her fault: she does not want to. Besides, she is (as her husband's letter of permission testifies) the spirit of negation, the obdurate puritan, the brutal censor, the angel of inhibition, public enemy number one, well deserving of her punishment. The position of Justine is similar. She reels from disaster to disaster in a kind of causal chain; at any point she might have broken the chain by not resisting, by accepting sexual uniformity, by not stalling. Her sufferings are identical to those of Mme. de Mistival. She chooses not to define as pleasure what is inflicted on her. She chooses to run, to break out, to pray and fight back—thus identifying herself as a counterrevolutionary and thus a victim. The fictional Pius VI of *Juliette* is horrible to the narrator only because of his integration into a sociomoral system and his allegiance to solidified values. Had he dissolved his obduracy into some fluid acceptance, the narrator could easily have applauded him and enrolled him in the party of redeemed libertines.

Another example is the torture and assassination of the Widow Rosalba and her daughters by Clairwil, Princess Borghese, Juliette, and their followers described in *Juliette*.[119] There is purpose in this particularly loathsome crime: the punishment and destruction of virtue and innocence. Juliette and her acolytes are not much different from some urban guerrillas working toward the renewal of the human being. Alice Laborde has shown in a particularly witty essay that the very mechanism of this renewal corresponds to the procedures employed (according to Mircea Eliade) by shamans, in order to destroy the profane frameworks of sensitivity and create a sensitive receptivity to the

supernatural.[120] Viewing crisis, ecstasy, and orgy as transitions toward
a new modality of being offers a convenient explanation for the initia-
tory nature of many Sadian texts, in *La Philosophie dans le boudoir* and
Juliette, in both of which revelation, teaching, test, and ceremony are
prominent. Most often the erotic exercises are accompanied by elaborate organizing rites—groups, positions, numbers, closed spaces, laby-
rinths. Such features strongly confirm the romantic-generative nature
of Sade's work.

Nor should Sade's work be seen as limited to a monomaniacal repetition of sexual structures. We are now much more aware than earlier
critics of the way in which Sade's thinking integrated crucial myths,
utopian images, and the mysteries of Masons and Templars into his
universal libertinage.[121] Saint-Just and Novalis were brought together
in Sade; Marcuse was his logical descendant.

Justified or not, the revulsion of the overwhelming majority of the
reading public against Sade was real enough. It was of the same caliber
as the hostility against Saint-Just and Hébert and it was followed
closely by the hostility and bewilderment with which somewhat fewer,
but still a majority, received the excesses of romantic visionarism. And
while the romantic model was moved by its own internal mechanics, it
undoubtedly responded also to outside responses or pressures.

BY COMPARISON to the radical romanticism of Saint-Just or Sade,
Chateaubriand's pre-1815 work seems more moderate. I am not dealing here with Chateaubriand's later work, which bears only faint traces
of romanticism and is quite close to the Biedermeier in its nostalgia for
Montesquieu, its arbitrary application or denial of the organicist label
to contemporary events, and hair-splitting distinctions between legiti-
mist and bourgeois monarchy.[122] His earliest work had been idyllic,
written under the influence of E. D. de Forges de Parny, Abbé De-
lille, Jean Regnault de Segrais, and Salomon Gessner. In the 1820s he
began to admire Mirabeau's letters and was impressed by the bourgeois simplicity of the Prussian royal family and the Biedermeier coziness of his ambassadorial neighborhood in Berlin; he opposed in many
ways Bonald and De Maistre, while befriending George Canning.[123]
Les Martyrs may be considered a forerunner of a whole line of novels
dealing with the overlap between Roman culture and Christianity,
from Nodier to Bulwer-Lytton, Sienkiewicz, and Pater; and Chateaubriand's earlier attraction to idyllic melancholy is patent. What could

be more telling than his insistence that he was born into a family as noble as any but humble enough to be in touch with everyday life, and what could be more revealing than the sad pleasure he took in the provincial charm of England: "Partout la petite église solitaire avec sa tour, le cimetière de campagne de Gray, des chemins étroits et sablés, des vallons remplis de vaches, de bruyères marbrées de moutons, de parcs, de châteaux, de villes, peu de grands bois, peu d'oiseaux, le vent de la mer."[124] Sainte-Beuve correctly described *Le Dernier Abencérage* as a "tableau d'Empire," even though he knew that: "Ce que Lamartine salue . . . sous le nom d'amour, de sensibilité et de tendresse, Chateaubriand le saluait sous le nom d'imagination, de Muses et de poésie."[125]

Nevertheless, we must judge Chateaubriand in terms of his central work: *René* (1802) and *Atala* (1800) with their framework study, the *Itinéraire* (1811) and perhaps *Les Martyrs* (1809). As to the degree of sheer romantic expansion and comprehensiveness existing in these works, there can be no doubt—historically and geographically (from Jerusalem and Athens to the Mississippi and the Ohio)—that Chateaubriand deals with vast areas in a stable and confident way; meanwhile, incest and mysticism, the passionate love of the farthest (Nietzsche's *Fernstenliebe*) and the innocent attachment to the nearest are accommodated with ease and authority. Chateaubriand was from this point of view the prototypical romantic. Particularly, his treatment of incest in *René* is masterly: the guilty destructiveness of Greek tragedy is avoided, and so is the sensationalism of English baroque drama. Even the mixture of eroticism and mysticism in the metaphysical poets or the medieval mystics is elegantly circumvented, and the meaning of the incestuous feeling is precisely indicated—it is a unifying symbol, the almost successful marriage of the self and the world. René says: "Amélie avoit reçu de la nature quelque chose de divin; son âme avoit les mêmes grâces innocentes que son corps; la douceur de ses sentiments étoit infinie; il n'y avoit rien que de suave et d'un peu rêveur dans son esprit; on eût dit que son coeur, sa pensée et sa voix soupiroient comme de concert; elle tenoit de la femme la timidité et l'amour, et de l'ange la pureté et la mélodie."[126] How would he not strive toward such an ideal, which synthesized reason, soul, and language and which already seemed close to transcendence? "Elle étoit si belle, il y avoit sur son visage quelque chose de si divin, qu'elle excite un mouvement de surprise et d'admiration" (p. 159). She is the universal, the necessary complement for the substanceless, empty, and alienated conscience: "Hélas, j'étois seul, seul sur la terre! Une langueur secrètc s'emparoit de mon corps. Ce dégoût de la vie que j'avois ressenti dès mon enfance revenoit avec une force nouvelle. Bientôt mon coeur ne fournit plus d'aliment à ma pensée, et je ne m'apercevois de mon existence que par un profond sentiment d'ennui" (p. 149).[127]

The similarities to the later Byronic hero (the sick, lonely, melancholy heart, the unrequited love, the haughty traveler, and the enigmatic woman) are obvious, but it is much more intriguing to observe the parallels to Wordsworth and the Dorothy of *Tintern Abbey* or *The Prelude* and to start reading *René* from there. René wants to capture total unity, lost vision, and supreme wholeness as much as Wordsworth's persona. But Chateaubriand's communication lines to Rousseau were shorter and more direct than were Wordsworth's; he was thus more familiar with the multiple possibilities of self-analysis and persona-creation. He was better aware of the theatrical and playful possibilities that could be provided on the road toward a renewed paradisial unity. The narrator of *René* is sad and helpless: he cannot influence the characters he has projected for us. The disagreement with the characters goes from admiration to envy to blame to regret. The typical contradiction involves the separating impact of religion (the primary connective force) on a different integrative attempt, which thus remains a mere project. The last European scene etched in René's memory is explicit: "D'un côté s'étendent les vagues étincelantes, de l'autre les murs sombres du monastère se perdent confusément dans les cieux" and also "La tempête sur les flots, le calme dans sa retraite . . . l'infini de l'autre côté du mur d'une cellule" (p. 165).[128] Infinity conflicts with infinity—hence defeat.

In *Atala* religion appears in the same ambiguous light. It is the balancing force among opposing agents of passion, but it is equally opposed to the passions, and thus itself in need of mediation. This is best seen in Father Aubry's Indian community, which is romantic, not Biedermeier. It might have been decreed by Saint-Just: "on va travailler dans les champs, et si les propriétés sont divisées, afin que chacun puisse apprendre l'économie sociale, les moissons sont deposées dans les greniers communs pour maintenir la charité fraternelle. Quatre vieillards distribuent avec égalité le produit du labeur. Ajoutez à cela des ceremonies religieuses, beaucoup de cantiques; la croix où j'ai célébré les mystères, l'ormeau sous lequel je prêche dans les bons jours, nos tombeaux tout près de nos champs de blé, nos fleuves, où je plonge les petits enfants . . ." Briefly it is "le mélange le plus touchant de la vie sociale et de la vie de la nature" or, more explicitly, "j'assistois aux noces primitives de l'Homme et de la Terre: l'Homme par ce grand contrat, abandonnant à la terre l'héritage de ses sueurs; et la terre s'engageant en retour à porter fidèlement les moissons, les fils et les cendres de l'homme" (pp. 88–90).[129] The regeneration of the backward and of the too advanced is equally marked by the perfect fusion of nature and culture. Atala is displaced and alienated; she finds her complement in Chactas, but also in the final narrator, one alienated and displaced for diametrically opposed reasons. Religion itself has become a pervasive and vague, but aesthetically energetic affect, as seen in the quotations above or in Father Aubry's pantheistic rituals when he has "pour autel un rocher, pour église le désert."

The breakdown of this society is due, however, to the separating power of Atala's mother's vows, to which Atala feels bound. It is again, as in *René*, the interference of religion as a competing integrative impulse that leads to the break. Nature and culture have to return to their respective spheres. In itself this separation should not seem too different from the Wordsworthian loss of vision or from Hölderlin's losses of divine substance; after all we do not know of any achieved and durable romantic recapturing of grace—they are all projects or moments. But two differences are suspicious. The first is the quality of the acceptance of loss in the epilog of *Atala,* otherwise a scene of great quietness. The acceptance of loss differs from Hölderlin's and Wordsworth's visions in that it is looked at, not integrated into a process: "Cette croix étoit alors à moitié entourée d'eau; son bois étoit rongé de mousse, et le pélican du désert aimoit à se percher sur ses bras vermoulus" and "il visita la grotte du Solitaire, qu'il trouva remplie de ronces et de framboisiers et dans laquelle une biche allaitoit son faon" (pp. 126–127).[130] All along the feelings of the narrator (a century later) substitute for those of Chactas or even of René the European from which they inevitably differ. The second difference is the manner in which loss occurs—through an external agent, rather than through some internal inevitability. Atala's suicide is only an apparent self-destruction. The culprits are elsewhere; they can be named and touched; they could be punished. This by itself seems to me more than enough to offset the profusion of colors and feelings, the paradisial community of the earlier part of the story.

In a word, I would call *Atala,* as well as *René*, high-romantic pieces placed in late-romantic frameworks. This will be even clearer to those who analyze the connection between *Atala* and *René* and the essays which accompanied the short stories when they were taken out of *Les Natchez;* these accompanying essays further defuse the violence of the central text with lukewarm theorization. But then *Atala* is further wrapped in protective narrative layers. The present narrator heard the story from a Seminole Indian who in turn had heard it from others who in turn "knew" that Chactas had told it to René the European around 1725 or so. The actual events took place well before 1700. As a consequence the story is almost statuary, and certainly de-subjectivised; the self declines responsibility for its own avatars, and a dose of historicism is injected. A thin melancholy neutralizes the high-romantic structure and pacifies the radicalism. Later on Chateaubriand proclaimed his distaste for egotism, pretending to ignore the difference between the transpersonal self and the all-too-personal one of the generation after 1820.[131]

MANY LAY MYSTICS, crank visionaries, and political fantasts of the age produced a thick paste of "texts" that proclaimed regeneration, expansion, and integration. These texts provided the black culmination of the French eighteenth century and its romantic release and explain the melancholy, defeated, and languid air of the late-romantics after 1815. This body of work was anticlimactic not only historically, but also from the point of view of the scorching intensity of the *écriture* of these magicians, scribblers, fanatics, and rhapsodists. The sources of these productions have been carefully shown by August Viatte, Brian Juden, and others to be no different from those detected by Abrams for English and German writings: Orphic and cabalistic traditions, Pythagorean mysticism, Neo-Platonic speculations, and Christian apocrypha.[132] A few names will suggest that, surprisingly, Béguin might have found the equivalents of Ignaz Troxler or G. H. Schubert or Heinrich Jung-Stilling in the texts of their French contemporaries. For instance, Michelet, Balzac, and Nodier were perfectly aware of Cousin de Grainville's apocalyptic reveries and visionary rhapsodies in *Le Dernier Homme* (1805). Louis-Claude de Saint-Martin was easily recognized by most of the leaders of the "French Biedermeier" after 1815 as one of their true fathers, not only owing to his quasi-pantheistic view of an omnipresent God, but also to his Hamannian perception of language as revelation. Probably less notice was taken of a Fabre d'Olivet and his Pythagoreanism (since his hobby horse was a theocratic empire) or Hérault de Sechelles' generic innovations in *Voyage à Montbard* (1785) or *Théorie de l'ambition* (1802). Maine de Biran was deeply involved in studies of somnambulism in the early years of the century. Meanwhile, Ballanche, perhaps the greatest of them all, mapped out quite clearly in his theory of *palingénèsie* a common ground of social and spiritual regeneration, the fragmentation of which was to define the European Biedermeier; equally important is the fact that he felt free enough to incorporate his thinking in more literary writings such as his *Antigone* and *Orphée* (both written before 1820).[133] Restif de la Bretonne was not only the quasi-realistic manufacturer of popular novels, but he was also the strange and visionary author of philosophy—sexual, pantheistic, and cosmic; works of Blakean inventiveness proclaimed the unity of a world in a huge organism, universal copulation, and the imminent advent of a unified religion of Father-Sun and Mother-Earth.[134] And perhaps Joseph de Maistre would be regarded with less terrified awe if looked at in the context of his exuberantly productive contemporaries, whose disciple and colleague he was (Saint-Martin, the Free Masons).[135]

The whole period was dominated by Gothic and sentimental novels (from Jacques Cazotte to Mme. de Genlis), it was teeming with the almanacs and pamphlets of the time,[136] dominated by the orators and journalists. Danton, Mirabeau, and P. V. Vergniaud can be analyzed in the same manner and in the same detail as Saint-Just and with rather similar results. It was also the period of experiments in the *fêtes nationales*, which attempted well before Wagner to create a *Gesamtkunstwerk*. Between 1792 and 1794 a number of parades, pageants, and mass demonstrations were staged, many conceived by David, all of them with clear themes, pervaded by light, music, and acting and sometimes culminating in the erecting of great statues. Their purpose was clearly the transformation of the people as a whole into a work of art. The *Marseillaise* and the hymns and other productions of Marie-Joseph Chénier and others all belong to the same order of endeavor.[137]

Recent studies, such as those of Peter Brooks, have again drawn attention to the rich melodrama and boulevard theater of the beginning of the nineteenth century.[138] I believe these works may also be considered "texts," that is direct, weakly aesthetic expressions of the same unmediated need for intensity and integrality.

My impression is that we cannot pinpoint a beginning for the high-

romantic period in France (unless we take the convenient 1789 date as
a landmark). This is an encouraging finding, because it is clear proof
of the highly integrated and organic nature of French literary development at this point. The works of the 1770s and 1780s slide imperceptibly toward romanticism. (The concepts of Monglond seem more
sensitive to the living movements of the literary body, than those of
either Moreau or Van Tieghem.[139]) The major events appear to be,
first, of course, Rousseau's *Confessions* and *Rêveries*. These were followed or accompanied by many others. Mercier's fantastic *Songes* no
less than his utopian vision of a France in 2440—with its working
priests, simple, functional architecture, bourgeois kings and cosmological religion—influenced J. M. R. Lenz and Chr. D. Fr. Schubart, to
some extent Herder and Goethe, and certainly Jean Paul.[140] The literary, theoretical, and scholarly work of Bernardin de St. Pierre, for example, his proposal to erect an ideal city on the banks of the Amazon,
along with the early writings of the radical Henri Linguet, who did not
hesitate to argue for terror in the service of collective happiness well
before Saint-Just and De Maistre (and who proclaimed bread a deadly
drug), or Marat's theory of revolution (*Les Chaînes de l'esclavage*) add
substance to our reading of romantic growth in France. In these works
all the ingredients of a triumphant core romanticism are already present, save one: the paradigmatic succession of phases which form the
romantic plot. These works are too soft, too malleable, too protean in
form—they are not crystallized, and they do not have the aesthetic
and philosophical direction that one finds at least in prominent figures
of the subsequent generation (Saint-Just, Saint-Martin, Sade, and
Chateaubriand). Furthermore, E. P. de Sénancour, ignored as he may
have been in his lifetime, had developed conceptual discriminations
quite similar to Coleridge's fancy-imagination opposition, while at the
same time experimenting with characters who were able to grasp the
universe as consciousness. Sénancour provided the link between Rousseauism and French high romanticism.[141]

I think we can now answer rather confidently a question asked at
the beginning of the chapter—yes, the French writers of the 1820s
and later were keenly aware of the high-romantic texts immediately
preceding them and strove to respond to them. Nodier's cosmological
reflections give unity to his work; they were borrowed from Ballanche.[142] Saint-Martin influenced not only the French late romantics,
but even German speculative mystics such as Baader.[143] Mme. de

Staël underwent her own Martinist-quietist crisis. Sénancour, Bernardin de Saint-Pierre, and Ballanche were equal promoters of Orphic harmony and determined the style and ideology of Lamartine and Felicité Lamennais. The mystical naturalism of Chateaubriand was heavily indebted to that of his older contemporaries and influenced more than anything else Vigny, Hugo, Nerval, and Gautier. Mercier was avidly read by Lamartine, Vigny, Nodier, Musset, Gautier, Balzac, and Baudelaire.[144] Lamartine was influenced by both Sade and Saint-Martin: when he or Musset spoke about the shattering avatars of their tired souls they were in fact talking about such predecessors, not about their own rather peaceful and pleasant lives. Saint-Just was not a direct influence perhaps, but the Revolution as a whole was. And scholars are now increasingly persuaded that Sade was well known by Borel, Manzoni, and Balzac; that in fact many readers assimilated him to Rousseau. The internal continuity of French romanticism is therefore based equally upon a continuity with the visionaries and the revolutionaries, and upon a reaction to them. This intimately national kind of dialectic continuity is precisely what makes French literature similar to other European literatures and integrates it into patterns that transcend the merely national.

APPLYING the patterns of European culture to the study of the general development of French romanticism from 1770 to 1840 reveals that the reader no longer has to postulate a multiplicity of romanticisms in order to accommodate the apparent temporal lag of French literature. It is quite clear that French romanticism, in spite of inevitable local, individual, and (to a lesser extent) national-historical peculiarities does not stray from the general European frameworks. Specifically, the differences in style and content between the central group of Anglo-German romantics and the French generation of the 1820s can be explained by the time in which they were writing. The French romantics of the 1820s and 1830s had no reason to write exactly like the Blakes and Hölderlins. They had much more reason to resemble their European colleagues of the 1820s and 1830s, and they actually did. French romanticism did not start twice: the fault is in the eye of the beholder. The tremendous but gradual build-up of the romantic human model during the eighteenth century in France and its dialectic movement did find release and implementation, no less than in English literature, and perhaps in a clearer way than in German literature. The difference is to be found in the different kinds of materials, in their quality and quantity. The conclusions of authors as different as Ernst Benz, Abrams, Viatte, and Béguin are strikingly similar: they find identical paradigms, visions, and purposes in the different authors. Still, it is relatively rare that we hear courageous voices such as that of Claude Pichois proclaiming: "Le romantisme français, le romantisme des manuels n'a qu'un point commun avec le romantisme allemand: le nom" and "Les vrais grands romantiques, il faut les découvrir avant la Révolution et après la chute des *Burgraves* (1843). Ce sont les 'preromantiques': Rousseau, Sébastien Mercier, Restif de la Bretonne, Sénancour."[145] I do not fully share his views, particularly as concerns Baudelaire, but I think Pichois has great merit in emphasizing that Sénancour developed, independently of Novalis, a visionary structure that was quite similar.

In the process of reflecting on the unfolding of French literature before and after 1800, we recognize again how large fictional frameworks can steer and shape human thinking and existence. To recognize their specific nature and impact is not to deny however that these frameworks are also engaged in transfers and substitutions. French high romanticism takes unusual forms *precisely* because the impetus and the transforming capacity of the French Enlightenment were tremendous and reached a degree of practicality that was unequalled in other literatures. Similarly, French late romanticism (once recognized as a phase following the core of the romantic explosion—complementary to it, modifying it, and taming it) can in good conscience be seen as a leading European literary movement, fully in accord with the age of Biedermeier.

4

EASTERN EUROPEAN ROMANTICISM: PATTERNS OF SUBSTITUTION

A modified and quiet romanticism is more evident and significant in Eastern and Central European literatures than anywhere else. However, two main deficiencies of research in this area have until now hampered the correct appreciation of this phenomenon by romantic scholarship. The first is the reluctance to seek earnestly for unifying traits in the area east of Germany. The second is the failure to understand correctly the relationship between romantic developments in different areas of Europe. As a consequence the general concept of romanticism was weakened and, repeatedly, uncertainties about the chronological borders of the period arose.

The transmission of literary phenomena inside a culture recognized as unitary has been analyzed *theoretically* even less than the reception of impulses from outside that culture. We know more about Arab influences on the Middle Ages or Chinese motifs flourishing in the eighteenth century than about the delicate mechanism through which baroque forms spread through Europe or about how romanticism came to travel from one center of initiative to many remote areas. Such omissions result from a failure to understand the peculiar pluralistic organization of Western culture (as opposed to, say, the Chinese or the Egyptian or indeed the Greco-Latin culture). The phases of romanticism and its internal growth can well be discussed as a unified model; how the succession of these phases actually occurred in different areas of Europe varied from case to case.

In his fundamental comparative studies of European industrialization in the eighteenth and nineteenth centuries, Alexander Gershenkron established a number of principles which have methodological interest even for those who do not subscribe to the stricter theories of socioeconomic determination of aesthetic constructs. Among these are the following:

1. The more backward a country's economy, the more likely was its industrialization to start discontinuously as a sudden great spurt pro ceeding at a relatively high rate of growth of manufacturing output.

2. The more backward the country's economy, the more pronounced was the stress of its industrialization on bigness of both plant and enterprise . . .

3. The more backward the country's economy, the greater was the part played by special institutional factors designed to increase supply of capital to the nascent industries and, in addition, to provide them with less decentralized and better informed entrepreneurial guidance; the more backward the country, the more pronounced was the coerciveness and comprehensiveness of those factors.[1]

Gershenkron also described areas as advanced or backward in terms of the sequence in which they used the following institutions during the stages of their industrialization as sources for their capital supply: factories from the beginning; banks and later factories; or state capital, then banks, and only last factories. In other words, Gershenkron showed that industrialization in various countries was similar in result, but that the processes of industrialization differed and that where the prerequisites of development (for example, according to the English model) were missing, substitutes occurred. In fact, Gershenkron explained, "the more backward was a country on the eve of its great spurt of industrial development, the more likely [were] the processes of its industrialization to present a rich and complete picture."[2] Once a model of development is chosen, a certain orderly predictability in its occurrence from country to country can be established by posing sets of patterns of substitutions.

CLEARLY neither the concept of backwardness nor that of development can be applied to a cultural situation lightly. Empirically, a case could be made for measuring whether a cultural situation is more or less advanced by the use of indicators such as literary editions, total number of authors, authors declared outstanding (according to some conventional set of criteria), and authors who are in tune with the prevailing trends in comparable countries. Such a sociological undertaking would be legitimate and interesting, but does not seem feasible in the near future. Even the concept of development is less than likely to coincide with some acceptable view of progress, as it does in economic history: in this respect even Marx had serious reservations.[3] In fact, I can hardly think of a modern literary history that conceives of its own theme as linear progress.

Nonetheless within limited periods of time of say 100 to 150 years, it would be easier to decide that there is a general direction of literary movement and that in terms of this *relative* movement an author or work can be seen as more or less advanced. Let me further qualify this statement by noting that this sense of the term *advanced* or *backward* is strictly limited to time and has little to do with quality or value; indeed, such are the dialectics of literary development that a valuable work that seems "chronologically displaced" is likely to seem after a while more challenging and influential than an equally important one that is fully integrated. I suspect that here some variant of the law of deviances (*écarts*) is functioning,[4] this time from a historical-literary rather than a strictly stylistic point of view.

Thus, assuming that the general European literary development includes the phases described in Chapter 1, namely: Enlightenment (neoclassic), Enlightenment (preromantic, or classicism modified in different directions), high romantic, and later romantic or Biedermeier,[5] it is clear that the full range of phases developed only in England and, to a lesser extent, in Germany and France. In most other countries one or more stages are missing, or the order seems dislocated, or one stage seems to absorb the others. The last case is most interesting, since it indicates a kind of "telescoping" (to employ a term used in the social sciences), a simultaneous occurrence of several phases over a relatively short period of time.

Eastern European social and literary historians tend to respond in three ways when faced with a Western pattern of development and the demand to apply it to a stubborn local context. The first is simply to proclaim that the literary-historical categories in Eastern Europe differ from those in the West and must be defined in their own way. Thus many historians of Russian literature refer to the late eighteenth and early nineteenth century as the "Age of Silver" or "Pushkin's age," or they limit the Russian Enlightenment to the latter half of the eighteenth century. Czech literary historians talk very often about a period of "national renaissance" (1780–1830), and so on. This kind of response tends to emphasize local historical circumstances, for example, the national, sociopolitical, sometimes revolutionary implications of romantic literature in the East, as opposed to the Western stress on imagination and individual completeness, and the reformist and moderate nature of the Enlightenment in East-Central Europe, as opposed to its radical implications in the West. The concept of *Goethezeit* sometimes provides a paradigm for the alternative Eastern European literary development.

The second response seems to be inspired by an epidemic vision of fixed cultural categories. These are seen as traveling from West to East like an infectious disease, changing conditions and contaminating vast populations. Each period or subperiod in the West has to find some kind of equivalent in the East, despite a possible lag of thirty or fifty years. Thus, Czech preromanticism is said by some to flourish between 1815 and 1830, Romanian preromanticism is sometimes pushed to 1848 or later, the Hungarian Enlightenment is generally situated between 1772 and 1820, and so on. This "contagious illness" vision was reinforced by the Marxist preconception that the phases of historical development (slave-owning society, feudalism, capitalism, socialism) must follow each other by necessity and in a complete chain for each separate country.

Only the third group of responses seems to approach Gershenkron's methodology in the social sciences. Authors such as Vera Călin or Istvan Söter contend that in Eastern Europe, at the end of the eighteenth and the beginning of the nineteenth century, a telescoping of periods takes place. Enlightenment and romanticism, both inspired by the West, overlap and thus create a new kind of cultural mix after 1770 or 1780. Obviously, this theory incorporates a bit of each of the preceding ones: the influence aspect from one, the locally specific aspect from the other. Perhaps the most convincing argument made is that most Eastern European societies (but particularly Czech, Hungarian, and Romanian) were throughout most of the eighteenth century in a state of stagnation and decline. Therefore even moderate proposals of reform could elicit passionate responses, high-flying sentiments of a romantic nature, visions of bliss and regeneration. In other words, Enlightenment produced romanticism, not in a dialectical succession, by contrast and continuity, but rather in a dialectics of simultaneity, as a contemporary outgrowth, a supplement.

It is this antihistorical side of the theory that I am uneasy with. I believe that a different explanation is valid for the periods 1780–1800 and 1820–1840 in these literatures. I shall first survey very briefly three East-Central European literatures and then outline my proposal and indicate in what way I believe the classification applies to other literatures.

*   *   *

ROMANIAN LITERATURE was dormant throughout the eighteenth century. There was a fair amount of cultural assimilation (translations and adaptations from French, or even English and German writers).[6] The technical means of cultural communication (printing presses and private, scholarly, or even public libraries) were dramatically improved; many of the traditional genres (chronicles, moral-religious writings, popular-mythical novels) continued to flourish, but there was little creative writing activity that could be correlated to European developments. Indeed seventeenth century and very early eighteenth century Romanian writings (D. Cantemir), seem by contrast to correspond more closely to the prevailing Western trends. Not until the late 1780s was there a significant literary change.

At that point, in Bucharest the Văcărescu brothers, following Greek and Italian models, developed an Anacreontic poetry. They paved the way for a new phase in Romanian literature, because their rococo eroticism was often mixed with heroic and nationalist strains; the influence of folklore themes and forms in their poetry is plain. More significantly, a group of philologists, historians, and critics later dubbed Şcoala Ardeleană (the Transylvanian School) discovered, after studies in Rome and Vienna, the Latin roots of Romanian and established the theoretical bases of the debate over national identity that was to rage in the nineteenth and deep into the twentieth century.[7] In the writings of Samuil Micu (1745–1806), Gheorghe Şincai (1754–1816), and Petru Maior (1760–1821) there was a strong radical-romantic component that turned into full romantic theorizing only a few decades later, in the work of their follower, Timotei Cipariu (1805–1887). The obsessions with linguistic and racial purity, return to the roots, history as fable, and the myth of regeneration after fall and decay are clear indications of their general thrust.

Although these movements clearly reflect the Enlightenment, it is difficult to share the opinion of most Romanian literary historians that a Romanian Enlightenment lasted until, say 1830, followed by a preromanticism, 1830–1848, and by a romanticism, whose highest achievements belonged to the 1870s and 1880s.[8] Paul Cornea, in his fundamental work on the origins of Romanian romanticism,[9] shows very clearly by analyzing the period 1790–1850 that elements of sentimentalist idyllism, Enlightenment neoclassicism, and didacticism, along with full-fledged romantic features, can be distinguished among the mass of minor poetic production of the time.

The most interesting problems are raised by the 1830–1860 period; its half-romantic nature is easily recognized. The main poets of the time were influenced by Lamartine, Hugo, and Byron: Grigore Alexandrescu, Dimitrie Bolintineanu, and Cezar Bolliac wrote melancholy meditations, colorful oriental and historical ballads, and rebellious social pamphlets, but usually kept away from the central concerns of romantic imagination and transfiguration. The greatest poet of the period, Vasile Alecsandri, was the soul of moderation: he added an academic or ironic polish to the marginally romantic motifs treated by his contemporaries, affected the serenity of Horace and the ironic sprightliness of Ovid, and touched all romantic themes with a graceful detachment, which indicates a lack of poignant involvement similar to that of the Biedermeier.

Among the main authors of fiction, Costache Negruzzi and Alexandru Odobescu wrote historical tableaux that can only be described as Biedermeier in their careful historicist manner, while Nicolae Filimon's novel *Ciocoii vechi și noi* (Old and New Landowners, 1863) evinces a post-Balzacian mixture of sensationalism and social realism—very far from the visionary intensities of core Romanticism. Bălcescu wrote history in the manner of Jules Michelet and Edgar Quinet; Ion Ghica's letters and Odobescu's *Pseudokynegetikos* are only the foremost among a vast body of conversational essays, strikingly close in manner, tone, and elegance to Lamb's and Xavier de Maistre's productions—with which they were hardly acquainted.[10]

The visionary romanticism of Mihai Eminescu in the 1870s is an anachronic but logical reconstruction of an aspect all but missing in the early nineteenth century;[11] the important qualification is that this phenomenon took place "underground," in unpublished projects and manuscripts. Titu Maiorescu, the sternly Victorian mentor of Romania in matters aesthetic, encouraged or even dictated their suppression, while promoting the realistic, serious, Biedermeier, and Victorian aspects of Eminescu's work. Eminescu's philosophy, a combination of Schopenhauer, J. F. Herbart, H. T. Buckle, Herbert Spencer, and Hegel, is largely responsible for the schizophrenic aspect of the poet's work: the "Neptunian," diurnal, discursive, and rational-social side ever opposed to the "Uranian," nocturnal, visionary, fiercely subjective, and mythical side.[12]

Somewhat similar processes occurred in the richer neighboring Hungarian literature. The eighteenth century was a period of literary decline after the flowering of Renaissance and even baroque writing in the previous two centuries; Hungarian Enlightenment is usually said to begin after 1772 and to go deep into the 1820s, while the "Reform Age" or "Vormärz" (roughly 1820–1844 or 1820–1850) is said to represent Hungarian romanticism.[13]

But what kind of Enlightenment do we discover when we look closely at the facts? There is no question that the ideas of Locke, Voltaire, and Montesquieu were introduced in Hungary, particularly by György Bessenyei and by his followers, who thought of themselves as representatives of Josephinism. But from the very beginning, there were mingled with these a stress on national sentiment, an admiration of the past, indeed of rugged conservatism, that seem to be, if anything, in *advance* of their time; at the very least they give a decisive preromantic coloring to the Hungarian Enlightenment. The prevalence of the extended topos of a societal idyll (often, but not always transposed into the historical past) is also a typical feature. Benedek Virág (1754–1830) and the circle of his admirers, Sándor Kisfaludy (whose most influential work appeared around 1800), and Dániel Berzsenyi (who, it is true, became known only after 1813) provide illustrations of this characteristic aspect. In all of them we encounter a peculiar mixture of the romance tradition (Horatian or Petrarchan) with a more nativist melancholy or exaltation of a dark golden age.[14] Among other examples are Mihály Csokonai Vitéz, who did most of his writing in the 1790s, and Mihály Fazekas, who wrote his one important work, *Ludas Matyi* (Matyas the Gooseboy), in 1804. The former displays a peculiar mixture of belated rococo and sentimentalism (*Dorattya* was clearly influenced by Pope's *Rape of the Lock*) with an intense quasi-romantic awareness of folk themes and folk-stylistic devices;[15] and his drama *Tempefői* is a good presentation of the myth of the *poète damné*, in spite of its amiable form and lack of bitterness. A similar mixture is easily recognized in *Ludas Matyi*.

In other words, it would seem that these preromantic writers slide imperceptibly into a kind of early Biedermeier while still preparing the romantic explosion. We may apply here the views of Alexandru Cioränescu regarding Romanian literature: namely, that compared to the stagnating cultural (and, I should like to add, social) situation in East-Central Europe, both Enlightenment and romantic features could be regarded as revolutionary departures, and thus used interchangeably.[16] There is no organic connection between a developing

Enlightenment model and its romantic outcome and negation. Rather, what we encounter is a combination, a kind of hasty averaging of features. In this early stage the quasi-Biedermeier features are perhaps not more than a coincidence; the retreating Western romanticism of the 1820s and 1830s tried to occupy a middle ground between high romanticism and a recuperated Enlightenment similar to that the Eastern Europeans were seeking in the 1780s and 1790s. But we must also take into account the sociocultural situation in which the decision that conservative-nostalgic and radical-didactic impulses are not incompatible was made even before the French Revolution.[17] In this respect Eastern Europe was more similar to England than to France and Germany.

Therefore it is not strange that the Hungarian "romantics" after 1820 differ from the preceding generation in value more than in substance. Mihály Vörösmarty's main works, the hexameter epic *Zalán futása* (The Flight of Zalan, 1825) and the historical tragedies, followed fairly closely the tradition of Csokonai and Berzsenyi. His historical plays of blood and revenge are in the manner of Victor Hugo. His political and philosophizing shorter poems have the ring of Jung Deutschland; they offer individual pessimism and doubt mixed with social and national hopefulness, which throughout Europe is indicative of the breakdown of the core-romantic paradigm.[18]

A number of minor figures could be termed purely Biedermeier: János Garay, whose *feuilletons,* short descriptive pieces, and humorous poems are in the spirit of Lamb and Hunt; Ferenc Toldy, a typical late-romantic historian and critic; Miklós Jósika, whose historical novels of the 1830s and 1840s adapted Scott's approach to Transylvanian history; Pál Vasvári, who philosophized in the manner of Saint-Simon, Fourier, and Michelet; or Mihály Tompa, whose assimilation of folk versification and themes was controlled by a Biedermeier seriousness and respect for industriousness.

The prime piece of evidence will be provided by Sandor Petöfi himself. Of his main poetic epics, *A helység kalapácsa* (The Hammer of the Village, 1844) was immediately recognized as antiromantic, deflating conventions and masterfully playing with the lower register halfway between Heine and Pushkin, and certainly not far from the manner of Mickiewiecz's *Pan Tadeusz. János Vitéz* (Childe John, 1845), on the other hand, uses the fantastic in the playful, deliberate manner of the later romantics, and certainly kept clear of the prophetic intensity of imagination of the first romantic generation. Naturally, one may debate whether in some of his shorter lyrics, in the short novel *A hóhér kötele* (Hangman's Rope), and some other writings of the years 1845–1846, Petöfi does not identify himself with a purer romanticism. It seems to me that, even after possibly answering this question in the affirmative, we shall find this high-romantic episode engulfed in a mass of idyllic, descriptive, and moody genre poetry, which includes *Az Alföld* (The Plain, 1844), *Winter Evenings,* and *The Standard-Bearer* (after 1847) and, indeed, his travel diaries and occasional prose pieces for *Pesti Divatlap.*[19] In *A Tisza* (1847) and the related genre and descriptive poems, we find Petöfi at his most characteristic: idyllic and tempestuous scenes alternate rather than organize themselves along a past versus future (alienation versus redemption) pattern of intelligible progress. What is more, Petöfi's characters show an awareness of Dickens' eccentrics and misfits, and close analysis of his treatment of structures borrowed from folk poetry shows how thoroughly he had "out-run" the romantics.[20] In a word, the progress from Csokonai to Petöfi is one of mastery or, perhaps, of aesthetic information, not a deeper one involving the self-shaping of human existentiality.

A FEW BRIEF comments on the periodization of Czech literature will, I hope, further clarify the specific romantic pattern of development in Eastern Europe. As William Harkins has shown, there has been a very serious debate on this subject and the conclusion rather generally accepted would have it that the Czech Enlightenment lasted well into the nineteenth century, followed by fairly short preromantic and romantic periods between roughly 1815 and 1860.[21] This view fits the second category of theories described above, the one which holds that all phases of the Western pattern must be rediscovered in identical sequence in the East, with an average lag of half a century. A closer look easily reveals a different situation.

The Czech Enlightenment had an explosively radical quality that makes it close kin to romanticism. That is why so many literary historians refer to it as the period of renaissance.[22] It would be impossible to overlook the many features pointing to romanticism even in the work of a rationalist like Josef Dobrovský, who was influenced by Herder, who admired the Schlegels, who thought that Indian and Slavic mythology had a common basis, and who tried to localize universal reason in the specific Slavic *Um.*[23] On the other hand, A. J. Puchmajer thought he could encourage or develop romanticism through poetry in the manner of the Göttinger Hain and rococo stylistics.[24] The same type of mixture is evident in the work and approach of the more nationalistic representatives of the literature of the time, such as Josef Jungmann of Ján Kollár. Jungmann disliked romantic poets and promoted the works of Voltaire and Wieland, Pope, Goldsmith, and Goethe (from among the latter's works he translated, significantly, *Hermann und Dorothea*). But at the same time he rhapsodized about a fantastically modified past of the Slavs and displayed intense nationalism. I shall not discuss the typical transitional ("preromantic") play of the fabricated manuscript collections of Králóve Dvúr and Zelená Hora (the imaginative work of Vacláv Hanka with the help of Josef Linda and others)—certainly prime examples of the imagination working with mixed theoretical and literary material.

But Ján Kollár and F. L. Čelakovský express even better the highly ambivalent attitude toward romanticism of writers belonging to the Czech "renaissance." These are people who were well aware of the main romantic figures in Europe (sometimes through personal contact) and who nevertheless were trying to find a middle road, specifically different from that of Western European core romanticism. During his German studies Kollár admired Goethe, Arndt, and Jahn; the ideas of Lorenz Oken, J. F. Fries, and Heinrich Luden were digested as suggestions for a patriotic-national vision of Slavic grandeur and mythical potential; better even than in Jungmann, we can observe the mechanics of structure transfer from the cosmic to the mundane in Kollár's poetic output or theoretical ramblings.[25] His courses and published or posthumous manuscripts on the identity of the Slavic zodiac with the Indian-Egyptian one or the fantastic-philosophical etymologies of the concept of *Slav* parallel similar attempts to structure poetically large areas of intellectual discourse throughout Europe in the early nineteenth century.[26] Such features of Biedermeier metamorphosis make even Kollár's later conservatism and admiration for A. S. Khomyakov irrelevant. Earlier, and perhaps more drastically than others, Kollár expressed the culture-civilization tension which from Herder on obsessed German and Eastern European intellectuals until well into the twentieth century.

Josef Mühlberger contends, correctly I believe, that the common, old Slavic concept of *Mir* with its implications of both peace and cosmos and its foundation in the matriarchal village-state with common ownership based on moderation and quiet growth was important to the shaping of the traditional perceptual assumptions of Czech literature.[27] It certainly provided, when rediscovered, a convenient historical and even religious legitimacy for a variety of holistic visions. It is easy to see how Puchmajer or others might in turn have related their rococo idyllism to this more vigorous and weightier construct. But it was left for Čelakovský to spell out the opposition in his two series of poems of 1829 and 1839: *Ohlas písní ruských* and *Ohlas písní českých*. Čelakovský himself claimed that he was pointing to differences between ethnic psychological morphologies in opposing the deep forests, rugged cliffs, and tumultuous waves of the Russian spirit to the open lawns, friendly bushes, and murmuring creeks of the Czech song.[28] I submit that Čelakovský was observing the transition from high romanticism to the lower but consistent harmonies that the Biedermeier was seeking.

The literary atmosphere of the 1830s and 1840s in Bohemia could never be thoroughly understood without the concept of Biedermeier. The main figures of the period certainly display Biedermeier features, and it seems surprising that almost none of the major literary historians (not even Wellek) were willing to tackle this fact. It is true that, for example, Josef Kajetán Tyl's musical plays, full of fairy-tale fantasy, black humor, and fiddling obsessions have always been compared to those of Nestroy and even Raimund. A brilliant, recent article by Milorada Součková has disclosed the wealth of implications in Tyl's famous poem, which later became the national anthem of the Czechoslovak republic *Kde domov můj?*[29] Although Součková's account is illuminating, I believe that her exclusive reliance on Cosmas's *Chronicon* is confining; whatever Tyl's sources, the responses to his poem were part of an intellectual climate in which a more modern idyllic model was shaping the perception of imaginative and empiric realities. The best evidence is provided by some of Tyl's contemporaries, such as František Jaromír Rubeš—the first important representative of the easy, humorous, miniature descriptive genre dealing with the ordinary life of ordinary people that was to inaugurate in Czech literature a tradition lasting from Karolina Světlá (d. 1899) all the way to Marie Pujmanová, Alois Jirásek (d. 1930), Jarmila Glazarová, František Táborský (d. 1940), Ignát Herrmann (d. 1935), and Karel Poláček (d. 1944) and indeed all the way to Jaroslav Hašek himself.

The acknowledged masters of this tradition came at its very beginning; contemporaries of Tyl and Rubeš, though younger, Božena

Němcová and Jan Neruda provided classical examples of Biedermeier writing by any standards. Němcová's *Babička* (Granny, 1855) with its static choices and multitude of vivid details illustrates the main strategy of this literary approach.[30] The examples of minute and credible harmony in the life surrounding us are multiplied to surfeit. They have to convince us that their mere accumulation suggests an all-encompassing harmony. Leslie Stephen and others have spoken of circumstantial realism in the writings of Defoe;[31] I suggest that Němcová similarly fuses the idyllism of the late eighteenth century with the hope that at least a fleeting outline of the primeval Slavic *mir* can be recaptured. But the cumulative effect proves stronger: the reception is one of atmosphere, not of comprehensive structure. The charge that this is sentimentalism—a mere mixture of sadness and humor—is, coming from a modern reader, neither more nor less justified than when applied to other contemporary writers: it only points to the deeper contradictions of any Biedermeier formula. Similarly, Jan Neruda in his *Malostránské povídky* (Small Side Stories, 1878) or in his earlier collections of stories insisted on the capacity of the smallest structures to reflect the complexity and diversity of the universe as a whole. Neruda has sometimes been compared to Gottfried Keller. There is no question that in any periodization scheme their function in their respective literatures would be quite similar. They both abandoned the confining schemes of later romanticism in favor of the nonpurposive description of realism. But although the schemes were abandoned, the thematic material remained the same—the life and habits of the small rural or urban bourgeois environment—and the range of possible combinations of events did not become broader. However, a better suggestion, in my opinion, is that Neruda paralleled Wilhelm Raabe, with whom he shares a slightly nervous use of humor and a rather bashful sentimentality. Many of Neruda's short stories relate psychologically sophisticated, almost "modernist" experiences, but they are placed in frameworks of hard stone: students at night smoking quietly on the Gothic roofs, surrounded by gables and gargoyles, or a teenager deciding to spend the night in St. Vencesles Cathedral, while other stories begin with lavish descriptions of the fat, smelly darkness of little houses. Thus the events are smothered and miniaturized by their own environment, not a rural, but an urban one. Layers of heavy civilization flatten out the would-be dramatic contours of events.

Czech literature certainly displays striking parallels to German literature; the two have probably the most orthodox and richly developed Biedermeier system. Czech literature has its equivalent of Heine or Jung Deutschland in the person of Karel Havlíček-Borovský who founded the epigrammatic-skeptical pole of the Czech Biedermeier, just as Rubeš had founded the idyllic one. Another stock character of the Biedermeier cast is also present—the leisurely, erudite, imaginative essayist. Indeed, František Palacký can be seen in the best of European company, with Michelet, Carlyle, and Quinet, as one of the greatest belletristic historians, whose ideological-polemical vision is informed by a dominant myth—the pragmatic version of the romantic paradigm of immanent transcendence. Palacký's stylistic olympianism combined with his later-romantic visionary brilliance make him an eminent representative of the European Biedermeier.

Karel Hynek Mácha is such an important figure that he has been discussed from a comparatist angle more often than others. René Wellek has been quite concerned with Mácha's status: in a famous article he shows that the parallel between Byron and Mácha is limiting and has to be replaced by categories of similarities to different authors (most of whom I would characterize as Biedermeier).[32] Let us note among the parallels enumerated by Wellek those with Bulwer-Lytton and with Scott. Although Mácha's lyrical intensity is much more impressive than that of his English colleagues, he did share some basic concerns with them. Chief among these seems to me realistic concealment. Like all later romantics, he shied away from the absolute hero, from the typical figure embodying the experience of mankind as a whole, but tried nevertheless to maintain the general abstract stages of this experience.

Even though he and his contemporaries would not have resorted to stark myth, and even though they did not have the courage to proclaim that they were writing on "the poet's mind" or the "world's soul," they were eager to tackle the subject somehow. Much as he differed from his conventional contemporaries, Mácha did strive for typical experiential stages in highly individualized circumstances. The abstract and symbolic scheme is hiding in realistic or melodramatic garb. It is not exaggerated to call this procedure a mimetic concealment, a deliberate attempt to throw the doubters off track and to illustrate the same general points with individual cases. This attempt required the increasing use of external "romantic" elements, that is, the spectacular romantic machinery that one finds in *Eugene Aram* or *The Last Days of Pompeii*, no less than *Cikáni* (The Gypsies) or *Máj*.

A different process is at work in Mácha's reception of Scott. The structure of Scott's historical novels is deformed in a high-romantic direction. This is a phenomenon that can be recognized in many literatures with a weak or even a missing high-romantic phase (French, Polish, Romanian, and others): the emergence of a substitute intensified romanticism at the tail end of the whole phase. *Křivoklat* or *Cikáni* are dense, fast-paced stories, in which suggestion and allusion come into their own as central devices, and energetic melodrama gradually acquires the shades of hermetism.

IN SPITE of Mácha's apparently ambiguous position, Czech literature, like Hungarian and Romanian, can essentially be divided into two phases: preromanticism and late romanticism (Biedermeier). The transition between the two is smooth. The more uniform character of the Eastern European romantic periods and movements prevents the sharp differences seen elsewhere, for example, between Goldsmith, Wordsworth, and Landor. Petöfi and Csokonai, Puchmajer and Rubeš, are close in style and matter, and the work of one continues smoothly from the work of the others.

This is not to say that such literatures lack pure Enlightenment features. Rather, a curious stratification takes place, perhaps as a consequence of the more elitist and stratified nature of Eastern European societies as opposed to Western ones: Enlightenment activities are bestowed from above, Enlightenment doctrines are designed to help the rising social groups. Not Dobrovský, but rather his humbler colleagues in the learned societies of Prague and Olomouc are true representatives of the Enlightenment. Václav Matěj Kramerius, with his journalistic and editorial production, is also such a representative. Echoes of the Enlightenment can be heard very late, in the statutes and work of the Matice Česká (after 1831).[33] For Eastern European literatures the Enlightenment is not a flourishing of the neoclassicist human paradigm, or the bold intellectual consequence of the structural tensions between elitism and egalitarianism, as it is for Diderot and Hume. Rather, it is a purely *practical* background of educational reform, importation of intellectual information, careful dismantling of religious absolutes by the addition of scientific or rationalist elements, renewal of social usage and intercourse. Most of these features had been rather secondary aspects of Western Enlightenment.

There is another major difference between the Western European and the Eastern European Enlightenment. In Hungarian, Romanian, and Czech literatures, the earlier phases of the Enlightenment were ignored and a strong late phase, already distorted in a preromantic direction, flourished. *Şcoala Ardeleană*, Kollár and Dobrovský, Csokonai and Fazekas are prime examples. However, many scholars would agree that the possibility of a strong romantic revolution depends on a fully developed Enlightenment base. It is indeed the complete implementation and dialectic *Aufhebung* (suspension—denial—preservation) of the Enlightenment program. The romantic human model does not emerge out of nothing; total expansion must proceed from gradual extensions. The absence of high romanticism in these Eastern European countries is not a quirk of fate, nor is it a matter of arbitrary choice. The cluster of values (Enlightenment plus preromantic) that appeared there in 1770–1790 had to develop its own momentum; it was simply not spacious enough, not comprehensive enough, not organic enough to lead to a spasm of transuniversal harmony. On the other hand, the same construction was well able to adapt itself to late-romantic (Biedermeier) configurations. In France, Lamartine and Musset represented a retreat from the temerities of Saint-Just and Sade; in England, Scott and Lamb moderated the absolute claims of Wordsworth's conscience; in Germany, Mörike and Heine reduced to scale the mythical intensities of Hölderlin and Novalis; but in Eastern Europe the entrance to the Biedermeier was effected smoothly, with merely a passing frown at the excesses of Western romantics. Indeed, in Mácha or Eminescu or Petöfi, the genuine intensities of romanticism were repressed or hidden.

The practicality of the Biedermeier—national and social bodies as agents of development—appealed to the historical forces at work there, while the idyllic and domestic side of the Biedermeier could well compensate for the agonies of historical change. To put it more forcefully, precisely because the Biedermeier was dualistic in nature, it had a wider appeal in Eastern Europe than the absolute unity postulated by core romanticism. The inherent conservatism of Eastern European political development that seemed so puzzling to outside observers was not "genetic" or "inevitable"; it just represented the unfolding of the specific model of their entrance into the modern age. This dualism explains how the smooth surface of continuous moderation is punctured by occasional outbursts, how social cohesion is challenged but not disrupted by harsh stratification, and finally how selfish materialism and social idealism coexist so placidly in this part of the world.

Thus, Gershenkron's suggestions can prove useful in many ways. The human model (the carrier of literature) develops in several phases; it is quite possible for a community to identify with a late phase and not with an earlier one. I believe that this is precisely what happened in Eastern Europe: there was no full-fledged Enlightenment, only a catching up with its *last* phase (preromantic warts and all). Analogously, there was no high romanticism—merely a powerful and complex Biedermeier (1820–1850), fully synchronized with the corresponding Western phase.

THIS COMMON, bipartite model for the substitution of Western patterns can also be applied to the highly developed Russian and Polish literatures. Western phases and trends can be most distinctly recognized in Polish literature, dating back to the Middle Ages. Polish literature did not suffer like neighboring literatures from the relative intellectual and aesthetic sterility of 1550–1750. In fact, both Russian and Polish literatures display a well-sketched (if not fully colored) Enlightenment phase, represented at its best by people such as M. V. Lomonosov and Antiokh Kantemir, by Bishop Ignacy Krasicki and Stanislaw Trembecki. One might therefore expect a full range of Western-model phases in steady progression.

Still, as soon as one nears the romantic period, there is a great deal of uncertainty in periodization and a marked reluctance even to use the term romanticism in connection with Russian literature. *When* the term is used, it is often accompanied by qualifying terms such as "Official, Bureaucratic, Full-Dress, Philistine, Bourgeois, Plebeian, Democratic, Aristocratic, Liberal, Progressive, Revolutionary, Conservative, Reactionary, Civic, Decembrist, Frenzied, Symbolical, Realistic, Subjective, Superficial, False, Pseudo, Ultra, Extreme, Counterfeit, True, Pure, Vulgar, and Lefty."[34] Prince Mirsky admits an age of classicism, but between it and the age of realism only a "Golden Age of Poetry" and an "Age of Gogol."[35] Yuri Tynyanov similarly avoids commitment to the term, and the Soviet critics of the 1930s and 1940s were not necessarily reluctant to speak about romanticism purely out of servile dogmatism.[36]

In Russian literature in the 1780s and 1790s neoclassicism was being weakened by sentimentalism but was not being discarded altogether. Although nobody could deny that Kantemir, Lomonosov, and even Ivan Krylov offer excellent examples of neoclassic Enlightenment, it may be doubted that the Horatian G. R. Derzhavin, particularly in his Anacreontic poems of 1804 or in *Evgenyu, Zhizni Zvanskaya* (To Eugene, Life at Zvanka, 1807), should be placed in the same category, particularly because the writers of the 1820s and 1830s considered him their forerunner.[37]

The opposition between Aleksandr Radischchev (1749–1802) and Nikolay Karamzin (1766–1826) is not interesting from our point of view, since it was based largely on politics.[38] Both authors clearly represented the peak of a distinct movement, even though Radischchev was less significant and productive. Karamzin was still part of the Enlightenment in his stylistic innovations and in his philosophy of history: but in his stories, particularly in *Bednaya Liza* (Poor Liza, 1792), and his translations (Thomson's *Seasons,* with their code value all over Europe), in his liberal journalism of 1802–1804, in his tempered Rousseauism, Karamzin showed himself a preromantic, as much as the more radical Radischchev. Prince Mirsky notes that "beginning as a reforming, almost revolutionary, force, Karamzin ended his career and passed into posterity as the symbol and most perfect embodiment of the official ideas of Imperial Russia."[39] This will not seem surprising to the attentive student of the period: the *Umfunktionierung* (remodeling) of liberal eighteenth-century ideas into conservative postrevolutionary tenets was common to the great literary and political figures of the age. Metternich's positions emerged by projecting Montesquieu onto the new, artificial, but inevitable equilibrium produced by twenty-five years of upheaval.[40] A deliberately delayed progressivism in intellectual matters becomes a static progressivism turned on itself. Ultimately, Radischchev too must be seen as a specialized segment of a more general "Karamzin statement" made by Russian literature in its phase of modified Enlightenment.

Nor should the line separating V. A. Zhukovsky from Karamzin or the Karamzinians be drawn too sharply. Zhukovsky's choice of works for translation did not place him in opposition to the previous generation, and even the stylistic and metrical decisions he made merely purified and modernized. They did not revolutionize but smoothly seem to have led the eighteenth century to its logical conclusion. K. N. Batyushkov and other members of the poetic society *Arzamas* considered themselves loyal followers of Karamzin. Postulating two Russian preromanticisms as some critics have tried to do is not only awkward, but it also distorts the basic aesthetic realities of the period by assigning top importance to the intentions and declarations of the period's main actors. From a European perspective, the "transitional" period 1780–1810 in Russian literature seems a coherent whole, and, much like the other Eastern European literatures, it offers a picture of late Enlightenment and romantic literary amalgamation.

The key complicating factor is that 1820, the date generally accepted as the beginning of Russian romanticism, seems, as in Hungarian or Czech literature, to bring with it a change merely in the value, not in the nature of the poetic output. The preparatory combination of a classical base with romantic superadded features led, in the West, to a purely romantic explosion, but not in Russian literature. An unstable mixture of romantic influences and classical traditions flows quietly and continuously from 1780 to 1840 or so. For instance, the features of Russian romanticism enumerated by Dimitry Chizhevsky and others do not sound convincingly different from those of the 1780–1810 "Sentimentalist" phase in Russian literature.[41] Liberation of poetic creativity from constraints does not mean too much—it is precisely the poets of the 1820s who were highly polished in form. Nationalism is not a feature of a strictly understood romanticism—was Wordsworth a nationalist in *The Prelude,* or Coleridge in *Kubla Khan,* or Novalis? The idea that mere allegiance to Rousseauism, Herderism, or *Sturm und Drang* might be signs of romanticism can be rejected out of hand as a simplified reading of the semiotics of cultural systems. Chizhevsky argues on the basis of quotations from F. I. Tyutchev that the key to Slavic romanticism is the opposition between reason and feeling.[42] This may well be conceded as an important feature of Eastern European romanticism, but it is highly doubtful that any of the Western high Romantics would have accepted it as such. Indeed, analogies will not be found in Wordsworth's or Novalis's overarching transrationality or in Coleridge's careful and precise disquisitions, but in handy prefabricated formulas circulated during the Biedermeier age. And so it goes with most other features cited by Chizhevsky: love of history and folklore, the choice of specific genre (the cosmic fresco, ballad, and epigrams), interest in madness and unusual personalities, and so on.[43]

The explanation I propose is that the main difference must indeed be sought not in style or in themes, but rather in attitude and literary conscience. As in Hungarian and Czech literature, the great Russian writing after 1820 differs more in quality than in structure from the prevailing formulas of 1780–1820; however its self-perception had changed in an obvious and radical way. By 1820 it was becoming impossible to ignore the explosive impact of the high-romantic paradigm in literature and in philosophy. Russian literature caught up with Western European trends at their most advanced point. Thus Russian literature skipped high romanticism, and "became Biedermeier." This was the outcome of deep-seated sociocultural decisions, not of literary-critical discussions. It is not that Pushkin and Gogol and Odoyevsky were ignorant or incapable of reproducing Blake and Hölderlin, any more than Lamartine or Leopardi were. They were simply implicated in a different, telescoping, and substitutive momentum, which in its way was richer and more significant than its modest British counterparts (for example, of the later 1820s).

PUSHKIN and Gogol were fully and immediately synchronized with their late-romantic colleagues in Vienna or Paris. A look at Pushkin's work from the point of view of the principles set forth here will show that he was neither the belated fine flower of the Russian Enlightenment nor the odd and uneasy romantic he is often made out to be, but a perfect late romantic of the Regency and Biedermeier age, in fact, perhaps the greatest in that generation of Mussets and Peacocks.

Pushkin is, among Eastern European writers, one of the least likely to be accused of ignoring what was going on in the rest of Europe. He opened himself to the influence of Byron and Scott (as has often been shown) because he felt they were relevant to his own aesthetic discourse.[44] He had a better understanding of Musset than most of the latter's French contemporaries.[45] He may not have actually read all his contemporaries (for example, Shelley or Keats), but theoretically he had certainly mastered the principles of romanticism. He had read in French A. W. Schlegel's work on drama; he was fully aware of the limitations of French critical theory and practice on romanticism, and in 1835 he accused the French of critical confusion, of failing to see the medieval bases of any true romanticism.[46] On the other hand, he felt free to accept the influence of Chénier, Gray, or Sterne precisely because for him they belonged to the past not less than Shakespeare. And, like many a German author after 1830, he liked to think of Goethe as a prototypical romantic. The main point is that Pushkin was not a *latecomer* in terms of reading or taste. When he chose to be, he was precisely synchronized with his European counterparts; when he was not, this was an autonomous and weighty aesthetic decision, which must be judged as such and its significance carefully considered.

There is rich evidence of the extent to which Pushkin's work is interwoven in the European literature of his time. True, his late-romantic skepticism can be easily confused with the Enlightenment "smile of reason." John Bayley compares the *Gavriliad* to Voltaire's lighthanded blasphemies. But it is much more appropriate to think of *Tsar Nikita i Sorok Yevo Docherey* (Tsar Nikita and His Forty Daughters, 1822) in comparison with Heine. It is written against the background of folk rhythms and motifs; it is a parody of *narodnost* (quintessential folk spirit) and of the world of nostalgic myth no less than of everyday realities. Similar parallels offer themselves at every step. *Boris Godunov* has been justly compared to Büchner's *Dantons Tod* in its episodic, atonal, and aleatory structure;[47] but it and *Stseny rytsarskikh vremen* (Scenes from the Days of Chivalry, 1835) can equally well be compared to Grabbe's cruel aestheticism; they are colorful and pregnant historic tableaux, streaked with mysticism and madness, historical color, and the disorderly picturesque. *Zimnyaya Doroga* (Winter Road, 1826) has been shown to have (by pure coincidence) similarities with Lenau's *Der Postillion*.[48]

Numerous parallels to Keats have, I believe, been overlooked. A few will be discussed later, but I shall mention off-hand *Tsarsoselskaija Statuya* (Fountain at Tsarskoe Selo, 1830)—both plastically and thematically a younger sister to the *Grecian Urn*. *Anchar* (The Upas Tree, 1828) has the severe pessimism of Vigny, and the many minor productions in the vein of Southey have been noted. Both *The Moor of Peter the Great* and *The Postmaster* begin like pieces of belletristic science, with the typical Biedermeier gesture of moving gradually from the general to the particular: this was standard procedure from Manzoni to Vigny, from Hugo to Stifter. It is groundless to claim, like N. A. Berdyaev, that Pushkin represented the Renaissance, and it is naive to stress too much the supremacy of laughter in Pushkin.[49] In a discrete and elegant way, Pushkin was no less devoted to the tragicomic or the grotesque than Gogol.

Pushkin's awareness of the idyllic societal model and of its implications is obvious. We do not have to go as far as Vladimir Nabokov, who at one point discovered the direct influence of Fontenelle's pastoralism; it is sufficient to say that both the older pastoral and the "revisionist" idyllic traditions were strong in Russian literature when Pushkin started writing, as well as later.[50] From V. K. Trediakovsky in 1752, with his strophes in praise of country life (*poselyanskomu zhitiyu*) to Derzhavin's *Life at Zvanka* this awareness is well documented, even though it may be doubtful whether until the 1820s the idyllic model received anything like a central position or that of a serious alternative system. Pushkin knew how to make use of the idyllic macro-image both directly and in a highly ironic manner—an interesting differentiating symptom, for Pushkin personally, as well as for Russian literature in general, since serious and ironic uses of the idyllic model are successive and opposing phases in English and German literature. While *Uedinyenye* (Seclusion, 1819) is merely a good-natured epigram, Pushkin's typical, rough, schizoid attitude toward idyllism is discovered best in *Derevnia* (In the Country, 1819).[51] There, the first twenty lines are sheer Winchilsea or Pomfret, but (after a virtuous proclamation, much in the vein of Wordsworth's *Ode to Duty*) the last twenty-five lines or so are in the manner of Crabbe. Their cruel and indignant realism is not really debunking. Pushkin fully admits the coexistence of two different universes in close proximity to each other: all-embracing romantic aspirations do not trouble him. The intermediate range is richly represented, whether by *Zima* (Here's Winter, 1829),[52] with its typical serene and cozy security, or by the strikingly Keatsian first stanza of *Oseny* (Autumn, 1829) or the superb little lyric *Vinograd* (Grapes, 1820).[53] The praise of tea, an idyllic signal from Voss to De Quincey, can be encountered in *Eugene Onegin* (III, 37). There is, to be sure, a certain light ironic overtone in all of these poems. It is not necessarily, as Nabokov says, that Pushkin "never quite made up his mind whether to satirize or praise (grotesque or fundamentally sound?) St. Petersburg society."[54] It is more that Pushkin, one of the greatest later romantics, was no longer willing to subordinate everything else to the unifying impulse: juxtaposition reimposed its rights. True, he could, when he wanted to, build a shattering scene such as that of the singing girls picking berries in *Eugene Onegin* (III, 39), with the horrifying and brutal social command behind it—a perfect example of synthetic, multidimensional writing. More often than not, such integration is shunned in favor of pleasant variety, significant paratactic confrontations, or the coexistence of contraries. Thus, Onegin can very well look at country life with squeamishness, boredom, and disapprobation, while the speaking persona can differ with him ever so politely (I, 55; II, 2–3)—and the persona itself, connecting Pushkin and Onegin, is one of the boldest and most complex achievements—the projection of a projection (VIII, 50).

*   *   *

PUSHKIN'S political and even philosophical opinions have always seemed a little irrelevant. The case for a religious Pushkin made by Leo Kobilinski-Ellis has not drawn much attention.[55] Whether we think of the young poet who moderately adhered to the most moderate wing of the moderately reformist Decembrist conspiracy,[56] or of the disgruntled middle-aged nobleman who may have been ready for the influence of P. Y. Chaadayev or even for a Slavophile nationalism à la *Klevetnikam Rosii* (To Russia's Calumniators, 1831), does not seem to make much difference.[57] There is a simple explanation.

Pushkin's *Weltanschauung* cannot be inferred from his declarations or activities, but rather from his consistent literary preconceptions. Pushkin's specific (and secondary) political and philosophical decisions are a consequence of his literary models or of his choices among the multiple variants of the Biedermeier. Very clearly Pushkin's basic decision was against pragmatic reduction and in favor of a skeptical irony that would preserve the shape of the high-romantic paradigm, while relativizing it. This decision explains, not only why we tend to overlook Pushkin's political gestures, but also why his work, which is stylistically quite close to Karamzin's, seems so different from it. The great gap between the two is the way in which they are integrated into European culture and is only visible from a comparatist approach: Karamzin looks forward to a coming human model, while Pushkin looks back with smiling nostalgia to something whose peak lies just behind him. But above all, this decision gives an informing unity and a precise focus to Pushkin's work, as can be readily seen by reading *Eugene Onegin* in the context of his other important works.

The central lyrical perception in *Eugene Onegin* (as distinct from its epic-dramatic level) is the gentle melancholy that follows the loss of identification with the rhythms of nature: these are perfectly perceived and understood (VII, 1–7), but empathy with them is imitative, not spontaneous.[58] It all happens as if a Wordsworthian imaginative sublime experience had just been irremediably lost. The loss of vision of the *Intimations* is accepted matter-of-factly. The jump into Being is now replaced by the polite simulation of Being. This attitude, succeeding as it does the great high-romantic bid, inevitably carries with it a subtle note of regret. Structurally, this subordinate analogy to essential rhythms can be encountered in the Enlightenment, too, but without the slight rueful smile, without the nostalgia, without the touch of piquant inadequacy. In the Enlightenment it is fully self-confident and, indeed, self-righteous in a sense in which Pushkin (as opposed to, say, Haydn) never wished to be. Tatyana may still manage to identify fully with the idyllic model (VII, 15, 18–19, 53), the "persona" may put on a brave face and summon vast reserves of stabilizing common sense, but Onegin knows better: the price of lucidity is incompleteness; he is not going to accept any self-stunting devices for the sake of a dubious, limited harmony.[59] After the explosive romantic revolution, the bitter forgiving smile accompanying the fragmentation of the world seems a more sincere solution than the only other possibility: an appropriate and judicious pragmatism. I am persuaded that the particular delicacy of Pushkin's writing results from the way in which he accepts the unifying harmony of the high-romantic paradigm as a thin film perceived in the distance which, like the rainbow, can never be touched; the colored sections of the arc are certain and palpable—though inert and unconnected, still preferable to a reduced, vulgarized version of the unifying paradigm as illustrated in either conservative or liberal political and social action.

Many of Pushkin's best works have as their theme the defeat of romanticism by the Biedermeier. Pushkin did not actually discuss which of the two romantic withdrawals (pragmatic or sectionalized) was preferable. He did seem to believe however that he had to defend his attitude, to show that romantic defeat was not only inevitable but (with a small relativizing smile and raising of eyebrows) desirable.

We do not know how Pushkin would have ended *Arap Petra Velikogo* (The Moor of Peter the Great, 1837), but we can draw an informed conclusion from the axiological alignments in the extant chapters. The conflict between Ibrahim and the Countess D——— is between black and white, passion and frivolity, nature and artifice, explosive power and peaceful domesticity. Can we for a second imagine that the first set of terms will win out over the second? Quite the contrary, it will be absorbed and neutralized like Peter the Great himself—the huge and splendid beast of prey, only the margins of whose behavior still glint with unpredictable danger—who is here well caught and kept in a web of pomp, humor, and homeliness, caught in the equivalent of a merry student drinking society, in a *Burschenschaft*, boisterous, but sedate (Ch. III).

The theme of *Kapitanskaya dochka* (The Captain's Daughter, 1836) is also the futility of romanticism. The paltry, musty Biedermeier of Ivan Kuzmich's fortress is there for everybody to use. Our hero can

lead a life of leisure and poetry inside it; young ladies can feel protected, quiet, and promisingly wifely; duels can be transformed from
tragic to comic without much fuss; one-eyed veterans (like Ivan Igna-
tych) can help with mushroom preservation (Ch. IV) or even with
sewing work (Ch. III). Nor is this an isolated instance. The scenes
(Chs. I and XIV) in our hero's home are very similar. Monsieur
Beaupré, former soldier and hairdresser, is quietly sleeping off the
"home-made Russian brews" and his amorous efforts with "fat, pock-
marked" Palashka the laundress and with the "one-eyed Akulka"; his
pupil is doodling over the map of Africa, though he would prefer,
given a chance, "chasing pigeons and playing leapfrog with the other
boys on the estate"; Andrey Petrovich reads the court calendar, while
his wife makes "some honey-jam by the window."[60] The city of
Orenburg squats stubbornly at the limits of frightening chaos, of
seething unruliness: one fictional world defended against another large
fiction, one myth against another. Orenburg is like Savyelitch in his
most glorious hour (Ch. IX), foolhardy when requesting his master's
belongings from the conquering revolutionaries: the maddest courage
humbled to the meanest of purposes, because property (particularly
small property) is more important than life. Pushkin, let us emphasize,
never hides the imperfections of the framework of normality: Grinev's
father is rough, unsympathetic, and insensitive; his colleague Shvabrin
has ample room for intrigue, harrassment, and maneuvering inside this
normal society; the chummy gambler Zurin does not hesitate to arrest
his former friend and to submit him to raillery, humiliation, and the
tribunal.[61]

Pugachev thinks that the eagle is right when it refuses to exchange
its diet of live blood (and its short life) for the raven's diet of carrion
and the resulting long life. When his prisoner points out that "to live
off murder and robbery is the same as pecking at carrion" (p. 436),
Pugachev is dumbfounded and pensive. Pushkin's descriptive strategy
is similar to that propounded in the eagle-raven fable: evenhanded and
melancholy. Pushkin can afford this attitude because he is convinced,
and his story loudly proclaims, that perfection is destruction. At Pugachev's table, Pyotr Andreyitch sees the new realm in action, the new
race of men talking and breathing, absolute love and unity incarnate;
what is more, he sees his luck decisively aided by these protective
black angels who grant him what normality grudgingly keeps from
him. Why is romanticism then impossible? The answer is easy: Shva-

brin. Normal imperfect man can only push to perfection his imperfections, once he identifies with the absolute paradigm of romantic change. Pyotr Andreyitch (like Waverley, Frank Osbaldistone, and Henry Morton) merely internalizes romantic changes and becomes the man of increased sensibility and tolerance, the man of partial redemption. Total romanticism is actually nonredemptive. Abrams's paradigm is again, in Biedermeier fashion, turned upside down: Imperfection-Perfection-Imperfection or Fall-Redemption-Fall.

In this kind of reading, *Medny Vsadnik* (The Bronze Horseman, 1837) must be seen as complementary to *Eugene Onegin.* The poor benighted victim, Eugene, stands for the Biedermeier crushed—a needless and perhaps ironic warning.[62] Peter the Great and the destructive Neva waters are not identical. On the contrary, they are adversaries. Peter's purpose had been precisely to control the Neva, to reorganize its natural environment, as the prologue explains. Nevertheless, in relation to Eugene (whose name derives not only from Onegin, but perhaps from Derzhavin's idyllic work, too), they act in full solidarity. Peter and the Neva cannot be imagined without one another, they need one another. They clasp each other as poles of a single tension. It does not matter that Peter has bridled or is bridling the Neva; it does not matter that the Neva is rearing from under the bronze rider. What matters is the prize—a new and absolute realm— and the level of the confrontation: the cosmic projection. That is why I find no contradiction between the poem and Pushkin's admiration for Peter. *The Bronze Horseman* tells us what might have happened if Peter had really won, according to Pushkin. In fact, life goes on much as it had before. Eugene may have suffered, but his suffering was private and untypical. The Neva's revolt was a mere isolated incident; Peter may look threatening but he is in fact just a statue, his pursuit the figment of a sick imagination; life actually goes on—banal, gray, at best cozy. And finally in *Eugene Onegin* we see romanticism defeated—that is, we see historical reality. Lensky is defeated by Onegin, and thus the potential volcanic outbursts of creativity are precluded. As Bayley, following a suggestion by Maurice Baring, correctly points out, Pushkin's novel in verse is close to Jane Austen's world of genteel intrigues and soft-spoken conflicts.[63] The life of Eugene in the countryside (for example, IV, 37–47) is the missing link between Biedermeier and dandyism. Pushkin intuits the dandy as philistine, as domestic romantic. In *Tsygane* (The Gypsies, 1827) Pushkin had demonstrated the incompatibility between modern soul and liberty, in *The Bronze Horseman* between modern man and absolute ideals; *Eugene Onegin* offers a rueful, ironic-melancholy solution.

GOGOL seems very different from Pushkin, but many basic patterns of their work are similar. As a young man, Gogol built for himself the persona of a Byronian dandy.[64] His repressed homosexuality gave his life a kind of permanent histrionic and playful quality, even in its gravest moments: when Gogol sternly lectures Aksakov on the best way to study Thomas à Kempis, we cannot suppress our amused mistrust of his solemn gesticulation—the persona has changed, but not the manner of his playacting.[65] Gogol's educated awareness of the European literary context was less elegant, but not less apposite than Pushkin's. He assimilated early Byron and Chateaubriand, admired Scott, but also Sterne, was steeped in Hoffmann and Tieck, was acquainted with Mickiewicz, and tried playful role-identifications with Hugo, Dumas, or Janin on his artistic friends.[66] Parallels to De Quincey or La Motte Fouqué have been demonstrated, and the general influence (perhaps indirect) of Schelling and others on him is widely acknowledged.[67]

There is a substantial, and often overlooked, part of Gogol's work that agrees fully with the fashionable and tame literary conventions circulating in the Europe of his time. This conforming, well-behaved Gogol can help us understand the ferocious one. The lesser writing of Gogol can be easily aligned with many productions of banal European Biedermeier extraction; it contains two groups of texts which deserve mention here. In one of them he gave free rein to his commitment to all varieties of belletristic and fake history. Gogol's fragmentary tragedy *Alfred* was obviously inferior to *Boris Godunov*, but it was similar to *Boris Godunov* in its adherence to the principles of the Barry Cornwall *tableau vivant*. His essays on the teaching of geography and architecture in *Arabesques* were sheer literature and the comparison to Coleridge[68] should be completed with one to Manzoni and the Hugo of *Notre-Dame de Paris*. Gogol's writing in *Arabesques* or *Selected Passages* was not different in method from his writing in *Taras Bulba*. It is no more and no less synthetic and artificial than the historical inventions of a mythical Ukraine.[69] His lectures, judging by the medieval essay in *Arabesques*, as well as by surviving reports, must have been composed in the same inventive vein.[70] The moralizing letters in *Se-*

lected Passages have to be read as formalistic exercises in the application of existential patterns to an ethical-political level of discourse; the result is the kind of secondary aesthetics that was the secret perversion of many Biedermeier writers.

In the second group of texts he let himself be seduced by the temptation of neo-neoclassicism, like other writers of the 1830s.[71] Viacheslav Ivanov claims that *Revizor* (The Inspector-General, 1836) is a classicist-allegorical work, with an abstract and classicist structure behind a facade of extreme localism and chaotic idiosyncracies. (This could actually serve as a general description of the Biedermeier: the split of romantic wholeness into an abstract basis and a colorful concreteness.) This view receives strong confirmation from those who, like Simon Karlinsky, point to the influence of A. S. Griboyedov and his school.[72] It is equally significant that Gogol was not immune to another stock motif of Biedermeier classicism—the alabaster *belle,* the pure, glacial, and simple damsel—that the Pre-Raphaelites would use later for purposes of their own.[73]

Gogol was also obsessed with the idyllic model. His first artistic instinct had led him to write the idyll *Ganz Küchelgarten,* the heroine of which was called Luise, like Voss's character. The title of the poem, whether Gogol knew it or not, neatly defined his later artistic dilemma: *Ganz* means (in German) "complete," "whole," while the family name of the hero could be translated as "little kitchen garden." Phonetically "Küchel" also suggests "little chick," or even "baked cake"; be that as it may, the opposition of domesticity versus totality imposes itself with mysterious energy. The societal idyll pops up in expected and unexpected places. Here is Manilov's pleasant and modest little room with its cozy tobacco reserves and (undoubtedly Empire) writing table, and there is the little town of N. N. with its lowlier and beastlier warmth, faded posters, crooked streets, soap-like cakes, and absurd shop signs.[74] Ivan Ivanovich, with his orchard, small red-roofed outhouses, and neatly inscribed melon-seed containers, is a growth of the idyllic garden (even though he later runs wild); and the city of Mirgorod is equally endearing and warm—Carlyle's Weissnichtwo in wood instead of stone.[75] Even in *Vecher nakanune Ivana Kupala* (St. John's Eve) the story proper begins with a quivering lamp, a grandfather resting on the earthen peasant stove, hermetically sealed windowpanes, a contentedly humming mother with cradle and spinning wheel, before it soars to diabolical laughter, trees steeped in blood, blue flames springing from earth, and flocks of misshapen monsters.[76] Even the scenes of brutal, but cozy fraternity in *Taras Bulba* betray the lingering nostalgia of the idyll.[77]

This sweetish, clumsy, and a little helpless side of Gogol firmly rooted him among his contemporaries and provided a common ground with many of Pushkin's minor admirers. But the deeper and more decisive similarity to the master must be looked for in an opposition to him. As I pointed out above, Pushkin openly recognized the defeat of the high-romantic experience and resolutely chose, among the alternatives, withdrawal. He rejected the possibility of maintaining the integrity of the (Abramsian) pattern, while reducing it to scale from the absolute to the intrahistorical, and thus to practical shapes and purposes. He preferred to watch the pattern crumble slowly, gather moss, or simply lose its active powers; and thus he preserved the ironic gentility of the relativist.

In our terms of reference, Gogol is the writer who wants to use both lines of retreat at once. On the one hand he wants to preserve the full, earnest import of the high-romantic pattern, to maintain in full force the absolute claim of the overall paradigm. On the other hand he is ready to reduce the elements of the pattern to (unredeemed and unredeemable) concrete, particular, and practical reality. Gogol did not work for the absolute regeneration of mankind and total expansion of the human model; instead he applied these principles of action to the most minute and factual limits of nature and society. Under these circumstances he could only remain within the confines of literature by choosing the most ravaging satire, by adopting the most negative stance; a positive standpoint could only lead out of literature into religion, and then perhaps out of this life—which is what eventually happened to Gogol. In any case, the inhuman, devastating force of Gogol's satire is quite clearly a result of the above-mentioned strident coincidence. Leon Stilman has brilliantly analyzed Gogol's yearning for absolute vision as symbolized by the horrifying Viy and as attempted in other works.[78] But absolute vision and absolute reality are bound to breed, in conjunction, the horror of Nothingness. In this sense, Merezhkovsky's remarks on the demonic nature of mediocrity are (anachronically) but the logical consequence of Stilman's and their illustration.[79] The all-encompassing sight of romanticism is based on or endowed with redemptive powers, but if we insist at the same time on the autonomy of the objects (again, a feature that Gogol shared with many Biedermeier writers), then they will turn their thus regained powers against us. The phrase "cosmic triteness" is an apt description of this procedure, and rhetorical analyses can discover it on the level of word choice, sentence structure, and so on.[80] Its appropriate background is Biedermeier tragicomedy.[81]

A look at *Starovetskiye pomeshchiki* (The Old-Fashioned Landowners) and its critical readings is most illuminating. In a mixture of fascination and disgust, Gogol is accused of slandering the idyllic way of life, and also of proposing an absurd state of fertility without sexuality.[82] The practical impossibility of consuming the amount of food described by Gogol has also been demonstrated.

Similar accusations had been leveled at Gogol's contemporary, Charles Lamb. The reply was that Lamb offered ingestion as a model of communication with the universe. High romanticism had imperiously established "organicism" and "assimilation" as categories of the imagination and of absolute consciousness itself; it was not far from there to the use of empirical ingestive models as substitutes for the loftier paradigm.[83] Afanasy Ivanovich and Pulcheria Ivanovna stand for high-romantic wholeness, for unhindered communication with the universe, for a paradisial existence that is literally fertility through grace, integrity, and creation without the need for dialectical antithesis and synthesis. The Old Landowners *are* the Romantic Paradise. But, unlike Pushkin, who is content with a relativizing smile, Gogol spells out details with the unrelenting vision of *Viy;* he actually gives us the details of at-rest-ness in a way which would have seemed unacceptable even to Blake. What can total communication be except Biedermeier over-stuffing? What can sexlessness be except just that—passive, subanimal perpetuation, a slow, dreamlike plunge into a vegetable and material level of being? Assimilation turns out to be mere accumulation: "the administration of Pulcheria Ivanovna consisted in an uninterrupted opening and shutting of the storeroom, in salting, drying, and baking of an immense quantity of vegetables and fruits."[84] What could they do to their guests except "treat them continuously with everything their property produced"? This is literally Holy Communion, since the sanctity of the existing materials has been preserved. From this angle, whether or not a small grain of sex (the common cat) is enough to explode this world, as Karlinsky ingeniously demonstrates, is less important than the fact that it does not have to be exploded. It is already black and corrupt; the paradise on earth is hell (exactly Pushkin's point with regard to Pugachev's latter-day saints) and the Tovstogubs are already monsters. It is all a matter of intensity of vision. A Biedermeier meticulousness applied to the redemptive paradigm will result in monstrous caricature for all but the most analytical readers, who can perhaps recapture a faint touch of infinite sweetness and a last trace of infinite longing.

The *Old-Fashioned Landowners* does not stand alone. Chizhevsky read *Shinel* (The Overcoat, 1842) as an obsession with particularity.[85] This is true, but it represents only the idyllic substratum of the story. Its fuller meaning becomes apparent when we look at the strategy of concomitant romantic intensity and minute exactness. The monstrous shriveling of Akaky Akakyevich is the outcome of formal pressures. When Valery Bryusov emphasized the hyperbolic nature of Gogol, he did nothing more than spell out what totalizing vision does to objects.[86]

Many critics nowadays accept Gogol's universe (or string of universes) as artificial and synthetic in nature, and few still speak about his "realism," "folklore influence," and the like. It may be time to take a step forward and recognize that Gogol actually belabors a model: the unifying romantic paradigm. The conclusion of Gogol's works is the inadequacy and breakdown of high romanticism. In this respect his views coincide with Pushkin's. But whereas in Pushkin this decision precedes and informs the act of writing, in Gogol the decision follows the writing: the decision is the outcome, recorded with agonized dismay, of a failed experiment. Sometimes I have the impression that Gogol does not expect the outcome of his short stories to be satirical, and that he is somehow enraged by it.

His philosophical and religious theories, which seem to many so outrageous and puzzling, are a logical consequence of Gogol's thematic and structural decisions. We have seen in what manner high romanticism acts as a substitute for or secularized version of a Christian and transcendent plot. Everything happens as if Gogol somehow envisions the romanticism as a front scene concealing Christianity; the collapse of romantic redemption therefore opens a vista, and the stark outlines of a patriarchal Christianity re-emerge. Gogol was not a pilgrim to religious fountainheads; religion confronted *him* as an ineluctable reality, imposed itself upon him. Thereafter a mechanical transfer of relationships took place: if behind the breakdown of a false mental reality we discover an older, more reliable level of reality, then is it not likely that politically, too, we can discover some noble columns behind the rubbish of corrupt appearances and decorations? And what can those columns be other than the time-honored traditions of *pravoslavnik,* pre-Petrine Russia? When all is said and done, the political views of Gogol are an adaptation of his aesthetic strategies. We are in fact strongly reminded of the ambiguity between mere wishful longing and the utopian prettification of the political present so widely and ambiguously spread in the years between 1815 and 1848 (the high romantics placed their more radical utopias in some other dimension). Utopia could already be here if only we had eyes to see it, or hands and minds to do a little work.[87]

Unquestionably there is an avant-garde and surrealist element in some of Gogol's writings; the pre-Kafkian Sukhovo-Kobylin understood this, and it is right to note this element in *The Inspector-General* or in the short stories. But unless we are bold enough to tackle directly the dilemmas of Bloomian inverse influence, we must accept that these are dimensions superadded by historical development: highly significant for any comprehensive value judgment, but not objective in the same sense as features morphologically consonant with his age. Gogol was, during his most creative period, an aestheticist; the worlds he evoked are, let me repeat, synthetic, but the general direction of his modeling remained fiercely Biedermeier.[88] A Heine and a Mörike all in one, Gogol allowed the fantasy and sentimentality of Mörike to turn savage and mordant. It is as if romanticism were turning in despair against itself.

Gogol's and Pushkin's relationship to many key Biedermeier orientations become more obvious for those who interpret their work in the vicinity of smaller, but even more strikingly Biedermeier figures. The theoretical writing of Apollon Grigoryev and V. F. Odoyevsky was merely organicist—it shied away from the absolute claims of high-romantic titanism. The overwhelming influence of Schelling on these, as well as on D. V. Venevitinov or the poet Tyutchev appears to be similar in nature to that which the German philosopher exerted on German intellectual life during the same period: a moderating, harmonizing influence. (Indeed, until deep into the 1920s, the intellectual Right and Left in Russia were divided, arguably, into a Schelling and a Hegel line of influence.) A. S. Khomyakov and the Kireyevsky brothers represented the national and pragmatic (ironic though the term may seem when used here) translation of redemptionist paradigms. (In the case of Ivan Kireyevsky one can literally follow the process as it went from Schelling to Slavophilism.) Slavophilism, not less than German nationalism, is a product of the Biedermeier. V. G. Belinsky, on the other hand, represented the Biedermeier Left; for him absolute change of human nature can only work as materialist and rational change of society.[89] The prose writers of the 1820s and 1830s, whether Scottians (like A. A. Bestuzhev-Marlinsky), Hoffmannians (like V. F. Odoyevsky), or Sternians (like A. F. Veltmann), are all closely allied to their Western contemporaries in their disillusionment and reliance on mere history. The literary environment was prepared for the emergence of Pushkin and Gogol.

POLISH LITERATURE might be said to be, in the 1820s and 1830s, the leading European literature, if we judge the intrinsic value of its most important writers and the way they express the chief trends of the age. It is, therefore, even more significant that Polish romanticism should be devoid of a high-romantic component (since, again, we cannot accept the idea that its equivalent is somehow located toward the end of the romantic period); Cyprian Norwid cannot be considered "romantic" in a historically meaningful sense of the word any more than Baudelaire or Rimbaud can. I have some doubts even as to the status of Zygmunt Krasiński, whose radical intensity of vision seems to transcend the limits of the Biedermeier.

According to Chizhevsky, a classicist and Enlightenment culture developed fully only in Poland and Russia (among Eastern European countries) because only these two countries had in the eighteenth century independent state organizations and attractive and supportive royal courts.[90] For Poland this explanation is valid, I believe, mostly in connection with the beginnings of neoclassicism and its connection with the baroque. In a negative way it may also explain why Poland's Enlightenment did not change into a high romanticism, as the Enlightenment had in England, France, and even Germany: it did not have a cumulative impetus of its own, but only a lingering momentum. It is difficult to point to writers born before the 1790s who did not think of the prevailing aesthetic and human models as satisfactory. It is quite difficult to point to any manifestation of high romanticism (not even a substitute one, as in France) in Poland in the period 1790–1820. The strength of the Enlightenment provided for the diversity of preromanticism in writers such as Trembecki, Bishop I. Krasicki, or the transitional J. U. Niemcewicz.

Mickiewicz emerges as a great figure of public cultural life in 1820–1822 with abrupt suddenness, but the tone of future romantic development had been set by Kazimierz Brodziński who, like theoreticians of his generation in Russia, Italy, France, and Hungary, was disclaiming the asperities of high romanticism and admonishing writers to caution and politeness. In Mickiewicz's earliest formation, beyond Polish models, the reference to contemporary writers who had already crossed the strict boundaries is obvious: Byron and Scott are good examples, and in a different sense, Goethe and Schiller. Mickiewicz's absolute fidelity to classical sources, Latin, as well as French, has never been overlooked.[91] Much more important, of course, is his actual integration into the texture of European literary life in the 1830s: the synchronic connection to Pushkin and James Fenimore Cooper, the aging Goethe and A. W. Schlegel, Vigny and George Sand, and many others.[92]

The first important sense in which Mickiewicz is set apart from high romanticism is the pervasive feeling of defeat and anguish in his work. This is not a matter of temperamental choice or aesthetic coloring, but one of ontological framework. Pessimism is offered not as one possibility among others, but as the solid foundation of knowledge and being. Like many writers of the Biedermeier age, Mickiewicz eliminated redemption from the model or turned it upside down. His writing grew as a creative response to the questions raised by a specific perception of a human situation. He used historical or visionary fragmentation in *Dziady* (Forefathers' Eve), and less obviously, in *Grażyna* or *Konrad Wallenrod*. He withdrew into the Parnassian refinement of the Crimean sonnets. He proclaimed, in the mystical nationalism of the *Księgi narodu polskiego i pielgrzymstwa polskiego* (Books of the Polish Nation and of the Polish Pilgrimage, 1832) the demotion of absolute transfigurations and of a unique history in favor of a cyclical, immanent system related to a specific nation and "practical" advice. (More than any other work, this shows what complicated telescopings take place between the different phases of romanticism itself; it should have been written at the beginning of Polish romanticism.)

It is in *Pan Tadeusz* above all that the nature of Mickiewicz's Biedermeier structure revealed itself.[93] Mickiewicz addressed himself to the problem of heroism reenacted, of the past recalled, of retrospection retrospectively viewed.[94] The story takes place in 1812, but the lyrical persona's main point of view, constantly emphasized, is that of the 1830s; the figures are stylized with careful love and touched up with minimal irony. At the same time, the figures themselves are "aware" of their own lapsed state—they have lost the tragic dimension of their ancestors; they no longer belong to a realm of definitive gestures and integral values. Judge Soplica, Tadeusz, even Count Horeszko are figures of a bourgeois society, spin-offs, not the genuine item: not the world of *Wallenrod,* not even the grand despair of *Dziady.* They are, moreover, permanently aware of it, and there is a continuous undertone of metaphysical hopelessness in the action: puppets reaching out for humanity. (St. Judas Thaddeus is in Roman Catholic tradition the patron of desperate causes: this goes some way toward explaining the choice of this character as title-hero.) But they are not puppets: they are only too human, yearning for the dignity of a titanic past. It is not Mickiewicz but the characters themselves who invent petty judicial suits, drunken brawling, and spontaneous rioting with the hope of spiritual revival in the violent purification of the *zajazd* (foray).

The key to the Biedermeier aspect of the poem is to be found in XII, 50–190, 220–250. A sophisticated sample of the confectioner's art is brought to the festive table, and the seneschal obligingly describes the winter scene: the gentry at a feast preceding elections, an orator speaking and

> beside him stands
> A man with hand to ear, who mutely twirls
> His great mustache and clearly gathers pearls
> Of eloquence to store in memory (XII, 97–100).[95]

The details continue with the orator abandoned, a new marshal elected; lonely nonpartisans and a priest followed by an altar-boy pass by with busy importance. Such is the skill of the confectioner, we are told (XII, 225, 242, 266), that as the successive layers of sugar melt at room temperature new scenes are revealed as if by magic. The winter scene gradually turns to vernal green, to the gold of summer, to the crimson of autumn, and, finally, to stark nakedness: sticks of cinnamon, twigs of laurel, seeds of caraway are revealed. The subject and its universe are thus repeated and relativized, made out of sugar: artificiality inside artificiality. The description has the odd charm of a music-box melody—counterfeit, nostalgic, touching in its mechanical helplessness, ever slower, ever more remote.

Inside this framework, worthy of the later Tieck, *Pan Tadeusz* teems with additional conflicts, resolved and unresolved. One of them is the ironic use of the idyllic societal model, in a way not much different from that of E. T. A. Hoffmann or Carlyle. Echoes of Goldsmith ("With such amusements, conflicts such as these, / Our village life in Lithuania stood") and Gray can be recognized in the first book.[96] The vegetable garden in II, 523–575 and the world of domestic birds in V, 67–99 are depicted in detail with Cowperian gusto and pleasure, though with more irony and with marked allusions to the action of the poem as a whole, since these nonhuman societies are little reflections of the provincial gentry of Lithuania as a whole. (Nevertheless, there are also passages of Georgic technical advice such as the best way to protect yard fowl against flying predators [III, 25–42].)[97] The storm at the beginning of X or the "symphony of the evening" with its birds of the field at the beginning of VIII reminds us more of James Thomson's palette. The present idyllic society (which, as I have just pointed out, is merely a nostalgic copy of another, more genuine world) is sometimes rendered in terms of idealized idyllic imagery: the younger gentry sleep in stables, and Zosia feeds the fowl, as if they needed to enhance their own participation in the rural world.

Equally pervasive is the nature-culture split of which Mickiewicz is only too aware. Book III is perhaps most typical in its proliferating oppositions. Count Horeszko seeks action. He is a young romantic crank (II, 161–165) who affects white English coats (II, 134), likes to call his servants "jockeys" and to have them dress accordingly (II, 136–140), is equally kind to neighbor, peasant, or Jew (II, 180), and is known for his fits of natural mysticism. He is thus a man of cultural idealism fascinated and surprised by Zosia, the embodiment of nature, who knows how to play with children, how to feed the geese, and how to blend with the bushes and vegetable patches. The opposition is enriched by reference to the different types of mushrooms, tame or wild (III, 312–350), by disputes over the stylistics of trees—cypress, lemon tree, and aloe versus honest local birch tree (III, 739–765)—and by distinctions between the quality of the sky in Italy and northern skies (IV, 799–829)—all of them ultimately a conflict between the typological approach of classical artifice and the rich variety of idyllic humanity. All these oppositions are finally concentrated in the contrast between Telimena—Frenchified, distinguished, and tasteful (III, 359–419)—and ruddy-cheeked Zosia. In typical Biedermeier fashion, it is the latter who will be united with Tadeusz Soplica, the young man of sensitivity, the Waverley passive hero who fuses the past and the present, reason and imagination, the hero of compromise. Robak's wholesome and innocent son will marry the daughter of Eva, for whose love his father had committed a crime. (Robak or Jacek Soplica is the only truly high-romantic character of the poem.) Meanwhile Telimena, the artificial flower of Biedermeier aristocracy, the latter-day Dido (VIII, 647–662), will become in a most appropriate and funny scene the victim of an attack by wood ants (V, 309–332) and will probably have to content herself with Count Horeszko.[98]

The nature versus culture opposition is seen in the struggle between Gerwazy and Protazy (the former represents the instinctual traditions of blood and kinship, war and revenge, the latter a more law-oriented system). But Mickiewicz shows nature and culture as intertwining serpentine lines, always pursuing each other: thus, the young Count Horeszko, who stands for "culture," is manipulated by his warden, Gerwazy, who stands for nature and who ultimately seeks alliance with the Dobrzynskis, the lower-class, brawling and farming gentry whom we must certainly view as representatives of nature.[99] Book XI supposedly brings a happy ending, a reconciliation of nature and culture, but this is ironic and ambiguous, since the reader knows as well as the poetic persona that everything is going to become much worse and that we have been offered just a graceful découpage. The cloud image at the end of XII, no less than the bittersweet irony of the conventional storytelling conclusion, underlines this.

Pan Tadeusz is romanticism embodied in a Meissen figurine reposing sedately in a Biedermeier china cabinet, and this is seen even in the character of an apparent exception such as Jacek (or Robak). He is (though Mickiewicz was probably unaware of Coleridge) the Ancient Mariner, carrying his heavy symbolic albatross through the military camps of an embattled Europe. The key difference lies not in place, time, or name, but in the heavy sociological and psychological explanations surrounding what had been for the high romantic an act of pure sin, transrational impulse coming from deep ontological centers.[100]

In terms of the Abramsian triad, what is missing or damaged is always the third term: paradise regained. *Pan Tadeusz* does not stand alone in its lack of conclusion, as a grasp of the structure of *Konrad Wallenrod* will reveal: the innocence of Alf is turned into the alienation of the false Konrad, but what paradise has been regained in the end? *Wallenrod* is a story of mutual defeat, not primarily because of its tragic ending, but simply because it indicates no regeneration, merely revenge. *Dziady* is perhaps closer to high romanticism, although Milosz's excellent description of the second part as a mixture of Enlightenment philosophy and folk fantasy indicates its Biedermeier attachments and therefore the somewhat kaleidoscopic character of the work.[101] These attachments are even more apparent in Part III, with its transformation of Konrad's egotism to proud political awareness and finally to the humility of the fighter for the common cause. Can *Dziady* be read as a variation of the redemptive cycle? It seems doubtful, unless one accepts a negative judgment of political activity in general; otherwise the scheme might seem more like gradual progress in purity of motives. And, certainly, sectionalization is a striking feature of this part of Mickiewicz's work. (Harold Segel points to simultaneity of events in disparate locations and episodic structure as typical features.)[102]

A SIMILAR sectionalization is characteristic of Słowacki's writings. It was noticed by Claude Backvis for one, who talks about the baroque as opposed to the romantic nature of Słowacki's work, the imagery of which stresses light and jewelry, dissonance and the fascinating brilliance of naturalistic detail.[103] He says that placed against gilded and silvery backgrounds and in a grotto's twilight, human bodies and natural scenery come to lose their palpable actuality and to play the role of signal or allusion.[104] It is thus not surprising that *Król-Duch* or even *Beniowski* seem lost in indetermination. This is not the infinity Schelling or Wordsworth are grappling to describe precisely or to approach. It is merely incompleteness, vagueness, the unfinished.

Balladyna and *Lilla Veneda* illustrate another side of Słowacki's Biedermeier involvement: the repeated shift from history to myth and back again. In *Balladyna* time is expanded to several years and then reduced to three days: precipitated historical and psychological evolution must fit the just and even temporal units of the fairy tale. The obsession with Popiel (the son of Ashes) links these two plays with the beginning of *Krol Duch*—this is not the myth of regeneration, but of a muffled original sin still echoing through a world which tries unsuccessfully to set itself up as history. The tragedy of *Balladyna* is that of characters trying to emerge into the light of rational history and merely gaining access to sin, crime, and failure (actively or as victims). Any such theme is based on the assumption that myth and history are two radically and qualitatively different ontological levels and that hence communication between them is, if not impossible, at least arduous and filled with risk. In this sense the play is closer to the two-level stories of Hoffmann than to the total fusion of Coleridge's *Ancient Mariner*.

Słowacki squarely comes to terms with the romantic paradigm in *Anhelli*. This is a long prose poem placed in a half-mythical, half-real Siberia of the 1830s, where countless Polish patriots have to pay for their hapless revolt against Russian occupation. Accompanied by the magic king of the land, Szaman, Anhelli observes with increasing horror and despair how suffering debases rather than purifies the exiles. Anhelli dies lonely, in humble despair, having been forbidden by celestial forces even the satisfaction of a heroic, redeeming gesture, and he will not rise even when the apocalyptic rider summons all the dead to a general uprising of people against the oppressors.

The connection with Dante and Vigny and the way in which the echoes of a biblical rhythm are filtered through Chateaubriand will not be discussed here.[105] More important for this study is that in the shape of this prose poem can be seen remotely, as through a colored and confusing filter, the outlines of the Abramsian concave curve. But both its ends are lost in extreme vagueness. There may have been or must have been a state of innocence before the fall into the hellish slump of the exiled martyrs. There may be or must be a kind of redemption for a few of the characters mentioned in the story, for Anhelli, for some of the women perhaps, but for how many of the others? And of what nature will this redemption be? We do not know precisely because we have no idea what the original state was. The final scenes are bathed in perfumed colors, and mild peace, but they are purely abstract. We have therefore a truncated curve, the central (low) part of which is thickened. Even inside this section we have further sectionalization: a series of self-contained episodes, well outlined, describing the decline from suffering to madness, crime, dehumanization, and ultimately disappearance. Moreover, the ambiguity extends to the very argument. Is it possible for one gifted individual to take upon himself the destiny of mankind and thus to substitute through his fullness the inadequacies of all? Can passivity become a true and satisfactory replacement for action, for any action, on the grounds that it represents potentiality and is thus richer than any actualization? Such dilemmas are, let us remember, the heart of the Biedermeier as a whole. The structure of *Anhelli* is related to Comte's or Darwin's "stages," rather than to the continuities, the wide, elegant arcs of the Enlightenment or of high romanticism. *Anhelli* is the negative counterpart of *Genezis z Ducha*.[106]

Krasiński's *Nieboska komedia* (The Undivine Comedy, 1835) equally well illustrates the decline of the complete curve. It is a tremendously ambitious work, for whose peers we must await the expressionist age. It begins with a family conflict. Sin and poetry, mother and son, morbidity and temptation prove too difficult for Count Henryk. He prefers to plunge into political action and to become the leader of the clerical-aristocratic army in its last stand against a cosmic social revolution. His defeat also signals in a mysterious way the defeat of his triumphant enemies.

I cannot agree with Harold Segel's contention regarding the Hegelian triadic nature of the work.[107] The third part, synthesis, is altogether missing. What we have may be described either as irreconcilable confrontation between two universal principles (good versus evil, structure versus chaos) or as an inverse evolutionary ladder—gradual victory of the featureless mass over organized, individualized humankind, gradual withdrawal. The interpretation of the last line of the drama is uncertain: Pancracy, the revolutionary, is overwhelmed by a terrifying vision and cries out a dying concession of victory to the crucified Galilean. It may indeed be read as the sudden and total change of defeat into victory—a type of change that can hardly be called Hegelian; it has more of the paradoxical-tragical ring of Krasiński's contemporary Kierkegaard. But it is more important to note that, no matter what significance we attach to the conclusion, it represents an *external* intervention. The natural course of things is entropic, humanity in and of itself will run aground and may be saved only by pure, arbitrary grace. Krasiński does not feel under the same obligation as Goethe, who endeavored to provide at least a shadow of justification for saving Faust; there is no indication that the courage or loyalty of Count Henryk finds a just reward. In other words, the organicity of the redemptionist paradigm is totally denied. There is no internalized progression of energy and no preprogrammed plan for salvation: restoration, if indeed it is that, comes from external sources and may be pure chance.

It would probably not add much to this overview to enumerate other ways in which Polish romanticism differs from high romanticism and draws close to the Biedermeier historicism of Victor Hugo and Walter Scott: the writings of J. I. Kraszewski, Henryk Rzewuski, Michal Grabowski, Zygmunt Kaczkowski, Ignacy Chodźko, or Seweryn Goszczynski in the 1830s and 1840s provide ample evidence. (Many of these, most notably Kraszewski, later wrote in a Victorian vein.) In a different manner, Alexander Fredro's memoirs *Trzy po Trzy* (Topsy-Turvy Talk, 1848) evince a combination of Sterne and Jean Paul, which is rather frequently encountered as a Biedermeier mode of discourse.[108] As yet unaddressed, but highly important, is the question of Andrzej Towiański's function in the cultural system of the period; a close reading of his work will have to decide to what extent his theories display a theoretical-practical rupture (Biedermeier) or the ineffable unity of human transformation, typical of Saint-Martin or even Ballanche.[109]

I BELIEVE that Polish literature between 1820 and 1848 represents the most striking illustration of Gerschenkron's substitution system applied to cultural evolution. Eastern European literatures, whether reawakening ones like Czech, Romanian, and Hungarian, or those based on a more continuous development like Russian and Polish, essentially skip over a phase of the standard development as represented by English literature. However, it is not *necessary* for one national literature to repeat all the phases of another or of the "general" European development. At the same time, we must not postulate the necessity of a time lag in certain literatures.

Eastern European literatures were not first in developing the core-Romantic paradigm. None of them was able to overcome the pressure of the Enlightenment and neoclassical momentum by itself. In fact in many of these literatures the Enlightenment mentality had managed to absorb the incipient modifications of its own *figura* and thus to change itself into a richer intellectual and psychological environment, capable of satisfying the developmental needs of intellectual elites. But once external impulses triggered the march toward romanticism, Eastern European literatures found it easy and natural to synchronize themselves with the prevailing European phase. This is true not only of the literatures surveyed all too briefly here, but also of others. In Croatian literature the founders of realism (August Šenoa, Ante Kovačić, and others) built on a strong pastoral-idyllic trend of the past. In the twin literature of Serbia, Jovan Steria Popovič (1806–1856) is roundly declared a Biedermeier writer by some modern critics.[110]

For many European literatures (English, French, even German), the new phase involved moderating radicalism and recovering the past, because in them the qualitative oppositions between romanticism and Enlightenment had been powerful. In Eastern European literatures there was less determinism in the historical continuity, but also less opposition; a limper later romanticism did not perceive its antagonism to an accommodating, broad late Enlightenment, richly purveyed with preromantic attributes. The sense of historical incongruence that echoes from the pages of Lilian Furst or Istvan Söter when they note that it is the *Sturm und Drang,* not German high romanticism, nor even the generation of Victor Hugo, that is tied in with East-Central Europe will thus, perhaps, be dispelled.[111] Literary advance can again be shown to represent a succession of syntheses: in our case the combination of an incomplete past with an intensely accepted contemporary phase. Eastern European romanticism is in many essential ways analogous to the Biedermeier, but it is aesthetically and socially more sophisticated than its Western counterpart.

The advantage of this counterpoint rhythm for a polycentric culture like that of Europe must be plain. Initiatives can be passed from one center or section to another. Periods of creative agitation can alternate with periods of respite, without actual overall stagnation. The more "synthetic" (or substitutive) periods can, it would seem, more easily provide suggestions for the future. Krasiński and even Słowacki point to twentieth-century expressionism and the avant-garde; Gogol is Kafkian and surrealistic; Mácha has been claimed by many modern groups.

5

ROMANTIC IRONY AND
BIEDERMEIER TRAGICOMEDY

A Biedermeier mentality sets in when romantic consciousness becomes so expanded, and its claims on the human model so broad and so absolute, that the center is no longer strong enough to hold the whole together. Previous chapters have provided illustrations of how peripheral areas begin to separate from central ones and how the circumference breaks into sections with some autonomy. Here I will try to explain how a key feature of romanticism, namely irony, can be shown to undergo a similar process. Irony is a part of the romantic model and is closely associated with other key concepts such as organicism, dialectics, lyrical intensity, and melancholy. Dialectical and ironic tensions are mutually dependent and, in fact, cannot be imagined without one another. Prophecy and irony are opposites, yet the romantic imperative of expansion insists on their collaboration. Even a visionary moment such as the Mount Snowdon episode in *The Prelude* has its share of romantic irony.[1] Romantic irony is part of romantic completeness and the romantic absolute, but it is also a mirror and repetition of that completeness and of that absolute. Romantic irony in fact seeks completeness through expansion; in turn it is subject to the centrifugal pressures that lead to the emergence of a Biedermeier intellectual and poetic environment.

The loosening and sectionalization of romantic irony provides the best explanation of the proliferation of tragicomic and grotesque phenomena in the literary production of later romanticism. After 1815 in France, as elsewhere, writers defiantly proclaimed their right to portray grotesque grinning, fright, and caricature. Victor Hugo's preface to *Cromwell* was a manifesto for the mixture of stylistic levels.[2] These phenomena can be related directly to their sociocultural environment and shown to express the fears and disappointments of the age, as well as some repressed rebellious tendencies. They can also be connected to some of the traditions of the theater and of the novel as they had developed in the eighteenth century: horror stories and Gothic tales, melodrama and *comédie larmoyante,* the renewed interest in folk ballads. But of at least equal importance is the net of intellectual ties between the tragicomic and the disintegration of high romantic irony.

A close look at these ties and at the historic dynamics of romantic irony (as literary practice and as theoretical comment) will help us understand dramatic discourse in the decades following the Congress of Vienna. It seems curious that a phenomenon as puzzling and as outstanding as the emergence of tragicomedy should be overlooked or avoided by many scholars. From Van Tieghem on, attempts were made to split the field into areas such as "poetic comedy," absurdist and expressionist experiments, bitter comedy, and the like. A better understanding of the steps by which tragicomedy emerges in this historical case should reestablish its place. When we look at this emergence from a typological point of view, we see that the unified tensions of the ironic mode are transformed into the unresolved and adversary tensions of the grotesque, and thence into the juxtapositions of tragicomedy, whose morphological principle is a paratactic rather than a hypotactic one. Simultaneously irony, which is regarded with something approaching grave respect, becomes itself relativized, sharing the fate of the romantic system as a whole. It loses not only its integrity, but also its gravity: irony is treated in tragicomedy in an ironic and offhand manner and thus loses its redeeming capabilities. A situation may arise in which irony can no longer "save the day"; a crisis may open into bitter sadness or tragedy, because the relativizing powers of irony have been themselves toned down.

FOR FRIEDRICH SCHLEGEL irony was something that deserved serious attention. Poetry, he said, was supposed to include critical reflection upon itself, as well as self-mirroring, "das Producierende mit dem Produkt."[3] Under the possible influence of Fichte, and certainly along a path parallel to the one Kleist would take in his essay on the puppet theater, Schlegel says, "Um über einen Gegenstand gut schreiben zu können, muss man sich nicht mehr für ihn interessieren."[4] This is a manner of achieving spontaneity, it is a return to nature, and it maps the road to completeness. This kind of poetic operation can be achieved best through irony. Philosophy must be the foundation of irony because it offers a transcendent vantage point from which the real and ideal appear united.[5] If we look closer we find that, for him, irony is a kind of dialectics, a permission for contraries to live together. Although this is not quite an entrance visa for classical serenity and *Vollendung*, it is a reach toward a somewhat different kind of wholeness, in which movement and dynamics are integrated.

According to some scholars, Schelling understands romantic irony much like Schlegel to the extent to which he maintains that irony is the basis of objectivity.[6] It would seem even more useful to read in this connection the works of less important figures such as Adam Müller and K. W. F. Solger, because they spell out in some detail what is only implicit in Friedrich Schlegel's fragments. Adam Müller in his little treatise "Die Lehre vom Gegensatze" of 1804, and in other works, specifically argues that the natural unity of life and death can be caught by irony only, which to him is synonymous with freedom. The idea of organic totality is strongly emphasized as cooperative with irony. Even more systematic is Solger, who is concerned with negation and affirmation as parts of true completeness. For him irony *is* the self-conscious and hence a negation that props up the affirmation contained in an aesthetic text.[7]

These "explanatory" authors justify the categorical conclusions of Ernst Behler: "die Schlegelsche Ironie . . . bezeichnet . . . die vorwärtstreibende Energie in der Bildung des Menschen. Sie wird zur Kraft, welche vor einseitigen, vorschnellen Verfestigungen bewahrt und den Geist, stets weiterdrängend, auf der Bahn hält."[8] Behler analyzes very closely the sources of Friedrich Schlegel and his successors, and he concludes that Schlegel and Adam Müller share a "dialectical philosophy of contrasts" out of which their views on irony grow freely.[9] Friedrich Schlegel undoubtedly included a note of anticlassical defiance in his praise of irony as the consciousness of the agility of the ontological fullness of chaos. Irony would thus be a viable alternative to the structured formalism of any classical rationalism; it would be better able to render the substance of the universe more truthfully.

In fact most of the German high romantics, no matter how much they may differ as to the definition and artistic handling of irony, have in common a respect for the gravity and significance of ironic procedures. In the case of Novalis for instance, we should not be misled by his rather cavalier treatment of the word (often used as a synonym for *parody, travesty,* and the like), but rather concentrate on the essential coincidence between his poetics and Schlegel's concept of irony.[10] It so happens that this inclusive, philosophically ambitious, and rather "serious" view of irony finds ample illustration in the actuual works of the German high romantics. The complementary interaction of events and comment can be seen in Clemens Brentano's *Godwi* and Ludwig Tieck's *Lovell,* as well as in short stories by them and by Arnim. The intimate fusion of "incompatible" sides of the world (pathetic-poetic versus ridiculous-earthy) is exemplified in Tieck's plays *Der gestiefelte Kater, Die verkehrte Welt,* and *Prinz Zerbino.* An even deeper and more internalized acceptance of irony as the key to the world, quite subtle and without openly comic effects, can be found in Heinrich von Kleist's works, perhaps most clearly in *Der Prinz von Homburg.* Goethe's *Faust* must stand as the supreme example of romantic subtlety and ambiguity. Much as Goethe may have frowned upon Friedrich Schlegel's aggressive definitions, he internalized better than anybody else the message of multiplicity and all-in-oneness that irony was seeking. In *Faust* irony is not jocular trifling, but rather a way of maintaining openness in the very substance of the action. Finally, at the end of the period, E. T. A. Hoffmann provides an example of total commitment to the principle of universal irony.

This view of irony is by no means generally accepted in other periods or by other intellectual traditions. The perusal of standard works on the subject such as those of Vladimir Jankélévich, Douglas Muecke, J. A. K. Thomson or Bert States gives us a rather different perspective. Thomson, who surveys Greek, Latin and English literature historically thinks of irony as a kind of detached amusement, a cunning chuckling.[11] Muecke specifically assigns romantic irony a place as a subcategory, linked to aesthetic motives; in fact he denies that irony is substantively real and prefers to find it in a situation, that is in a relationship between beholder and event.[12] And Jankélévich, who openly professes his preference for Heine over the early German romantics, tells us that although any beginning of conscience and reflection is implicitly ironic, full-fledged irony shuns intimacy, shows cruelty, is aware of opposing distances, remains an "art d'effleurer."[13] Even Cleanth Brooks who, among the modern theoreticians of irony is perhaps closest to the romantics, ultimately sees in irony a balance of contraries, a field of tension rather than holistic completeness and fusion.[14]

It is perhaps even more significant that in the very generation following the high romantics there was severe criticism that amounted to a break with high romanticism. Hegel in the mid-twenties (both in *Vorlesungen über Aesthetik* and in a critique of Solger published in 1828) launched vitriolic attacks against Schlegel's irony as a self-indulgent, superficial, empty and vainglorious feeling which might undermine the bases of human dignity and value. From a different direction, but equally devastating is Kierkegaard's attack in his essay on irony. He accused the romantics (Schlegel and Tieck) of reducing everything to universal negativity and hedonistic aesthetics. He proposed instead an irony that should control reality and limit or define events more precisely, that should clarify and describe empirically.[15]

These angry rebuttals reveal much about the changes inside the romantic world model. For the early generation of pure romantics "irony" could capture simultaneously a situation's opening toward the infinite and its limitations, the ideal and the real; it did so by presenting a fact as well as its negation. Where the somewhat reductive sarcasm that seems to prevail in much of seventeenth- and eighteenth-century writing tried to cut pretensions and yearnings down to size by occupying a safe middle ground, romantic irony tended to spread out in all directions, to relativize both thesis and antithesis, one *through* the other. As understood by Schlegel and Tieck, by Jean Paul and Kleist, romantic irony was a statement on the complexity of the world, an investigation of the dialectics of reality. Like so many other exalted attempts of the romantics, this exalted view was not able to maintain its effectiveness. The Biedermeier period witnessed a different kind of irony, often bitter and debunking, the irony of Heine and Byron for instance, which could be pushed by them or by others in an openly nihilistic direction.[16] The confident world-unifying claims were therefore replaced by anxiety in the face of a world the unity of which seemed less and less credible. After all it is, methodologically, a small step from seeking the unity of appearance and essences to merely juxtaposing them. Whereas Friedrich Schlegel had been separating in order to unify better, in the 1820s and the 1830s the unification was believed to be impossible. Opposition was recognized as a kind of connection, sufficient to a skeptical poetic view. Setting contradictions side by side must be enough; the two sides will somehow interact with each other on the page or on the stage, by the mysterious virtues of the text itself; the efforts of the interacting author are weakened or abandoned. The road from high romanticism to its lower reaches is one from fusion to interaction and thence to juxtaposition.

Tragicomedy thus suddenly grew in importance. The classical doctrines current in the seventeenth and eighteenth centuries had repudiated unseemly mixtures, and even Shakespeare, let alone other baroque dramatists, fared badly at the hands of irate guardians of orthodoxy. *La comédie larmoyante* and other sentimental productions had not really made a dent in these attitudes. Only the Biedermeier period, by its decision to put into everyday practice the lofty fusionary principles of its high romantic predecessors, managed to break the stubborn opposition of almost two centuries. The fact is striking and deserves some attention since tragicomedy actually flourished in only three periods of Western literature; the genre seems to require a rather particular intellectual climate and favorable cultural circumstances. One of them is the period around and after 1600 when the baroque was in full growth. Another is the modern period when with few exceptions all valid theatrical writing is tragicomic (Ionesco and Beckett, Artaud and Dürrenmatt); and the cruelty and oneiric modernism of our own period certainly "influence" (in a Bloomian sense) Musset.[17] The other period was the age of later romanticism. Tragicomedy as a genre could accommodate this new kind of irony, which derived from the loftier romantic irony yet differed from it in important ways. A brief discussion of some of the prominent European dramatists of the 1820s and 1830s will provide material for a more detailed explanation of this process.

ALFRED DE MUSSET'S writing is a good example of the way in which the later romanticism established itself as a distortion of core romanticism, through tragicomic orientation. Heine once said about him: "La muse de la Comédie l'a baisé sur les lèvres, et la muse de la Tragédie sur le coeur."[18] But even a cursory glance shows that this neat separation (tragic in content, comic in form) cannot be maintained as such. Rather, in many of his dramatic productions different types and degrees of serious and frivolous actions intermingle and motivate each other.

One recurrent pattern, particularly obvious in his later plays, indicates that conjugal bliss, harmony, and order are to be achieved only through intrigue and confusion and by fully taking advantage of the intricate dialectics of appearance versus reality. Up to a point this fits the traditional scheme of vernal comedy as described by Frye. But more often Musset, in a Biedermeier vein, shows himself interested not in the creation of a new world, but in the recapturing of some troubled, preexistent idyllic situation. Thus, in *Louison* (1849) the outcome of the Duke's amorous expeditions is reconciliation with the Duchess; similar aims, in a more deliberate and artificial fashion, are pursued in *Un Caprice* (1837) and other plays. In these short plays harmony is reestablished as a consequence of open transgressions; without such violations slow deterioration would have continued unimpeded. The plays' form imitates in a mock frivolous way a historical pattern: social harmony–social sickness–revolution–harmonious Restoration.[19] In most cases, Musset avoids simplicity and directness. Thus, the conclusion of *Louison* is ambiguous. It is not clear whether Louison (the agent of reconciliation) will finally marry Berthaud. She certainly does not love him, so the lower social level, which traditionally should have been a mirroring or confirmation of harmony on the upper social level, is still unsettled and vague; the conclusion is relativized.[20]

Similarly in *Il ne faut jurer de rien* (1836), intrigue leads toward a happy and peaceful family life. Valentin, the cynical dandy, tries to expose Cécile, the well-bred young lady his family had chosen as his future wife, largely for pecuniary reasons, and to prove to himself the truth of his skeptical and suspicious philosophy of life. Not only is he proved wrong, not only does his cold ethical system suffer a defeat, but even his technique, his "superior" intellectual game, is shown inferior to straightforwardness and purity. "Suis-je un renard pris a son piège, ou un fou qui revient à la raison?" and "Ou j'ai près de moi le plus rusé démon que l'enfer ait jamais produit, ou la voix qui me parle est celle d'un ange, et m'ouvre le chemin des cieux," he exclaims over and over when he realizes that most of the time he had been manipulated by the "naive" Cécile.[21]

In a more melodramatic vein, early plays such as *La Quittance du diable* (an adaptation of fragments of Scott's *Redgauntlet*, written perhaps in 1830) display conclusions in which love is the outcome of death, intrigue, and demonic intervention, and *La Coupe et les lèvres* (1832) offers abundant space for love-death imagery and for a staged, mock burial (Act IV) which is supposed to test and break conventional reactions to death, friendship, and love.[22] In *Lorenzaccio*, Musset's most acclaimed play, the good-through-evil theme figures prominently. The liberator and tyrannicide revels in hypocritical dissipation; he wears the mask of cowardice, sloth, and comic degeneracy. Lorenzaccio is for most of the play a comic figure in a tragic setting, and the proliferation of his nicknames indicates a tenuous, slippery nature and the uncertainty of his reality.[23] But the conclusion of the play is tragic; evil carries the day. In the light of the conclusion, we must say that Lorenzaccio had to take on the mask of (comic) evil in order to function in a world that is evil, but he also had to accept a (tragic) punishment for taking part in this combination of evils. The comic is ultimately swallowed up by the tragic.

Is this necessity or mere chance? As Fantasio says: "jouer avec les mots est un moyen comme un autre de jouer avec les pensées, les actions et les êtres" and "Qui est-ce que pourra me dire au juste si je suis heureux ou malheureux, bon ou mauvais, triste ou gai, bête ou spirituel?"[24] And a character in another play muses (in connection with cardplaying, but obviously with an eye to human destiny): "La Fortune, dès qu'on l'appelle, peu importe par quel moyen, accourt et voltige autour de la table, tantôt souriante, tantôt sévère; ce qu'il faut étudier pour lui plaire, ce n'est pas le carton paint ni les dès, ce sont les caprices, ce sont les boutades, qu'il faut pressentir, qu'il faut deviner, qu'il faut savoir saisir au vol."[25] What emerges from such passages is the image of a world in which serious and frivolous, tragic and comic elements are hopelessly intermingled and arranged in a purely aleatory fashion; everything is interchangeable and the course of action is not predetermined. Necessity *is* chance. Thus, it does not come as a surprise that some characters actually *worry* about the outcome of the dramatic situation and try to shape it. In *Bettine* (1851) the main character is disturbed by the treacherous disappearance of her lover, Baron Steinberg, and wants to stop people from laughing, to avert comedy, so to speak.[26] Similarly, in the better known *La Nuit vénitienne* (1830), Razetta, the betrayed villain, proves to be a conformist who wants to preserve his reputation in the eyes of the public;[27] he carefully spells out the different possibilities for turning comedy into tragedy, that is, into an environment where his honor might be saved.[28] *Le Chandelier* (1835) hovers between the purely comic and the dramatic exploitation of pity and defection; the dramatic focus is on Fortunio's ultimately successful attempts to change from a ridiculous character into a serious one, to change his erotic status and fortune through a change in the shape of the drama. Characters who are aware of their *formal* function, who gain autonomy and strive toward self-definition, illustrate the ways in which Biedermeier drama foreshadows the dilemmatic twentieth-century modernism. They are part of a world in which the principle of uncertainty reigns supreme and in which security is a prized goal. Musset's plays are clearly founded on the distortion and relativization of a core-romantic scheme (the synthesis of harmony and trouble). But in some of them the author merely indulged in playful experimentation with the human or aesthetic possibilities of the situation. In others he took full advantage of a specific possibility: that of combining tragic and comic situations. These can be said to represent the fully crystallized center of Musset's theatrical thinking.

Only two of Musset's plays, *Les Caprices de Marianne* (1833) and *On ne badine pas avec l'amour* (1834), seem to me to fall into the latter category. In both, a typical comic situation leads finally to tragedy: Marianne, the wife of Claudio, a solemn and boring magistrate, is—in the first of the two plays—courted by the helpless, shy, and sentimental Célio. Her cousin Octave, an adventurous, high-spirited, elegant, and ironic rake, mocks the pair, consents to act as an intermediary, encourages them, and is finally at the point of supplanting Célio in the heart of Marianne. But Claudio, driven to mad jealousy, hires assassins, and Célio is caught in a deadly ambush to which his friends unwittingly send him. Octave, broken-hearted, abandons Marianne, as well as his youth, his adventures, and his dissipation. As the title shows, the main motive element is the change of attitude (and, we must conclude, standard of value) of Marianne during the play—from pious propriety to sulky vengefulness and finally to full love. But the tragic outcome could not take place if she were not faced with an equally unstable partner: Célio and Octave as parts of one and the same character (Lorenzaccio cut in two, as E. Gans suggests).[29] Octave is expression without content. Célio content with no expression.

Structurally, we may speak here of the comic searching for a tragic possibility—by trial and error, as it were—and finally finding it. In *Les Caprices de Marianne* the mobility of comedy turns into the rigidity of tragedy. Célio is a fairly stable character; his values are sublime love, unyielding honor, passion, and faith. As long as he is isolated with these anti- and supersocial values, he can do neither good nor harm; it is only when Marianne in her erratic search for a convenient stance *adopts* the same values (though their object is different) that a tragic situation is created—because confrontation turns into conflict.

This point will be confirmed by a look at *On ne badine pas avec l'amour*. Perdican, the son of a baron, wants to marry Camille, his cousin; he is a sprightly and engaging scapegrace who is looking for domestic harmony and stability. Camille is, like Marianne, seeking identification with a set of values: should she return for good to the convent? should she devote her life to the predictabilities of a pre-arranged marriage? or will she be able to experience total loss of self in a consuming love? Most of the play is taken up with the changing of position of the two main characters toward each other, along with some marginal influences of other characters. Finally, Perdican draws humble Rosette into an affair; she dies or commits suicide when Ca-mille is reunited with Perdican, and Camille leaves Perdican for good. Rosette is the exact counterpart of Célio: the carrier of values such as absolute love, faithfulness, honor, purity. The moment Camille's search has reached its object, that is, the moment she has invested her interior energy in values that are similar to those of Rosette—tragic conflict strikes with lightning speed. At this point mobility turns into ridigity. The situation differs from that of *Caprices* because the desired object (Perdican) is fairly well defined and stationary. But the morality of the structure is the same in both cases: the extremes of passion and idealistic devotion are tolerable only in isolation; the moment they "connect," the moment they begin to create alternative societies, the moment they are converted into reality, tragedy ensues.

In the Musset canon, play after play celebrates conjugal peace and faithfulness (*Barberine, Louison, Un Caprice, La Nuit vénitienne, Car-mosine*), or at least (and more significantly) reaches for it, much as Ra-zetta grasps for a serious ending. Intrigue turns to innocence (*Il ne faut jurer de rien*); dandyism turns upon itself and changes into its contrary; the societal idyll is gained through social confusion and the mixing of levels (as in *Louison,* I, iv, or II, v), even when Musset is enough of an artist to leave open the ambiguity of a lower social level which may have remained troubled after acting as an instrument for the restoration of harmony in the upper levels of the society presented. It is easy to agree with the opinion that Musset's great achievement in his dramas is the integration of the libertine in the community.[30]

Musset's ultimate mansuetude tallies well with his cultural tastes and preferences: with his personal dandyism, with his early admiration for Schubert and Mendelssohn over Mozart and Beethoven, with his infatuation for Jean Paul and Hoffmann, Scott and Byron, even for De Quincey (a translation of the latter seems to have been his first work).[31] It agrees with the views expressed in *La Confession,* which are as often as not patently antiromantic. There the persona reveals an inclination toward Wertherian idyllism (Pt. III, Ch. 3), is deeply worried by the relationship between innocence and knowledge or reality and evil (Pt. V, Ch. 4), inserts harangues against perfection (Desgenais in Pt. I, Ch. 5), and feels trapped by the separation between self, nature, and love (Pt. I, Ch. 8). All these passages and others indicate revolt against the existential premises of a romantically colored age. *La Confession* is a story of paradise lost and not regained as seen in the break with Brigitte (Pt. V, Chs. 5 and 7), in the regret for innocence, and in the theory that absolute love is "supersocial" and thus unrealizable (Pt. I, Ch. 5). Infinity and perfection are experienced as slowly fading away, out of the reach of personal action. If we speak often about the opposition between appearance and reality in Musset, it is precisely because, as Gans says, it has become "un rapport ésthétique."[32] At one point in *La Confession* we are told: "les douleurs passagères blasphèment et accusent le ciel; les grandes douleurs n'accusent ni ne blasphèment; elles écoutent."[33] The constant fear and pain of not being able to experience the Great Pain is a feature of Biedermeier sensibility that Musset understood and expressed very well.

DRAMATIC STRATEGIES and problematics strikingly similar to those of Musset can be encountered in the writings of Juliusz Słowacki. In *Mazeppa* the choice of material is extraordinary. Pushkin was interested in the shattering dilemmas of an aging yet insecure hero (*Poltava*). Hugo and Byron were eager to investigate the psychological horrors of the young courtier's deathly cavalcade, bound on the back of a galloping steed: strong colors and sensationalism, but also a heralding of future greatness. Słowacki, closest to the hero, in a geohistorical sense and perhaps most likely to admire him, ignored all this and wrote a play on the hero before he becomes a hero, that is, a play on Mazeppa as a young page, on the lusty king, Jan Casimir, on an elderly Voivod and his pure wife, and on their high-strung stepson Zbigniew. The conclusion is tragic or at least highly melodramatic: the Voivod plunges a dagger into his heart, after his much tortured wife and her adoring stepson have lost their own lives; the philandering Jan Casimir finally decides to act as a true ruler; Mazeppa is tied to the horse and whipped away into the steppe. But what ends in melodrama had begun as highly ambiguous comedy. The old husband jealously guarding a much younger wife eagerly pursued by courtier bucks, and instigating Madam Castellan Robroncka, in her middle-age poised between coquettishness and lechery, the elegant bantering of a jocular, pert, ironic Mazeppa—all the trappings are here. Mazeppa is protean, at one point he courts Amelia by taking on the cynical mask of the utter nihilist who jests because he will not believe in anything; the next moment he is ready to play Leporello to the king's Don Juan (II, 2). But by the end of the first act, when the young man cuts his own hand to save Jan Casimir's honor, there already are intimations of change. These had been linked all along with the glum and intense Zbigniew, the third wooer of Amelia, who might be said to stand like Esmeralda in *Notre-Dame de Paris* in the eye of the hurricane, an emblem of some absolute natural balance. Zbigniew, as we get to understand him, is Mazeppa's other side: they are united like Octave and Célio.[34] The explanatory scene is to be found in Act II when the duel between the two young men is followed by passionate reconciliation. Mazeppa maintains the distance of a lucid though mild amusement on this occasion, while Zbigniew reveals his common denominator with his newfound "brother": nihilism and pessimism.

From this point on the action veers between the macabre comic and serious melodrama. The Voivod hardens into a murderous maniac, the king pushes his jocular irresponsibility to treacherous cynicism, Amelia's schizoid tendencies reach the point of no return. Słowacki's intention may have been merely to delineate how a budding hero coped with traumatic and opposing pressures. What the play demonstrates in fact is something rather different. It is the explosive potential of comic conflict. Mazeppa comes in all seriousness and with no ulterior motive to Amelia's room to give her a fair warning. He finds himself trapped there by the bumbling and fuming old husband—a comic scene. His good intentions combined with those of Amelia and Zbigniew (the seekers of the absolute) lead him to the tragic and horrifying situation of being walled in the alcove where he had sought refuge. The return of the king brings back comedy: honor is relative; error reigns in human life; and even the Voivod—a Corneillean hero in a hysterical mode—enhances the zaniness. The suicide of Zbigniew and the revelation of his love for Amelia will, in turn, crush the old husband and his comic potential.

Apparently *Mazeppa* is a comedy that ends in tragedy. But Słowacki introduces an additional and decisive ambiguity. The survivor is the comic character, the symbol of openness and indifference. Those who perish represent the "old world" of fixed values. Cynicism and the fluidity of the real world are vindicated; Mazeppa can embark on his heroic adventure because he has rid himself of illusions. Rigidity is self-defeating. Purification appears in the guise of freedom from morality, energy, and high aspiration.

Fantazy is not too different from *Mazeppa* in its ultimate outcome, but much more explicit in admitting cultural morphology as its reference system; it is also much more explicit in the reflection of the characters on their own tragicomic situation. Fantazy declares: "The devil himself is playing a comedy with me . . . and the saddest at that"[35] or "My mocking tones were the last pain of my soul" (p. 306), or "Just see what jesters Poland produces; they can amuse you to the death" (p. 308), while his pedestrian friend and famulus Rzecznicki observes: "I had no idea, you see, whether a wedding or a funeral would result from the enterprise" (p. 290), and even flighty Idalia cautions: "You'll be left to play a comedy in the graveyard" (p. 296).[36]

As to the "morphocultural" level of reference, it seems to be our chief help in understanding an otherwise confusing and obscure play. The characters are grouped in three tiers. In the back there is the gross rationalism and materialist commonsense of Rzecznicki and Count Respekt, accompanied by the conventional idyllic posing of the Countess, who wants to transform the estate into a large pastoral *tableau vivant* (I, 4) with little basket-weaving peasants, fishnets, goatherds, and Ukranian folk songs by the cascade of water. In the front we have the tragic group of the patriotic hero Jan, the passionate and faithful Diana, and the enigmatic, self-sacrificing Russian major. These characters emerge from a recent past that many would like to see buried and forgotten. They act out the drama of idealism, purity, and vision in the midst of an embarrassed and often unsympathetic audience. Nevertheless they offer suffering and fulfillment in an absolute form. In between there is a third, central group, represented chiefly by the title hero, Count Fantazy Dafnicki and Countess Idalia. They stand for the ironic hopelessness and nihilistic elegance of an age grasping for substitutes for the lost absolute of romanticism. They provide a self-conscious, mocking, and elaborate imitation of romantic processes staged for the needs of a stodgy and insensitive audience. The stridency, the fantasy, and the pert cynicism of their antics is due partly to a desperate loss of ideals, but also to the need to impress rather gross eyes and ears. At the same time their connective function is positive. In Act V, Fantazy calls Rzecznicki "this famulus of mine" (p. 308);[37] at the same time both he and Idalia admire and "emulate" Jan and Diana.

In Act I the scene is set up for a farcical demonstration. Fantazy, already preceded by his "romantic" (late romantic) reputation as a melancholy Mediterranean traveler and feverish letter writer, perhaps even a mystic and a poet, returns to Poland for a largely prearranged marriage of convenience. But very soon two complementary disasters are revealed. One of them is "the return of the dead"—Jan, the martyred hero, emerges briefly from Siberian exile, and Diana does not hesitate to choose his authenticity over Fantazy's arabesques of imagination. The other disaster is Fantazy himself, who is engaged in a perpetual negation of his own reality, in doubt and deprecation. Fantazy is described by the author, and understands himself, as a creature of instability, built out of contradictions that are temporarily held together by broad gestures and histrionics. He aspires to the pure romantic experience of totality but does not ignore his own inability to achieve it; his cold, sometimes mean fury at the world is a mirror-image of self-contempt. He is ready to fall in love with Diana as soon as she rejects, him (I, 14, 15), even though a few minutes earlier he had proclaimed with ringing pathos: "she's the kind of person who needs wounds. Her lips are made for the drinking of poison" (p. 264). Idalia displays a mixture of fantastic aspiration and cynical self-mockery.

The difference between this pair and the foreground circle around Jan is best seen in comparing their language. Jan may often use the same high register as Fantazy, for instance throughout his conversation with Stella (II, 2): "the seven stars bound together that you showed me once, my golden astronomer . . . above the terrible image of frozen misery—of an extinguished life, of a snowy hell" (p. 270). But there is, as the reader is never allowed to forget, an iron solidarity between these words and his action, indeed his whole life. More than the others, Idalia recognizes this. In Act II, Scene 3 after Jan's lonely song, she slips easily into the role of Biedermeier passive spectator to high-romantic substantial action. Indeed she proclaims: "With the masters gone, the lackeys are dressing themselves in their clothes and conducting romances in their places" (p. 279).[38] This is clearly an existential, not a social, statement. Her sophisticated and self-conscious discourse is seen as madness by a puzzled Jan; pure verbalism is beyond his ken. The opposition comes to a head in the rapid alternations of life and death, ridiculous and earnest, that mark with their speedy and hysterical rhythm the last scenes of Act IV and the beginning of Act V. After Diana's true feelings become public knowledge, Fantazy and Idalia act out in the graveyard an incoherent scene of despair, sardonic laughter, and suicide, which, needless to say, will be unconsummated. It will be swept aside unceremoniously by the intrusion of a higher reality: the actual sacrificial death of the Russian major which forms a bond between Diana and Jan.

Fantazy is thus a very odd comedy—its comic effect results, in a way, from the conflict between romantic and Biedermeier mentalities, between genuine tragedy and mock despair. Respekt, Rzecznicki, and others are butts and victims of this transcendent joke. And is the link between Jan and Diana invoked as the beginning of Eden, of exemplary perfection? Is it not more likely to result in the foundation of a further variant of Biedermeier socializing, spectacularly unhappy in the Siberian snows or in lukewarm country squire coziness? Thus, as in *Mazeppa*, the apparent victory of a tragic feeling of life seems idle; the Major has exploded the redeemed society through his death. Romantic irony would have been based upon the coexistence of this society and the girl's parents, for instance. The interposition of a relativizing middle level must decisively obstruct such ironic wholeness. Moreover, Fantazy will now have the field to himself, precisely because he has remained in the twilight area of tragicomedy. The characters keep using theatrical imagery and asking (with almost detached curiosity) about the outcome of their own tangled affairs. The answer, in the spirit of late-romantic tragicomedy is clearly more questioning, and an enduring painful openness.

Such works as those of Słowacki and Musset can be better understood when looked at in connection with other works that use tragicomic touches only occasionally, for instance, Słowacki's *Balladyna*. A poetic drama, heavily indebted to Shakespeare's oneirism and scenes of lyrical madness (from *Midsummer Night's Dream* to *King Lear* to *The Tempest*), *Balladyna* is bathed in historical incertitude, is rich in identity changes, and systematically substitutes natural doom for ethical decisions. Above all it plays a daring game with time, concentrating a lifetime of events into a very few days; the peremptory energy of Słowacki easily modifies proportions and the meanings of actions. These are the circumstances under which tragic and comic elements begin to nudge each other, to combine or even to be translated into each other in the play. Goplana, a local Slavic Titania has fallen in love with a strapping country fellow name Grabiec. Since the latter is in turn in love with a girl called Balladyna, Goplana in her comic infatuation uses the services of two grumbling rustic spirits (or half-spirits) in a complicated scheme: she punishes Grabiec by turning him temporarily into a willow, while Balladyna is skillfully pushed into the path of temptation when Krikor, a tense, high-minded count begins to woo her.

Goplana's delicately comic intrigues trigger the tragedy of Balladyna's precipitous ascension. Her ambitious scaling of heights is strewn with horrifying crimes (killing her sister, torturing and starving her mother, hanging the old hermit, destroying her husband, poisoning her accomplice and lover Kostryn), and her hasty jump—within 3 days—from peasant-girl to queen is unseemly and bumbling. Her attempts to fabricate a past for herself as a persecuted and lonely offspring of the dynasty in Trebizond are certainly comic. And so—in a sly way—are the ostentatious *collages* used by Słowacki: like Lady Macbeth, Balladyna strives in vain to wash off the raspberry spots that may well be the blood of her butchered sister; like Goneril she taunts and repudiates her mother; like Macbeth himself she tries to exorcise the ghosts of her victims; like Richard III she freely mixes sex with violence to reach the top. Balladyna seems to revel in proclaiming her own literariness, thus undermining the reader's horror of her crimes. And of course the beginning of the downfall of the beautiful, evil, peasant princess is similar to the beginning of the ascension, as it is put under the sign of the comic. In Act V the second accuser is the sentimental and literary shepherd Filon, the former *soupirant* of her sister Alina, who has now discovered the corpse, the knife, a jug of raspberries, and other incriminating evidence. Filon's verbal habits, his invocations to Apollo, and his comparison of Orpheus begging his wife from Pluto are certainly reminders of the hilarious and sustained scene (I, i) when Filon, like Fantazy, raves about imaginary sorrows in the face of the hermit's intensely tragic experience and perception of the universe. Thus Biedermeier tragicomic scenes mark the beginning and the end of the play. The same tragicomic spirit accompanies the action throughout. Balladyna is shocked by the mocking overtones of a sad ballad played by Cochlik and Skierka, but she joins wholeheartedly in the proclamation of the dunce Grabiec first as fake "Diamond" King, then as potential pretender (IV, i). In the same scene Grabiec laughs in all good nature, convinced as he is that the pathetic, starving old widow is a figure in a peasant masquerade. Grabiec can be better understood as Balladyna's counterpart if we remember his behavior during his successive transformations: first into nature, then into culture (III, iv)—as soon as he is aware of his extraordinary powers, he begins to degrade nature by a series of mock laws, grotesque tax levies upon rabbits and flowers, and the like.

Infusions of the comic and grotesque are needed in order to determine the purely fictitious and playful nature of the text. In a melancholy-lyrical universe, gently decaying, comic features act like shocks. Through contrast they can lend depth and additional "reality" to the main line of action, as has indeed been one of the traditional duties of comic inserts in tragedy, ever since Shakespeare. It can be argued however that here and in similar contemporary works, comic episodes have a more specific function: they relativize the action, cast aspersions on the reliability of the directors, the author, and even the audience. Like grinning skulls thrown by an odd joker in the middle of a ceremony, they embarrass and slow down the proceedings.

Such a function differs from the pattern of tragicomic usage described in Musset, but only in degree, not in essence. It may be said to be the *Urgrund* out of which a "Mussetian" usage is crystallized. A few examples of the diffuse, unstructured use of the tragicomic may be justified, in order to show that the experience of Słowacki does not differ in this respect from that of his other contemporaries.

THE NAME of Grabbe comes readily to mind. His *Don Juan und Faust* is by any standard a heavily Biedermeier play, based on a programmatic separation of eros and knowledge. Both the main characters are defeated, both are incompatible with the world. Both are aware of Biedermeier dilemmas, as shown during their dispute (III, iii) over the relationship between the human (Biedermeier) and the superhuman (romantic). Don Juan argues like a dismayed skeptic: "wozu übermenschlich, / wenn du ein Mensch bleibst?" Any play of the imagination or any mere aspiration must remain pointless as long as it does not find a placement in space and time and thus in effect transfigure reality. Faust parries shrewdly: "Wozu Mensch, / Wenn du nach übermenschlichen nicht strebst?"[39] For him humanness itself requires that functioning of creative imagination for which Don Juan (we understand) is raising absurd expectations; human nature can only be fully itself when it includes a visionary and transcendent moment. This is not really an answer, but rather a rearrangement of the terms of the problem. Still, Donna Anna thinks of Faust as a divinity of the abyss (III, ii), while he presents himself as a Byronic hero, tortured by the vision of his weeping wife far in the north. Meanwhile people are laughing at both, and comic scenes, like the one (II, ii) in which Signor Rubio and Signor Negro are confronted with Don Juan, reestablish the perspective.

I think that such touches of tragicomedy, included in a play that wants to be above all an intellectual debate, are explained by Grabbe's preoccupation with the conflict between the integral tragic potential of high romanticism and the failed aspirations of late-romantic tragicomedy. The last act of *Hannibal* has often been read as a sarcastic ending to a straightforward and genuinely dramatic play. Sengle draws our attention to the unfinished parody of the *Cid* and to some lower register passages in the *Hermannsschlacht* which have a comic, though perhaps unintended, effect, such as the death of Varus.[40] Even in a play like *Napoleon oder die hundert Tage* (which can be seen as Biedermeier chiefly because it uses the popular form of a suite of historical scenes), the organizing motif is the incongruous return of the recent past: Napoleon the absolute fanatic caught in the web of mediocre peacefulness. Napoleon reaches a Wordsworthian perfection of harmony and a grasp of wholeness in the midst of nature (IV, vi) and finds his apotheosis in destruction (V, vii).[41] König Ludwig points out in a long speech to the Duchess of Angoulême the opposition between his own balancing and peacemaking function and Napoleon's conquering impetus (I, iii). In a symmetrical later scene (I, ix) Napoleon drives the same point home in a talk to Bertrand. Hortense exclaims: "Bedenke was würde die Welt, wären alle wie du!" (III, iii).[42] And in the one outburst of truly Biedermeier irony, the German army expresses the belief that Waterloo is but a poor, banal counterpart of the truly high-romantic, Napoleonic epic that had preceded it.

Aschenbrödel, a less than distinguished production, frankly imitates Tieck, but a few unexpected touches here and there suggest the character of epigonic originality attached to some of the writing in the 1820s and 1830s. These have to do with witty reversals of the natural turned into the social. Olympia, the youngest of three sisters, persecuted and lovely, dreams of communion with nature, of floating through the cool forest air and over the waves of grain, but her aim is really the light and glamour of the royal dining hall (II, i). This ironic reversal is illustrated in a graciously grotesque manner in the very next scene, when the Rat is turned into a coachdriver, the Cat into a lady's maid: natural into social. The pure juxtaposition of the highly poetic with the low comic occurs almost as an afterthought, as in Act III, Scene ii, when the gross scuffles of Isaak and Rüpel are interrupted by the young king's lofty declaration of love to Olympia.[43]

This brings us to a major contention around Grabbe's work. Karl Guthke, a leading contemporary authority on German tragicomedy, maintains that *Don Juan und Faust* is Grabbe's most significant tragicomic effort; he tends to play down the importance of *Scherz, Satire, Ironie und tiefere Bedeutung*.[44] The latter had been considered by all those who paid attention to Grabbe's own characterization of the play as an embodiment of "laughter in despair" as the top production of Grabbe's tragicomic genius. Guthke argues chiefly that Faust and Don Juan are mirror images of one and the same reality, namely drive, or aspiration, or the attempt to transcend the immediate. Don Juan is ridiculous because of his earthbound and physical manner, Faust transmutes aspiration into the spiritual and thus in his failure reaches tragic heights. There is some merit in the argument, but it pushes the differences between the two heroes too far.[45] On the other hand Guthke is unduly suspicious of the ability of a comedy to carry a tragic burden also (a belated Hegelian influence perhaps). Grabbe himself is much less timid. His Scipio der Jüngere tells Terenz (in *Hannibal*): "was tragisch ist, ist auch lustig und umgekehrt. Hab ich doch oft in Tragödien gelacht, und bin in Komödien fast gerührt worden."[46] Moreover, the reading of Grabbe's contemporaries will persuade us that comic verve is not always paired off with the tragic, but often with the poetic, or simply with earnestness and gravity.

In *Scherz, Satire, Ironie und tiefere Bedeutung* the corrosiveness of the comic slides from an attack on serious reality to despair and (almost) tragedy. The keynote comes at the beginning: "Schnapps with sugar!—*utile cum dulci!*" and a little later "A country oaf and the first declension . . . a crow trying to put on a starched dickie."[47] The play can be regarded as a comedy only by those who pay attention to the action. But obviously the characters and their movements are mere pretexts, absurd and grotesque carriers of the feelings that have to be conveyed to the audience.[48] It is the emotions that are indeed tragicomic. Their tragicomic nature is bred in the same disorderly and aleatory environment as that of Słowacki and Musset; the chief difference is the wildness and the radical dismissal of realistic pretense. At least Liddy, the main feminine character, has the substance of a Fantasio, Leonce, or Fantazy. (Thus she says to the Schulmeister: "Sie besahen sich zufälligerweise im Spiegel, und da ihnen Ihr Gesicht zu schlecht vorkam, so strichen Sie es aus."[49]) Not so the Freiherr von Mordax, Herr Mollfels, the poet Rattengift, or even the Devil, who freely change identities and are mostly mouthpieces for positional systems. They kill, destroy, enter pacts with the devil, sit legs akimbo on the sarcophagus of the baronial family vault, all without the slightest compunction. When things get really dangerous, Mordax explains furiously to Liddy's father, the Baron von Haldungen, that he is just an actor playing a baron and quickly disappears in the orchestra pit.

All this might conceivably be seen as "pure" grinning comedy were it not for the *tiefere Bedeutung* mentioned in the title and provided by the Schulmeister; he is the character who, though still in his middle age, is able to connect the heroic age of a past romanticism with a musty and rudderless age cozily wallowing in mud. His bouts with alcohol are due to disappointment. He still has moments of patriotic reverie (beginning of II, iii) though he now merely hopes for practical improvements: education of farmers, trees to be cut for use as school benches and the like. When deeply drunk he reveals to himself his gnawing pain (III, i): "O ihr schönen, schwärmerischen, unwiderbringlich verschwundenen Tage, wo ich—" and earlier: "*Fuimus Troes*, die goldenen Flegeljahre sind dahin."[50] The Schulmeister's regret is not just the melancholy of maturation, it is addressed specifically to the heroic age of romantic upheaval. Soon after his tirade he engages in homosexual play with Mollfels, in a scene that could well have signified for the author (and for his immediate audience) the substitution of an incomplete, empty act for the wholeness of genuine love. This symbolization of the "second best" (Mollfels, and in his way the Schulmeister too, are in love with Liddy) as well as of a tragicomic mixture of substances reinforces the confessions of the play's main "serious" character. The Schulmeister's despair is fully disclosed at the very end of the play in his furious, impotent outburst against Grabbe—against his creator. The scene brings a whiff of doom and terror as the silent Author, halting and inexorable at the same time, steps through the dark forest toward the lonely house carrying a ghostly lantern and bringing The End. The Schulmeister's tantrum is directed against his own existence.

Mollfels (whose name combines the hard and the soft, stonecliff and mush, a further suggestion of tragicomic polarity) chooses the safer path of inauthentic existence. He identifies with the purely verbal level of romanticism and revels in long tirades, some of them nostalgic in the vein of *Sartor Resartus* ("Sieh, da liegt es, das väterliche Dorf! Horch, auf seinem grauen Kirchturme klingt die Vesperglocke! Wie anmutig sie mir nach vierjähriger Abwesenheit entgegentönt!—Auch das altertümliche Schloss ist noch unverändert geblieben, stolz und stattlich erhebt es sich dort aus der Mitte seines sommerlich blühenden Gartens, und in seinen mächtigen Fenstern spielt purpurn der erste Schimmer des Abendrots!" II, iii), others exaltedly erotic ("welch reizendes Weib! Man hört die Musik ihrer Bewegungen. Wie zwei geistige Naphtafeuer glänzen die unauslöschlichen Flammen ihrer Augen, und wie ein See über seiner Quelle wogt ihr Busen über ihrem Herzen," II, iv).[51] Although his grotesque ugliness almost provides an anchor to reality, Mollfels remains the most typical character of the play, precisely because he is the most purely verbal. His final union with Liddy is not as accidental as it might seem. It is Grabbe's dismayed and sarcastic statement about the "valid" survivals of a lowered romanticism, in the same way in which the Schulmeister represents the desperate and hopeless revolt.

Scherz, Satire, Ironie und tiefere Bedeutung might be called a post-tragedy. Its characters, statement, and feelings are the outcome of an explosion: the defeat of the high-romantic adventure. They are scattered pieces flying in all directions. That is why they are, deliberately, improbable as rounded live characters. And that is also why they are lost in a limbo between comedy and tragedy. Grabbe's play differs from those of Musset and Słowacki in that a tragic solidification never occurs. Manfred Schneider claims, rightly I believe, that in fact the whole of Grabbe's dramatic work is focused on destruction and splintering. Grabbe's interpretation of reality draws its basic models out of a fragmentary world, a world built out of shards, ruins, and disconnected pieces; an integrating will or a concept of perfection survive merely in decadent form, broken by parody or colored by irony. His heroes are desperate, hate-filled, disappointed in a word, rudimentary humans.[52] He goes on to argue that the use of heroic, superhuman figures is an attempt to overcome this fragmentation. Obviously the failure of such an attempt even to get started is the main reason why the play discussed above fails to gel in either the direction of comic reconciliation or genuine tragedy, thus refusing to define itself as a tragicomedy.

GRABBE'S CONTEMPORARY, Büchner, uses many similar strategies. His "serious" plays—*Woyzeck* and *Dantons Tod* contain their share of jocular references, and particularly of sarcastic and grotesque touches. *Woyzeck,* the tragedy of seediness, is spiced with heavy doses of earthy obscenity, as in the exchanges of the noncommissioned officers about Marie, as well as in the catty, lust-filled clash of Marie and Margreth over the good graces of the drum major. These and other scenes go beyond the general tragic irony of the play. In *Dantons Tod* such touches are even more frequent. Jocular frivolity establishes a distance between man and his fate, or life and death, and relativizes both.

The reverse is true in *Leonce und Lena.* Sadness and tragedy are superadded elements that change the general frivolity and merriment into a threatening world picture; the sad and the tragic relativize the comic. Büchner's purpose in *Leonce und Lena* is to pit his irony against romantic irony. Even the choice of the main character's name is suggestive. It is a pun on the name of Büchner's own highly serious romantic hero Lenz; it reminds us forcefully of Brentano's *Ponce de Leon* and, as Majut has shown, confirms the use of the name in works such as Mme. de Staël's *Delphine,* Mme. Cottin's *Isola Bella* (German translation 1833), Grillparzer's *Weh dem, der lügt* (The Cook Boy Leon), and later George Sand's *Tévérino.* (Majut concisely defines Leonce as "die biedermeierliche Form des problematischen Menschen."[53])

Ludwig Büttner shows graphically the opposition between Friedrich Schlegel and Büchner in terms of their attitudes toward leisure. The former talks about the creativity and nobility of leisure and the power of imagination. Leisure is called in *Lucinde* "die Lebensluft der Unschuld und der Begeisterung."[54] Büchner refuses such high-romantic aspirations and perceptions—for him leisure is emptiness, imagination is an idle, wildly titillating toy. Not only Leonce, but the other characters are also tired; they move slowly, often recline. They have stylized, languidly foppish gestures.[55] Leisure is for them not primarily the space of freedom and creation, but the symbolic preparation for death. Leonce is a Mussetian character or one who might also be encountered in some of Pushkin's works.[56] His skepticism and boredom are designed to hide sensitivity, yearning and aspiration, even a touch of despair. Leonce's drama is real, in spite of its ridicule. At every point his fantasy flies off on a tangent, and (almost) breaks away from the body of his existence; Leonce barely manages to hold on to his social environment. (Therefore, in my opinion, those who seek satirical implications in the play are bound to be disappointed.) Leonce fears conformity more than anything, but precisely by fleeing it, he falls into it (the conventional marriage). This is the best explanation of the famous exchange between the two young people toward the end of the play:

> Lena: "Ich bin betrogen"
> Leonce: "Ich bin betrogen"
> Lena: "O Zufall."
> Leonce: "O Vorsehung."[57]

It is arguable that a Leonce who would not have run away would have had a better chance to achieve a genuinely romantic goal. At any rate the ending is highly ambiguous, and many questions remain open. Has Leonce indeed given in to conformist pressures? Is he now tamed? Has he decided that fantasy can be secret, that it can be accommodated in a miniature framework, by small places and among small things?

We can understand the full weight of such questions only if we admit that the ironic treatment of irony must inevitably give birth to a tragic dimension in literature. Ludwig Büttner correctly observes that the idyllic and cozy little principality with its secluded leafy bowers stands on dark and shaky ground.[58] Those who ignore the tragicomic mixture do so at their own risk: they have to overemphasize the light satirical touches into heavy criticism and protest, or else they could not explain the grave seriousness that often seems to breathe out of so light and playful an action. Even the insights of some able critics are thus distorted.[59] Karl Viëtor is more judicious, and his opinions may provide the most reliable starting point for a discussion of the tragicomic in *Leonce und Lena*. The melancholy in this comedy is essentially the same as that in Büchner's two tragedies, Viëtor finds after a colorful enumeration of the play's ingredients that would certainly fit *Measure for Measure*.[60] Viëtor is also impressed by the cruelty, misanthropy (*Welthass*), and deadly earnestness of many rejoinders (p. 176). Leonce's exclamation "ich bin so jung und die Welt ist so alt," followed by the expressionistic anxiety of "Die Erde hat sich ängstlich zusammengeschmiegt wie ein Kind, und über ihre Wiege schreiten die Gespenster" (II, ii), captures exactly the pervasive fear by which the merriment and jocularity of the action are so effectively neutralized.[61] Viëtor touches only slightly upon what is left: ambiguity, the lack of substance of the characters symbolizing the hovering intellectual and social uncertainties of the age, boredom as the mother of melancholy.

More radically it can be claimed that, conversely, boredom is the outcome of melancholy, or, even better, of despair. The arguments for reading Büchner's play as the irony of romantic irony are compelling. They include the figure of Leonce (the pale, impotent, skeptical version of Danton or Lenz); the figure of König Peter who, like Teuffelsdröckh, relativizes romantic idealistic philosphy by resorting to the metaphor of clothes and running around the room naked to illustrate the *Ding-an-Sich* (I, ii); Valerio's mockery of romantic communion with nature: "Ich werde mich indessen in das Gras legen und meine Nase oben zwischen den Halmen heraus blühen lassen und romantische Empfindungen beziehen" (I, i);[62] and the openness of the ending. But we must not overlook the opposite perspective, from which the play is a tragedy without the tragic release of catastrophe. The almost panic feeling of generalized fear pervading the play is part of this syndrome. It grips not only the sensitive, but even König Peter, and in fact the whole of nature and society (Lena, Rosetta, even Valerio). The death wish remains just yearning, as in the case of Fantazy. The love encounters between Leonce and Lena have a strange somnambulistic quality with many references to impending death. Valerio, who is often interpreted as the simple man of sound common sense, should be understood instead as a destructive, careless pragmatist. His language is similar to that of Leonce in extravagance and cynical word choice, but he has deliberately eliminated the touches of hope, the occasional softness and delicacy. Looked at closely, Valerio turns into the grinning figure of coming modernity. His final tirade is more than an irony, it is a brutal threat against the distraught attempts of Leonce to build a thin web of protective illusion around his life.

Beyond even Valerio's questioning is the radical questioning of the characters' validity and right to existence by Büchner himself. Leonce tells his companion "Mensch, du bist nichts als ein schlechtes Wortspiel. Du hast weder Vater noch Mutter, sondern die fünf Vokale haben dich miteinander erzeugt" only to receive the answer "Und sie

Prinz, sind ein Buch ohne Buchstaben, mit nichts als Gedankenstri-
chen" (I, iii).[63] Whereas Grabbe's Mordax was retreating into
verbalism in order to escape death or punishment, here the characters
in the fullness of their "life" recognize their own lack of reality—an
additional token of tragedy. But even their verbal reality is problematic. As Jürgen Schröder has shown quite convincingly, the language
of the play must be related all the time to nothingness. It is not self-
sustaining, but rather an attempt to fill a void (to shut up the silence, if
I may add a stress here).[64] In other words, the characters are not only
sucked back into the purely fictional level of textuality, they are further diminished by the relativization of the text itself. A tragic ending
would have restored some dignity, some finality to their existence.
The denial of a tragic ending means that Leonce and Lena are fixed in
eternal ambiguity and uncertainty. The illusions they express in the
final scene are not only a whistling in the dark, they are consciously
exposed as illusions and concessions of defeat. Tragedy eludes them
and that signifies that existence itself eludes them. This loss is itself
their greatest tragedy, precisely because they are not really the type of
puppet figures that Grabbe had staged.[65]

BEFORE USING these works to draw any conclusions about Biedermeier tragicomedy, we should pause and reflect on the predilection for
the grotesque that seems to be a feature of the age in its entire literary
production, not just in drama. Although eighteenth-century literature
is by no means devoid of figures and situations that we would nowadays call grotesque, the writers as well as the audience did not perceive
these characters as autonomous or endowed with their own integrity.
Smollett's Lishmahago for instance is perceived as deviant from an implicit norm; similarly Sir Roger de Coverley may be defined as the
neoclassical human standard (in fact Mr. Spectator) plus some pleasing
quirks. When not the object of amusement, such figures are showered
with contempt (or are even presented as hateful) for what is perceived
as their failure to live up to a level of normality (by Swift for instance).
A shift in attitude is noted only after the 1760s or 1770s and is signaled by what seems to have been the first definition of the grotesque
as an independent aesthetic category, Justus Möser's essay, *Harlekin
oder Verteidigung des Grotesk-Komischen* (1761). In any case before
the romantic age it would have been impossible to imagine grotesque
figures such as Hugo's Quasimodo or E. T. A. Hoffmann's Nathanael

in *Der Sandmann* invested with tragic dignity. And before the romantic age it would have been impossible to expect to contemplate the
sheer quantitative increase of grotesque scenes and figures in all kinds
of literature.

Practically the whole of Gogol's work can be divided according to
various kinds of the grotesque. These may be illogical syntactical combinations of the type: "All the others were more or less educated people: many were reading Karamzin, many 'Moskovskie Vedmosti,' and
there were even some who didn't read anything at all" or "What a
capital fellow Ivan Ivanovich is. The police commissioner of Poltava
knows him, too."[66] They may be based on brutal metaphorical combinations of the animate and the inanimate. Among these the "nose"
and the "overcoat" come easily to mind, but it is not unusual to encounter a description of an old woman as a "perfect coffee jug in a
night bonnet."[67] They may be fully elaborated scenes such as the
witches' sabbath with its amorous animal demons in "The Lost Letter" or other scenes in the Dikanka series such as that of the dancing
old women.[68] But even Pushkin, whose outlook was more serene,
mentions approvingly (in an unpublished fragment probably written
around 1825) the mixture of comic and tragic, suggesting that the
reader's interest is thus unified. (He was working on *Boris Godunov* at
the time.)[69] Immermann who controlled the whole range of Biedermeier effects, did not ignore the grotesque in his *Münchhausen*. The
influence of Hoffmann created a powerful tradition in Eastern Europe,
as well as in America and France, seen in the multiplication of doubles,
robots and marionettes, jeering contorted figures, nightmarish imps,
and in other manifestations. England was easily able to build its own
stock of demonic caricatures, since there was the Gothic tradition to
fall back upon. Sir Oran Haut-ton in Peacock's *Melincourt*, Mary
Shelley's Frankenstein, De Quincey's mock-sinful personae, even
C. R. Maturin's Melmoth or J. J. Morier's Hajji Baba are just some
figures in the gallery.

The pervasive presence of grotesque situations and characters in all
kinds of shapes in the literature of the 1820s and 1830s raises the
question of the exact relationship between categories of the tragicomic
and the grotesque. The two roughly correspond and, without the proliferation, they could well be taken as synonymous, as they usually are.
But for practical classification purposes, an effort at discrimination is
necessary. The claim has been made that the tragicomic (any combina-

tion of tragic and comic elements) is quite general, while the grotesque is a special subcategory. Over and beyond the combination of tragic and comic elements the grotesque contains an ingredient (a leer, a caricature, a touch of the bizarre) which will set it apart from an ordinary tragicomic work. This view is tenable particularly if we accept the somewhat circular argument of the critics of the leading theoretician of the grotesque, Wolfgang Kayser. Kayser had emphasized rather heavily the demonic and monstrous elements in grotesque works, and he had asserted that a subversion of reality and an implicit threat lurk under their surface in all such works. His adversaries replied that while demonic features are always prominent, they are also neutralized by comic elements, so that ultimately the grotesque appears as a "humorous disarming" of the "terrible outcroppings" of the underworld.[70] If either Kayser or his critics are right, then clearly the grotesque designates a rather small number of literary objects, all of which are also comprised in the broader category of the tragicomic.

The realities of Biedermeier literary production seem to disprove this view, its possible theoretical merits notwithstanding, chiefly because of the astounding frequency of grotesque phenomena in all areas of cultural life. If for no other than strictly pragmatic reasons, we are prompted therefore to resort to some of the older theories of the grotesque, which confined themselves to more general definitions. Thus for Hegel the grotesque is a feature of "primitive" literature and art—unbalanced, twisted, confused. In spite of its arbitrary historical identification with Indian and other arts, this definition seems more appealing, precisely because it disregards overly detailed analyses, as more recent critics do not. Perhaps even more persuasive is the opinion of Wilhelm Michel, an early authority who emphasized that the grotesque, which he also called "universal grin" (*Weltgrimasse*), must be based on duality and contradiction.[71]

Distortion and contradiction seem indeed to characterize the grotesque in the work of Gogol, Hugo, Peacock, or Büchner, rather than demonic intensities or humorous gentleness. Similarly Grabbe's devil is neither infernal nor merely amusing—he is the distorted answer to the needs of a nihilistic situation. In the most general sense, the grotesque in later romanticism appears as the consequence of the breakdown of romantic integrity. The latter sought regeneration in a maximum extension of human faculties in their full and organic connection. The area covered by a thus expanded conscience and by all the values it tried to assimilate went well beyond the traditional human norms (particularly neoclassical norms) and embraced aesthetic or moral or psychological features that would not have been considered acceptable only a few decades before. Wordsworth's *The Thorn* is one example of such areas of deformation which were, however, closely linked to a central body of values. Wordsworth's *We Are Seven* might easily be seen as grotesque were it not for the anchoring of its more extreme claims to traditional views by some qualifying touches of surprise (and implied disagreement); the speaker is, he suggests, on the side of the reader, even though he seeks understanding for the children. Coleridge's Ancient Mariner is a bizarre, ludicrous, even demonic apparition at the beginning of the poem. He is no longer so at the end because he is now integrated in a huge mythical framework. The grotesque is here a superadded ornament in a way, but it is chiefly a piece of evidence, one that shows the myth's capacity for inclusiveness. The human model is stretched to the limits of the possible.

By the time we reach Hoffmann and Hugo, no such inclusiveness ties the grotesque peripheries to the mythical center any longer. The two can and will function separately. Hoffmann's Nathanael is autonomous, not redeemed by integration. Quasimodo or L'homme qui rit are based on the stark contradiction between their forms and content. Fantasio toils hard at his own grotesqueness with a kind of defiant zest, because he *wants* separation. It seems unquestionable that in these and many other cases, the grotesque is turned from a mere part into an independent whole. Gogol's *Nose* is the literal statement of this process, a demonstration in which metaphoric tenor and vehicle fully coincide.[72]

If this is so, then we can assert that at least inside the Biedermeier it is the grotesque that represents the more general category, while tragicomedy represents a much more limited and specialized aesthetic situation. On the one hand tragicomedy is confined to the world of the stage. On the other, it represents a specific kind of modification, one that goes from integrating irony to the divisive duality of language. The grotesque meanwhile epitomizes the period dynamics of the age in their entirety: it is the separation of central areas of significance from the marginal provinces temporarily annexed by the expansion of romanticism. The similarity and the difference between the two can be best illustrated if we compare *Leonce und Lena* with *Woyzeck*. The first of these two plays is chiefly a tragicomedy: the tragedy of nothingness is resolved into the comedy of nothingness. There are occasional grotesque moments, like the naked philosophizing of König Peter (I, ii) or the drilling of the peasants by the Landrat and the Schulmeister into suitable expressions of enthusiasm for the princely festivities (III, ii)—an episode worthy of the pen of Gogol. The second play is too gloomy to be seen as tragicomedy, though it combines the lower register (language, behavior, and social extraction of characters) with the high stylistic register (the relentless pressure of doom). In *Woyzeck* the grotesque is much more dominant: the quarrel of the sexually heated Marie and Margret over the legs of the drum major, the ethical theorizing of the Hauptmann as he is being shaved, the scenes at the country fair, and many more. It is plain that of the two *Woyzeck* has a broader sweep and encompasses more human situations. *Leonce und Lena* could be placed in it, not the other way around. Arguably, if *Woyzeck* were chosen to illustrate the general anxiety of the Biedermeier age or the decay of romanticism as a chief root of the Biedermeier, it would be because of the prevalence of the grotesque.

For Büchner in *Woyzeck,* as for Gogol in most of his writings, the grotesque really means a world from which the spirit has withdrawn or keeps withdrawing; in consequence the world becomes material, mechanical, "marionettenhaft"; it is "de-organicized," indeed "deromanticized." Of course the process takes on truly catastrophic proportions in an Orthodox-Byzantine cultural context, where it becomes apocalyptic and signals the disappearance of God. In the context of a *Filioque* culture (that is, of Protestantism or post-Cartesian subjectivism), the break between reality and imagination may have provoked less anguish, and the transcendent meaning of spiritual withdrawal could be interpreted in many ways, while for Gogol the withdrawal of God left society or nature incapable of fending for itself. This is the kind of problem that, as we have seen before, does not really arise in the tragicomic stage works of the period. However, the latter can be fully understood only as a subdivision in the broader category of the grotesque. The concluding analysis below will try to evidence some of the sociocultural directions of the tragicomic.

THE FUNDAMENTAL possibility of the interference between tragic and comic elements must be sought in the very structure of these modes. Both the tragic and the comic can be described as (usually unequal) segments on an axis. Comedy ensues when the segments (which represent values) are fairly equal, fairly mobile on that axis, and without a stable, precise point of impact. That is why no brutal clash occurs and hence no destruction of one of the parts. By contrast, tragedy could be represented as a rigid and unequal segmentation of the axis and by confrontation at a precise, stable point of impact. This must lead necessarily to tragic catastrophe and to the destruction of the smaller (weaker) of the two segments. In a highly abstract structural manner then, tragicomedy could be defined as the change from one segmental organization of the value axis to the other.[73] The mobility of comedy is replaced by the rigidity of tragedy, by fixed and thus collision-prone structures within the dramatic space of merely five acts. This at least is one way in which tragicomedy may come about.

In the Biedermeier age, however, the key strategy may be described as the uncertainty of uncertainty. The reader is pulled toward a fascinated observation of an action wavering between the two types of "segmentation." The Biedermeier period provides a state of affairs in which at least two of the determining conditions for the emergence of a tragicomic tradition are fulfilled. (A third one, which Cyrus Hoy describes as the permanent conflict between the ideal and the real human state, is of course always with us, and thus nonhistorical.)[74] First there is the mixture of levels. It is almost universally accepted that a tragicomic situation is connected with the mixture of stylistic levels. Erich Auerbach in particular argued very persuasively that in Shakespeare's plays the combination of rhetorical voices which had been confined to the tragic or comic register, respectively, led to powerful innovative effects.[75] Inevitably such rhetorical combinations are based on social mixtures: the noble Capulets with the lowly nurse, Prince Hal and Falstaff, and so forth. Logically, such an aesthetic outcome may well be expected under the conditions given in the period here discussed. Circumstances in which a great deal of instability, class mobility and mixture prevail—or are perceived to prevail—such as those after 1815, should provide a fertile ground for the emergence or development of tragicomic literature. Instability and combination go hand in hand.

The second determining condition is the one described by Gustav René Hocke and accepted by Marianne Thalmann and others.[76] The origins of tragicomedy are to be found, according to this view, in the ritual labyrinthine dance invented by Daedalus for Ariadne. The labyrinth is an attempt to secularize the innermost mystery of the universe

into a solvable enigma; it may serve thus as an analogy to the secularization of the tragic into the comic, by revealing and emphasizing the
former's incompatibilities. Nevertheless, Hocke contends that the
tragicomic has intrinsic features and structures which are other than a
mere repetition on the tragic and comic ones; the tragicomic is not de-
rivative. Daedalus's dance is meant to exorcise confusion and entanglement and to search for the center of order; however it mocks
grotesquely the self-deception of a reestablished pattern. The origins
of the tragicomic, Hocke contends, must be sought in an ingenious
quarrel with something apparently unreachable and in a dialectical dis-
tancing from the inevitable.

This second origin of tragicomedy, which is not I think incompatible with the first, nor even radically different from it, is also present in
the intellectual make-up of the decades following the Congress of
Vienna. The loss of a firm center or, more exactly, the loss of a firm
grasp on the wholeness of reality, elicits a whole array of responses.
One among them is the desperate laughter combined with artful manneristic combinations which are the foundation of tragicomedy. The
loss of an axis seems to be both feared and welcomed in the plays we
have discussed above. Conversely, the characters act as if they were
searching for some hidden answer and solution, yet dreading and
shunning it at the same time.

Hocke points to many interesting examples all the way from Men-
ander and Euripides to G. B. Andreini and Pierre Du Ryer. But he
seems to be in error when he stresses too much the work of Tieck as
the only romantic embodiment of tragicomedy. Hocke fails to take
into consideration some historical distinctions and this in turn leads
him to ignore the transition between an earlier and a later romanticism. He also fails to notice that inside tragicomic literature there is a
fairly constant division between a tragicomedy of *crisis* and a tragicomedy of *serenity*. Admittedly these two kinds of writing have so much in
common that distinguishing between them is often a rather subjective
business. It becomes less subjective, however, if we decide to take into
account the intentions of the age and even the intellectual background
of the individual writers. Thus it would seem fair to assert even without cumbersome, detailed demonstrations that most twentieth-century
writers, such as Beckett, Ionesco, or Dürrenmatt project a problemati-
cal existence, fissures and contrasts, multiple perspectives, the anxieties of uncertainty; we see their characters functioning like tightrope

dancers without a safety net. Büchner's, Musset's, and Słowacki's plays also abound in similar features. But these are overshadowed by an attraction toward *relativity*. Surprising as it may seem, the late-romantic playwrights share a background of meekness. They are above all the enemies of intransigence, absolute claims, indisputable truths. They may well respond to their own intellectual tenor with a show of sardonic despair, but they are certainly not confined to this, as is sometimes believed.

If we look at the specific mechanism for conversion of the comic into the tragic in Musset's plays, we can best observe the philosophical roots of Biedermeier tragicomedy. The repeated transformation of the comic into the tragic illustrates the impossibility of organizing the world coherently according to the high-romantic (or core-romantic) scheme. The organic unity of the world is irremediably shattered, and an attempt to fuse ideal and real is doomed to trigger disaster. The only harmony possible in later romanticism is a microharmony or a sectional harmony—the harmony of family and home, the harmony of limited social groups and landscapes, the harmony of uprooted ideals, or perhaps the purely sociopolitical harmony of radicalism—but not the harmony of high romanticism, which transcended contradictions and also transcended the tragic-comic opposition. A Biedermeier world view and state of mind will involve a dramatic world with a random distribution of frivolous and serious elements, and will therefore have a basically comic outlook. Tragedy will grow out of the tendency to see these elements *organized* in an intelligible fashion. Paradoxically then, the type of insecurity expressed in Musset's plays is for him (and for his readers) a kind of security; it offers protection from the cosmos-shattering consistency of romantics.[77] The cynical and frivolous overtones are really "soothing"—the essence of life is a random succession of serious or comic elements; we have to restrict our expectations and actions, we have to avoid the hubris of large-scale systems. Musset quotes in *La Confession* a passage from Ecclesiastes, wondering at the indifference with which everything is happening to everybody; his response is a retreat to either cynicism or modest virtue; under these circumstances tragedy would become possible only through rigidity.[78]

Slightly different, but basically similar conclusions can be drawn from the reading of the other authors discussed above. In them also tragicomedy signals the relaxation of romantic tensions and the taming of romantic irony. At the same time the continuity between the two phases of romanticism is plain and unmistakeable. No comparable spread of grotesque and tragicomic features can be noticed after 1850. The dramatic problems of Hauptmann and Sudermann, of Ibsen and Tolstoy were totally different. In fact even the "lower class" dramatists between 1815 and 1848, such as R. C. G. de Pixérécourt, with their melodramatic simplifications, are closer to the intellectually demanding Słowacki and Musset.

6

THE BIEDERMEIER
HISTORICAL NOVEL AND THE
DECLINE OF COMPROMISE

GOETHE'S *Hermann und Dorothea,* the high-water mark of European idyllism, the consummate expression of graceful organicism, has a curious ending. Hermann, the guardian of tradition and continuity, the restorer and soother, the inheritor of microhappiness, is suddenly, in the fever of his nuptials gripped by an access of "edler menschlicher Rührung." In a ringing baritone he delivers a threatening tirade. Not only are "allgemeine Erschüttrung," "die fürchterliche Bewegung," and the "schwankende Zeit" abhorrent, he exclaims, but "der schöner Güter Besitztum" imposes new attitudes and new habits.[1] He will be only too glad to offer his manly chest to the enemy and fiercely enjoy the battle for hearth and fatherland. In fact, he theorizes, peace is nothing but the outcome of power opposing power, a kind of equilibrium of forces. According to Hermann, the idyllic system can only survive as a soft core encased in a hard shell; it is merely the gentle opposite of hard aggressiveness, much like Brecht's Szechwan hero. How to keep the idyllic system free of disruptive outside influences is a question that had plagued many eighteenth-century writers and had been the topic of works ranging from Goldsmith's *Vicar of Wakefield* and Smollett's *Humphry Clinker,* to Jean Paul's *Siebenkäs* and even to Goethe's *Faust.* The dilemma was clearly one between a fragile idyll kept away from outside influences and a strong, mundane, idyllic world that would be altered in its innermost core by learning to cope with the outside world. Hermann's question was not new, his radical answer was. Its toughness destroys or suspends the idyll it tries to defend. The development of the historical novel in the age of Biedermeier is closely linked to this kind of evolution, from support to obliteration of the idyll. Stifter's *Witiko* represents the end point of this larger movement, the destruction of the idyllic model as a prop or supporting structure for the narrative endeavors of Biedermeier romanticism.

Later romanticism is, as argued above, an adaption of high romanticism, a reduction to scale, a lowering of sights.[2] Inside this diminished and softened shape further "decays" may occur. The historical novel illustrates how Biedermeier ideals, modest as they might seem, are discarded at the end of the movement's own historical evolution. One of the most important types of change to the high-romantic vision of mankind proposed in the Biedermeier is the translation of the concept of wholeness or synthesis into that of conciliation. The high-romantic vision (Novalis, Saint-Just), the argument tacitly runs, errs by being too linear, in spite of its apparent spirality or circularity; it actually tries to sell us on the idea that paradise regained is the outcome of some quantitative accumulations, which must inevitably turn into the revelation and opening of the new world. What happens in fact is that transition is a smoother but also more selective process: not the total gain and total loss of the high-romantics. It is a reformist blending. Historical change can best be effected according to both liberal and conservative thinkers of the Biedermeier age by the transfer and maintenance of earlier historical values into an idealized or hopeful present (that is, immediate future).

The historical novel appears after 1815 as the metaphoric vehicle for the exploration of these ideative processes (of these *Gedankengänge*), and that is why we do not really think of pre-Scottian productions as historical novels, even though they may deal with historical events or realities of the past. The historical novel grows neither out of eighteenth-century realism as Lukács claims to believe (his whole demonstration shows otherwise), nor out of a mechanical opposition to romantic-revolutionary tenets (as Lukács actually believes).[3] It grows, rather, out of a desire to *accommodate* those tenets, to adapt them flexibly to the possibilities of the real world. Placing the epistemological exercise in the past is merely a strategic gesture; the visibility is better, the outlines are clearer, the writing is neater, the moral at the end is more compelling.

The Biedermeier historical novel strengthens itself, from the very beginning, by using the idyllic model as a sketch of the desirable "final state." By this time there was already a long tradition of purely functional use of the idyllic model, for example, as a foil for romantic exalted states or as a moderating influence for many writers of the eighteenth century. Therefore authors resorted to this convenient metaphorical framework without qualms. Besides, there was a natural affinity between the intrinsic assumptions of idyllism and the moderate compromise sought by Biedermeier writers. A state of *plausible* paradise, as opposed to one of regenerated perfection, would perhaps display those features of natural society, graceful balance, sensible reason, organic coherence, and crisis-free evolution that were traditionally attributed to the model of the societal idyll. The trap of which Goethe was ironically aware—the *excess* of functional use, the change of the model into a sheerly didactic construct—was not avoided. The movement from *Waverley* to *Witiko,* with some reference on the way to Manzoni, shows what happens.

OUR PRESENT understanding of Scott was shaped (almost in a dialectical progression) by three moments. First came Lukács's strong affirmation of Walter Scott as a nonromantic, indeed in some ways, an antiromantic writer. Whatever other light Lukács may have thrown on Scott seems pale compared to the definitive shattering of the misconceptions put into circulation by late French and Russian romantics about one of their peers.[4] Then David Daiches effectively described the tension between the "prudent Briton and the passionate Scot" and thus drew our attention to the bipolar and dialectical nature of Scott's work (in a fashion much more dialectical than Lukács).[5] Next several critics observed that this tension was not merely historical but philosophical. F. R. Hart, with whose name I would like to associate this view, argued in favor of essentializing Scott's conception. By recognizing Scott's "ambiguous view of human history" Hart showed how a typological strategy rather than a historically mimetic impulse directs Scott's narratives.[6] In fact even Scott's scenery (castles, waterfalls) is now said to be "not actual landscapes, but previous artistic and, more especially literary descriptions"; literary conventions serve as mediations and codes of representation.[7]

I believe the moment has come, after full and grateful acceptance of this typological approach, to return it to its historical basis. We can do so by recognizing a connection between the "essentialized" epic game and the actual dilemmas in Scott's life and sociocultural situation. We can do so by recognizing that while for Scott the actual historical relationship between patriarchal Scotland and its Hanoverian-capitalist conquerors was important, another historical relationship—that between himself and romantic revolution—was crucial and decisive. The first of these relations was somewhat less important simply because it was less topical than the second and because it involved just coming to terms with the past, not facing a present problem. Scott adroitly uses the first of these oppositions as a metaphor for the other one. Many readers have therefore concluded that Scott's main concern is a loving rejection of the past (that is, medieval Scottish history) in favor of an Augustan England continued into the present. In fact, the reverse is true. The Scottish historical past is Scott's metaphor for the present, that is, for revolutionary danger and romantic excess, as it was in a way for the Byron of *English Bards and Scotch Reviewers.* Sometimes the equivalence is plain to see. In *Old Mortality* the young, intelligent, and heroic fanatic Reverend Ephraim Macbriar is a portrait of Saint-Just, while the conflicts between the moderate and radical factions of the revolutionary Covenanters seem faithful copies of the struggle between the Girondin and Montagnard factions of the French *Convention.* In a more general way, the Gothic turbulence of the past stands for the revolutionary fervor of the emergent future. Indeed it is significant that in most of the *Waverley* novels archaism is manifested through disorder or revolution, a case of simple metaphorical contamination. The concluding chapters of *Old Mortality* incorporate an important idea: the alliance of the committed quasi-republican revolutionary Balfour with the inflexible reactionary aristocrat Claverhouse, his former opponent, in the hope of thwarting the orderly conservative social progress that followed the Glorious Revolution. All along Scott, much like Jane Austen, is indeed pleading for the past, but it is for the Augustan past, the past of Swift and Dryden. The formidable image of Gothic Scotland serves him well for romantic power; to bolster his factual-historical scaffolding, Scott assimilates to this image not only the sensitivity developed by Coleridge and the Gothic novelists, but also the aesthetic procedures of Goethe's still fully high-romantic *Götz von Berlichingen,* Bürger's *Lenore,* the writings of Tieck, and the revived German ballads with which he was so well acquainted.[8] But Scott's real rapport with this image was one of control and manipulation; he had toward it the fond feelings of the owner and master toward his land and dogs, not those of the piously awed descendant to the revered ancestor. Scott "acquired" the historical past much as he acquired Abbotsford—with genuine affection, but not with organic *désinvolture*. The past thus acquired had to serve him: it must be put often in incongruous positions; more then once it could stand for its very contrary: the threatening radical future. This paradoxical attitude is consistent with Scott's political *Weltanschauung*.

Scott's conservatism was of a reformist kind, closer in style to that of Louis Philippe than to that of Novalis or even De Maistre. He is socially a type often encountered after 1815: the upper-middle-class entrepreneur who "joins" the aristocracy on the basis of financial success. Both England and France knew this process. Later, T. S. Eliot was even going to praise it as the sign of a healthy society.[9] The only difference is that this time the gentrified bourgeois wizard had built his wealth on best-sellers, processing his own talent commercially. He does not acknowledge authorship among other things because he could thus praise his own work; privately, he was even able to disparage his own work and did not hesitate to say that to him prestige was indifferent and, one deduces, inferior to financial gain.[10] He knew when and how to give good advice about the commercial success of a literary journal; even as a voracious young reader he knew what to buy, and when, and what the uses of writing were; when visiting the Duke of Queensberry he liked best the change of the dungeon into a wine cellar; he loved the industrial-commercial side of printing and sought solutions to industrial conflicts.[11] Archibald Constable and Robert Cadell, his publishers, speak about him as they would about some raw material.[12]

By contrast his conservative feats or expressions are merely those of a solid reliable citizen. He is glad he is not living in 1745;[13] he cherishes a lock from King Charles I's head,[14] thinks of Napoleon as demonic (I, 367), gives militaristic advice (I, 281), plans to launch an anti-Jacobin paper (I, 689), brawls with Irish dissident students (I, 102), worries about protection when governments are changed, and is not beyond other politicking (I, 723; II, 359, 1102); he rants against parliamentary reform (II, 1157, 1164–66, 1178), and indulges in some monarchic flattery (I, 704). Perhaps Scott's only unsavory aspect is his readiness to take up arms for "law and order," for example, after "Peterloo," though even then he shows himself more of a populist than expected (I, 690, 694). Scott is fully himself when, in the introduction to the two *Tales*, he brings together characters and framework narrators from some *Waverley* novels and presents them as preparing a commercial and productive venture. Fiction and economy

serve here as referential images for each other; life and literature in-
tertwine in an exemplary manner.

The scheme of Scott's life is the scheme of his work. The transposi-
tion of systems of values or of the essence of such systems from one
kind of environment to another is always his main concern and his
main success. To convey this concern he resorts unabashedly in his
earlier novels to the capitalist metaphor of the lost inheritance and to
the treasure hunt. What is it that all characters in *The Antiquary* are
concerned with? It is the possession of the past (II, 1255) and the nature of that possession.[15] Dousterswivel wants a capitalistic-materialis-
tic possession, straight physical ownership. Oldbuck has a quite
different, much more sophisticated vision of what such a possession
should be like; sitting at the center of an idyllic little world: "You have
a competent and easy fortune—are generally respected—may, in your
own phrase, *vacare musis,* indulge yourself in the researches to which
your taste addicts you; you may form your own society without-
doors—and within you have the affectionate and sedulous attention of
the nearest relatives."[16] He is integrated into this world by exchange
and support: with the post office, with the provost and council, with
the mourning fishermen, but above all by correcting and aiding the
others—Sir Arthur Wardour repeatedly, but also Lovel and M'Intyre
in one direction, the women again in another; and he is certainly the
main factor in bringing Glenallan back into the mainstream of sociable
life. Oldbuck, the title hero (but then are not *all* the main characters
"antiquaries" in one sense or another?), wants to preserve this world,
and in order to preserve it he has to accumulate, to shore up his world
against incoming dangers and waves (it was he who saved the War-
dours and Lovel from the storming tide), to fortify its foundations.
The treasure is that strength of the past which should not be wasted.
Oldbuck's method of detecting and choosing it is rough and ready: su-
perstition is bad, historical tradition is good, as even Elspeth and Edie
know[17]—and that accounts ultimately for his comic pedantry—but
Oldbuck is just a mock-comic character. Sir Arthur Wardour is placed
between Dousterswivel (materialist and phantast-magician, scientific
and immoral, much like Irving Babbitt's worst apprehensions of romantic danger) and Oldbuck. Like Oldbuck, he tries to "shore up"
the present with the past, possession with inheritance, but like Dousterswivel he tries to do it by physical means: the "warden" and the
"ardour" present in his name never fuse, they remain in uneasy bal-

ance. Sir Arthur's ultimate salvation and preservation will come about through the marriage of his daughter with Glenallan's son, erstwhile Lovel, in a unification of the two central metaphors of *The Antiquary* (mirroring each other): search for treasure and search for family. Lovel is in a real sense Oldbuck's son, a son who is immediately recognized, wooed, saved from dangers, advised, befriended. Oldbuck recognizes in Neville, Eveline, whom he had loved and deserved. Thus Wardour does not serve Glenallan, nor vice versa, which would have been absurd—it is Oldbuck who takes over and props up both tottering houses. (And, incidentally, the sexually suspicious reader may ask himself whether the effete and depressive Glenallan was not cuckolded by a buck who twenty some years ago was far from old and who even at the time of the action enjoys pointed bantering with the girl whose "father in law" he is destined to be,[18] in other words, whether Lovel was the natural as well as the spiritual son of the antiquary.)

Thus the ironical reversal of the story and the final outcome of all the bustling antiquarian search is that the present (Oldbuck the moderate, the Burkean Whig) helps the past (the great houses), not the other way round. This is confirmed by the nature and adventures of the treasure itself: it does not belong to the past at all, but rather to the present; it comes from Lovel, and it is just disguised in romantic garb. Edie Ochiltree, the soul of the people, the man of the physical concrete, the custodian of common sense, the original Adam (his usually overlooked Christian name)—is in fact merely the handyman of Lovel and Oldbuck, their convenient and picturesque extension. Nature serves civilization.

But, after all, what are Oldbuck, Lovel, and perhaps Isabella Wardour fighting against? A close reading of this sly and tricky novel (yes, "comic" as Donald Davie says,[19] but with a kind of ominous and admonitory twist to its comicality) in the light of its conclusion can only show that the dangers being faced are those that undermine the continuity of the idyllic present: the navy of revolutionary France on a par with the rages of sea, the suspected incest of Glenallan on a par with Wardour's financial irresponsibility, M'Intyre's foolhardiness on a par with Dousterswivel's resort to the homeopathic terminology of Hahnemann.[20] And a combination of these features offers a recognizable, if distorted, picture of high romanticism, which of course we must complete with picturesque details, as well as with echoes such as the Hoffmannian dream of Lovel (Ch. 10), the Ofterdingen-like descent into the bowels of the earth (Ch. 21), the Tieck-like insert of Martin Waldeck's story (Ch. 18), the neo-Gothic castle on Griselda's head (Ch. 6), the grand ruins of Elspeth's mind (Ch. 28). In *The Antiquary* the idyllic world is constituted after the sane, compromising Augustan has overthrown the past-future excess (or potential excess) and after it has simultaneously severed the grand romantic vision from itself. The dialectics of value transfer is presented squarely, but with genuine concern for the complexities involved.

WE HAVE long known that there is in Scott's work a foreground level of imagery that epitomizes many of the text's meanings. Christabel Fiske in what probably remains the most conscientious analysis of imagery in Scott's novels proves quite conclusively that the "world-in-simile" is a simpler but more coherent and certainly self-sustaining universe, more pointedly oriented than the broader novel in which it is embedded. Her analyses indicate a level of reference constituted by the ancient Mediterranean epic. Elemental economic activities (farming, metal forging, stock breeding), landscapes such as sea, mountain, torrent, warriors attacking or repelling, and the horse and the dog all figure here.[21] Fiske's analysis seems to provide a very solid argument in favor of reading almost any novel by Scott warily, with an eye to hidden structures and motivating systems. We may want to expand Fiske's findings and assume that the text of the novel as a whole is a "world-in-simile," a simpler, self-sustaining, coherent illustration of the broadest system of meanings which really concern Scott.

Novel after novel is an exercise in the procedures of *value transfer;* they are experiments in the migration of essential values into the body of a new system of phenomena. The concern of the artist is to maintain continuity of soul when there is discontinuity of body. As we have seen by looking at *The Antiquary* or at *Waverley* (in Chapter 2 of this study), the rejection of romanticism is plain: there is no primeval paradise or natural sacredness to recapture; revolution is not the solution but the problem. Paradise is a continuing possibility and a disposition of growth, a world of healthy civility and social harmony. Scott in life (like many of his spokesmen in the novels) is quite ready to settle for Hanoverian compromise if, in some of its trappings, it will signal continuity with the Jacobite past. Contrasted with the text, this position appears not to be Hegelian tryadic progress but rather a subtle version of stagnant conservatism. Revolution is illness because it is growth by loss; meanwhile, restoration is simply growth by evenhanded exchange of elements. But as the exchange amounts to a neatly balanced sheet, there has been no real modification: look closely, Scott is telling us, and you will see that paradise regained is nothing but paradise maintained. Ivanhoe knows this, not Cedric; young Everard does, but not Sir Henry Lee (*Woodstock*); Henry Morton (*Old Mortality*) discovers it, when he decides that, as a character, he is closer to Burkean continuity than to the heroic solo; young Osbaldistone (*Rob Roy*) discovers it after his plunge into Highland intrigue and into Edinburgh's underground. Conversely, Cousin Rashleigh knows perfectly well how to unite in himself the reactionary aims of the north and the mercantile and mechanistic rapidity of mind of the south. (He is on the point, within a few short weeks, of taking over the whole business network of his uncle.) In Rashleigh, Scott discloses his deepest fears and animosities: the rugged monstrosities of the past are perhaps nothing but tokens for destructive agents of the present. Rashleigh stands for the acid fervency of romanticism, not less than for the utopian leveling of the Enlightenment. Both are equally dangerous deviations from the underlying construct of a harmonious paradise, with its slow motions. Preserving the past is dangerous, precisely because it is revolutionary. What has to be preserved is the axiological content of the past, not its external forms or sections.[22] The stark opposition between tradition and progress is dismissed, and so is the facile result of a mere synthesis. Compromise is not needed where there is continuity.

The bearer of the solution is indeed a "new man," much as Blake or Novalis would have demanded, but a "new man" who may legitimately claim continuity, a creature fusing reason and sensibility, Augustanism and romanticism (whether the old Gothic one or the new revolutionary one), the man who manages to maintain and repair a modest paradise. Not all Scott's novels hide their tracks as well as *Rob Roy,* where the excesses of the capitalist Enlightenment are fused with a romantic-irrational essence (Rashleigh), while Die Vernon acts in support of both reality and rationality by her opposition to Rashleigh. (She is an angel who cleanses paradise by acting from the inside, not from the outside, by subverting the romantic danger and substituting rationality at key points.) But *Rob Roy* shares with others the so-called passive hero, who somehow mysteriously turns out to be a carrier and product of regeneration.[23]

Certainly none of these heroes (Waverley, Frank Osbaldistone,

Lovell) is more passive than Darsie Latimer in *Redgauntlet*. Not only do his feelings for Herries (Ch. 4) closely resemble those of a flighty girl toward a brawny, gruff, husky male ("I could not help running mentally over the ancient heroes, to whom I might assimilate the noble form and countenance before me"—after he had "raised me in a trice to the croupe of his horse," where he is repeatedly thrown and pressed "on the shoulders of the athletic rider"), but he suffers the fate of many a Richardsonian and Radcliffean heroine: imprisonment, anxious waiting, and thin-voiced protest.[24] Indeed, he finds himself repeatedly dressed up as a girl when transported in the open.[25] Darsie's total passivity is driven home in so far as his fate is reified in the person of Redgauntlet, destiny in anthropomorphic shape. But even in this rather extreme case Darsie's passivity is, as F. R. Hart argues, "more akin to the wise passiveness, the mixture of alertness and somnolence, of creativity and openness, described by Wordsworth and Keats."[26] This seems confirmed by Lars Hartveit: "The drug-like effect of the most heroic moments in *Waverley* indicates that the hero moves about in a kind of trance" and "the heroic past of the hero is based on a dream."[27] This trancelike state, so close to romantic ecstasy and change is necessarily transitional, leading to the improved and higher state; it is not demeaning, but rather a sign of election; it prepares the hero and turns him into the solution maker. It is for Darsie's soul that the battle is being waged between contending forces. At the level of the action, if Darsie abandons his "cause," the battle is lost.

Redgauntlet is in many ways a *Bildungsroman,* something usually not noticed but true of many Scott novels (particularly *Rob Roy*). Hartveit correctly observes that *Redgauntlet* is full of people of no fixed abode, wandering and unstable, but admits that in the case of Alan Fairford "the pilgrimage is proof of his humanity."[28] It would be more apposite to say that it is the unfolding or actualization of his humanity, thus a true *Bildungsroman.* But Alan of course is only to some extent an independent character. He can be seen equally well as one with Darsie, as a part of the same hero (Frank Osbaldistone cut in two—sentiment and reason). Darsie's character and rationality have to be strengthened; Alan has to be improved in terms of experience (empirical sense perception) and sensitivity. And of course, in the end they *are* reunited, as one family, through Greenmantle (the opposition in name to Redgauntlet should also be noted).

Alan's own pilgrimage, though less dreamlike, has something oddly gliding about it: he is passed on mechanically from hand to hand until he reaches the still eye of the hurricane, the royal center of the counterorder (Ch. 17, p. 332). In the process, however, he realizes that his perceptions of life have been incomplete and discovers the picturesque, the variety, the diversity of human existence. Things had been "hidden" from him: the potential goodness of the Catholic minority (Ch. 16, pp. 322–323), smugglers, equivocating dissidents (Pate-in-Peril), vagabonds. This whole underground is symbolized by a literal descent into hidden chambers (Ch. 12, pp. 286–290). Both his and Darsie's pilgrimage are confrontations with romanticism. Redgauntlet stands for both the past and the present. He is a revolutionary, allied with the lower orders of society, an outlaw; at the same time he is an archaic figure, a curious rock formation of violence, of burdened heredity, fanaticism, cruelty, sterility, defeat, and horror. His is the volcanic outbreak of the primal substratum of instinct and naked power—he is more than historical, he is a geological force. Nanty Ewart is much like Hoffmann's Elis Fröbom, and the mazes remind us of all labyrinthine descents in literature as a *topos* (pp. 305–307, 290–292).[29]

But the essential point to be made is that Alan and Darsie's dreamlike adventure, which for them means transformation to a higher level of humanity, a filling up, is the outcome of a simultaneous *emptying* of the opposing camp. Alan and Darsie *absorb* into themselves the romantic substance of Redgauntlet and of his half-hearted allies and leave empty shells behind. The intensities of high romanticism become impossible: they have been neutralized into the broader idyll which is Hanoverian England. The comic aura of the Herries-Geddes conflict can be explained easily: it is not a real conflict, merely the cozy squabbling inside a societal idyll where right and wrong are mixed. And the device of a spurious historical episode pertains to the same strategy of unreality: Alan and Darsie reach a fuller reality by defeating a phantom, that is, an illusion or an illusory reality. They were looking for a treasure (inheritance, identity, love) and implemented a transfer of values—exactly as did the characters in *The Antiquary*. Paradise is maintained. The idyllic society is strong.

Last but not least, an observation on narrative mechanism which as much as anything else connects *Redgauntlet* to subsequent European historical novels. The rebellion breaks down not so much because Geddes and Fairford bring harmony and rationality into the turbid society at the inn (pp. 414–415), but rather because the Pretender categorically refuses to subordinate his individual and familial interests to the values of the community (pp. 414–420, 425–426). The Pretender thus subscribes to a basic rule of the idyllic world: the priority of small size. The England of the 1760s can remain a large idyllic world, because nobody *seeks* to create a large idyllic world.

I tried to show in Chapter 2 how Scott's novels transfer the scheme of visionary high romanticism from absolute consciousness or mythical truth into practical and limited situations (historical and political). In the pages above, an investigation of a few characters and situations has revealed, I believe, three things. First, Scott maintains the integrity of the paradigmatic romantic world even in the new reduced form. It is no mean achievement to institute (through the generic prototype of the historical novel) a new and rounded vision of the universe that is plausible. The second is that under these circumstances, that is, when the scope of the romantic expansion contracts dramatically, the idyllic model can serve as a substitute for "paradise." The third and most important is that the mechanism of phase succession becomes a complex dialectic of exchange, compromise, preservation, and renewal. The imposing, visionary, tripartite structure is subdivided into many small areas of negotiation, and yet the framework is somehow preserved intact. It is fascinating to trace in the further development of the historical novel how this solution in turn reveals itself as provisional and unstable.

THE FIRST "ominous" signs in a major work appear in Manzoni's *Betrothed.* There the relationship between large and small is already different and the balance between "to restore" and "to maintain" is clearly unstable. The similarities to Scott are great, as they may well be expected to be. Manzoni shares Scott's ideological background, and like Scott he has been the object of many puzzled or contradictory reactions.

Let me recall a recent polemic. Alberto Moravia (as well as Salvatore Battaglia) attacked Manzoni, saying that much of his work is the Catholic equivalent of what was later to be "realist socialism." To this, answers came from Carlo Emilio Gadda, Carlo Bo, and Enzo Noé Girardi among others, defending Manzoni as the author of a self-contained and aesthetically autonomous construct.[30] This dispute repeated in its way some conflicts of the Fascist period in Italy and, as a matter of fact, those times during the nineteenth century when, for instance,

the early attacks of Luigi Settembrini against the passivist and demo-
bilizing character of *I Promessi Sposi* appeared. His were severe words:
"un libro que loda i preti e i frati e consiglia pazienza, sommissione e
perdono" and also, ultimately, "la sommissione nella servitù, la nega-
zione della patria e di ogni generoso sentimento civile." It was followed by attacks from the opposed aestheticist camp.[31]

Such polemics have little intrinsic significance; they merely betray
an insufficiently historical thinking and a lack of dialectic understanding of Manzoni's subtle art of compromise. They stem from ignorance
of the deeper polarities sustaining the Biedermeier, a period which
more than any other finds coherence in the solidarity of its own contradictions. Naturally enough the leading novelists of the period—
Manzoni as well as Scott—were preoccupied with the theory and
practice of compromise.

In the case of Manzoni we usually notice the contradiction between
his political liberalism and his deeply felt spiritual conservatism, or
sometimes the opposition between the early, progressive, and Napoleonic Manzoni, and the later Catholic convert. One critic has argued
that the whole issue of Manzoni's Jansenism is moot, since it is an impression produced by the arbitrary combination of incompatible
facts.[32] There is, I think, a better way of formulating the reality of
ideological mixture. Antonio Rosmini, and particularly Vincenzo
Cuoco, Manzoni's foremost mentors, had provided him from the beginning with a moderate liberal and Christian combination that he
found attractive and epically useful. In addition we have ample documentation of the influence of Augustin Thierry, Claude Fauriel, and
even François Guizot on the Italian novelist, all ideologists of compromise in their way; the Jansenism of the converted Manzoni is homologous with the "racist" determinism (at that time, lest we forget, still a
left-wing doctrine) of some French sources.[33] Pessimism was the most
important consequence of the Jansenist connection; that is why the
defeated "race" of the *tiers état* was for Manzoni not an object of glorification (as for Thierry) but merely of compassion—and that is why he
seeks as a solution the "providential" (compromising) idyll. The mild
Catholicism of Manzoni's mentors and the liberal conservatism of his
contemporaries did nothing but reinforce the basic tenets Manzoni
had acquired in his young years in France from the late illuminist
ideologues who tended to consider values as being above the social
classes that carried them.[34] It is helpful, in my opinion, to identify the

Abbé Sieyès, M.J.A.N. Condorcet, P.J.G. Cabanis, and above all Destutt de Tracy, who mostly flourished during the Directory (1795–1802) and were connected with it, as representatives of the earliest European manifestation of a withdrawal from high romanticism.[35] This becomes more obvious if we take into account (as Simonini correctly does) the direct filiation between them and the generation "between Enlightenment and Restoration"—the Staëls, the Sismondis, the Benjamin Constants.[36] (In a Marxist mode, Simonini gathers that Renzo *must* end up as a small entrepreneur, because Manzoni seeks a refuge both from the old aristocracy of blood and from the riotous multitudes of the fourth estate.)[37] Manzoni's most natural environment is this early Biedermeier that had been growing in the very heart of high romanticism, modifying and tempering it. Adding Enlightenment ingredients was Manzoni's most important concern in his dealings with the romantic wave. A return to what had been progressive literary and philosophical values as a means of tempering the energies of high romanticism was for Manzoni, as for Scott, Austen, Pushkin, or even Metternich, a key strategy. Political contradictions arose, but they were secondary under the circumstances. Other analogies or influences are fused in this general mixture: even that of Voltaire for instance (comparisons with Heine and Musset have been proposed as to the intensity of that influence, and Renzo has often been compared to Candide), while the Catholicism of Manzoni must be measured against that of Chateaubriand and Lamennais.[38]

In the broadest sense, therefore, we can detect as many eighteenth-century "survivals" in Manzoni as in Scott. We have to understand them as Biedermeier recuperations of a past denied in theory or in practice by romanticism and revolution. Manzoni's work is an act of response to European culture with all its problems; it cannot be said for a moment to be based on his ignorance of contemporary trends. In typical Biedermeier (Metternichian) fashion he takes advantage of the ambiguous nature of yesteryear's progressivism to blunt present-day trends—and in this he is perhaps closest to Scott.[39] As has been said, Manzoni reacts to European literature as a whole: from Rousseau and Ann Radcliffe to August Wilhelm Schlegel and Schiller.[40] A very specific example of his way of "reacting" is his treatment of the "persecuted girl" motif which of course had grown from modest Richardsonian and Gothic beginnings to the lurid intensities of "Monk" Lewis, Diderot, and particularly Sade. Writers such as Victor

Hugo (for example, in the Esmeralda-Claude Frollo episodes of *Notre-Dame de Paris*) and Manzoni (in the Monaca di Monza episodes no less than in the pursuit and capture of Lucia by Rodrigo and the Innominato) preserve the framework of the motif with its structural positioning of characters and slyly take advantage of the readers' lurid expectations.[41] At the same time, they tone down the naked romantic violence of Sade and replace it with general disquisitions on psychological motives, social circumstances, ironic coincidences, moral choices, and the like. The stark outlines of act and scene are often lost in this undergrowth. Hugo, Manzoni, or others decide that changes in the outcome of the scenes are in order. We see Claude Frollo groveling at the feet of Esmeralda, and we see Lucia bravely and successfully resisting her persecutors.[42] Gertrude, the future abbess of Monza, submits to pressures, but the outcome is after all not disastrously unhappy; it is not infamy, vice, or humiliation, it is simply the realistic psychological warping, the complex, victorious though defeated Monaca di Monza. In effect the absolute is being diluted until it becomes relative and just vaguely poetic.

One more example, too well documented to warrant a detailed discussion here, is Manzoni's "classicist" bent. Formulas such as "romanticism as purified classicism" and "conversion of neoclassic poetics into romantics" have been bandied about. The influence of Virgil and Catullus has been noted.[43] All these observations merely point to a habitual aspect of writing in the Biedermeier age: classical aspects are no longer perceived as an opposition; they are either integrated and used, or they become the object of playful, manneristic refashioning. Manzoni recovers classical influences and rehabilitates them; he is not simplistically following age-old rules. Like Scott, he returns to the eighteenth-century world as much as he continues it. This explains why both authors were so decisively influential in the generation immediately following the publication of their books. (Manzoni's influence on writers outside Italy is often overlooked.)[44]

In a word, as Gianni Scalia demonstrates, Manzoni is not a *grande reazionario* in his views and philosophy, as is often still claimed, but merely a *grande borghese:* "Il suo compito e quello di mediare i contrari, non di bloccare il progresso."[45] To reach this conclusion Scalia shows that Manzoni's novel is predicated on a system of exchange of forms based in turn on a general equivalence of models and real data. For Manzoni social-historical reality *is* a system of exchange, and his method is an internalization of the capitalist processes, done with deliberate mastery. We do not have to follow Scalia in his conclusions regarding the ultimately static character of *The Betrothed* ("il borghese si pensa nella forma dell'essere e non del divenire, del divenire-altro") to appreciate his conclusions on the intentional circularity of Manzoni's structures, which are meant to depict a movement without change, contradiction absorbed by eternity, and the all-governing principle of mediation—between the natural and the historical as well as inside history itself.[46]

It is perhaps here that we come to the end of the striking structural and ideological similarities between Manzoni and Scott and start noting those differences which indicate how the Biedermeier historical novel was changing under the impact of its own internal logic, but also in keeping with the broader machinery of the culture as a whole. There are three main areas in which Manzoni takes the Biedermeier historical novel away from Scott and into a direction that was perhaps inevitable but also inevitably fatal to it. They are structure, the use of the idyll, and intentionality.

THE FIRST area is the structure of the novel. Scott pretends to play around with point of view, but he is not genuinely an experimentalist. The "author of Waverley," the different introductory characters, the historical notes at the end are sometimes more poetic ornaments (perhaps comparable to Eliot's notes to *The Waste Land*) or more likely, protective devices, means by which a layer of plausibility and credibility is placed around the central romantic or sensational narrative. In any case they remain purely external. Manzoni's procedure is different; he uses long historical, documentary chapters, ostensibly without any narrative adaptation. The reasons for introducing such "offensive" blocks of raw information are the same as in Victor Hugo and a score of other contemporary authors: hypertrophy of cause, the compulsive need (ideologically motivated) to present an ironclad explanation of the events.[47] But the stark, almost defiant presentation of historical documentation and description seems curious until one realizes that it is in fact a writing strategy. In his very thorough works, Fausto Nicolini has shown that, at least in some shape, the anointers had been historical reality, suspects with a repugnant moral figure, while their judges were fair and well-intentioned individuals, not profiteers of public hysteria; Manzoni changed not only the interpretation, but also deformed some facts to fit his prejudgments.[48] Similar defor-mations from a medical point of view are detected by Michele Mazi-telli who shows that Manzoni repeatedly applies nineteenth-century epidemiological information to seventeenth-century situations.[49] Thus we have to return to an observation as old as De Sanctis's, that the du-ality in Manzoni (poetry versus documentation) is less important than the unity of impact on the audience.[50] I want to go even farther and maintain that in *I Promessi Sposi* the documentation is almost com-pletely absorbed and turned into a necessary aesthetic element. It is aesthetically effective because it does no more than masquerade as documentation; we have to regard these chapters as large images de-noting the power of abstract and unseen forces, as well as the meshing of rationality and absurdity. Of such decadent (indeed expressionist-sounding) daring, Scott was incapable, and that is perhaps the real reason why Lukács suspected Manzoni of "provinciality"; he smelled antimimetic heresy.[51] Scott's historical documentation was evenly spaced out as part of the texture, while the occasional notes are like whimsical afterthoughts and adornments. Manzoni actually uses docu-mentation as a building block, even though it is in fact a carefully pro-cessed documentation (something the reader does not normally find out). There is in this respect from Scott to Manzoni a decrease in fic-tionality and representation, as well as an increase in theoretical ab-straction. Even more important, there is a little less confidence in Manzoni than in Scott of the writer's ability to make the two sides co-here. The seeds of the historical novel's generic disintegration are al-ready sown.

The second is the idyllic circularity. In spite of voices to the con-trary,[52] there can be little doubt that the construction of Manzoni's novel is meant to suggest that stalling an idyllic process will lead to confusion, agonizing quest, and destruction. The idyllic normality of the mating of two young peasants is interrupted by outside forces: this leads to huge disturbances not merely in their life, but in everwidening circles in the life of the village and the country. Only when, after a long detour they are reunited again is the world too set at rest, or at least it regains a kind of precarious balance. Meanwhile the novelist provides severe punishment for those guilty of the sin of unjoining. But the important observation here is the *pointlessness* of the whole ex-ercise. Renzo's adventures do not represent an expiation or purifica-tion: there is nothing of which he was culpable. Nor are they really a process of growth, at least not one that would have been indispensable.

Renzo is neither wiser nor more mature at the end—he is merely more cunning or more knowledgeable; his learning has been rather Pavlovian and mechanical. Experience is exposed as futility and sham—hence the rather unusual wry humor at the end of the novel: the author is not (and the reader should not be) taken in by Renzo's naive boasting and storytelling.[53] Lucia similarly had nothing to gain from her expedition; she may have proved herself capable of sacrifice, open to spiritual experience, courageous, and noble, but none of these did she gain as a result of her misadventures. Others may have won or lost something, but they were not part of the opening and closing structure of the idyll. The main exception is Don Rodrigo, who was instrumental in hindering the idyllic process. His destruction indicates that in Manzoni's opinion, there is a tremendous energy hidden in idyllic inertia—interfering with it may lead to total destruction. The difference from Scott is obvious and striking. Scott's novels are novels of growth and synthesis, Manzoni advances toward circularity and analysis. Scott is an advocate and illustrator of compromise, but Manzoni never believes that compromise is a process of becoming: it is or it is not. The idyll is powerful enough to simply *be*, it does not need manipulations.

Mediation of course brings to mind the figure of Don Abbondio. Some have claimed that he should be seen as a central figure in the novel. Angelandrea Zottoli argues that Don Abbondio was for Manzoni "la volpe nascosta sotto le vesti."[54] She says that Don Abbondio embodies the spirit of empirical realism, of crafty calculation, of earthy common sense. Neither cowardly nor stupid, this man of arithmetic (p. 72) who is neither just nor truly unjust is the hypothetical person whom Manzoni had tried to persuade in his essay on Catholic morals: the one who would be efficiently good in a good world, and whose failings are a judgment on the one in which he lives at present. Manzoni is reconciled with him in the end, indeed he admits Don Abbondio to a kind of coauthorship (p. 130).

Perhaps it is more revealing to say that we are faced here with a personification of the good-natured inertia of matter. The author's love-hate relationship with the prelate defines better than anything else the transitional place of Manzoni in the historical novel of later romanticism. On the one hand Manzoni has a powerful and harmonious vision of order and justice (which Goudet who makes this argument, calls "Catholic," but which should with more historical accuracy be called "high romantic"[55]); on the other hand, Goudet argues,

Manzoni recognizes that his vision is incompatible with the actual state of society and the universe (Biedermeier disappointment)—the outcome being disillusioned humor (p. 496), the anxieties of the landscape (pp. 503–18), or the sadness of secondary characters—"promenades aux bords de l'angoisse" (p. 575). But when all is said and done, and this *must* be seen as Manzoni's answer (or else nothing is—which, in turn, would confirm, not disprove our argument here), a relative compromise has to be achieved as symbolized in the idyllic marriage of the more spiritual "light-filled" Lucia and the more instinctual-material Renzo. Don Abbondio should by rights reinforce this trend, he should be part of the final harmony and herald or illustrate the solution; he should be the ecclesiastic counterpart of the realm of the possible which—the reader has every right to assume—Renzo and Lucia are trying to set up. Instead he is the first to wriggle his way out of it and set road blocks for those who want to come in. Don Abbondio is the unmediating mediator. Manzoni seems bent upon proving that the historical compromise of the Biedermeier is a paltry and unsatisfactory business at its best, and he chooses Don Abbondio to make his point.

We can therefore discover in *I Promessi Sposi* (and this is the third area of difference from Scott) an ambiguity grafted upon an ambiguity: it is a historical novel that is ambiguous about the ambiguous tradition it represents. Scott knew how to foster a sturdy, cheerful ambiguity—in the reader, certainly, but perhaps also in his own heart. Manzoni has serious doubts about whether the idyllic synthesis is feasible or desirable. Underneath the pretended unity and simplicity of the novel, there is a multiplicity of narrators and angles, some inside the text, others outside it, some of the type of the omniscient narrator, others simply "il narratore sentenzioso."[56] This multiplicity is explained and imposed by the beginning decay of the vehicle chosen.

As mentioned before, Moravia accuses Manzoni of being a precursor of "socialist realism." If this accusation has any meaning at all, then it is only in the sense that he resolutely opts for *psychomachia* over pedestrian realism in his manner of writing. Manzoni abandons Scott's checks and balances in favor of a deceptive but consistent use of objects for overall purposes and ironic combinations. Giuseppe Raimondi documented how details (sometimes raw and naked) "sono risucchiati nell'aria e nello stile della composizione."[57] The favorite object of scrutiny for such distortive strategies has always been the famous episode of Renzo's vineyard (in Chapter 34 as the young man returns to his village, searching for Lucia) which was seen as a masterful mixture of order and disorder—an emblem for the state of a deidyllized Italy. A little known but delicate and precise study by Gina Alani speaks of "compenetrazione estetica e etica"[58] and provides additional examples: the sun always appears indirectly in the story, through light reflexes (p. 12), space expands as the novel proceeds (pp. 20–21). Also, some main characters are just crystallized outcomes of the flowing and turning action.[59] Even more obvious (perhaps too obvious) are the descriptions of the lofty, gloomy, and dangerous lairs of the robber knights Don Rodrigo (Ch. 5) and the Innominato (Ch. 20):

> Il castello dell'innominato era a cavaliere a una valle angusta e uggiosa, sulla cima d'un poggio che sporge in fuori da un'aspra giogaia di monti, ed è, non si saprebbe dir bene, se congiunto ad essa o separatone, da un mucchio di massi e di dirupi, e da un andirivieni di tane e di precipizi, che si prolungano anche dalle due parti ... Dall'alto del castellacio, come l'aquila dal suo nido insanguinato, il selvaggio signore dominava all'intorno tutto lo spazio dove piede d'uomo potesse posarsi.[60]

These are clusters of high-romantic signals, not photographs of actual landscapes. They stand here in order to be defeated. The heart of the Unnamed may well be softened by Cardinal Federigo, but its true defeat comes at the hands of such as Don Abbondio, with the Perpetuas and Agneses in his train who invade and domesticate the castle. Their idyllic dowry is quite plain. We recognize it in the last nostalgic glances (end of Ch. 8) cast by Lucia toward the land of her birth, much like those of Teufelsdröckh in *Sartor Resartus;* we recognize it in the homely meal offered by the good tailor to Don Abbondio and his companions (Ch. 30); we recognize it even in the old-fashioned irony of the framework voices. The castles will be swamped.

Some of the elements mentioned before (the manipulation of historical data, the bending or softening of situations from Sade or Chateaubriand, the uses of tradition) are examples of broader devices that exemplify psychomachia. They reinforce the conclusions above and allow us to see *I Promessi Sposi* as a high-water mark in the Biedermeier historical novel, owing to its nimble subtlety and resourcefulness in grasping for compensatory devices. At the same time these elements reveal the crisis of the vehicle itself.

Scott was under the direct influence of the regenerative vision of high romanticism. He affirmed, by and through his novels, that a fusion of reason and sensibility would be a convenient substitute for the new paradisial humanity of the early romantics. He believed that the process of growth in that direction was shaped by the high-romantic paradigm, though embedded in empirical history. He clearly believed that a societal idyll with its moderation, imperfect harmony, rational compromise and continuity of values could serve as a substitute for a recaptured paradise, a kind of practical paradise as it were. He thought that all these processes grew out of narrativity as an expression of the nature of things. Manzoni's novel reveals a loss of confidence in narrativity, in the idyll, in organic progress and, in the feasibility of compromise—but not a radical loss of confidence. The ambiguity imposes some authorial manipulation, but not the resort to decadent formalism that Stifter's or Flaubert's deeper doubts were soon to require.

Where Scott had achieved the taming of high romanticism and its compromise with the world in the contents of the novel, Manzoni does so only in the form, that is, in his own manner of writing. The shaper of reality is no longer the character, it is the writer. Miraculously, the unity of natural law still holds in the midst of the diversity of objects—but it does so only because (be it said without ethical invidiousness) Manzoni is cheating. By a deft sleight-of-hand he conceals his own disarray; the melancholy of the novel is the melancholy of the author's doubts and of his uncertainty about the truth.

ADALBERT STIFTER, who is often considered the embodiment of the Biedermeier or its grand master, is in fact the one who signs its death warrant. He represents the breakdown of later romanticism, the admission that solutions have to be sought in other ways and in other directions. Nowhere is this seen better than in *Witiko*, Stifter's last major completed work, a historical novel whose action is placed in twelfth-century Bohemia. However, since this work comes at the end of Stifter's development (and is often overlooked by readers and critics alike), it may be useful to make a few comments on the meaning of his work as a whole and perhaps in the process to correct some widely held misapprehensions.

Stifter was not merely imbued with Biedermeier ideology—he was, if one may say so, a Biedermeier personality, that is, a deeply neurotic and insecure person who needed a stabilizing and pacifying world view as an auxiliary construction. Lamb and Mörike represent this pathological type who resorts to cultural remedies; Gogol does, too, though in a different way. Stifter conceded defeat by committing suicide, but only after a long and valiant struggle to exorcise the demons of chaos and unsettled existence.[61] His work, the testimony of this struggle, is a lucidly, purposefully erected set of ramparts. This point needs emphasizing because often he is tacitly assumed to be the spontaneous producer of soothing beauty and stylistic sophistication, a nostalgic peasant, the Robert Burns of marmoreal description. An attentive reading proves otherwise.

For one thing, unlike Scott or to a certain extent Manzoni, Stifter did not "invent" the Biedermeier, did not combine originally romantic and Enlightenment views; rather, he drew from an already constituted, almost formalized, Biedermeier ideology, as provided by Metternich's constitutional and ethical system. He was not satisfied with it and sought an even broader support for his construction of serenity. This he found in the Leibnizian teachings as streamlined by Benedictine and other Catholic sources. The harmonious universality that could be inferred or constructed from Leibnizian traditions was popular in Austrian culture and constituted the raw material for many a philosophic system. In fact both the first and the second half of the nineteenth century in Austria and in Bohemia were strewn with attempts to adapt Leibniz's philosophy to an ethics of the whole and to economic or juridical versions of the law of harmony between nature and society.[62] Stifter was influenced by Justus Möser, a very thoughtful idyllist sociologist.[63] Other influences worked in the same direction. His use of biblical, Homeric, and *Nibelungen* elements shows that more than others he intentionally resorted to epic and dignifying processes.[64] He chose with exact precision from the preceding generation those works and ideas that could be of use to him: the elder Brentano, the Olympian side of Goethe. Stifter knew, admired, and respected Scott, as some famous quotations in his letters show. He admired particularly *Old Mortality* because of its understanding of the psychology of large groups and communities. Connections with Manzoni have been observed, though rarely.[65] Jean Paul remains perhaps the only sprightly, intriguing, and impish influence on Stifter.

There is already in the earliest works of Stifter something deliberate and relentless in his insistence on peace, order, and harmony. As a result of the romantic onslaught, the idyllic model is used after 1815–1820 either ironically or didactically. In Stifter the didacticism is overwhelming, offered with massive insistence. His confidence correctly summarizes the Olympian age of the bourgeoisie—an age to which Flaubert, in a quite different manner, also belonged.[66] We must conclude that Stifter, like Scott and Manzoni, is a "grande borghese," and by no means a feudal or reactionary type.[67] In *Nachsommer* Freiherr Risach, who comes closest to being a character paragon is modeled after Andreas Freiherr of Baumgartner (1793–1865), a self-made man of modest origin, a managerial technocrat who was professor of physics, president of the Academy of Science, and member of the cabinet as secretary of departments such as Public Works and Commerce. Stifter himself, to the extent to which he was politically and socially active, was a paleo-liberal rather than a pugnacious neoconservative. In his stories tradition, property, and *Heimat* are ultimately subordinated to the freedom and growth of the individual person. A close analysis of his proposed and rejected *Schullesbuch* reveals it devoid of the nationalistic and *linientreu*-dynastic overtones of similar works of the time, devoid even of an orthodox religious dimension.[68] To Freiherr von Helfert, the Undersecretary for Education who rejected Stifter's project and was an admirer of Russian Czarist administrative methods, Stifter seemed a liberal, almost a revolutionary, and his mistrust and distaste can still be felt in his memoirs, written seventeen years after Stifter's death and over a quarter of a century after the aborted textbook affair.[69] Stifter should not be measured against some late twentieth-century standards but rather placed in the context of his own time. Of course, Stifter looked upon 1848 as an unmitigated disaster, but he repeatedly had words of severe blame and contempt for "all das Bubenhafte, das in unseren äusseren Zuständen ist" and he tended to place at the same level "Zügellosigkeit, Despotie and Reaction."[70] Some recent critics go so far as to see in him a left-liberal.[71] Ranzoni, an admiring disciple, reports Stifter's empathetic understanding of Robespierre.[72] This may or may not be relevant. It is certainly part of a broader liberal philosophy, generous and harmonious at the same time. The cornerstone of this practical philosophy was "Bildung," a belated echo of the Enlightenment, and "Mässigung"[73]—a direct application of harmony to the bourgeois system, under which an upper class has a marginal presence and is saddled with serious duties.

The centerpiece of Stifter's machinery for rebuilding the Biedermeier is a pedagogically tinged neoclassicism. Stifter's judgments on the artists of the day and his activities as an art critic illustrate well how tenuous and bothersome the attempt to reconcile Biedermeier values with the academic mannerism of the day must have become.[74] His preferences were equally for classical tradition, baroque architecture and furniture, and naturalism in painting. His own painting moves from an early romanticized classicism (*Vedutenmalerei*) to moralized symbolism, sometimes with preimpressionist touches.[75] It is not as if Stifter's work as a plastician were of any aesthetic value. Nevertheless, to the extent to which we accept the consistency of Stifter's personal tendencies, we may say that we have, in a small and grosser fashion, the outlines of the work as a whole. Stifter appears by this token almost as a fake Biedermeier author. Even in his early work, even in *Nachsommer*, his compromise is no longer chiefly between romantic and Enlightenment, but rather between Biedermeier and Victorian. His Biedermeier world is recognizably aesthetic and manneristic in a way that removes it sharply from Mörike and Immermann, Scott and Austen. Stifter is groping. He is tentative, artificial, and insecure—closer to a *fin de siècle* decadent than to a Biedermeier stalwart. Because he distrusts the validity of this body of ideas, as a compensation he affirms it loudly in a challenging and dandyish manner.

To take Stifter's didactic proclamations at face value is regarded as kitschy even by many of his greatest admirers. To polemicize with Stifter's so-called harmonious *Weltanschauung* strikes me by the same token as faintly ludicrous. Thus, Horst Albert Glaser will rant about "Rentnerutopie," "Pensionopolis," about the coldness of love as an index to the impotence of society, complaining resentfully (and correctly) that the novel is shot through with the ideology of legitimate bourgeois property rights.[76] It is not as if Glaser were mistaken about the mixture of slyness and truth in the utopian imagery in *Nachsommer* or the bourgeois confidence of Biedermeier rationality. But the level of truth at which these statements or others such as "die restaurative Utopie ... will den Kapitalismus, aber nicht den der Klassengegensätze" function[77] is the same as that of Nadler summarizing the usual points about organicism, personality, tradition, nature, moral duties, and social integration or Günther Müller presenting Stifter as the bard of pure Catholicism;[78] it is the same level at which Konrad Steffen praises Stifter for having offered us "Heimat als Erlebnisform des Hierarchiegedankens"—the retrospective depiction of durability, natural regularity, ordering custom, *Ordnungsgemeinschaft*, and the unifying patterns of ecclesiastical centers.[79] At the level we are talking about, Friedrich Hebbel could easily call Stifter "a comma in evening dress" ("Das Komma im Frack,"), while Emil Kuh was able to summarize as early as 1868 in a reasoned and persuasive way most of the later arguments deriding the author's "gläubige Zufriedenheit mit Welt und Leben."[80] With equal justification Hermann Kunisch explains to us how the big and the small are connected by Stifter and unified as "das Göttliche im Gewande des Reizes." Kunisch agrees with Lukács or Glaser, but he gives a positive appreciation (from a Guardinian point of view) to his findings.[81]

Examples of the same kind could be freely multiplied, but this line of research is entirely unproductive. Any serious research on Stifter must start from an entirely different point; it must come to terms with the paradoxical ability of his works to combine gross didacticism with the voluptuous weltering in seas of natural sensation.[82] The answer can possibly come only by looking at Stifter as part of a morpho-historical sequence. In doing so we will do well to keep in mind the frameworks just mentioned: Stifter's political-ideological moderation, his deliberate choice of influences, the manneristic boundaries that he drew for himself. These interact practically in his work and determine its general direction.

One of Stifter's key, stealthy, strategic moves was the repeated replacement of the settled peace of the idyllic with the grander structures of ideal meaning. In *Nachsommer* the peace of the concrete and the peace of the abstract are often presented as interchangeable. Thus when the "Marmorgestalt" offers to Heinrich Drendorf "the aesthetic vision of a fundamental reality" this is both a victory and a defeat.[83] The idyll (an aesthetic construct) recognizes itself as an aesthetic construct and loses its creative ambiguity (which even the ironic idyll still preserved). It becomes openly aesthetic, but also can and does remain didactic; because it has turned Victorian on the way to modernism. Manzoni was using documentary material for aesthetic purposes. Stifter turns even the pseudo-documentary convention of the idyll into purely aesthetic material.

Every Biedermeier writer, as we have seen, is dominated by the vision and memory of the high-romantic paradigm and, at the same time, seeks some means by which to conciliate it with the earthly or scruffy realities of everyday life. Stifter pretends to repeat this procedure, to show the *Weltplan* in action, to offer a plausible idyllic world. But he no longer believes even in the acrobatic implementation of a

Manzoni. The impossibility carries with it much tension, suffering, nostalgia, hopefulness, and anxiety, as I will explain later—but it also has a tremendous liberating effect. Stifter can use the materials of sensory and social perception in a totally arbitrary fashion, according to resolutely aesthetic decisions which the reader himself can then freely interpret didactically. His aesthetic harmony can be total because he has lost totally the grip on *real* becoming. He no longer trusts the manipulative capacity of his own art and therefore transfers his field of action onto a different level. I will illustrate this convoluted failure and creation by three instances: Stifter's treatment of nature and space, Stifter's concept and handling of *Dinge* (objects, things), and Stifter's attitude toward style, already mentioned in passing.

For a writer who is popularly so admired for his nature feelings and in whose work material descriptions seem so frequent, Stifter is oddly ambiguous toward nature. His nature is definitely not the nature—all-embracing, all-life-giving, beyond good and evil—of the romantics, the unifying force of God and consciousness. It is first of all, as it is for every Biedermeier writer, an exterior object, something with which dual relationships can be established (an attitude different from that of Wordsworth or Chateaubriand). Moreover the implication that nature is dangerous and has to be kept in bounds (*gezähmt*) is never absent.[84] That is why descriptions have to fuse the elemental and pure with the artificial (socially controlled) in nature. Hills and vales are covered with orchards and plowed fields, gardens play an important part, and, most significantly, the very disposition and make-up of the mountain forests betray human intervention. The spirit of the park prevails even in the remote *Waldeinsamkeit*. Gardens are the models and centers of Stifterian landscapes. But the effects of human activity are more often than not perceived without an actual human presence. Indeed even animal life is rarely indicated, and traces of any Darwinian competition seem carefully expunged.[85] The ensuing emptiness and stillness signify fear and anxiety, but they also connote geometrical perfection. (Stifter's nature is often like a cityscape by Giorgio De Chirico: the abandoned battlefield of action, hope, and passion.) Its full meaning is disclosed only in connection with its geological dimension: biology is surface, a latecomer in the economy of the world, not close enough to the Prime Mover. In *Nachsommer* the geological metaphor (a joy for Novalis, a danger for Hoffmann) replaces the biological one.[86] Cause becomes a noble, saving category; revolution can be absorbed in a broader, almost predivine unity.

The contradiction in Stifter's perception and estimation of space becomes plain if we consider the relation between limits and their transgression. Stifter's work is full of mighty wanderers, of individuals who, much like characters in a Wordsworthian poem, traverse huge distances, observe avidly, and take into possession through all senses sizable chunks of the world.[87] Simultaneously Stifter indicates his respect for borders and sees encroachment of spatial rights as a major crime, obscurely undermining the whole world order.[88] Christine Wohlbrandt explains some of the mechanisms of this compatibility-incompatibility. She says that (particularly in later works) Stifter resorts to a hierarchical and concentric spatial organization.[89] There is an extreme outer limit of chaos and danger, instability, death, and muteness, represented by the steppe or by the highest mountains. Only inside this do we encounter the known, steady nature loosely shaped by man (for example, the *Hochwald,* or even more so the plastically shaped area of agriculture—the area where earth has been given a face and healed). Inside this are home and garden, protected, well-built, proof of maturity and weight. And then, finally the reified man—a sacred and inviolable space; there, disorder expresses lack of love (*Der Hagestolz*). Hence *Wandern* is the contemplation of microspace, the knowledge of one's limiting horizon, and, in turn *Reisen* is ordering one's interior, healing by subjecting oneself to the vast rhythms of macrospace organization: the interior is reordered by beginning to vibrate.[90] This is a good example of how Stifter overcomes in an aesthetic direction a purely practical incompatibility and probably also indicates in what sense he himself (as opposed to many of his readers) would consider didacticism still feasible.

This impression is strengthened by the specific attitude toward objects in most of the Austrian master's stories. "Stillstehen, Zeigen und Nennen: diese drei gehören für Stifter wesentlich zusammen" (in *Witiko,* in *Granit,* in *Nachsommer,* as well as in *Der Waldsteig*), one critic observed.[91] The favorite goal of the "monumental" wanderers seems to be rest on a bank or a large rock. Observation leads to precise naming, to a stabilized world of separate units. Many readers have noticed the peculiar uses of the term *Ding* by Stifter. Stylistic analyses have shown that it can replace whole series of nouns and is used in many new combinations such as *Pelzdinge, Wurfdinge, Kletterdinge,* and a dozen others. Such a stylistic analysis catches both the late-Biedermeier contradiction of Stifter and its solution (outside the Biedermeier): the divine, not human, measure is placed in the center of the universe, yet this divine standard finds its symbol in the world of objects, in the landscape.[92] It may be said that *Ding* acquires an almost magical value—it expresses a search for essentiality, reality, truth (that is, large-scale structures) which might somehow still be embodied in immediate and palpable entities. Such a use of *Ding* is in fact not limited to one writer, we find it even in the writings of Metternich.[93] In a sense, the attempt was doomed to failure. Biedermeier was coming full circle back to the dilemmas of high-romantic fusion, which it had been set up to solve. It was losing its ability to compromise, but was predictably still unable (or less able than ever) to employ earthly dust for starbound perfection.

At the microstylistic level this is seen in the victory of "decadent" paratactic over integrating hypotactic structures, in the victory of mere juxtaposition and addition over combination and building. Hans Wysling enumerates among the most important features the lack of antithesis; Stifter speaks at best of "einige—andere," not "die einigen—die anderen"), substitution of seriality for relation, preference for retention over tension. He also notes that Stifter generally avoids connectives such as "und, auch, aber, doch, je, sogar" between his sentences, that is, most connectives which might make for flowing transitions.[94] It has even been argued that in concentrating on *Sammeln und Hegen,* Stifter leaves the Biedermeier altogether.[95] To concede this would mean accepting a somewhat limiting view of the Biedermeier; rather, Stifter actualizes all its potentialities and thus achieves its *Überwindung* by showing its limitations and drawbacks as well as the directions of its future development. The concern for objects, for miniatures and gathering, becomes an actual phenomenological obsession with intrinsic things, with basic models of simple life ("Grundformen des einfachen Lebens") and points toward reality as essentiality.

This paradoxical simplification is seen in broader stylistic categories and preferences, too. Stifter's option for classical shapes, in the Goethean sense of the word, may seem obvious in the earlier phase of his writing, and its emblem is the famous "Marmorbild" in *Nachsommer,* a piece of Thorwaldsen bordering on the kitschy. To understand such an academic mode we have to place it in the context of later writings, which explain Stifter's purposes retrospectively. It is perhaps not literally correct to say that in Stifter's mature work the world becomes more colorless, is drained of light and brilliance, that a lovely world of beauty is replaced by a rigid world or regularities, that the grandiose replaces the pleasant.[96] Nevertheless, such formulations summarize well some very early intuitions or observations. In the 1860s critics had already begun to speak about Stifter's prehistoric and fossil style, paradisial syntax, or even, with more malice, about regression in artistic barbarity and appearing *en negligée* in the parlors of art; one of them pointed disparagingly to parallels with a certain Belgian school of painters which stiffly, lifelessly imitates Van Eyck and Memling, and another at about the same time sensed primitivistic biblical imitation and chronicle faddishness.[97] With the hindsight of over a century we can associate Stifter's style with the later D. G. Rossetti and Burne-Jones, or with the slightly earlier Ph. O. Runge, with the Pre-Raphaelites and their contemporaries all over Europe. Large areas of speculation are open for those who want to proclaim this style a predecessor to *Jugendstil* or even *Neue Sachlichkeit.* Closer to literary relations, we shall concur with Hohoff when he says that: "Die gewollte Naivität des *Witiko* entspringt der philologischen Romantik," that is, it is the outcome of the reading of Palacký or Raumer as much as of Homer and the Bible.[98] In practice this results in an almost total lack of psychological motivation of characters in *Witiko,* where everything is figural, scenic, and linear-ornamental. Lack of psychology and ritual repetition are used by Stifter to release the potential which had been protected and restrained and hidden by a misleading classicist facade in the earlier works. Polysyndeton, replacement of full verbs by *sein/werden,* and symmetries are just some of the devices used to signal perennity.[99] The dissection of simple everyday gestures to achieve an air of festivity goes, in my opinion, well beyond pedantry. It is in fact the best example of the manner in which Stifter hopes to transcend the opposition between aesthetic and didactic purposes, between dilettantic and mercenary impulses.

An analysis of Stifter's stylistic tendencies, or even of his expression of nature, therefore shows as a central feature of his work the abandonment of Biedermeier and a return to the starker outlines of early romanticism, mythical and abstract at the same time, simplified and visionary. However, such are the inevitable connections of literary existence that a regression from a "sentimental" to a "naive" type of romanticism was not directly possible. It needed the mediations of nostalgia and, ultimately, a prescriptive artifice. In resorting to these,

Stifter's work becomes of course quite different from that of the early romantics and quite similar to that of modernist mannerists from Barbey d'Aurevilly to Paul Ernst. The capture of the elementary carries its own dangers: the essential can easily become abstract or pseudo-naive decoration.

IF THE ABOVE description of Stifter's literary makeup is at all correct, then the key position of his lone historical novel must become immediately apparent. Far from being an afterthought, a belated epilog to an already closed canon, it was the point toward which the works of that canon had been directed all along, the logical outcome of an entire evolution. This is by no means a value judgment, and in turn it does not disqualify the novel from an inclusion in a European as opposed to a merely personal pattern.

Although the character of Witiko is invented, the story gave a historically careful description of twelfth-century Bohemia. Stifter conscientiously studied histories and chronicles and was painstakingly exact in noting the geographical route of the young man who rises from relatively modest circumstances (though he had distinguished forebears) to a position of leadership and begins an aristocratic line.[100] Thus *Witiko* would seem a novel of tradition seen from its beginning, not its end.[101] While partially true, this impression would not establish the interest or the originality of the novel. Throughout the nineteenth century, all the way to Conrad, the future or progress is seen as an orderly continuation of the present with mostly quantitative changes. Stifter is adept at sliding back and forth along the line of progress, smoothly substituting past, present, and future. *Witiko*—tradition "in progress," in movement—mixed up past, present, and future in ways which infuriated even some conservative critics who found the assemblies of Bohemian noblemen too reminiscent of parliamentary democracy.[102] In Scott's novels we see at work a precise and well-oiled machine for switching past and present. In Stifter the mixture of temporal meanings is deliberate and announces the loss of hope. The purpose is here to achieve totalization, that is, synthesize past, present, and future into a kind of permanence. The narrative resumptions strive to turn each episode into a kind of Leibnizian monad, reflecting the whole in a formalized unit.

Totalization is the operative term here—it replaces compromise almost entirely and points to a return (from a different direction) to high-romantic ambitions. But there is an ominous difference this time. The gap between the secular and the divine, or the everyday and the absolute, can apparently no longer be closed by compromise as it was in the Biedermeier age. The arbitrary and defiant aestheticist freedom of the earlier work is itself no longer satisfactory. Even less acceptable is the powerful vision of high romanticism: the paradigm of transfiguration *happening,* just happening without artful manipulation. Therefore *Witiko,* a masterpiece of despair, decides for its readers that the paradigm of order and perfection must be *imposed.* We might conceivably agree that a Stifterian corpus, excluding *Witiko,* must abandon excessive mobility as a sacrifice—if it wishes to be "vollkommen gewordenes Leben das sich überwunden hat, ohne den eigenen Übergangswert zu leugnen," a sophisticated ideal to which Scott might still have subscribed.[103] *Witiko* changed all that and probably changed by implication the makeup of the corpus as a whole. It represented the departure from the crucial view "dass sich Gemeinschaft nicht organisieren lässt, sondern organisch wachsen muss wie ein Garten," that is, the idyllic view, and its replacement by aggression and open didacticism.[104] We are leaving the realm of freedom and entering the realm of necessity; we are moving from a "naive" to a "sentimental" Biedermeier. As in *Nachsommer,* in *Witiko* the author knows all along, and the alert reader senses, that the order and stability postulated as natural are impossible, and hence artificial. An almost cynical complicity is thus established which gives a perverse tang to the texts.

Stifter himself in his private statements exposed frankly why and how the chrysalis of "das sanfte Gesetz" turns into the black butterfly of "das harte Gesetz." Thus he wrote to Heckenast in a letter of April 10, 1860, about "die schreckliche Majestät des Sittengesetzes welches die hohen Frevler . . . zerschmettert, und ihre Gewaltpläne wie Halme nickt."[105] By the time he finished the novel, he owned up to his hope that the work would make the Germans "etwas körniger und höher" as a matter of civic duty.[106] Much like Vigny he claims that he would prefer wolves and elephants to the human race were it not for "savior" individuals, for Isaiah's remnant, so to speak. He says "weil die gegenwärtige Weltlage Schwäche ist, flüchte ich zur Stärke und dichte starke Menschen und das stärkt mich selber."[107] We hear again Hermann's martial tones proclaiming that action will permeate and transform a structure of compromise that can no longer sustain itself.

It is by no means surprising that some twentieth-century activists felt they could convert for their own ideological purposes the conclusions of *Witiko*. Of course, racism and nationalism could not by any stretch of the imagination be read into a text which is abundantly contemptuous of the difference between Czechs, Germans, and so on.[108] On the other hand, it was enthusiastically praised as a rejection of liberal individualism and description of the rise of a line of leaders from the seed of an old, legitimate, and tried source[109] or because it deals with the growth and becoming of a nation and its leader, or even because it renders action, not talk. Quite a few Nazi ideologues strove hard to convert the Stifter of *Witiko* into a prophet of the coming millenium (*Seher des Reiches*).[110] Somewhat more independently Adolf von Grolman spoke of the entanglement of youth, service, and growing conquering aristocracy "auf dem deutschrechtlichen Grundsatz der Genossenschaft."[111] Perhaps in answer to such views, others have launched into Marxist diatribes against the portrayal of Friedrich Barbarossa or have argued that Stifter was actually issuing a warning against the misuses of naked and arbitrary power and the coming of totalitarianism.[112] Even very careful analyses such as the one by Erik Wolf do not seem to go much beyond the conclusion that "das sanfte Gesetz" is compatible with dangerous action and heroic life. Wolf says "Es wird weder der mittelalterliche noch der germanische noch ein idealer Ständestaat als politisches Postulat behauptet," largely because a still continuing Enlightenment and liberal influence was exerted during Stifter's early law studies.[113]

But a strictly juridical or political-ideological analysis of *Witiko* can touch only on relatively minor aspects of the work. Stifter's avowed intentions quoted above are achieved, according to Von Grolman, who observes (perhaps under the influence of Nadler's distinction between *Kunstlehre* and *Geschichtslehre*) that the action and phenomena (the structures) of *Nachsommer* are present in *Witiko*, but "alles ist . . . in der Mehrzahl."[114] We must be ready, however, to go even beyond this and recognize some qualitative differences. Even though we may be persuaded that at the end of his life Stifter did nothing more than lay bare some of the assumptions that had always been inherent in earlier works, the end result was still striking. I would therefore emphasize not only and not so much the plural as the size. Any foray into the realm of the "macro-idyllic" is bound to be suspect, as we have seen elsewhere. There was clearly a sharp change from the aesthetic-federalist proposals of Risach, which led to his resignation, to the expansionism of Friedrich in *Witiko*. Risach actually seeks a separation of areas and the cooperation of individuals in small units, that is, the dismantling of even large cooperative worlds.[115] In *Witiko* we see the combination of small units in ever larger aggregates: Witiko–the forest people–Bohemia–Germany–the known world. Similarly, the "klein-Familie" is replaced by the clan, as the basic unit. The ever-larger frameworks are supposed to provide protection for the central idyll and to guarantee its integrity, but in fact they replace it by a dynamic, outward looking imperialism. The building of the home, ultimate protecting shelter and spatial organization, is placed in the center (almost the mathematical center) of the book, but it is not the goal, nor the crowning achievement, nor the motivating purpose of *Witiko*. There had been all along in Stifter's work an inclination toward the *esprit de géometrie* and away from the *esprit de finesse*. Emil Staiger draws attention to the deeper meanings of the petrified titles of many shorter stories, as well as to the attraction for mathematics of people such as Drendorf and Risach.[116] The full victory of symmetry and abstraction is experienced only in *Witiko*. The small circle of Witiko's forest world is wrapped into the larger arc of the Bohemian state and this in turn receives its full significance only through peace and blessed subservience to Barbarossa's world empire. Moreover, the possibility of the small idyllic world, its very condition of existence, is that of a larger framework, Stifter now suggests. Witiko's growth is not plantlike, he makes a career in the wide world, receives outside sanction, and is only thereafter enabled to build a family and an estate.

The "souring" of the idyll is produced not only by an abrupt break in the dialectics of small and large (which had been expounded so eloquently in the introduction to *Bunte Steine*), but also by the perhaps inevitable conflict between the principle of hierarchy and the idyllic principle. The societal idyll was based on the reduction and taming of hierarchy, but not on its abolition. Now the principle of external (wide-world) realism is transported back into Witiko's own mountainous region. The rise of a feudal lord is accompanied by the unpleasant odor of exploitative goodness and class differentiation. Zacharias der Schenke summarizes the acquiescence of the populace: "und es ist alles gut."[117] Each craftsman promises voluntarily and with some enthusiasm to contribute to the building of the new lord's castle.[118] Plainly Stifter's intention was to show the cooperation of the parts in an organic whole: but the whole is not the community; it finds a *Stellvertreter* in the concrete person of the hero. It is not only that mid-nineteenth-century individualism and hero worship deform idyllism when they get mixed up with it, but also that we are dealing with a desertion of modeled reality in favor of (abstract) symbolism. The merciful readers may want to overlook the *kitschig* Wilhelmine procession, parade, and festivity at the inauguration of the castle.[119] They cannot overlook the two essential political speeches of the novel. While in the first Old Bolemil in Vishehrad pleads for legitimacy, continuity, and tradition, Witiko himself takes a less conservative and more "democratic" line.[120] He urges the populace, after the castle has been built, to join him in Wladislaw's campaign. He does so in the name of the "little man" and the "one leader" principle; he already sees himself as embodying the aspirations and best interests of a rather uniform mass of people: "Bei uns ist nur der hocherlauchte Herzog der Herr, dem wir Kleine Gaben senden und der uns beschützt" and "Der Herzog wird . . . immer ein Freund der Geringen sein, er wird mit uns leben, und wir werden mit ihm leben."[121]

This type of argumentation is in keeping with the crucial decision of the novel, the break with legitimacy in favor of aggression. Strict legitimacy would have required the succession of Wladislaw the son of Sobeslaw. The arbitrary decision of the noble assembly in favor of the other Wladislaw is based, to be sure, upon considerations of merit; within the book this merit is undeniable. But at least part of it is a capacity for aggression that the legitimate heir lacks. Manipulation replaces chance; aggression replaces indifference. The foregrounding of aggression in the book's action expresses the more fundamental aggression of Stifter as narrator against the reader, the novel, and the literary paradigm that provides his background. This aggression consists in the imposition of an arbitrarily contrived compromise on the universe. In the subject matter of his historical novel this is merely mirrored by Witiko's decision to turn from natural legitimacy to the rational and (dubiously) legal succession of the other Wladislaw, in fact a gesture of adherence to power politics justified by a long speech: "Dein Vater hat dir den Rat gegeben, dein Recht auf die Nachfolge in der Herrschaft der Länder hinzugeben, dass das Heil des Reiches nicht zerstöret werde." The key is the reference to a renewed justice and right which has supplanted the old legitimacy.[122]

The connection between microidyll and legitimate large state (the ostensible theme of the book) is soon turned into an apology for an aggressive and expansionist universal state.[123] Thus *Witiko* acknowledges itself as a Victorian neoromantic work and admits failure where Smollet, Scott, and the young Carlyle had succeeded: energy can no longer be accommodated inside the idyllic world, it must be placed outside it, as an adjuvant in the shape of aggression.[124] Although such crass parallels should be avoided, the brutal elitism and smug positioning of *Witiko* growing out of idyllism, as it does, will remind us of the analogous demonstration of National Socialist ideology (or large parts of it) growing out of philistinism (*Spiessertum.*) It must be added in all fairness that Stifter was much less offensive in his nationalism than many of his German contemporaries or than Charles Kingsley, whose *Westward Ho!* (1855) or *Hereward the Wake* (1866) represents with much less art a similar kind of driving Victorian jingoism and the regression from the idyll to the primitive.

This analogy would have some justification if indeed *Witiko* could be separated from the rest of Stifter's work, as quite a few indignant contemporaries and some later critics believed it could.[125] The revelation of Stifter's death by suicide led to the hysterical outrage of some, but it also meant, ironically, the beginning of revaluation. In the eyes of any modernist this suicide was Stifter's redemption and salvation. It drew attention with a sudden jerk to the hidden depths and dangers underneath the "luxe, calme et volupté" of an Olympian style. F. Klatt talked at length about the demons of Stifter and their exorcism;[126] Jens Tismar included him among the authors of "damaged idylls";[127] Lee Byron Jennings spoke about systems of chaos in *Die Narrenburg* and emphasized the grotesque in *Turmalin* ("an insane man and his deformed daughter . . . live in a basement room of an old, dilapidated house. They carry on a queer, stunted existence, in almost complete isolation").[128] Jean-Louis Bandet tackled such subjects as the impotence of nature and education in *Katzensilber,* the similarity of Stifter's procedure to a psychoanalytic cure, as well as paradox, dread, and disorder.[129] Thomas Mann, who was a sincere admirer of *Witiko,* gave a classical definition of the mechanism whereby excess, pathology, and the elementary-catastrophic are somehow *necessarily* placed behind the apparent serenity and quiet warmth of its style.[130]

There is no reason to quarrel with these findings. Exaggerated though they sometimes may be, they point to an undeniable reality: Stifter was no longer capable or willing to play the game of compromise which was at the very heart of late romanticism. His early works are not humble, but haughty aestheticist-decadent proclamations of the idyllic world and of the prefections of the romantic paradigm on earth; they are placed alongside or in front of a pale and vague demonic background. The tension between the two is perceptible. In *Witiko* the game of security and self-confidence in turn can be played no longer; the demons rise and mingle freely in the foreground world. Aggression, lack of laughter and sentiment, the dryness of stylization, the search for grandeur follow necessarily from the integration of evil and the grotesque into the prevailing world image. For the late Stifter, the rebellious barons in Bohemia and Moravia, no less than the independent-minded trading city of Milan, are now guilty of the sin of diversity; they no longer really represent "die Hintergründigkeit der Welt" (the enigmatic depth of the world), although for a reader faithful to Biedermeier traditions they are not credible ugly demons—on the contrary, they seem rather close to Risach's views. Stifter's actual pacification involves a release from the tension with demonism. He achieves what he may have wished all along: to integrate the demons into a uniform, covering crust.

WHAT THEN does a scrutiny of the historical novel in its evolution contribute to our understanding of the Biedermeier period as a whole? It will be quite obvious by now that I tend to side with those who, unlike Avrom Fleishman or Robin Collingwood, consider discussions of the historical imagination as perhaps interesting but of secondary importance.[131] True, I would not like to see the historical novel simply merged in a mass of novelistic writings, on the grounds that after all any novel is based on some past, close or remote, and that temporal distance should be ignored. It is quite reasonable to admit that the historical novel is an aesthetic artifact similar to a novel; but that it chooses to be a specific artifact (a historical novel) tells us something important about the intentions of the author. There is undoubtedly a difference between a work that resorts to relatively neutral, nonresonant, or connotation-free materials and one that chooses materials already shaped by the "original" historical imagination or placed in a discursive space and subjected to previous intertextual embraces. The decisive role of attitude can be observed by contrast. Why do we think of *Cromwell* as historical drama and not Corneille's *Cinna?* Why is *Richard II* perceived as more of a historical drama than *Anthony and Cleopatra?* Why is *War and Peace* less often thought of as a historical novel when V. F. Odoyevsky's *Sebastian Bach* is immediately recognized as one? Why are we less reluctant to call Pater's *Marius the Epicurean* a historical novel than Faulkner's *Sartoris*? I submit that we simply acknowledge the author's intention. We perceive the historicity as placed in the foreground. The novelist (Scott, Hugo, Manzoni, or Stifter) is eager to use the historical novel to some purpose. In the case of these founding fathers of the genre, the purpose seems plain. They wanted to stake out an intermediate area between the absolute metaphysical and cosmological speculation of the poets and philosophers (Wordsworth and Coleridge, Schelling and Hölderlin) and the area of immediate preoccupations and secular realism. The constitutive principle of the historical novel is none other than that of late romanticism itself: compromise, reconciliation. A novel is historical—it debouches into the idyllic world—because its author wants to accommodate the vision of rebirth and paradise to tangible circumstances or, in a grosser way, to let the burgher enjoy the delight of a danger that cannot actually reach him.

Three main things seem to have happened to the practitioners of this craft over four decades or so. First of all they were overtaken by the hypertrophy of cause, the seeds of which were planted by Scott himself but were not apparent until the very logic of its development led to an explosion. Injecting cause into the visionary (and slightly miraculous, a-causal) circuit proposed by high romanticism was one of the ways in which it could be scaled down and become manageable or probable. Scott could treat this with a light hand, by concentrating on the flow of the action. In Hugo's novels the pattern of congestion and explosion becomes apparent in the style: melodrama prepared by long, "calmly scientific" passages. In *The Betrothed* the even more swollen causal episodes are integrated "as if" they were aesthetically valid and deliberate in the texture. With Stifter (and, again, with Flaubert's *Salammbô*) the hypertrophy of cause becomes crushing: it is no longer subordinated to evolution ("flowing" with it and inside it), but builds its own unwieldy clanking machines. The proliferating geology in *Nachsommer* had been only an omen. Now characters with a cadaverous color are manipulated mechanically. The outcome, that partial and ironic paradise, is lost to sight. Cause for the sake of cause is already art for the sake of art.

Curiously enough the second destructive agent seems to be symmetrically opposed to the first. It might be described as the liberation of composing elements. In *Witiko,* that grand opera of cause (at the level of the novel as a whole), juxtaposition reigns supreme among the smaller narrative units. Sentences do not follow each other causally. Witiko does not explain why he lets the rebellious princes get away. Bertha's love for him does not grow: it *is*. *Sein* detached from *Werden* has often been described as reification. Besides this, it indicates an impressionist animus, the separation of elements and observations, which is more typical of the chronicle than of history. Thus natural descriptions seem abandoned and the often mentioned "forest" origin of the people is symbolic rather than real. Similarly, religion is a detached, objective ritual, the bishops are feudals, prayer is a symbol—not an informing force as in Manzoni. There is a basic and almost nihilistic difference in *Witiko*. Ranke had taught his time that historicism is good because there is no linear progression: all historical periods are immediate to God ("unmittelbar zu Gott").[132] Hence a shoulder-shrugging indifference: I can take any period I want to, it doesn't matter anyway. Pieces are moved around with almost cruel coldness.

The last of these three forces has already been mentioned. It is the breakdown of the idyllic model owing to the fact that Stifter takes too literally the idea of an aesthetically structured community.[133] According to Erik Lunding, Stifter's purpose in *Witiko* had been the salvation of history; he thinks the search is for "beglückende existentielle Beruhigung," in a hopeless struggle to idyllize history and impart an optimistic meaning where none is possible.[134] I am afraid that, more seriously, Stifter was already aware of the limitations of the idyll and had given up on it. Imposing idyllic forms on overlarge structures was both the outcome and the cause of the loss of compromise. Victorian breaks and the unleashing of neoromantic uncontrollable Dionysian eruption had already begun. The dynamism of decadence flowers out of the Biedermeier. If Stifter is a political writer no less than Karl Gutzkow, if we look upon him with some melancholy, as upon a gravedigger of his age, we must also admit that his scientism and his luridly scintillating scenes seem more compatible with Baudelaire, Georg Trakl, and Kafka than we would have thought.

Manzoni as we have seen, covers up by adroit technique his doubts about the ability of consciousness to come to terms with the world. His novel suggests that a unified framework for the recuperation of an integral world may be impossible in itself; but Manzoni indicates that our will to manipulate reality may be sufficient in hiding the crack. Impression restores natural harmony and may in itself be enough to offset the unlikelihood of that kind of harmony. A strange and ambiguous balance is thus created, and a fateful precedent is set. Creation of the idyllic world (as a specific embodiment of a regenerated humanity) is postulated as a prerogative of the author: it may be imposed or decreed. The conclusions are fully drawn in Stifter's *Witiko*.

Scott had set up the Biedermeier historical novel as a vehicle for reasonable compromise and idyllic imperfection. The historical novel was supposed to be an acceptable substitute for romantic regeneration and salvation. For over fifty years or so there is a steady decline in the belief of this feasibility; authors resort to sleight of hand to present a plausible version of this proposition. *Witiko* is pushed by the logical momentum of this development to the point where the theory is totally implausible. Stifter does not want to abandon it. He therefore chooses to impose it by authorial fiat, distorting the figures and situations in shapes borrowed from the mechanical aesthetic and mineral; the outcome will be a universe of glory and hope closer in some ways to the salamander-world of Hoffmann (*Der goldene Topf*) or Novalis (in Klingsor's tale in *Ofterdingen*) than to Scott or even Manzoni, but close to *Salammbô, Là-bas,* or the tales of William Morris. There is nothing to indicate that such a decisive turn was taken by abandoning preexisting pressures and drives. In the light of *Witiko* Stifter's early work appears no longer as either bourgeois or transcendently serene. It appears as aggressively aesthetic. By the 1840s and 1850s Stifter would seem already to have been doubtful about the Biedermeier, whose claim, let me repeat again, had been the relative restoration of harmony inside limited worlds. As in *Witiko,* though less obviously, he had conjured by will and magic stylistic power a decorative-manneristic world in *Nachsommer* or *Der Waldsteig* or *Kalkstein.* Nietzsche's paradoxical sympathy for Stifter can thus be understood; he liked the Austrian's arbitrary inventiveness, his strong-arm tactics. The willed artificiality of *Witiko* lent his work the magic and hallucinatory qualities that he expected from art as a strong substitute for reality. The similarities to Gotthelf or Mörike are misleading; Stifter uses the same images but for radically different purposes—he proclaims the separation of world and consciousness and their hostility. In doing so he plays a dangerous game, but he is neither a didacticist nor a utopian. Rather he is the first great writer for whom artistic and ideological conservatism is an expression of morbidity and decadence, rather than of mere nostalgia.

AFTERWORD

SEVERAL assumptions underlie the discussion in the preceding chapters, and I will comment on them in the following order: methodology, the concept of period, and the uses of Biedermeier research.

As to methodology, I have sought in this book and elsewhere to work against a pluralist background, keeping in mind the widest range of possible explanations of any given literary phenomenon. Applying a rigidly Laplaceian causality to the understanding of human events has long been under suspicion. Nowadays, under the influence of radically changing concepts in the exact sciences, the practice (though not always the theory) of criticism takes univocal explanations as a thing of the past. We have seen some rather strict methodologies (Marxist, Freudian) opening the doors to an exciting variety of alternative possibilities (for example, structuralist and reader-response criticism). We have seen the downfall of the once mighty New Criticism effected above all by the widely held perception that it claimed to possess binding and homogeneous explanations. We have seen a curious kind of practical agreement between the pluralistic approach of traditional viewpoints (Wayne Booth) and the relativistic innovators (Stanley Fish, reader-response, Derrideans). So, when embarking upon further work in the explanation of literary history, it seems only natural to postulate a state of affairs in which some version of multiplicity prevails. Causal multiplicity seems the most plausible theoretical ground for the literary historian simply because of the complex nature of his object. Any single literary explanation is the projection of a multidimensional reality onto a simple horizontal plane. Small wonder that multiple projections from different angles are necessary even to begin to approximate what is given in the immediate experiential grasp of literature by subjectivity.

Thus it is quite obvious to me that the concept of Biedermeier as a controlling category does not supplant or cancel other explanations, partial or comprehensive. The whole production of the age could be described in a quite satisfactory way by an integrated set of myths, submerged images, and psychological moves. The search for an absent father and for the inheritance are the most obvious among these and have been mentioned in several chapters. The parable of the profligate brother is also frequent. The prevalence of maternal femininity (for which large, embracing, and protective communities, such as the national or local ones, could be emblems) I have barely mentioned, although it is equally important and in fact closely linked to the paternal ambiguity. Incest undergoes an interesting change. In high romanticism, for René and Lucille, for Laon and Cythna (as well as, in different ways, Wordsworth, Blake, or Byron), incest is a form of wholeness; it signals the joining of self and cosmos and pleads for a restoration of unity. For later romantics, however, incest becomes a scandal, a danger, or a perverse temptation—it is a sensational and not a substantial matter. With these and other elements a fairly comprehensive psychomythic reading of the age could be sketched.

A direct sociological explanation of the period's literature would be perhaps even more powerful. At different points in this book (and particularly in the first chapter) I pointed out the solidarity of a number of social trends or historical events with literary ones. Beyond this, an explanation of Biedermeier literature as a direct outcome of some historical novelties would not be difficult to outline. One could start with a mentality growing, almost by necessity, out of the size of towns. Around 1800 Vienna, St. Petersburg, Moscow, and Berlin had 250,-000 inhabitants or so. Except for London and Paris, other European cities were smaller; they provided both coziness and alienation; in them growth, poverty, and culture were inextricably connected. The new transportation provided a tantalizing possibility of closeness and yet preserved the difficulties in distance. The general phenomenon of the "parvenu" in France and in German-speaking areas is another important precondition of Biedermeier literature. This social type combines upward mobility and a good share of dynamism with the desire for security and stability, and even with nostalgia for its own simpler past—the ideal soil for the growth as well as for the reception of late-romantic views. The Biedermeier style in furniture was largely the outcome of austerity. The emerging bureaucracy could act as a unifying force above the classes, promoting the ideals of education, efficiency, cultural value, meritocracy, and, of course, contentment and appeasement. The great financiers were disliked by small businessmen or farmers (who envied the access of the former to easy credit terms) more than even by the laborers as E. J. Hobsbawm contends. Hence their preference for a bureaucracy that was leveling but not egalitarian and that could provide a unifying coziness for the shattered aristocracy, the artisans nervous about the new market economy, the intellectuals seeking state service, and many other groups. Idyllic bonding was amply provided by the large households on estates as well as in the middle-class households, even while the economic structure described as the "hometown economy" was slowly coming to an end.[1] Within all these broader or narrower social frameworks irony and disappointment, cultural fantasies and moderate rebellion could draw emotional nourishment and project their insights on a literary scene. The golden age of the European bourgeoisie ("eine Stunde des Bürgertums mit der Chance einer gediegenen Herrschaft des Besitzes und der Bildung, mit regelrechten Verfassungsbestrebungen unter freiheitlichen Parolen, mit politischen Revolutionen gemässigter Art") is engendered out of many small and specific material incidents.[2]

Needless to say, a purely national mode of writing history (or even *in extremis* an ethnic one in the manner of Nadler) can present its own narratives and has done so with great eloquence. We are only too familiar with the *Goethezeit* theory of German literature, with the explanation of a persistent classicism and rationalism that colors French intellectual life and letters; we are familiar with the importance of national aspirations for the Czechs, Italians, and Romanians. These are mighty realities, and compelling explanatory contexts, that nobody can wish away. In fact, the nominalist criticism of Lovejoy and the comparative theories that emphasize national differences, such as those of Lilian Furst or Margery Sabin, have their own kind of justification. Other factors can be added in the dialectical web of the post-1815 period: for example religious and ideological or linguistic and stylistic.

However, none of the above can displace the presence of broad continent-wide connections, patterns, and correspondences. Reasonable disagreement may arise on the relative importance of one set of probabilities or the other, as well as on the way they relate among themselves. But I think that the spontaneous experiential agreement on a "romantic" quality in works otherwise widely different (language, geographic area, style, theme, philosophical views), coupled with an analytic recognition of these differences, presents literary study with a very basic dilemma. The only promising approach to this dilemma seems to me the historical one of period dynamics. I have attempted here to articulate the dilemma and explain its consequences.

The second matter of possible controversy is the use of the concept of period. There can be little doubt that the objectivist pretensions of *Geistesgeschichte* have been rejected by the academic community at large. Few would speak about "the baroque" as about a hermetically sealed universe with complete internal consistency, and it is unlikely that "romantic" man or "classical" man—spiritual races located not in physical geography, but in a sort of ideal history—can be accepted even as working hypotheses. The glib and speculative productions of this post-Hegelian current strove to define period as a unit, a *forma mentis* determining the whole of an epoch (or a culture or a nation) in all its manifestations. The determinism of it seems more offensive than the unifying aims. René Wellek provided an alternative acceptable for several decades by defining periods as time sections "dominated by a system of literary norms, standards, and conventions." This approach has some of the advantages and disadvantages of any chiefly rationalistic view. It is interesting that most of the attempts to either qualify or disqualify it have circled round the concept of "domination," rather than around "standards," for instance. These corrective efforts have shown a preference for "currents" or polarities within a neutral time frame and have tried to drop the privileged position of any set of norms.[3] However, it seems that the dangers of aleatory nominalism cannot be avoided; arbitrary time units, antihistoricism or simplifying causalities arise to fill the conceptual vacuum that obtains when even the instrumental role of periods is questioned.

Several kinds of answers are possible. One was suggested at the beginning of this afterword to emphasize constantly the modest role of concepts such as period (as well as genre or theme) among many others. Another answer is to admit that period should be seen as purely artificial but, at the same time, as a beneficial tool in teaching and writing. In this study I have taken a different approach, one that regards literature as part of a larger existential and cultural unity. The "human model" underlying this approach to periods was described briefly in the first chapter. This powerful but inchoate mental reality is hypothetical but thereby experiential in nature. Jeffrey Barnouw in a different argument aptly says that "the impulse at work in a literary text is less one of expression or communication than of grasping and making sense of self and world." Thus categories of works will display a common "effort, endeavor or intentionality"; they will also display a "common dimension of consciousness and experience." The chief character of the intentionality or potentiality active in each of these individual works is that they are "responses which reveal deep affinities where otherwise only divergence is apparent."[4] The mains strategic move of Barnouw's approach is to displace period from a level of thematic certainties and answers to one of the questions and dilemmas, potentialities and hypotheses of an age's self-awareness, while preserving a level of transpersonal subjectivity. I believe that, in using the "human model" as the referential level for literature and in treating literature as the processing and shaping of this level, we gain epistemological advantages that are similar to those gained in Barnouw's period theory. At the same time the emphasis of the model theory on the period's implicit self-images provides us with a better focus and with better crystallized responses. The dilemmatic and tentative structure of a work's relationship to its age is highlighted by both.

In a curious way, the dilemmatic and anxiety-ridden substratum of the age of the Biedermeier illustrates the illusive, hypothetical, and crisis-laden substance of any period. Nevertheless, the question of why we should postulate a European Biedermeier may arise. Is there any increase in our knowledge, and is our understanding clarified by using this conceptual framework rather than another one?

Roger Bauer once spoke of the "Austrianization" of German romanticism, that is, of its becoming more local and more modest in aims.[5] I have tried to describe the way in which European romanticism as a whole undergoes a similar process. We do not have to call it Biedermeier, but we cannot deny its strong similarities to the German Biedermeier. The "Austrianization" is a European process. Accepting this conclusion will help us understand better why French and Eastern European romanticisms have a special shape. It will help us understand better the significance of some genres and modes (historical novel, tragicomedy and the grotesque, the idyllic) in their historical context. It will help us understand the sense of conclusiveness and reification brought by the *answers* of realism—a closing down of solutions much different from the awkward and flustered openness of the Biedermeier. (Victorian polarities are clear-cut and seem to escape the smoldering crisis before 1848.) Thus John Speirs's argument that Wordsworth (*Michael*), Crabbe (*Tales in Verse*), and Byron (*Beppo, Don Juan*) continue the tradition of the eighteenth-century English novel but pave the way for the more poetic Victorians (Dickens, Charlotte Brontë, even Eliot and Conrad) could benefit from a better historical grounding.[6] It could be reformulated as an impulse toward the more firmly prosaic Victorian realism through the transitional poeticality of the later romantic narrative.

Broader historical propositions can be advanced, most of them probably open to discussion. I will mention a few. The romantic explosion occurs earlier than we usually consider, that is, in the late 1780s and early 1790s. The revolutionary movement of the 1790s is a consequence of romanticism, or at most one of its forms, rather than its cause. The Restoration begins in England as well as in France around 1800, even though it gains full momentum after 1815. Literatures without a core-romantic production tend to evolve a final phase between romanticism and Victorianism or symbolism (hence Mácha, Krasiński and Norwid, Eminescu, Nerval, Poe). Diagonal correspondences enrich dialectically simple historical evolution,[7] and there is a particularly close relationship between the German *Frühromantiker* and the symbolist movement, as both Béguin and Furst have pointed out. The eighteenth-century Enlightenment is in a sense fully responsible for the emergence of romanticism, in another sense symmetrically opposed to it. To dwell a little upon this last proposition: the visionary romanticism of Blake or Novalis is the consequence of Enlightenment dynamics, in that in their work key elements of the Enlightenment model turn into a dialectical opposite (reason versus imagination, education versus nature, social versus individual, mirror versus lamp, and so on). But a second and different relationship emerges in Biedermeier later romanticism: then direct influences are again and gratefully accepted as a counterweight to romantic intensities.

These and other propositions, though controversial, are of great interest in the investigation of literary history; they become possible largely through the introduction of the concept of Biedermeier and, more generally, through attention to period dynamics. The broad perspective of this concept can be helpful everywhere, in the small matters of analytical detail, as well as in our compulsive philosophizing on the destiny of human culture. It may help us to compare Words-

worth's daffodils to Mörike's winter dawn. We can, I think, notice
better the precise shape and the pantheistic breath animating the first,
as well as the certainty of their coinherence in the poet's memory. We
can contrast this to the blurred impressionism of *An einem Wintermorgen, vor Sonnenaufgang* and with the certainty of its fleetingness.
We can place this contrastive design in a sociocultural framework with
the reasonble hope that we are not damaging it too much.

At the other end of the spectrum of critical work we can meditate
more grandiosely on what "taming" involves. We can recall Byron
and Gide on taming romanticism. We can reverently appeal to Leo
Spitzer's thoughts on classicism as a muted and subdued baroque. We
can think of the Kuhnian paradigmatic change as an analogy to the
fading of human models. We can muse on the inevitable decay of
mystical intensity into political pragmatism. We can reflect on the
power and uses of imperfection in the human world. We can evoke the
passing of cultures and the mighty sway of time. But we will then have
left quietly behind us literary examination and all its small delicious
twinges of guilty uncertainty.

NOTES

1. THE DYNAMICS OF THE ROMANTIC PERIOD

1. Karl Immermann, *Werke,* ed. Benno v. Wiese, 5 vols. (Frankfurt am Main: Athenäum, 1971), II, 110–111, 312–313, 554–555, 585, 502, 621, and elsewhere. References hereafter parenthetically in the text.

2. Benno v. Wiese, *Karl Immermann* (Bad Homburg: Gehlen, 1969), p. 175.

3. Günter Böhmer, *Die Welt des Biedermeier* (1968; Elville: Rheingauer Verlagsgesellschaft, 1981), p. 114.

4. H. J. Halm, *Formen der Narrheit in Immermann's Prosa* (Marburg: N. G. Elwert, 1972), p. 129.

5. Hermann August Korff, *Geist der Goethezeit* (1923; Leipzig: Koehler und Amelang, 1954), 5 vols.

6. Paul Gottfried, *Conservative Millenarians: The Romantic Experience in Bavaria* (New York: Fordham University Press, 1979). The generally accepted view is in Fritz Martini, *Deutsche Literaturgeschichte* (1949; new rev. ed. Stuttgart: Kröner, 1977). The East German Marxist view is, as regards periodization, quite similar. See Hans-Günther Thalheim et al., eds. *Geschichte der deutschen Literatur von den Anfängen bis zur Gegenwart,* 10 vols. (East Berlin: Volk und Wissen, 1975), VIII, pts. 1 and 2.

7. A very good handy selection is in Elfriede Neubuhr, ed., *Begriffsbestimmung des literarischen Biedermeier* (Darmstadt: Wissenschaftliche Buchgesellschaft, 1974), Wege der Forschung, vol. 118, with the relevant bibliography.

8. Charles A. Williams, "Notes on the Origin and History of the Early Biedermeier," *Journal of English and Germanic Philology,* 57 (1958), 403–415, presents the emergence of the term. Kussmaul had been amused and incited by the discovery in 1853 of a 500-page collection of poems published eight years earlier in Karlsruhe, in a kind of vanity press, by Samuel Friedrich Sauter, a retired village schoolmaster. Sauter became for him the prototype of the philistine poetaster of what came to be called the Biedermeier age. Cf. Böhmer, *Die Welt des Biedermeier,* pp. 9–13, and Rudolph Majut, "Das literarische Biedermeier. Aufriss und Probleme," *Germanisch-*

romanische Monatsschrift, 20 (1932), 401–412, for term history. Neubuhr, *Begriffsbestimmung*, pp. 8–31 and elsewhere discusses the growth of Biedermeier studies in Germany.

9. A good example is the tortuous article of Hermann Pongs, "Zur Bürgerkultur des Biedermeier," *Dichtung und Volkstum*, 36 (1935), 141–163, which tries to demonstrate that the "orderly" and "wholesome" Biedermeier must be ideologically acceptable. A close reading reveals an attempt to save this area of research from brutal rejection by the regime's chief ideological spokesman, Alfred Rosenberg.

10. Franz Koch, *Geschichte deutscher Dichtung* (Hamburg: Hanseatische Verlagsanstalt, 1937), pp. 195–259. Walter Linden, *Geschichte der deutschen Literatur* (1937; Leipzig: Reclam, 1940), pp. 360–408. Josef Nadler, *Literaturgeschichte des deutschen Volkes*, 4 vols. (1912; Berlin: Propyläen, 1939), vol. III. Paul Fechter, *Geschichte der deutschen Literatur von den Anfängen bis zur Gegenwart* (Berlin: Th. Knaur Nachfolger, 1941), pp. 525–639.

11. Martin Greiner, *Zwischen Biedermeier und Bourgeoisie* (Göttingen: Vandenhoeck und Rupprecht, 1953), pp. 179–278. Jost Hermand, "Allgemeine Epochenprobleme" in Jost Hermand and Manfred Windfuhr, eds., *Zur Literatur der Restaurationsepoche 1815–1848* (Stuttgart: Metzler, 1970), pp. 3–61. See also Hermand's two seminal anthologies, *Der deutsche Vormärz. Texte und Dokumente* (Stuttgart: Reclam, 1967) and *Das Junge Deutschland. Texte und Dokumente* (Stuttgart: Reclam, 1966).

12. Hermann Pongs, "Ein Beitrag zum Dämonischen im Biedermeier," *Dichtung und Volkstum: NF des Euphorion*, 36 (1935), 257.

13. Majut, "Das literarische Biedermeier," p. 421.

14. Friedrich Sengle, *Biedermeierzeit: Deutsche Literatur im Spannungsfeld zwischen Restauration und Revolution 1815–1848*, 3 vols. (Stuttgart: J. B. Metzler, 1971–1980).

15. Lee Byron Jennings, *The Ludicrous Demon* (Berkeley: University of California Press, 1963), U. C. Publications in Modern Philology, vol. 71, pp. 150–152, 141–142.

16. Sengle, *Biedermeierzeit*, II, 83–320.

17. Walter Weiss, *Enttäuschter Pantheismus. Zur Weltgestaltung der Dichtung in der Restaurationszeit* (Vorarlberg: Dornbirn, 1962).

18. E. J. Hobsbawm, *The Age of Revolution, 1789–1848* (New York: Signet-Mentor, 1962), p. 221.

19. Ibid., p. 168.

20. K. E. Rotschuh, "Deutsche Biedermeiermedizin. Epoche zwischen Romantik und Naturalismus 1830–1850," *Gesnerus*, 25, no. 3–4 (1968), 169–187.

21. Otto F. B. Bollnow, *Die Pädagogik der deutschen Romantik von Arndt bis Fröbel* (1952; Stuttgart: Klett-Cotta, 1977). The illustrations in

Fröbel's *Mutter—und Koselieder* of 1844 were executed by Friedrich Unger (1811–1853).

22. Böhmer, *Die Welt des Biedermeier,* pp. 236, 195. But see, for instance, Edwin Redslob, *Die Welt vor hundert Jahren. Menschen und Kultur der Zeitwende um 1840* (Leipzig: Reclam, 1940), pp. 111–134, 284–286, 384–396, for a glowing account of the epoch's achievements in science.

23. Günther Weydt, "Literarisches Biedermeier," *Deutsche Vierteljahrschrift für Literaturwissenschaft und Geistesgeschichte,* 9 (1931), 628–665. See Neubuhr, *Begriffsbestimmung,* p. 55.

24. Böhmer, *Die Welt des Biedermeier,* pp. 110, 114–115.

25. Marcel Brion, *Daily Life in the Vienna of Mozart and Schubert* (1959 Fr. ed.; New York: Macmillan, 1962), p. 74. Much detailed information and some bibliography also in Marianne Bernhard, *Das Biedermeier: Kultur zwischen Wiener Kongress und Märzrevolution,* Hermes Handlexikon (Düsseldorf: Econ, 1983).

26. Böhmer, *Die Welt des Biedermeier,* pp. 260, 262. Brion, *Daily Life,* pp. 48–49, 56.

27. Brion, *Daily Life,* pp. 184–185.

28. Anne Hollander, *Seeing Through Clothes* (1978; New York: Avon, 1980), p. 12.

29. Böhmer, *Die Welt des Biedermeier,* pp. 166–167, 171.

30. Paul Bernard, *Rush to the Alps: The Evolution of Vacationing in Switzerland* (Boulder and New York: East European Quarterly and Columbia University Press, 1978), pp. 5–29, 86–105. David Robertson, "Mid-Victorians Amongst the Alps" in Ulrich Knoepflmacher and G. B. Tennyson, eds., *Nature and the Victorian Imagination* (Berkeley: University of California Press, 1977), pp. 113–136.

31. J. C. Loudon, *The Suburban Gardener and Villa Companion* (London: 1838), p. 8, quoted in Knoepflmacher and Tennyson, *Nature and the Victorian Imagination,* p. 50.

32. Anthony Dale, *Fashionable Brighton 1820–1860* (London: Country Life, 1949), pp. 13, 17.

33. Brion, *Daily Life,* pp. 188–189.

34. Böhmer, *Die Welt des Biedermeier,* pp. 185–186.

35. Norbert Fuerst, *The Victorian Age in German Literature* (London: D. Dobson, 1966), p. 89.

36. Brion, *Daily Life,* pp. 158–159.

37. J. L. Talmon, *Political Messianism: The Romantic Phase* (London: Secker and Warburg, 1960).

38. Donald Charlton, *Secular Religions in France, 1815–1870* (Oxford: Oxford University Press, 1963); George Boas, *French Philosophies of the Romantic Period* (Baltimore: Johns Hopkins University Press, 1925).

39. Adolf v. Grolman, "Biedermeier-Forschung," *Euphorion*, 36 (1935), 311–325. Ferdinand Joseph Schneider, "Biedermeier und Literaturwissenschaft," *Preussische Jahrbücher*, 240 (1935), 207–223, reprinted in Neubuhr, *Begriffsbestimmung*, 175–193.

40. Virgil Nemoianu, *Structuralismul* (Bucharest: ELU, 1967), pp. 14–16, where I develop Damáso Alonso, *Poesía española. Ensayo de métodos y límites estilésticos* (1952; 5th ed. Madrid: Gredos, 1966), pp. 212–216, who in turn was perhaps influenced by Benedetto Croce and Nicolai Hartmann.

41. Neubuhr, *Begriffsbestimmung*, p. 3; Jeffrey Barnouw used the term "intentionality" of an age (although not in connection with the Biedermeier) in "The Cognitive Import of Period Concepts," in *Comparative Literature: Proceedings of the VIIth Congress of the I.C.L.A. (Montreal)*, (Stuttgart: Erich Bieber, 1979), II, 21–32.

42. Sengle, *Biedermeierzeit*, I, pp. 1–82.

43. Wilhelm Bietak, "Vom Wesen des österreichischen Biedermeier und seiner Dichtung," *DVLG*, 9 (1931), 652–672, reprinted in Neubuhr, *Begriffsbestimmung*, 61–83.

44. Neubuhr, *Begriffsbestimmung*, p. 80.

45. Ibid., pp. 120–121. Paul Kluckhohn, "Biedermeier als literarische Epochenbezeichnung," *DVLG*, 13 (1935), 1–43.

46. Neubuhr, *Begriffsbestimmung*, pp. 108, 116.

47. Sengle, *Biedermeierzeit*, I, pp. 34–47.

48. Neubuhr, *Begriffsbestimmung*, pp. 17, 234. For other short formulas see ibid. Also Jost Hermand, *Von Mainz nach Weimar. Studien zur deutschen Literatur* (Stuttgart: Metzler, 1969), pp. 99–129, who argues that many works by Gotthelf or Grillparzer should be understood as allegories exploring the relationship between harmonious order and the revolutionary titan.

49. Irving Babbitt, *Rousseau and Romanticism* (1919; Boston: Houghton Mifflin, 1935); Fritz Strich, *Deutsche Klassik und Romantik* (Munich: Meyer und Jessen, 1922); Paul van Tieghem, *Le Romantisme dans la littérature européene* (1948; Paris: Albin Michel, 1969): Albert Béguin, *L'Ame romantique et le rêve*, 2 vols. (Marseilles: Cahiers du sud, 1937; rev. ed., 1947); Mario Praz, *The Romantic Agony* (1933; Oxford: Oxford University Press, 1970); René Wellek, "The Concept of Romanticism in Literary History," *Comparative Literature*, 1 (1949), 1–23, 147–172, often reprinted, for example, in René Wellek, *Concepts of Criticism*, ed. Stephen G. Nichols, Jr. (New Haven: Yale University Press, 1976), pp. 128–198. Of the many anthologies of romanticism the two most relevant for the purposes of this chapter are Robert F. Gleckner and Gerald E. Enscoe, eds., *Romanticism: Points of View* (1962; Detroit: Wayne University Press, 1975) and Harold Bloom, ed., *Romanticism and Consciousness* (New York: Norton, 1970).

50. Henry H. H. Remak, "West European Romanticism" in Newton P. Stallknecht, and Horst Frenz, eds., *Comparative Literature: Method and Perspective* (Carbondale: Southern Illinois University Press, 1961), pp. 223–259. Northrop Frye, "The Drunken Boat: The Revolutionary Element in Romanticism" in Northrop Frye ed., *Romanticism Reconsidered* (New York: Columbia University Press, 1963), pp. 1–25. Harold Bloom, *The Visionary Company* (Garden City, N.Y.: Doubleday, 1961; rev. ed., 1971), as well as his "The Internalization of Quest-Romance," *Yale Review*, 58, no. 4 (1969), 526–535, Geoffrey Hartman, "Romanticism and Antiself-consciousness," *Centennial Review*, 6, no. 4 (1962), 553–565, often reprinted and revised.

51. Meyer H. Abrams, *Natural Supernaturalism* (1971; New York: Norton, 1973), pp. 61, 65, 68, 90–92, 174, 179. References hereafter in parentheses in the text.

52. Michael Cooke, *Acts of Inclusion: Studies Bearing on an Elementary Theory of Romanticism* (New Haven: Yale University Press, 1979), pp. 47, 137–141.

53. Marshall Brown, *The Shape of German Romanticism* (Ithaca: Cornell University Press, 1979), p. 36.

54. Paul de Man, "Intentional Structure of the Romantic Image" in Bloom, ed., *Romanticism and Consciousness*, pp. 65–76 (first published in French in 1969).

55. Thomas MacFarland, *Romanticism and the Forms of Ruin* (Princeton: Princeton University Press, 1981).

56. Hartman, "Romanticism and Antiself-consciousness." See Bloom, *Romanticism and Consciousness*, p. 53; also p. 49.

57. E. D. Hirsch, *Wordsworth and Schelling: A Typological Study of Romanticism* (New Haven: Yale University Press, 1960).

58. "Romantic thinkers . . . try to explain the process of cosmic becoming itself as a path of return to a lost unity; in doing so, they resort to myths that are all informed by the idea of the fall"; "Reintegration will occur at the moment when the language of dream regains its primal integrity." Béguin, *L'Ame romantique*, pp. 129, 214.

59. Istvan Söter, *The Dilemma of Literary Science* (Budapest: Akademiai Kiado, 1973), p. 123, has thoughtful comments on the somewhat excessive reliance of Van Tieghem on preromanticism.

60. Virgil Nemoianu, *Micro-Harmony: The Growth and Uses of the Idyllic Model in Literature* (Bern: Peter Lang, 1977). Paul Hazard, *La Crise de la conscience européene, 1680–1715*, 2 vols. (Paris: Boivin, 1935), II, 120–138. Tudor Vianu, *Transformările ideii de om* (Bucharest; Traditia, 1946). Alexandru Duțu, *Eseu în teoria modelelor umane* (Bucharest: Editura Stiințifică, 1972). C. S. Lewis, *The Discarded Image* (Cambridge: Cambridge

University Press, 1964). Victor Tapié, *Baroque et classicisme* (Paris: Plon, 1957), pp. 231 ff.

61. Raymond Williams, *Marxism and Literature* (Oxford: Oxford University Press, 1977), p. 106.

62. Frederic Jameson, *Marxism and Form* (Princeton: Princeton University Press, 1971), p. 10.

63. "A boundlessly energetic will toward ideals and joy, huge claims from the social structures, indeed from nature herself, a yearning for the infinitely remote and states of exorbitant happiness." Wilhelm Dilthey, *Das Erlebnis und die Dichtung* (1905; Leipzig and Berlin: Teubner, 1913), p. 397.

64. Bloom, *Romanticism and Consciousness*, p. 11.

65. MacFarland, *Romanticism and the Forms of Ruin*, pp. 409-410.

66. "We must avoid regarding the philosophers of nature merely as apologists for the nocturnal sides of life, who ignore conscious activity. The myth of unity lost is also the myth of unity regained." Béguin, *L'Âme romantique*, p. 159. See also pp. 112, 113.

67. Béguin, *L'Âme romantique*, pp. 124, 130, 142. See also pp. 111-112, 100, 26.

68. "Hamann envisages the state of our earliest ancestors as an alternation of profound sleep with 'vertiginous' dances; long immobilized in 'the torpor of awed wonder and meditation' they would suddenly speak up 'in soaring rhetoric'." Béguin, *L'Âme romantique*, p. 105.

69. Dieter Arendt, *Der poetische Nihilismus in der Romantik*, 2 vols. (Tübingen: Max Niemeyer, 1972), Studien zur deutschen Literatur, vol. 30. See particularly I, 8-35.

70. Strich, *Deutsche Klassik und Romantik*, pp. 46-49, 92, 57, 37.

71. MacFarland, *Romanticism and the Forms of Ruin*, p. 165.

72. "A change of this kind by which totally separated things will melt into each other as shadows do, is the natural consequence of such conceptions." "Only one thing—a negative conclusion—is quite plain. We grasp the world only as an analogy of our self. However the analogical reference is not to the rational structure of the self, but rather to its seething depths, mysterious to ourselves, elemental in their eruption: will, feeling or imagination." Dilthey, *Das Erlebnis und die Dichtung*, pp. 305-307.

73. Bloom, *Romanticism and Consciousness*, p. 24.

74. MacFarland, *Romanticism and the Forms of Ruin*, pp. 15-16.

75. Karl Jaspers, *Schelling: Grösse und Verhängnis* (Munich: Piper, 1955), pp. 74-89 and passim.

76. Dilthey, *Das Erlebnis und die Dichtung*, p. 412.

77. Emil Staiger, *Spätzeit. Studien zur deutschen Literatur* (Zurich and Munich: Artemis, 1973), p. 125.

78. Morse Peckham, "Toward a Theory of Romanticism," *PMLA*, 66,

no. 2 (1951), 5–23. See also Söter, *Dilemma*, p. 123, who seems aware of this two-step process.

79. Peckham even sketches the view of romanticism as analogous to the Christian plot: "A man moves from a trust in the Universe to a period of doubt and despair of any meaning in the universe, and then to a re-affirmation of faith in cosmic meaning and goodness, or at least meaning. The transition from the first stage to the second we may call spiritual death; that from the second to the third, we may call spiritual rebirth." "Toward a Theory of Romanticism," p. 16.

80. Williams, *Marxism and Literature*, p. 39.

81. Cf. Arendt, *Der poetische Nihilismus*, I, 27.

82. "This specific Romantic view of historical fiction differs by a wide mark from the later one which tried to lay bare the essence of history in its factual reality and felt quite dependent upon it." Strich, *Deutsche Klassik und Romantik*, p. 103.

83. George Levine, "High and Low: Ruskin and the Novelists," in Knoepflmacher and Tennyson, *Nature and the Victorian Imagination*, p. 137.

84. Praz, *Romantic Agony*, p. 71.

85. Babbitt, *Rousseau and Romanticism*, p. 140.

86. Praz, *Romantic Agony*, pp. 99, 115, 126–128, 173–175, 179, 183 is very persuasive in this respect, particularly when discussing the Sadian themes.

87. Hobsbawm, *Age of Revolution*, p. 307.

88. Mörike, *Werke*, 2 vols. (Stuttgart: Cotta, 1954), I, 51.

89. Ibid., I, 26.

90. Sengle, *Biedermeierzeit*, I, 244.

91. Francesco de Sanctis, *Storia della letteratura italiana* (1870–1871; Milano: Feltrinelli, 1967), pp. 824–864. Olga Ragusa, "Romantico-Romanticismo" in Hans Eichner, ed., *Romantic and Its Cognates* (Toronto: Toronto University Press, 1972), p. 293. Francesco Flora, *Storia della letteratura italiana*, 5 vols. (1940; Milano: Mondadori, 1959), IV, 28. Hans Sckommodau, "Italienische Literatur in der romantischen Epoche" in *Die europäische Romantik* (Frankfurt: Athenäum, 1972), p. 247. These references in standard works indicate the existing consensus on the peculiarities of Italian romanticism.

92. J. G. Robertson, *Studies in the Genesis of Romantic Theory in the 18th Century* (New York: Russell and Russell, 1972).

93. W. Krömer, "Die Romantik in Spanien" in *Die europäische Romantik*, pp. 270–332. See also Ricardo Navas-Ruiz, *El romanticismo español* (Salamanca: Anaya, 1971). Donald Shaw, *A Literary History of Spain: The Nineteenth Century* (London: Benn, 1972), as well as the standard accounts of Diaz-Plaja and Valbuena Prat. See Susan Kirkpatrick, "On the Threshold of

the Realist Novel: Gender and Genre in 'La Gaviota'," *PMLA,* 98 (1983), 323–341.

94. Shaw, *Literary History of Spain,* pp. 44–53. Documents on *costumbrismo* in Ricardo Navas-Ruiz, *El romanticismo español. Documentos* (Salamanca: Anaya, 1971), pp. 241 ff. For more detailed analyses, see José Montesinos, *Costumbrismo y novela* (Berkeley: University of California Press, 1960), Vincente Llorens Castillo, *El romanticismo español* (Madrid: Castalia, 1979).

95. Sengle, *Biedermeierzeit,* II, 743–802.

96. Nemoianu, *Micro-Harmony,* pp. 93–112.

2. SUPPORT FOR AN ENGLISH BIEDERMEIER

1. Norbert Fuerst, *The Victorian Age in Literature,* (University Park: Pennsylvania State University Press, 1966), pp. 68–79.

2. Friedrich Brie, "Literarisches Biedermeier in England," *Deutsche Vierteljahrschrift für Literaturwissenschaft und Geistesgeschichte,* 13 (1935), pp. 149–162.

3. Carl Dawson, *Victorian Noon,* (Baltimore: Johns Hopkins University Press, 1977), pp. 149–162.

4. L. H. C. Thomas, "German Literature and British Mid-Nineteenth Century Novelists," in R. W. Last, ed., *Affinities* (London: O. Wolff, 1971), p. 45.

5. Ilse Hecht, "Dickens' Verhältnis zum Biedermeier," *Deutsche Vierteljahrschrift für Literaturwissenschaft und Geistesgeschichte,* 22, no. 4 (1944), 439–470. Pius Wolters, "Das Drollige bei Dickens als charakteristisches Stilelement der Biedermeierkunst," *Germanisch-Romanische Monatsschrift,* 33 (1952), 283.

6. Mario Praz, *The Hero in Eclipse in Victorian Fiction,* trans. Angus Davidson (London and Oxford: Oxford University Press, 1956).

7. Otto F. Bollnow, *Unruhe und Geborgenheit im Weltbild neuerer Dichter,* (1953; reprint, Stuttgart: Kohlhammer, 1968), pp. 255–259.

8. Graham Hough, *The Romantic Poets* (Tiptree, Essex: Arrow Books, 1964), pp. 25–97. Allan Grant, *A Preface to Coleridge* (London: Longman, 1972), pp. 88–97. Recently Marilyn Butler, *Romantics, Rebels and Reactionaries* (New York and Oxford: Oxford University Press, 1982), has argued that the Lake Poets had been conservative from the beginning, an interesting but simplifying view.

9. Or, as Alethea Hayter put it in *Opium and the Romantic Imagination* (Berkeley: University of California Press, 1968), "Opium was a symptom, not a cause of Coleridge's tragedy" (p. 207).

10. *Manfred,* III, 1, 138–145, in Byron, *Poetical Works,* ed. F. Page and J. Jump (London: Oxford University Press), p. 403.

11. Butler, *Romantics,* pp. 75–77, shows herself aware of the phenomenon and provides some empirical explanations which are pedestrian, but correct from a cultural point of view.

12. Jack Stillinger, *The Hoodwinking of Madeline* (Urbana: University of Illinois Press, 1971), p. 130.

13. Thomas MacFarland, *Romanticism and the Forms of Ruin* (Princeton: Princeton University Press, 1981), pp. 217–218.

14. See for instance Geoffrey Hartman, "Blessing the Torrent: On Wordsworth's Later Style," *PMLA,* 93, no. 2 (1978), 196–204. This refers specifically to one sonnet, but reaches conclusions on change valid for Wordsworth's work as a whole.

15. Vincent De Luca, "The Type of a Mighty Mind: Mutual Influence in Wordsworth and De Quincy," *Texas Studies in Language and Literature,* 13, no. 2 (1979), 239–247, quotes on pp. 241–242, 245.

16. Jerome McGann, *Don Juan in Context* (Chicago: University of Chicago Press, 1976), pp. 123 and 115. Further references in parentheses in the text.

17. Virgil Nemoianu, "The Dialectics of Movement in Keats' Autumn," *PMLA,* 93 (1978), 205–214.

18. E. C. Pettet, *On the Poetry of Keats* (Cambridge: Cambridge University Press, 1957). Douglas Bush, *Mythology and the Romantic Tradition in English Poetry* (1937; New York: Norton, 1969), pp. 81–128. See also Walter Evert, *Aesthetic and Myth in the Poetry of Keats* (Princeton: Princeton University Press, 1965).

19. "Literary and Lake Reminiscences" in Thomas De Quincey, *Collected Writings,* ed. David Masson, 14 vols. (Edinburgh: Adam and Charles Black, 1889), II, 113–454. First published in 1839–1841.

20. Fred Randel, *The World of Elia: Charles Lamb's Essayistic Romanticism* (Port Washington, New York: Kennikat Press, 1975), pp. 21–112.

21. Virgil Nemoianu, *Micro-Harmony: The Growth and Uses of the Idyllic Model in Literature* (Bern: Peter Lang, 1977), pp. 47–93. See also Irving Babbitt, *Rousseau and Romanticism* (Boston: Houghton Mifflin, 1919), pp. 91–92, and Max Byrd, *London Transformed* (New Haven: Yale University Press, 1978).

22. Praz, *Victorian Hero,* p. 67. He also mentions Lamb's lack of interest in politics and indifference to Parisian sights.

23. For a detailed discussion see Albert Goldman, *The Mine and the Mint: Sources for the Writings of De Quincey* (Carbondale: Southern Illinois University Press, 1965).

24. Mario Praz, *Romantic Agony* (1933; reprint, Oxford: Oxford University Press, 1978), p. 179.

25. Virgil Nemoianu, *Calmul Valorilor* (Dacia: Cluj, 1971), pp. 116–124.

26. Praz, *Victorian Hero,* pp. 83–85. He also underlines De Quincey's preference for Jean Paul over Goethe and even Sterne (p. 79).

27. M. H. Abrams, *Natural Supernaturalism* (New York: Norton, 1971), p. 347.

28. Gilbert K. Chesterton, *The Victorian Age in Literature (*1918; reprint, Oxford: Oxford University Press, 1966), pp. 4–7.

29. William Hazlitt, *The Complete Works,* ed. P. P. Howe, 21 volumes. (London: J. Dent and Sons, 1930–1934), V, 161–162. Parenthetical references in the text hereafter.

30. See Ralph Wardle, *Hazlitt* (Lincoln: University of Nebraska Press, 1971), p. 175.

31. Elizabeth Schneider, *The Aesthetics of William Hazlitt* (New York: Octagon, 1967), pp. 184–189.

32. Roy Park, *Hazlitt and the Spirit of the Age: Abstraction and Critical Theory* (Oxford: Clarendon Press, 1971), pp. 2, 78, 88–91.

33. Hazlitt's essay "On Gusto" first appeared in *The Examiner,* 26 (May 1816).

34. Marilyn Butler, *Peacock Displayed* (London: Routledge and Kegan Paul, 1979), p. 183.

35. Howard Mills, *Peacock: His Circle and His Age* (Cambridge: Cambridge University Press, 1969), pp. 163, 140.

36. For a parallel between *Don Juan* and *Nightmare Abbey* see Carl Dawson, *His Fine Wit: A Study of Th. L. Peacock* (Berkeley: University of California Press, 1970), p. 308.

37. That is how I explain the puzzling conclusions of A. E. Dyson, "The Crazy Fabric" in Lorne Sage, ed., *Peacock: The Satirical Novels. A Casebook* (London: Macmillan, 1971), pp. 186–189, regarding the dialectics progressive-conservative in Peacock.

38. For a discussion see Dawson, *His Fine Wit,* pp. 210–211.

39. Warren Roberts, *Jane Austen and the French Revolution* (New York: St. Martin's Press, 1979).

40. Scott commented on Austen in *The Quarterly Review,* 18 (March 1816), pp. 188–201.

41. Marvin Mudrick, "Jane Austen: Irony as Defense and Discovery" in Brian C. Southam, ed., *Jane Austen: Northanger Abbey and Persuasion. A Casebook* (London: Macmillan, 1976), pp. 82–83. Northrop Frye, *The Secular Scripture: A Study of the Structure of Romance,* (Cambridge: Harvard University Press, 1982), p. 138, made similar observations about *Emma:* "Emma imposes a romance pattern on her friend Harriet, whose parentage is unknown, and who therefore, by all the rules of romance, must be of some quite exceptional birth. Emma's discovery that Harriet is, in parentage as well as character, pretty well what she appears to be is the discovery that liberates her from illusion."

42. R. F. Brissenden, "La Philosphie dans le boudoir; or A Young Lady's Entrance into the World," *Studies in Eighteenth Century Culture,* 2 (1972), p. 128.

43. Robert Kiely, *The Romantic Novel in England* (Cambridge: Harvard University Press, 1972), p. 121.

44. Alistair Duckworth, *The Improvement of the Estate* (Baltimore: Johns Hopkins University Press, 1971), pp. 57–91. Other observations of the same type are in William H. Helm, *Jane Austen and Her Country-House Comedy* (London: E. Nash, 1909), and Charles Murrah, "The Background of *Mansfield Park,*" in *From Jane Austen to Joseph Conrad: Essays Collected in Memory of James T. Hillhouse,* ed. Robert C. Rathburn and Martin Steinmann, Jr. (Minneapolis: University of Minnesota Press, 1958), pp. 23–34.

45. Jane Austen, *Mansfield Park,* ed. John Lucas (Oxford: Oxford University Press, 1970), p. 218; of course, there is an ironic note. References hereafter in parentheses in the text.

46. Avrom Fleishman made this point very cogently in *A Reading of Mansfield Park: An Essay in Critical Synthesis* (Minneapolis: University of Minnesota Press, 1967), pp. 15–17, 34–35.

47. Tony Tanner, "Jane Austen and the Quiet Thing" in Brian C. Southam, ed., *Critical Essays on Jane Austen* (London: Routledge and Kegan, 1968), p. 142.

48. Roberts, *Jane Austen and the French Revolution,* pp. 203, 205.

49. Marilyn Butler, *Jane Austen and the War of Ideas* (Oxford: Clarendon 1975), pp. 194–195, 180.

50. Irvin Ehrenpreis, "Jane Austen and Heroism," *New York Review of Books,* 8 February 1979, p. 40.

51. Ibid., p. 43. Roberts, *Jane Austen and the French Revolution,* pp. 65–67.

52. Edgar Johnson, *Sir Walter Scott,* 2 vols. (New York: Macmillan, 1970), I, 469.

53. George Lukács, *The Historical Novel* (London: Merlin, 1937; rev. ed. 1960), pp. 30–63, explains Scott's historical novel as a resumption in a bourgeois tone of the grand postures of epic.

54. Walter Scott, *Waverley* (Edinburgh: Adam and Charles Black, 1871), pp. 31–49. References hereafter in parentheses in the text.

55. Walter Scott, *Rob Roy* (Edinburgh: Adam and Charles Black, 1871), pp. 60–79.

56. Meyer H. Abrams, *Natural Supernaturalism* (1971; reprint, New York: Norton, 1973), pp. 236–237.

57. Alexander Llewellyn, *The Decade of Reform: The 1830's* (Newton Abbott, England: David and Charles, 1972), pp. 23–25, 120.

58. Llewellyn, *Decade of Reform,* pp. 201–203.

59. Donald Low, *That Sunny Dome: A Portrait of Regency Britain,* (London and Totowa, N.J.: Dent, Rowman and Littlefield, 1977), p. 171.

60. Ibid., pp. 174-179.

61. Ibid., pp. 46-47.

62. Harriet Bridgeman and Elizabeth Drury, eds., *The English Eccentric* (London: M. Joseph, 1975).

63. Willard Connely, *The Reign of Beau Brummell* (London: Cassell, 1940), pp. 127-130.

64. Edmund Blunden, *Leigh Hunt* (London: Cobden-Sanderson, 1930), pp. 34-38.

65. Ian Jack, *English Literature 1815-1832* (Oxford: Oxford University Press, 173-174).

66. Virgil Nemoianu, "The Structure of Classical Periods: The Classical Age of Romanticism," paper presented at the IXth I.C.L.A. Congress, Innsbruck, 1979.

67. Margery Sabin, *English Romanticism and the French Tradition,* (Cambridge: Cambridge University Press, 1977).

68. Beth Nelson, *George Crabbe and the Progress of the 18th Century Narrative Verse* (Lewisburg, Pa.: Bucknell University Press, 1976), p. 16.

69. John Barrell, *The Idea of Landscape and the Sense of Place 1730-1840* (Cambridge: Cambridge University Press, 1972), pp. 146-152, 187-188.

70. Northrop Frye, *The Secular Scripture* (Cambridge: Harvard University Press, 1976), pp. 146-147, discovers important archetypes in *Handley Cross:* Jorrocks as Actaeon.

71. For superb comments on the prose writing of the essayists see Michael Cooke, *Acts of Inclusion* (New Haven and London: Yale University Press, 1979), pp. 186-187, 242-249.

72. John Speirs, *Poetry Towards Novel* (New York: New York University Press, 1971), pp. 11-12, 287-305.

73. Cf. also Bernice Slote, *Keats and the Dramatic Principle* (Lincoln: University of Nebraska Press, 1958), pp. 117-119.

74. John Carey, *Thackeray: Prodigal Genius* (London: Faber & Faber, 1977).

75. Praz, *Hero in Eclipse,* pp. 201, 220-221, 246-249. Robert Colby, *Thackeray's Canvass of Humanity: The Author and His Public* (Columbus: Ohio State University Press, 1979).

76. Tennyson, *The Poetic and Dramatic Works,* ed. W. J. Rolfe (Boston: Houghton Mifflin, 1898), pp. 51-52.

3. FRENCH ROMANTICISM: TWO BEGINNINGS?

1. Pierre Moreau, *Le Classicisme des romantiques* (Paris: Plon, 1932).

2. Albert Béguin, *L'Âme romantique et le rêve* (Paris: Cahiers du Sud,

1937). The collection *Littérature française* (Paris: Arthaud, 1964–1974) is edited by Claude Pichois. The first volume on romanticism covers 1820–1843, the third 1869–1896. Mario Praz, *The Romantic Agony*, trans. A. Davidson (1933; reprint, Oxford: Oxford University Press, 1970), also extends his analyses to 1900. Kenneth Clark, *The Romantic Rebellion* (London: J. Murray, 1973), considers Rodin a great romantic.

    3. Philippe Van Tieghem, *Histoire de la littérature française* (Paris: Fayard, 1949), pp. 287–373. The next chapter is entitled "Romantisme et réalisme (1830–1885) where romanticism is bolstered by the annexation of Balzac, George Sand, Baudelaire, and the Parnassiens; even François Coppée and Catulle Mendès are called up in despair.

    4. Thus Pierre Abraham and Roland Desné, eds., *Manuel d'histoire littéraire de la France*, 6 vols. (Paris: Editions Sociales, 1965–1975). But also Pierre G. Castex et al., *Histoire de la littérature française* (1977; reprint, Paris: Hachette, 1979), who resorts to a transitional chapter "Du siècle philosophique au siècle romantique (1795–1820)." Their common model is probably the prestigious work of Joseph Bédier and Paul Hazard, *Histoire de la littérature française*, 2 vols. (Paris: Larousse, 1923–1924). This work had at least the advantage of ending its first volume around 1700; more recent two-volume works are split around 1789, which only compounds their problem. See Pierre Brunel et al., *Histoire de la littérature française*, 2 vols. (Paris: Bordas, 1977).

    5. Daniel Mornet, *Le Romantisme en France au XVIIIe siècle* (Paris: Hachette, 1912).

    6. Thus in effect Pierre Martino, *L'époque romantique en France 1815–1830* (Paris: Boivin, 1944), pp. 19–35.

    7. Henri Peyre, *What Is Romanticism?* trans. Roda Roberts (1971; reprint, University: University of Alabama Press, 1977), pp. 26–41.

    8. "Uncertain, agitated / And tossed about by the winds on the waves of doubt"; "hearts resounding with storms"; "as soon as for a moment the wind has fallen asleep, / smoothes again the surface on which the heavens once shuddered." See Alphonse de Lamartine, *Oeuvres poétiques complètes*, ed. M. F. Guyard (Paris: Pléiade, 1963), pp. 306–311. Idyllic overtones, e.g., in "Souvenir d'enfance ou la vie cachée," which is part of "Harmonies poétiques et religieuses" (bk. 2, 12), or "Milly ou la terre natale," ibid. (bk. 2, 2). Cf. Lamartine, pp. 378–385, 392ff. "La cloche du village" (pp. 1160–1162) is a nice imitation of Gray's *Elegy*. Helmut Hatzfeld, *Literature Through Art*, University of North Carolina Studies in the Romance Languages and Literatures 86 (1952; Chapel Hill: University of North Carolina Press, 1969), pp. 158–159, quotes the scenes of *Jocelyn* under the heading "The Family Idyl."

    9. Lamartine, *Oeuvres*, pp. 577–580 ("Ier mai 1786").

10. Lamartine, *Oeuvres*, p. 947 (in the passage "Les Laboureurs" of May 16, 1801, in Valneige).

11. "On the banks of the Tiber, of the Nile, and of the Ganges"; "empire, glory, freedom," "transported by youth and hope, / I will again challenge the waves and the storms." Lamartine, *Oeuvres*, pp. 36–38.

12. "Your vaster spirit covers the whole horizon; / And embracing the world's scenery, / The torch of study shines upon your reason." Lamartine, *Oeuvres*, p. 37.

13. Lamartine, *Oeuvres*, pp. 56–59.

14. "roaming soul"; "an often deceived eagle"; "the rustic enclosure, planted by my forefathers." Lamartine, *Oeuvres*, p. 58.

15. See, for instance, *Adieu* in the first series of *Méditations Poétiques:* "Quand mes cheveux auront blanchi, / Je viendrai du vieux Bissy, / Visiter le toit solitaire." Lamartine, *Oeuvres*, p. 67.

16. I believe that Albert Joseph George, *Lamartine and Romantic Unanimism* (New York: Columbia University Press, 1940), pp. 12–67, fails to distinguish between the declarative expository version of organic pantheism to be found in Lamartine's work and the deeper organic principle governing the very growth of high-romantic language and imagery (in De Man's sense).

17. "I murmured low: oh, why am I not one of you!" "to shine on the brow of beauty supreme, / Like a pale jewel of its sacred diadem." Lamartine, *Oeuvres*, pp. 124–127. It is the fourth of the *Nouvelles Méditations Poétiques* of 1823.

18. "Changed form and contour"; "Yes, in this heavenly air, life's heavy cares, / The contempt of mortals, their hatred or envy, / No longer accompany man." Lamartine, *Oeuvres*, pp. 135–137, the eighth of the *Nouvelles Méditations.*

19. Lamartine, *Oeuvres*, pp. 159–165, the fifteenth, sixteenth, and twenty-fourth of the *Nouvelles Méditations.*

20. Georges Poulet, *Metamorphoses of the Circle* (Paris: Plon, 1961; Baltimore: Johns Hopkins University Press, 1966), pp. 119–136. Jean-Pierre Richard, "Vallon et horizon: Thématique de l'ouvert et du clos chez Lamartine," in *Sainte-Beuve, Lamartine: Colloques 8 Novembre 1968,* Publications de la Société Littéraire de la France (Paris: Armand Colin, 1970), pp. 62–76. Others have underscored the importance of water imagery. The sea or the lake provide both stability and determinacy; water conveniently suggests a cosmic dimension without actually committing Lamartine. See Jeanne-Louis Manning, "Les Images aquatiques dans la poésie lyrique d'Alphonse de Lamartine" and Marcel Schaettel, "L'Occident, poème cosmique," in *Journées européenes d'études lamartiniennes: Actes du Congrès III* (Mâcon: n.p., 1969), pp. 221–224, 197–206.

21. "The self, well protected in its retreat, or else securely attached to

its perch, no longer is afraid to plunge—visually, or in imagination—into all the far horizons which now seem devoid of any iniquity. His watchtower is so safe, that all risk of dispersal and loss is precluded." Richard, "Vallon et horizon," p. 73.

22. See B. Zolnai, "Irodalom es Biedermeier," *Acta Litterarum et Scientiarum Reg. Univ. Hung. Francisco-Josephinae,* 7 (1935). See also D. Baroti, "Biedermeier izlés a francia irodalomban," *Études francaises publiées par l'Institut de l' Université François-Joseph,* 21 (1942). Both are quoted and summarized in Henry H. H. Remak, "The Periodization of XIXth Century German Literature in the Light of French Trends: A Reconsideration," *Neohelicon,* 1–2 (1973), 177–194. Colette Dimić has made thorough and persuasive studies of Biedermeier features in the prose of Fromentin and in some of George Sand's pastoral novels of the 1840s. "Dominique de Fromentin dans la perspective du Biedermeier" and "Les Traits Biedermeier dans les romans champêtres de George Sand" (unpublished, communication of the author).

23. "I would have needed in some corner of the world, / but an innocent peace, a lonely hut." Sainte-Beuve, "Sonnet II" of "Vie, Poésie et Pensées de Joseph Delorme," in *Poésies complètes* (Paris: Charpentier, 1908), p. 35.

24. "All this is, for just one day, intoxicating / But let, oh let tomorrow come" Sainte-Beuve, "Bonheur champêtre. A mon ami E. T.," in "Delorme," *Poésies complètes,* pp. 56–59. His idyllic interests were of course based also on critical readings of bucolic Greek, Latin, or French authors. See Ruth Muhlhauser, *Sainte-Beuve and Greco-Roman Antiquity* (Cleveland: The Press of Case Western Reserve University, 1969), pp. 181–197.

25. "Far of the beaten paths; hardly by the hunter / known"; "lizard or viper under your steps." Sainte-Beuve, "Le Creux de la valée," in "Delorme," *Poésies complètes,* p. 103.

26. Sainte-Beuve, "Au loisir," in "Delorme," *Poésies complètes,* pp. 32–33.

27. "and the abundant harvests, / And the numberless apple-trees with their round leafy heads, / As well, the cherry-trees shining all red with fruit; / The neighboring farms whose noises I so loved"; Sainte-Beuve, "Pour mon ami Ulric G., V," in "Poésies diverses," *Poésies complètes,* p. 177.

28. "The enclosure lined with weeping larches and laburnums and judas trees, / shrubbery hidden to daylight, secret lanes"; "these lawns watered by her / these curving paths over which a lovely whim / freely reigns"; "Pour mon ami Ulric G., II" in "Poésies diverses," *Poésies complètes,* p. 173. See also Sainte-Beuve, "A Villemain" in "Pensées d'Août," *Poésies complètes,* p. 379.

29. "Oh! I have always dreamt of living solitary / In some hidden ruin of an ancient monastery, / of having my obscure room, with, behind stout

bars, / A narrow stained-glass window," Sainte-Beuve, "A Fontaney," in "Les Consolations," *Poésies complètes,* p. 229.

30. "Portals, steeples, and belfries, / And the age-old houses hiding in huge backyards." Sainte-Beuve, "A mon ami Boulanger," in "Les Consolations," *Poésies complètes,* p. 251.

31. Sainte-Beuve, "Mes Livres. A mon ami Paul L., le bibliophile," in "Delorme," *Poésies complètes,* p. 79.

32. Saint-Beuve, "Les Rayons jaunes" in "Delorme," *Poésies complètes,* p. 68. Regarding Sainte-Beuve's preference for semi-urban retreats, see Gerald Antoine, "Introduction," *Vie, poésies et pensées de Joseph Delorme* by Sainte-Beuve (Paris: Nouvelles Éditions Latines, 1956), l-li.

33. Sainte-Beuve, "Pour mon ami Ulric G., III" in "Poésies diverses," *Poésies complètes,* pp. 175–176.

34. "and so we must heaven, before night falls, / demand for our hearts some unhappiness, some duty." Sainte-Beuve, "Pensée d'Août" in "Pensées d'Août," *Poésies complètes,* p. 295.

35. "Flowers, do not hurry to blossom; / February is not yet over, / oh, no, winter is not over," Sainte-Beuve, "Espérance. Á mon ami Ferdinand D," in "Delorme," *Poésies complètes,* p. 128.

36. "And I, with eyes moist and with shining brow, / Head uncovered, in adoration, recited the Ave." Sainte-Beuve, "Sonnet, à madame P." in "Pensées d'Août," *Poésies complètes,* p. 343. It is typical that Sainte-Beuve, a professed admirer of the Lake Poets, should have considered Cowper one of them. Antoine, "Introduction," li.

37. Sainte-Beuve, "A Madame V. H.," which opens "Les Consolations" and may be said to give its tone, *Poésies complètes,* p. 208.

38. Sainte-Beuve, "Monsieur Jean, Maître d'école" and "A Madame la C. de T . . ." in *Poésies complètes,* pp. 306, 406, respectively.

39. Sainte-Beuve, "A Mon Ami Boulanger," in *Poésies complètes,* p. 251.

40. "Kneeling, drop by drop to sweat your agony." Sainte-Beuve, "A Mon Ami Boulanger," p. 255. This study does not deal with Sainte-Beuve's criticism, but there are notable morphological similarities. Sainte-Beuve creates a seventeenth century that should provide him with a Restorationist balance between an "excessive" romanticism and a dried-out eighteenth-century neoclassicism; methodologically he juggles history with artistic devices and yokes artistic devices to scholarly purposes to achieve a synthesis of moderate humanism. See Raphaël Molho, *L'Ordre et les tenèbres ou la naissance d'un mythe du 17e siècle chez Sainte-Beuve* (Paris: Armand Colin, 1972), or Roger Fayolle, *Sainte-Beuve et le 18e siècle ou comment les révolutions arrivent* (Paris: Armand Colin, 1972).

41. See the sensitive description of Claude Roy, *Les Soleils du romantisme* (Paris: Gallimard, 1974), pp. 165–167, 173.

42. "Our wheat is now all safely in the barns; I am setting up and improving a brandy distillery since from our grapes we can get the finest *cognac*." Letter to Busoni of August 11, 1848. See Vigny, *Correspondance 1822–1863*, 2 vols. (Paris: Séché, 1913).

43. Alfred de Vigny, *Oeuvres complètes*, ed. Paul Villaneix (Paris: Seuil, 1965), p. 58.

44. "The merchants are envious. / Gold rains from under the coals of the passing steam" and "Each will glide on his line, / Fixed in the rank already assigned at departure, / Plunged in cold, mute and deliberate scheming." Vigny, *Oeuvres*, p. 91.

45. A rich, but somewhat undiscriminating discussion of Vigny's sociopolitical views in Pierre Flottes, *La Pensée politique et sociale d'Alfred de Vigny*, Publications de la Faculté de lettres de l'Université de Strasbourg, 37 (Paris: Les belles lettres, 1927).

46. "But we must conquer both time and space"; "Well, let everything move"; "On the iron bull that smokes, blows and bellows / Man too early has climbed."

47. "fatal rocks of human slavery"; "Poetry! oh treasure! pearls of thought!" The poetic jewel also appears in *Les Oracles* (ll. 125–133, in the Post Scriptum). It has been suggested that Heine introduced this image in France when he talked about pearls as the malignant growths of underwater shells. Cf. Vigny, *Les Destinées*, ed. Alphonse Bouvet (Paris: Bordas, 1971), p. 48. See François Germain, *L'Imagination d'Alfred de Vigny* (Paris: José Corti, 1962), pp. 145–148, 206–219.

48. Vera Summers, *L'Orientalisme d'Alfred de Vigny* (Paris: Champion, 1930), pp. 97–137.

49. "Vigorously fulfill your long and heavy duty / on the path chosen for you by Fate; / Thereafter, like myself, suffer and die without words." Vigny, *Oeuvres*, pp. 102, 11, 86–88.

50. Vigny, *Oeuvres*, pp. 40–49.

51. Vigny, *Oeuvres*, pp. 66, 68.

52. "We should admit that the true is just secondary; it is nothing but one more beautifying illusion, one more inclination that we have to flatter." Vigny, *Oeuvres*, p. 145.

53. Vigny, *Oeuvres*, pp. 149ff.

54. "Happy the man who does not survive his own youth and illusions, and who thus carries away to the grave his whole treasure." Vigny, *Oeuvres*, p. 150.

55. "The young men laughingly applauded, and they all stepped back up to the dancing hall as if they had been fighting." Vigny, *Oeuvres*, p. 237.

56. Vigny, *Oeuvres*, pp. 218, 254–255.

57. "Parliament is dead, one of the men said, the nobility are finished:

Let's dance, we are now the masters; the old cardinal is on the way out, there's nobody left but the King and us." Vigny, *Oeuvres,* pp. 270–271.

58. Charles Villiers, *L'Univers métaphysique de Victor Hugo* (Paris: J. Vrin, 1970), pp. 21–27, does not agree, but quotes Denis Saurat, Jacques Heugel, and Auguste Viatte as opposing authorities. He admits that his is a minority opinion.

59. Claude Gély, *Victor Hugo, poète de l'intimité* (Paris: Nizet, 1979). Cf. M. Barrère, *La Fantaisie de Victor Hugo* (Paris: José Corti, 1979), I, 247–302.

60. "Yes, this is truly the dale! dark and peaceful dale! / Here the coolest summer blossoms in the shade"; "I love the lofty oak less than the mossy nest; / I love the breeze in meadows more than the harsh storm"; "through the bright leaves / Her window, small and somehow amazed, / Blossoms by the Gothic portal." Victor Hugo, *Oeuvres poétiques,* ed. P. Albouy (Paris: NRF Pléiade, 1947), I, 782, 1038.

61. "First, there was a wide, immense, confused clamor, / Vaguer than the wind in the leafy trees, / Full of striking chords, of delicate rumors"; "the sun still glitters through their shades / . . . / Vague horizons are being contested with the mists; / The fall on dark lawns carves out / what might be large ponds of light." Hugo, *Oeuvres,* I, 726.

62. Hugo, *Oeuvres,* I, 770–774. Marcel Raymond, *Romantisme et rêverie* (Paris: José Corti, 1978), pp. 259, 265–278, uses this example to claim continuity in Hugo's poetic output. I think it is a rather isolated example.

63. Hugo, *Oeuvres,* I, 510–512.

64. Charles Dédéyan, *Victor Hugo et l'Allemagne* (Paris: Lettres Modernes, 1964), II, 528–550.

65. See Fernand Gregh, *L'Oeuvre de Victor Hugo* (Paris: Flammarion, 1933), pp. 78–110, 152–183.

66. Geraud Venzac, *Les Origines réligieuses de Victor Hugo* (Paris: Bloud et Gay, 1955).

67. Ibid., 85–88, 218–282.

68. Eric Voegelin, *From Enlightenment to Revolution* (Durham, N.C.: Duke University Press, 1975).

69. Perhaps based on the title of VIII, 6, "Trois coeurs d'homme faits différement." Wolfgang Holdheim, *Die Suche nach dem Epos* (Heidelberg: Carl Winter, 1978), p. 22, thinks the binary and ternary structures in the novel are incompatible.

70. Dédéyan, *Victor Hugo et l'Allemagne,* II, 285–320.

71. Victor Hugo, *Notre-Dame de Paris* (1831; reprint, Paris: Furne, 1844), II, 140–142 (Bk. VIII, Ch. 4).

72. Hugo, *Notre-Dame,* II, 288 (Bk. X, Ch. 4).

73. Hugo, *Notre-Dame,* I, 273 (Bk. V, Ch. 1).

74. Hugo, *Notre-Dame,* II, 288 (Bk. X, Ch. 4). For Quasimodo as nature, see IV, 3. René Girard, *Critique dans un souterrain* (Lausanne: L'Age d'Homme, 1976), p. 157, says Quasimodo is a gargoyle. See also Holdheim, *Die Suche nach dem Epos,* p. 40.

75. Incidentally, I suspect Djali was not a goat at all, but possibly *ovis ammon,* the Mongolian wild sheep called *argali,* whose fur and horn formation may make it look like a goat to a European. Obviously, Hugo needed a goat for symbolic reasons.

76. Hugo, *Notre-Dame,* Bk. II, Chs. 4 and 6 or Bk. X, 1–3.

77. Hugo, *Notre-Dame,* Bk. VIII, Chs. 4 and 5; Bks. VII and VIII; Bk. VIII, Chs. 1–3; Bk. VI, Ch. 4; even Bk. II, Ch. 3. See esp. II, 302–303 (the ending of Bk. X, Ch. 4) and II, 413–418 (Bk. XI, Ch. 2).

78. " 'In the very heart of the underwater cave, suddenly gripped by a cold and viscous lash, Gilliet recognized the devil-fish!' Period, paragraph, new chapter: 'The devil-fish is an octopode which . . .' There follow ten or twenty pages in Buffon's most didadic vein, in which usually some antithetical images will be strewn at random, which swell up, bulge, and finally burst with hardly any consequence." Roger Ikor, "Le Romancier populaire," in *Victor Hugo,* ed. Jacques de Lacretelle (Paris: Hachette, 1967), p. 140.

79. Hugo, *Notre-Dame,* II, 187–206 (Bk. IX, Chs. 1 and 2).

80. Hugo, *Notre-Dame,* II, 9–15 (Bk. VII, Ch. 1). Similarly, Quasimodo's flogging, I, 357–363. Hatzfeld, *Literature Through Art,* pp. 144–145, quotes this scene as typical of the sensational picturesque.

81. Jean Maillon, *Victor Hugo et l'art architectural* (Grenoble: Allier, 1962).

82. Hugo, *Notre-Dame,* III, 1.

83. Hugo, *Notre-Dame,* I, 272–273, 286–289 (Bk. V, Chs. 1 and 2).

84. Hugo, *Notre-Dame,* I, 293–297.

85. Holdheim, *Die Suche nach dem Epos,* pp. 39, 66, 68.

86. Hugo, *Notre-Dame,* II, 150–152, 372–375 (Bks. VIII, Ch. 4; Bk. XI, Ch. 1).

87. Hugo, *Notre-Dame,* II, 280–281 (Bk. VIII, Ch. 4) also I, 4.

88. Hugo, *Notre-Dame,* II, 56–60, 341–347 (Bk. X, Ch. 5, or Bk. I, Chs. 1 and 3, or Bk. II, Ch. 3).

89. Van Tieghem, *Histoire de la littérature francaise,* p. 421. Antoine, "Introduction," pp. xcv-c, squarely links Sainte-Beuve to these and other minor writers.

90. H. Van Der Tuin, *Les Vieux Peintres des Pays-Bas et la littérature en France dans la première moitié du XIXe siècle* (Paris: Nizet, 1953).

91. For a good general presentation of these changes and useful bibliographical hints, see Abraham and Desné, *Manuel d'histoire littéraire,* pp. 442–443, 450–460.

92. "Ecstasy falls back upon anxiety . . . Human nature herself would

not suffer a protracted siege. So we pass from capture to languor, from ecstasy to normal time, from innocence to guilt," and "satanic hope interrupted by occasional anxieties." Armand Hoog, "La Révolte métaphysique des petits romantiques," in Francis Dumont, ed., *Les Petits Romantiques Français* (Marseilles: Cahiers du Sud, 1949), p. 22.

93. Victor Brombert, *La Prison romantique: Essai sur l'imaginaire* (Paris: José Corti, 1975), pp. 53–57.

94. Cf. note 22.

95. Paul Louis Courier, *Oeuvres complètes,* ed. Armand Carrel (1829; reprint, Paris: Firmin Didot, 1839), pp. 83–88. His petition in favor of Sunday dances is made in the spirit of Goldsmith. The self-labeled "vigneron de la Chavonnière" was quite competent in ancient pastoral literature, as his edition of Longus shows.

96. Voegelin, *From Enlightenment to Revolution,* pp. 173–176.

97. François Furet and Denis Richet, *La Révolution française* (1965; reprint, Paris: Fayard, 1973), p. 486.

98. Howard Mumford Jones, *Revolution and Romanticism* (Cambridge: Harvard University Press, 1974), p. 487.

99. See Roman Jakobson, "Linguistics and Poetics," in *Style in Language,* ed. Thomas Sebeok (Cambridge: M.I.T. Press, 1960), pp. 353–364. Jan Mukařovsky, *Aesthetic Function, Norm and Value as Social Facts* (1936; Engl. ed. Ann Arbor: Michigan Slavic Contributions, 1970). The difference I set up is mainly one of self-awareness. A text that wishes to consider itself literary *is,* in a practical sense literary. Its stress, as Jakobson says, will be on the independence of the message among the different components of communication. Literary and textual materials are, in fact, mutually convertible: some pieces of literature can be turned utilitarian (*Uncle Tom's Cabin*), texts can become literary (Montaigne's *Essais*), intermediary cases abound (*La Marseillaise*).

100. Saint-Just's *Organt,* an epic in verse, has strong pornographic touches—a possible connection to Sade.

101. Louis de Saint-Just, *Oeuvres choisies,* ed. Dionys Mascolo (Paris: Gallimard, N.R.F., 1968), pp. 307–366, 123–144. I decided to use this handy little volume (the first edition of which had appeared in 1946) because the larger editions are not much more reliable and are not yet recognized as standard (e.g., the Soboul edition or even the prolix Vellay edition of 1908). Hereafter page numbers in parentheses in the text.

102. "The division of France into departments is maintained: each department has a capital center . . . The population of each department is divided into three districts: each district has a capital center . . . The urban and rural population within each district is divided into communes of 6 to 200 voters: each commune has a capital center" or "Each citizen expresses his

will by yes or no . . . The will of the majority is the will of the commune. The president apprizes the directories of the commune's will. The directory immediately makes public the will of the district's communes . . . The directories apprize the Minister of Ballotting of the communes' will . . . The Minister of Ballotting reports the results to the National Assembly, as soon as they are in."

103. "Public force is the people in its entirety, armed to ensure the execution of the law . . . The armies are part of the nation . . . There is no supreme commander . . . In triumphal parades, generals shall walk behind their troops . . . A French army can never surrender without casting infamy upon itself."

104. "The French people proclaims itself the friend of all nations; it will scrupulously respect all treaties and banners; it offers in its ports asylum to all the world's ships; it offers asylum to all great men, to the unfortunate virtuous from any country; on the high seas its ships will offer protection to foreign ships against the elements . . . The Republic . . . refuses asylum to homicides and tyrants . . . The Republic shall never take up arms to enslave and oppress people . . . She never makes peace with an enemy who occupies her territory . . . She shall not sign any treaties that do not have as purpose the peace and happiness of all nations . . . The French people votes the freedom of the world."

105. "Children are reared in the love of silence and the contempt of rhetoric . . . They must be forbidden all games which involve declamation and must be accustomed to truth unadorned"; "Children from five to ten must learn to read, to write, to swim"; "Children must be dressed in linen at all seasons. They take their rest on mats and sleep eight hours each night. They shall take their meals in common and be fed only roots, fruit, vegetables, dairy products, bread and water"; "They can only put on the habit of the arts after swimming across a river, on the day of the youth festival, in the presence of all people."

106. "Six elders remarkable for their virtues, whose duty it is to pacify seditions . . . The elders are decorated with a tricolor sash and white tuft; when they appear wearing their regalia, all people shall preserve silence and arrest anybody who continues the tumult"; "If one of the elders is murdered, the republic will mourn a whole day and all labors will be suspended"; "Each family receives a small plot for its graves. The cemeteries are pleasing landscapes; the tombs are covered with flowers, planted each year by the children. Blameless children place above the gate of the house the portraits of their father and mother."

107. "The council protects agriculture, maintains abundance, administers direct contributions, submits to the National Assembly projects for improvement, indemnities and rewards . . . It oversees the maintenance of

roads, the postal system, fortifications, internal navigation, mines, forests, the national estate; it supervises the production of weapons, of gun powder . . . it disposes the triumph of armies, it protects the arts, all talents, the public institutions"; "the courts are guardians of morality and trustees of the law: they are inflexible."

108. "Murderers must dress in black all their life long, under pain of execution"; "Nobody shall eat meat the third, sixth and ninth day of a decade"; "Strasbourg, eleventh day of the second month of Year II. The French Republic receives from and sends to its enemies only lead"; "I despise the dust that I am made from and that speaks to you"; "In battle, friends shall be placed by each other's side. Those who remain close all their life will be buried together. Friends will wear mourning for one another."

109. "If moral habits were firm, nothing further would be needed; institutional systems must purify them . . . all else will follow naturally"; "what will save us from corruption? . . . Institutions."

110. Cf. Maurice Dommaget, *Saint-Just* (Paris: Editions du Cercle, 1971), pp. 132, 124–128.

111. Roland Barthes, *Sade / Fourier / Loyola* (Fr. edition 1971; transl. New York: Hill and Wang, 1976), p. 177. Petrus Borel acted as a popularizer, Hugo and Musset were also influenced, as Sainte-Beuve and Viel-Castel knew. Connections to Thackeray (through Soulié), Manzoni, and Jane Austen were recently suggested. Diderot influenced Janin through Sade. See Mario Praz, *Romantic Agony,* chap. 3.

112. Michel Foucault, *Madness and Civilization* (Fr. edition 1961; transl. London: Tavistock, 1967), p. 283.

113. Barthes, *Sade / Fourier / Loyola,* pp. 31, 32.

114. Thomas Molnar, "Kakotopia: The Politics of Sade," *Political Science Reviewer,* 3 (1973), 143–161. The term "Kakotopian" is meant to suggest a perfection of evil and ugliness, that is, an inverse of utopia.

115. Marcel Jean and Arpad Mezei, *Genèse de la pensée moderne dans la littérature française* (Paris: Correa, 1950), p. 37.

116. Foucault, *Madness and Civilization,* p. 283.

117. Jean and Mezei, *Genèse de la pensée moderne,* p. 38.

118. Sade, *La Philosophie dans le boudoir* in Marquis de Sade, *Oeuvres complètes,* 16 vols. (Paris: Cercle du Livre Precieux, 1966), ed. Gilbert Lély, vol. III–IV, "Septième et dernier dialogue."

119. Sade, *Juliette,* in *Oeuvres,* IX, 152–218, 388–394.

120. Alice Laborde, *Sade Romancier* (Neuchâtel: La Baconnière, 1974), pp. 131–149.

121. Roger Lacombe, *Sade et ses masques* (Paris: Payot, 1974).

122. A. Ages, "Chateaubriand and the philosophes," in *Chateaubriand Today,* ed. R. Switzer (Madison: University of Wisconsin Press, 1970), pp. 230, 240. Owen Aldridge, "Chateaubriand: The Idea of Liberty and Latin

America," in *Chateaubriand Today,* pp. 203, 204, 268, shows how he discriminates between the legitimate, earned liberty of the USA and the anorganic struggle of the Spanish colonies. He said at one point: "Républicain par nature, monarchiste par raison et bourbonnien par honneur, je me serais beaucoup mieux arrangé d'une démocratie si je n'avais pu conserver la monarchie légitime, que de la monarchie bâtarde octroyée par je ne sais qui." Quoted in André Maurois, *Chateaubriand* (Paris: Grasset, 1938), chap. 10. ("A Republican by nature, a monarchist by deliberation, and a Bourbon loyalist for honor's sake, I would have much preferred to live in a democracy, if legitimate monarchy could not be preserved, than to put up with the mongrel monarchy decreed by God knows who.") See Switzer, *Chateaubriand Today,* pp. 181–182, 189, 30–31, 36–37, 42. Ultimately Chateaubriand was a paternalist who applied aesthetic (and idyllic) patterns to political situations.

123. Maurois, *Chateaubriand,* pp. 317ff; see pp. 289, 273, 313.

124. Chateaubriand, "De l'Angleterre et des Anglois" in *Oeuvres complètes,* 12 vols. (Paris: Garnier, 1929), VI, 373. Cf. Chateaubriand, *Mémoires d'outre tombe,* Bk. 27, Chap. 11.

125. "What Lamartine salutes . . . under the name of love, sensibility and tenderness, Chateaubriand used to salute under the name of imagination, Muses and poetry." Sainte-Beuve, *Chateaubriand et son groupe littéraire sous l'Empire* (1861; Paris: Garnier, 1948), II, 75, 43.

126. Chateaubriand, *Atala. René,* ed. Gilbert Chinard, Collection Budé (Paris: Fernand Roches, 1930), p. 151. Hereafter references in parentheses in the text. "Amélie had received some divine attribute from nature. Her soul had the same innocent grace as her body; her feelings were surpassingly gentle, and in her manner there was nothing but softness and a certain dreamy quality. It seemed as though her heart, her thought, and her voice were all sighing in harmony. From her womanly side came her shyness and love, while her purity and melody were angelic." Translations are from Chateaubriand, *Atala. René,* transl. Irving Putter (1952; Berkeley: University of California Press, 1967), p. 100.

127. "So beautiful was she, so divinely radiant her countenance, that she brought a gasp of surprise and admiration from the onlookers" (p. 106), "Alas! I was alone, alone in the world! A mysterious apathy gradually took hold of my body. My aversion for life, which I had felt as a child, was returning with renewed intensity. Soon my heart supplied no more nourishment for my thought, and I was aware of my existence only in a deep sense of weariness" (p. 98).

128. "On one side I could see the vast expanse of shimmering waves, and on the other the somber walls of the convent vaguely reaching up and fading away in the skies"; "Storm on the waves and calm in your retreat . . . infinity on the other side of a cell wall" (p. 111).

129. "Then we go off to labor in the fields and although properties are

divided in order that all may learn to live in organized society, the harvests are placed in community granaries, and thus we may all practice brotherly charity. Four elders distribute equally the fruits of the farming. Add to this our religious ceremonies, a great many hymns, the cross where I celebrate the mysteries, the elm beneath which I preach on fair days, our graves close beside our corn fields, our rivers where I immerse little children . . ." (p. 56); "the most charming harmony of social and natural life" (p. 54); "I was witnessing the primal wedding of man and the earth, with men delivering to the earth the heritage of his sweat, and the earth, in return, undertaking to bear fruitfully man's harvests, his sons and his ashes" (p. 55).

130. "This cross was now partly submerged in water; the wood was overgrown with moss, and the pelican of the wilds liked to perch on its decaying arms" (p. 81); "He went to see the hermit's grotto and found it full of brambles and rasberry bushes, with a doe suckling its fawn" (p. 81). In the preceding paragraph Fr. Aubry has "for an altar a rock, for a church the wilderness" (p. 54).

131. Moreau, *Le classicisme des romantiques*, pp. 92–93.

132. Auguste Viatte, *Les Sources occultes du romantisme: Illuminisme. Classicisme. Théosophie 1770–1820*, 2 vols. (1927; reprint, Paris: Honoré Champion, 1965). Brian Juden, *Traditions orphiques et tendances mystiques dans le romantisme français* (Paris: Klincksieck, 1971). Among the many works of Antoine Faivre, the most comprehensive is *L'Esotérisme* au XVIIIe siècle en France et en Allemagne (Paris: Seghers, La Table d'éméraude, 1973).

133. Pierre-Simon Ballanche, *Oeuvres complètes* (Genève: Slatkine Reprints, 1967).

134. See Viatte, *Les Sources occultes du romantisme*, I, 238. See also the meticulous, but somewhat too cautious analysis of Mark Poster, *The Utopian Thought of Restif de la Bretonne* (New York: New York University Press, 1971).

135. Recently the utopian and illuminated dimension of De Maistre was discussed by Paul Gottfried, "Utopianism of the Right: Maistre and Schlegel," *Modern Age*, 24, 2 (1980), 150–160.

136. Abraham and Desné, *Manuel d'histoire littéraire*, pp. 29–32.

137. Ibid., pp. 44–47, 65.

138. Peter Brooks, *The Melodramatic Imagination* (New Haven, Conn.: Yale University Press, 1976), pp. 24–68. See also Reginald Hartland, *Walter Scott et le roman frénétique* (Paris: Honoré Champion, 1928), Chs. 4 and 5.

139. André Monglond, *Le Préromantisme français* (Grenoble: Arthaud, 1930), 2 vols.

140. Hermann Hofer, ed., *Louis-Sebastien Mercier précurseur et sa for-*

tune (Munich: Fink, 1977), pp. 37–135. L. S. Mercier, *L'An 2440: rêve s'il en fut jamais*, ed. R. Trousson (Paris: Ducros, 1971). Mercier may be considered a full romantic in his theory of the imagination as well as in his sensibility toward nature. See Henry Majewski, *The Preromantic Imagination of L. S. Mercier* (New York: Humanities Press, 1971), pp. 25–78, 137–159.

141. Beatrice Le Gall, *L'Imaginaire chez Sénancour*, 2 vols. (Paris: José Corti, 1966).

142. L. M. Porter, "Charles Nodier and Pierre-Simon Ballanche," *Orbis Litterarum*, 27 (1972), 229–236.

143. Antoine Faivre, *Mystiques, théosophes et illuminés au siècle des lumières* (Hildesheim and New York: Georg Olms, 1976), pp. 1–30.

144. Hofer, *Louis-Sebastien Mercier précurseur.*

145. "French romanticism, the romanticism of textbooks has only one thing in common with German romanticism: the name"; "The truly great romantics must be sought for either before the Revolution, or after the fall of the *Burgraves* (1843). They are 'pre-romantics': Rousseau, Sébastien Mercier, Restif de la Bretonne, Sénancour." Claude Pichois, "Surnaturalisme français et romantisme allemand," in *Connaissance de l'étranger: Mélanges offerts à la mémoire de Jean Marie Carré* (Paris: Didier, 1964), pp. 386–387.

4. EASTERN EUROPEAN ROMANTICISM

1. Alexander Gerschenkron, *Economic Backwardness in Historical Perspective* (1952; reprint, Cambridge: Belknap Press of Harvard University Press, 1966), pp. 353–354. See pp. 5–30, 354–364.

2. Ibid., p. 358.

3. Karl Marx and Friedrich Engels, *Werke* (Berlin: Dietz, 1956), XIII, 640–642. This is an often quoted passage from one of the mss. of the *Kritik der politischen Ökonomie.*

4. See Samuel Levin, *The Semantics of Metaphor* (Baltimore: Johns Hopkins University Press, 1977), Ch. 1.

5. See Chapter 1.

6. Alexandru Duțu, *Coordonate ale culturii românești în secolul al XVIII-lea* (Bucharest: Editura Pentru Literátură, 1968).

7. A recent presentation in Ion Lungu, *Școala ardeleană* (Bucharest: Minerva, 1978). The one significant literary work associated with the group is *Țiganiada* by I. Budai-Deleanu, a Voltairean mock-heroic poem in which some preromantic notes can be detected.

8. Typically, Alexandru Dima et al., eds., *Istoria literaturii române* (Bucharest: Editura Academiei R.S.R., 1968), II, 9–229.

9. Paul Cornea, *Originile romantismului românesc* (Bucharest: Minerva, 1972). See Vera Călin, "Aspects de la superposition des courants littéraires

dans la littérature roumaine au cours de la première moitié du XIXe siècle," in *Actes du Ve congrès de l'Association Internationale de Littérature Comparée* (Belgrade: Mouton, 1969), pp. 225–230. Călin speaks mostly about the simultaneous reception of classicism, Enlightenment, preromanticism, and romanticism in Romanian poetry.

10. Mention could also be made of Nicolae Filimon's *Escursiuni în Germania meridională* (1860), or his many artistic, musical, and economic reviews. Mihai Kogălniceanu published in the 1840s a large number of delightful observations (ironic and objective) on Moldavian social customs; see *Scrisori: Note de călătorie*, ed. Augustin Z. N. Pop and Dan Simonescu (Bucharest: Eminescu, 1967). Vasile Alecsandri's fragmentary memoirs and some of his prose (*Istoria unui galbăn și a unei parale*) belong to the same category.

11. A conceivable exception is Alecu Russo, *Cîntare României* (1850). But even Russo was influenced by Xavier de Maistre—an author greatly appreciated by Romanian literati of the time—in his minor writings.

12. Ion Negoițescu, *Poezia lui Eminescu* (Bucharest: EPL, 1967).

13. Tibor Klaniczay, Joszef Szauder, and Miklos Szcabolcsi, *History of Hungarian Literature* (London: Collet's, 1964) is Marxist. Julius von Farkas, *Die ungarische Romantik* (Berlin: Walter de Gruyer, 1931) is Nadlerian. A typical position (widely shared by traditional Eastern European Marxists) is that the problem of periodization should be subordinated to a belated nation-forming process, which drew from different sources simultaneously. It is put forward by Laszlo Sziklay, "La Formation de la conscience nationale moderne dans les littératures de l'Est de l'Europe Centrale," in *Les Lumières en Hongrie, en Europe Centrale et en Europe Orientale*, ed. Bela Köpeczi (Budapest: Akademiai Kiado, 1971), p. 56. Interesting and sophisticated is Istvan Söter, *The Dilemma of Literary Science* (Budapest: Akademiai Kiado, 1973), pp. 101–240—both on the theory of periodization in European literature, and on the way this can be applied to Hungarian literature. He applies the *Goethezeit* model and relies a lot on expanded *Sturm und Drang;* ultimately he takes 1817 as the starting date.

14. One of the many parallel examples in neighboring literatures is provided by the Slovak J. I. Bajza's *René* (1783–1785). Usually characterized as an Enlightenment novel, it might well be understood as showing romantic features. See Jan Tibensky, "Les Traits fondamentaux et les principaux représentants slovaques de l'époque des lumières," in Köpeczi, *Les Lumières en Hongrie*, p. 66.

15. It should be noted that Csokonai's *Dorottya* has often been compared to *Pan Tadeusz* and *Onegin*. See, e.g., F. Szilágyi, "Les Changements du léxique de la langue littéraire et courante hongroise à l'époque des lumières, en rapport avec les changements de la conscience (collective) linguistique (stylistique)," in Köpeczi, *Les Lumières en Hongrie*, p. 86.

16. Alexandra Cioranescu says: "le romantisme ne peut être conçu comme renversement ou comme réaction que là où il y a eu préalablement un classicisme" (*Revue de littérature comparée*, 48, no. 1 [1974], 160–161). This opinion is shared by many Eastern European specialists. Besides Vera Calin (n. 9), see the opinions of K. Horvath and L. Sziklay in Köpeczi, *Les Lumières en Hongrie*, pp. 59 and 101, on simultaneous reception.

17. Both in Hungary and in Romania. See Andrew Janos, "Modernization and Decay in Historical Perspective: The Case of Romania," in *Social Change in Romania 1860–1940*, ed. K. Jowitt (Berkeley: Institute of International Studies, 1978), pp. 72–117. See also Janos, *The Politics of Backwardness in Modern Hungary, 1825–1945* (Princeton: Princeton University Press, 1981).

18. A possible exception is his philosophic fairy play in verse *Csongor es Tünde* (1831), much indebted to the atmosphere of *A Midsummer Night's Dream*.

19. The parallel examples of Mácha, Eminescu, Hugo, and, in another sense, Norwid and Nerval are mentioned elsewhere.

20. Söter, pp. 196–197.

21. William Harkins, "The Periodization of Czech Literary History, 1774–1879," in *The Czech Renascence of the 19th Century: Essays Presented to Otakar Odložilik*, ed. Peter H. Brock and H. Gordon Skilling (Toronto: University of Toronto Press, 1970), pp. 3–13.

22. Vaclav Flajšhans, *Pisemnictví české slovem i obrazem od nejdávnějších dob až po naše časy* (Prague: Grosman a Svoboda, 1901). Arne Novak, *Die tschechische Literatur*, Handbuch der Literaturwissenschaft, 18, ed. Oskar Walzel (Potsdam: Athenaion, 1931), pp. 1–114. (Novak later changed his mind.) See Arne Novak, *Dějiny české literatury*, 3 vols. (Prague: Práce Československé Akademie Věd, 1959–1961).

23. Matthias Murko, *Deutsche Einflüsse auf die Anfänge der Böhmischen Romantik* (Graz: Styria, 1897), p. 23.

24. Ibid., p. 18.

25. See ibid., pp. 197–216, 234; see also the interesting sonnet analysis of the way in which a new "wholeness" is created out of separate parts by a mimetic process, pp. 213–214.

26. Ibid., pp. 269–270.

27. Josef Mühlberger, *Tschechische Literaturgeschichte* (Munich: Ackermann-Gemeinde, 1970), pp. 4–5.

28. Novák, *Die tschechische Literatur*, p. 46.

29. Milorada Součková, "*Locus Amoenus*: An Aspect of National Tradition," in Brock and Skilling, *Czech Renascence*, pp. 26–32.

30. Božena Němcová, *Babička* (Prague: Pospisil, 1855). A recent translation is Edith Pargeter, trans., *Granny* (Prague: Artia, 1962).

31. Leslie Stephen, *Hours in a Library,* 2nd ed. (London: Smith and Elder, 1877), I, 13, 15.

32. René Wellek, *Essays on Czech Literature* (The Hague: Mouton, 1963), pp. 148–179. Parts of the essay were published in 1937 and 1938. Milorada Součková, *The Czech Romantics* (The Hague: Mouton, 1958), pp. 39–86.

33. Stanley Kimball, "The 'Matice Česká,' 1831–1861: The First Thirty Years of Literary Foundation," in Brock and Skilling, *Czech Renascence,* pp. 53–73. Similar organizations were created by the Transylvanian Romanians (in fact, Archbishop Șaguna was directly inspired by his Uniate philologist predecessors—Micu and Șincai) and the Serbians: *Astra* and *Matica Srpska.* For a more general Czech background, see Arne Novak, *Die tschechische Literatur,* pp. 35–37.

34. Lauren C. Leighton, *Russian Romanticism: Two Essays* (The Hague: Mouton, 1975), p. 6.

35. D. S. Mirsky, *A History of Russian Literature,* ed. Francis J. Whitfield (1926; reprint, New York: Vintage-Random House, 1958), pp. 73–177.

36. Leighton, *Russian Romanticism,* pp. 4, 5.

37. Specifically A. A. Bestuzhev and Wilhelm Küchelbecker. See Leighton, *Russian Romanticism,* p. 7.

38. A. Gukovsky, *Pushkin i russkyi romantizm* (1937; Moscow: KL, 1965).

39. Mirsky, *History of Russian Literature,* p. 83.

40. Heinrich v. Srbik, *Metternich* (1925; reprint, Munich: Bruckmann, 1957), I, 60–66, 227–228, and elsewhere. It is interesting that the same argument should have been made about Pushkin, namely that as a conservative liberal he does nothing but subscribe to the conceptions of Fénelon and Montesquieu (and the later Byron). See Pushkin, *Eugene Onegin,* 4 vols., ed. Vladimir Nabokov (New York: Bollingen Foundation and Pantheon, 1964), III, 336–338. (Hereafter cited as Nabokov.)

41. Dimitrij Chizhevsky, *Comparative History of Slavic Literatures,* trans. Richard Noel Porter and Martin P. Rice (1968; reprint, Nashville, Tenn.: Vanderbilt University Press, 1971), pp. 119–149. Leighton, *Russian Romanticism,* p. 9.

42. Chizhevsky, *Slavic Literature,* p. 121.

43. Ibid., pp. 122–145.

44. Viktor M. Zhirmunsky, *Bairon i Pushkin: Pushkin i zapadnye literatury* (1924; reprint, Munich: W. Fink, 1970). John Bayley, *Pushkin: A Comparative Commentary* (Cambridge: Cambridge University Press, 1971), pp. 348–353. N. L. Stepanov, "Paths of the Novel," in *Russian Views of Pushkin,* ed. D. J. Richards and C. R. S. Cockrell (Oxford: William Meeuws,

1976), p. 227. It is also important to note the interaction with Mickiewicz. See, e.g., the studies by John Washburn and Marian Jakóbiec in *Adam Mickiewicz: Poet of Poland,* ed. Manfred Kridl (New York: Columbia University Press, 1951), pp. 144–170.

45. Pushkin, *Critical Prose,* ed. and trans. Carl Proffer (Bloomington: Indiana University Press, 1969), pp. 125–126. In unpublished notes dating from 1830.

46. He had probably read Hazlitt. See Pushkin, *Critical Prose,* p. 245. For attitudes toward the French see John Mersereau, "Pushkin's Concept of Romanticism," *Studies in Romanticism,* 3, no. 1 (1963), 38. Also Pushkin, *Critical Prose,* p. 35.

47. Bayley, *Pushkin,* pp. 169, 173.

48. *Pushkin Threefold,* trans. Walter Arndt (New York: Dutton, 1972), p. 27. A useful account of the wider problem of Pushkin reception is in Harold Raab, *Die Lyrik Puškins in Deutschland (1820–1870),* Veröffentlichungen des Instituts für Slawistik, 33 (Berlin: Akademie Verlag, 1964), esp. pp. 19–49.

49. D. D. Blagoi, "Pushkin's Laughter," in Richards and Cockrell, *Russian Views* (an article first published in 1968), pp. 243–256; see p. 208.

50. Nabokov, III, 223. In connection with *Eugene Onegin,* VIII, 35–36.

51. Pushkin, *Polnoe sobranye sotchinenii,* 10 vols. (Moscow: Izdatelstvo Akademyi Nauk, 1949), I, 359, 366.

52. Ibid., III, 125. See Pushkin, *Eugene Onegin,* V, 2–7.

53. Nabokov repeatedly stresses the filiation with Thomson's *Seasons,* II, 179; III, 69; in connection with *Eugene Onegin,* VII, 1–3. This, of course, is a rather typical Biedermeier symptom.

54. Nabokov, II, 297.

55. Leo Kobilinski-Ellis, *Alexander Pushkin: Der religiöse Genius Russlands* (Olten: Otto Walter, 1948).

56. Nabokov, III, 345–350.

57. My own tendency is to argue that all those changes were just specialized forms of organicism. It is significant to note that while in his own generation Pushkin shared only with Küchelbecker an admiration for the grand-master of organicism, the younger generation (D. V. Venevitinov, Prince V. F. Odoevsky, S. P. Shevyrev) felt close to Goethe as a teacher. See André von Gornicka, *The Russian Image of Goethe* (Philadelphia: University of Pennsylvania Press, 1968), pp. 115–168. Pushkin's reactions were complete and personal, pp. 65–68.

58. Bayley, *Pushkin,* p. 265, quotes Shklovsky's excellent remark that Pushkin's subject is not the story of Tatyana and Onegin, but a game with this fable. See also ibid., p. 267, on Art (Eugene) versus Life (Tatyana).

59. Bayley, *Pushkin,* pp. 241–244, has some extremely perceptive analyses of the significance of incompleteness for *Eugene Onegin.* It should also be pointed out that he is one of the very few critics aware of which contemporary authors are relevant for understanding Pushkin (for example, Constant, p. 250, and Cornwall, pp. 209–210, 222).

60. Pushkin, *Complete Prose Tales,* trans. Gillon Aitken (London: Barrie and Rockliff, 1966), pp. 338–339.

61. Ibid., pp. 445–446.

62. Pushkin, *Eugene Onegin,* III, 222. Bayley, *Pushkin,* p. 142. W. Lednicki, *Pushkin's The Bronze Horseman* (Berkeley: University of California Press, 1955), pp. 40–41. I do not really want to add to the multitude of overambitious explanations (Lunacharsky's individual vs. historical necessity, Merezhkovsky's Christian stand vs. historical necessity, etc.), but I cannot help noting that even for an empirical pragmatist the temptation of the allegorical approach is great. See Bayley, *Pushkin,* pp. 153, 156, 162–163 (the critic's emphasis on "the unpainted fence, the little house, and the willow" is revealing). See also the interpretation by Lednicki, *Pushkin's The Bronze Horseman,* pp. 79–81.

63. Bayley, *Pushkin,* pp. 243–244. At the same time, note the ironic or disparaging references to romantic literature in the work: *Eugene Onegin,* VI, 23, 39; VII, 22, 24; and perhaps VIII, 35.

64. Vsevolod Setchkarev, *Gogol: His Life and Work,* trans. Richard Kramer (New York: New York University Press, 1965), pp. 13–19.

65. Simon Karlinsky, *The Sexual Labyrinth of Nikolai Gogol* (Cambridge: Harvard University Press, 1976), p. 243.

66. F. C. Driessen, *Gogol as a Short-Story Writer: A Study of His Technique of Composition* (The Hague: Mouton, 1965), p. 222. A. Stender-Petersen, "Gogol und die deutsche Romantik," *Euphorion,* 24 (1922), 628–653. Setchkarev, *Gogol,* pp. 36, 137–138.

67. Karlinsky, *Sexual Labyrinth,* p. 100; Setchkarev, *Gogol,* p. 132 (quoting the studies of Vinogradov). Setchkarev, *Gogol,* pp. 36, 51, 95, 114, 118–119, 122–123, 132–133; Karlinsky, *Sexual Labyrinth,* pp. 78, 100, 157.

68. Karlinsky, *The Sexual Labyrinth,* p. 77.

69. Ibid., p. 31. Valerian Pereverzev, *Evolyutsiya tvorchestva Gogolya* (1914), Chs. 2–4, quoted in R. Maguire, ed., *Gogol from the 20th Century: Eleven Essays* (Princeton: Princeton University Press, 1974), pp. 136–137.

70. Setchkarev, *Gogol,* pp. 40–41.

71. Landor, Platen, and the Nodier of *Smarra* come to mind.

72. Setchkarev, *Gogol,* pp. 147, 149, 161, 185. Vyacheslav Ivanov has gone so far as to speak of the classicist-allegorical nature of *The Inspector-General,* i.e., of an abstract, regular structure behind the forefront of extreme

localism, peculiarity, idiosyncrasy, thereby describing rather correctly a Bie-dermeier strategy. Cf. Maguire, *Gogol,* pp. 199–215.

73. Among these: *Alcinoe,* the Polish beauty in *Taras Bulba,* Annunziata in an incomplete fragment, etc. Karlinsky, *Sexual Labyrinth,* p. 209.

74. Gogol, *Sobranye sochinenii,* 6 vols. (Moscow: GIHL, 1959), V, 6–12, 32–33.

75. Ibid., II, 196, 215–216, 245.

76. Ibid., I, 43–45.

77. Ibid., II, 54–55, 115.

78. Leon Stilman, "*Vsevidyashchee oko'* u Gogolya," *Vosdushnye puti,* 5 (1967), 279–292, quoted from Maguire, *Gogol,* pp. 376–384. The anxiety of vision signals, I contend, the breakdown of pure romantic totalization and the incapacity of the late romantic to establish himself as the total knowledge factor, much more than a moral problem.

79. D. Merezhkovsky, "Gogol' i chert," in *Polnoe sobranie sochinenii* (1906; reprint, St. Petersburg: M. O. Volf, 1911), quoted from Maguire, *Gogol,* pp. 66–67, 77.

80. Setchkarev, *Gogol,* pp. 204–205, 186–188.

81. See Chapter 5.

82. Renato Poggioli, *The Oaten Flute: Essays in Pastoral Poetry and the Pastoral Ideal* (Cambridge: Harvard University Press, 1975), pp. 241–264. Karlinsky, *Sexual Labyrinth,* p. 63.

83. The accuser was Denys Thompson. See Fred Randel, "Eating and Drinking in Lamb's Elia Essays," *ELH,* 37 (1970), 57–76.

84. Gogol, *Sobranie sochinenii,* II, 13.

85. Dmitry Chizhevsky, "O 'Shineli' Gogolya," *Sovremennye zapiski* (Paris), 47 (1958), 172–195, quoted from Maguire, *Gogol,* pp. 300–320.

86. Valery Bryusov, "Ispepelenyi," *Vesy* (1909), p. 4.

87. Cf. Setchkarev, *Gogol,* pp. 237–239, 242–243, 246. Karlinsky, *Sexual Labyrinth,* 239–242, 252–259.

88. Setchkarev, *Gogol,* pp. 126–127; Karlinsky, *Sexual Labyrinth,* p. 309, n. 41. Boris Eichenbaum, "Kak Sdelana 'Shinel' Gogolya," in *Skvoz' Literatury* (Leningrad: Academia, 1924), from Maguire, *Gogol,* pp. 270–271; also ibid., pp. 136–137, 112.

89. Of course, I am speaking of the later Belinsky, the one of the 1840s. But then does not his own evolution from the organicism of Schelling to a conception of art as servant of reality prove something about the Bieder-meier? Cf. Victor Terras, *Belinskij and Russian Literary Criticism* (Madison: University of Wisconsin Press, 1974), pp. 33–39, 77–91.

90. Chizhevsky, *Comparative Literature,* pp. 106–107.

91. Wiktor Weintraub, *The Poetry of Adam Mickiewicz,* Slavic Print-ings and Reprintings II (The Hague: Mouton, 1954), pp. 21–31. See Czes-

law Milosz, "Mickiewicz and Modern Poetry," in Manfred Kridl, ed., *Adam Mickiewicz: Poet of Poland,* p. 59.

92. Weintraub, *Poetry of Adam Mickiewicz,* 9–45. Tadeusz Sinko, *Mickiewicz i Antyk* (Wroclaw and Krakow: Narodowy im Ossolińskich Wydawnictwo Polskiej Akademii Nauk, 1957). Waclaw Lednicki, ed., *Adam Mickiewicz in World Literature* (Berkeley: University of California Press, 1956). Also Kridl, *Adam Mickiewicz,* pp. 129–273.

93. References in the text are from Adam Mickiewicz, *Pan Tadeusz,* trans. Watson Kirkconnell (New York: The Polish Institute of Arts and Sciences in America, 1962). References to the Polish original are given in the notes from Adam Mickiewicz, *Dziela* (Warsaw: Czytelnik, 1955), vol. 4.

94. I enjoyed the witty parallel to Proust in Józef Wittlin, *"Pan Tadeusz,"* in Kridl, *Adam Mickiewicz,* p. 85.

95. Mickiewicz, *Pan Tadeusz,* XII, 36–182, esp. 66–88.

96. Mickiewicz, *Pan Tadeusz,* I, 148–204 (Gray), 906–907 (Goldsmith). Karel Krejci, *Geschichte der polnischen Literatur* (1953: reprint, Halle/Saale: Max Niemeyer, 1958), pp. 196, 214, and elsewhere, emphasizes the importance of the idyllic model in the late eighteenth and early nineteenth century.

97. Mickiewicz, *Pan Tadeusz,* II, 403–433; V, 57–84; III, 23–36. There is even a little book identifying and depicting the plants in the poem: Bolesław Hryniewicki, *Adam Mickiewicz a flora Litwy* (Warsaw: Ludowa Spółdzielnia Wydawnicza, 1956).

98. Mickiewicz, *Pan Tadeusz,* II, 105–143; III, 260–289, 580–603, 630–653, 296–342; VIII, 512–527; V, 263–281.

99. Maciej, for instance, is presented as one closely associated with animals in Mickiewicz, *Pan Tadeusz,* VI, 581–601.

100. See Weintraub, *Poetry of Adam Mickiewicz,* pp. 241–242.

101. Czeslaw Milosz, *The History of Polish Literature* (New York and London: Macmillan-Collier, 1969), p. 216.

102. Harold Segel, ed. and trans., "Introduction," *Polish Romantic Drama: Three Plays in English Translation* (Ithaca: Cornell University Press, 1972), p. 37.

103. Claude Backvis, "Słowacki et l'héritage baroque," in *Julius Słowacki 1809–1849: Księga zbiorowa w stulecie zgonu* (London: The Polish Research Centre, 1951), pp. 87–94, 31–42. One assumes that the author follows the definition of D'Ors of the baroque as a generic family of historic forms. Fragmentation and independence of imagery are pointed to in Jerzy Pietrkiewicz, "Metafora ruchowa u poezji Słowackiego," in *Julius Słowacki,* pp. 160–170. By contrast, Jan Miroslaw Kasjan, *Przysłowia i metaforyka poloczna w twórczosci Słowackiego* (Torun: Towarzystwo Naukowe, 1966), stresses the large number of set, "prepackaged" elements. Cf. Manfred

Kridl, *The Lyric Poems of Julius Słowacki,* Collection Musagetes (The Hague: Mouton, 1958), pp. 54–56. A better explanation of the same imagistic material is offered by a comparison to the historical contemporary Eichendorff. See Hermann Buddensieg, "Vom unbekannten Eichendorff," *Mickiewicz-Blätter,* 19 (1962), p. 25.

104. Backvis, "Słowacki et l'héritage baroque," p. 91.

105. Wladyslaw Folkierski, *Od Chateaubrianda do Anhellego* (Krakow: Gebethner i Wolff, 1934), deals with Chateaubriand, Hugo, and Vigny, mostly as sources, rather than as contemporaries of Słowacki. Musset is ignored.

106. This work, written in 1844, is often said to be Słowacki's philosophical credo. See Milosz, *History of Polish Literature,* p. 240. In it a cosmic evolution from animal to spiritual is outlined, though phases of decline and revolution are not ignored.

107. Segel, *Polish Romantic Drama,* pp. 55–56.

108. Milosz, *History of Polish Literature,* pp. 247–266. Maxime Herman, *Histoire de la littérature polonaise (des origines à 1961)* (Paris: Nizet, 1961), pp. 171–179, 225–289. Krejci, *Geschichte der polnischen Literatur,* pp. 202–210, 299–321, and elsewhere.

109. Sensitivity in pointing out the influence of Towiański on Mickiewicz and Krasiński, of Mochnacki and Lelewel on Słowacki and others, though without a consistent analysis, can be noted in Edouard Krakowski, *Trois Destins tragiques: Słowacki, Krasiński, Norwid* (Paris: Firmin-Didot, 1931), pp. 83–84, 87, 95–96, 192–193.

110. Aleksander Flaker, "Kovačić's Novel *In the Registry* and the Stylistic Formation of Realism," *Comparative Studies in Croatian Literature* (Zagreb, 1981). Dragysha Zhivkovich, *Evropskie okviri srpskie knizhevnosti,* 2 vols. (Beograd: Prosveta, 1970, 1977).

111. Lilian Furst, *Romanticism in Perspective* (London: Macmillan, 1969), p. 49. Söter, *Dilemma of Literary Science,* pp. 121, 208. Söter's awareness of the problems I raised here is complete. He realizes that nothing like the "Jena romanticism" is to be found in Eastern Europe, and that in these literatures romanticism cannot be "unequivocally considered as the negation of the enlightenment" (p. 140).

5. ROMANTIC IRONY AND BIEDERMEIER TRAGICOMEDY

1. Michael Cooke, *Acts of Inclusion* (New Haven: Yale University Press, 1979), pp. 21, XIII. Also Frederick Garber, "Nature and the Romantic Mind," *Comparative Literature,* 22 (1977), 207ff.

2. Victor Hugo, *Oeuvres Complètes* (Paris: Hetzel & Quantin, 1881), I, 17, 23, 49, 69.

3. Helmut Prang, *Die romantische Ironie* (Darmstadt: Wissenschaftliche Buchgesellschaft, 1972), p. 12.

4. "To write truly well about a topic, you must first lose interest in it," ibid., p. 10.

5. Ibid., p. 9.

6. Ibid., p. 17. Ingrid Strohschneider-Kohrs. *Die romantische Ironie in Theorie und Gestaltung,* Hermaea, Germanische Forschungen, Bd. 6 (1960; reprint, Tübingen: Max Niemeyer, 1977), pp. 88–92.

7. Prang, *Die romantische Ironie,* pp. 22–26, Strohschneider-Kohrs, *Die romantische Ironie,* pp. 194–202, 162–185, 93–97.

8. Ernest Behler, *Klassische Ironie. Romantische Ironie. Tragische Ironie. Zum Ursprung dieser Begriffe.* (Darmstadt: Wissenschaftliche Buchgesellschaft, 1972), p. 93.

9. Ibid., pp. 85–104.

10. Beda Allemann, *Ironie und Dichtung* (1956; Pfullingen: Neske, 1969), pp. 119ff.

11. J. A. K. Thomson, *Irony: An Historical Introduction* (Cambridge: Harvard University Press, 1927), p. 33.

12. Douglas Muecke, *The Compass of Irony* (London: Methuen, 1969), p. 14. Also pp. 159–215.

13. Vladimir Jankélévich, *L'Ironie* (1936; Paris: Flammarion, 1964), pp. 21–39.

14. Cleanth Brooks, "Irony and Ironic Poetry," *College English,* 9 (1947–1948), 231–237. An older specialist tries to solve the problem by distinguishing between "kleine Ironie" and "grosse Ironie," the latter being quite close to the concept developed by Schlegel and his school; see Rudolf Jancke, *Das Wesen der Ironie: Eine Strukturanalyse ihrer Erscheinungsformen* (Leipzig: Barth, 1929).

15. For a brief summary of this celebrated controversy see Prang, *Die romantische Ironie,* pp. 78–85, and Strohschneider-Kohrs, *Die romantische Ironie,* pp. 215–222. The texts are in G. W. F. Hegel, *Sämtliche Werke,* ed. H. Glockner (Stuttgart: Frommann, 1927–1940), XII, also XX, 141–184. Sören Kierkegaard, *The Concept of Irony,* tr. Lee Capel (London: Collins, 1966), originally published in 1841.

16. J. B. O'Leary, "Irony in the Plays of Alfred de Musset" (Ph.D. diss., University of Michigan, 1970).

17. David Sices, *Theater of Solitude: The Drama of Alfred de Musset* (Hanover, N.H.: University Press of New England, 1974).

18. "The muse of comedy has kissed his lips, the muse of tragedy his heart," quoted by Jean Giraud, *L'Ecole romantique française* (Paris: Armand Colin, 1927), p. 132.

19. Frederic Jameson, *Marxism and Form* (Princeton: Princeton University Press, 1972), pp. 4–45 and elsewhere.

20. Alfred de Musset, *Théâtre complet,* cd. Maurice Allem (Paris: Pléiade, 1947), pp. 492–495, also p. 461.

21. "Am I a fox caught in a trap, or a madman slowly recovering his senses?" "Either I have by me the most cunning demon ever conceived in hell, or I am listening now to the voice of an angel opening for me the road to heaven," Musset, *Théâtre complet,* pp. 367–406.

22. For interesting comments see Eric Gans, *Musset et le "drame tragique"* (Paris: José Corti, 1974), p. 107, and Herbert Gochberg, *Stage of Dreams: The Dramatic Art of Alfred de Musset (1828–1834)* (Geneva: Droz, 1967), p. 111.

23. Gochberg, *Stage of Dreams,* p. 170.

24. "To play with words is just one more way among others to play with thoughts, actions, and beings." "Actually who could be able to tell me if I am happy or unhappy, good or evil, sad or cheerful, dumb or witty?" Musset, *Théâtre complet,* p. 202 (in *Fantasio*).

25. "Fortune, as soon as we call her, no matter how, will come running up and flit around the table, now smiling, now frowning; to please her you have to study neither the printed cardboard, nor the dice, rather you have to surmise whims and sallies, to guess them and to catch them in midair," Musset, *Théâtre complet,* p. 611 (in *Bettine*).

26. Mussct, *Théâtre complet,* pp. 614–615.

27. Gans, *Musset,* pp. 81, 84, thinks the play should be read as "un premier pas vers la quasi-intégration du libertin à la communauté" and that Razetta will accept anything provided his attitude gets some public exposure and applause.

28. Love grows out of convention, deliberation, and rationality rather than out of free fantasy. See Gochberg, *Stage of Dreams,* p. 72.

29. Gans, *Musset,* p. 169. See also Gochberg, *Stage of Dreams,* p. 146.

30. Gans, *Musset,* p. 81.

31. Maurice Toesca, *Musset ou l'amour de la mort* (Paris: Hachette, 1970), pp. 69, 54, 71. Gochberg, *Stage of Dreams,* pp. 13–22. Musset even thickened De Quincey's dreamlike imagery.

32. Birds, roses, water, and animals have a unifying function in Musset's work, according to Michael J. Herrschensohn, "Imagery in the Works of Alfred de Musset" (Ph.D. diss., University of Pennsylvania, 1970). Even these patterns express the dilemma of an ideal love struggling against the real world; the impossibility of materialization leads to a traumatic life-in-death and to the masochistic acceptance of this state of affairs.

33. "Ephemeral pains blaspheme and arraign the heavens; deep suffering does neither, it merely harkens." Musset, *La Confession d'un enfant du siècle,* ed. Maurice Allem (Paris: Garnier, 1968), p. 129 (Part III, Ch. 2).

34. Mazeppa occasionally acts and talks like Zbigniew. Juliusz Słowacki, *Mazeppa*, trans. Marion Moore Coleman (Cheshire, Conn.: Cherry Hill Books, 1960), p. 9. See Juliusz Słowacki, *Dziela Wybrane*, ed. Julian Krzyzanowski (Wroclaw & Warsaw: Zaklad Narodowy Im. Ossolinskich, 1974), IV, 227–228.

35. Juliusz Słowacki, *Fantazy* in Harold Segel, ed. *Polish Romantic Drama* (Ithaca: Cornell University Press, 1977), p. 263. Hereafter references in parentheses in the text. For the original see *Dziela*, IV, 384, in Act. I, Scene 13, ll. 412–413.

36. Słowacki, *Dziela*, IV, 463, in Act V, Scene I, ll. 9–10, and, respectively ibid. IV, 466, in ll. 77–78 and earlier IV, 431, in Act III, Scene 8, ll. 361–362 and IV, 443, in Act IV, Scene 2, ll. 84–85.

37. Słowacki, *Dziela*, IV, 465, in Act V, Scene 1, ll. 60–61.

38. See Słowacki, *Dziela*, IV, 387, in Act I, scene 13, ll. 466, and respectively IV, 397, in Act II, Scene 2, ll. 68–71 and IV, 403, Act II, Scene 3, ll. 233–235.

39. "Why be superhuman / if you remain just a man?"; "Why be human / if you do not strive to overcome your state?" Christian Dietrich Grabbe, *Gesammelte Werke* (Düsseldorf: Sigbert Mohn, 1964), I, 154.

40. Ibid., III, 176–177.

41. Grabbe, *Werke*, ed. Roy C. Cowen (Munich: Hanser, 1977), II, 118, 159–161.

42. "Think what the world would be like, if all were like you!" Ibid; I, 30, 37–40, 89.

43. Ibid., II, 180, 207.

44. Karl Guthke, *Geschichte und Poetik der deutschen Tragikomödie* (Göttingen: Vandenhoeck und Rupprecht, 1961), pp. 200–206, with some further nuances, regarding in particular elements of the puppet theatre and of the *commedia dell'arte*. This view is shared by Fritz Böttger, *Grabbe, Glanz und Elend eines Dichters* (East Berlin: Verlag der Nation, 1963), pp. 209–211.

45. See also Wolfgang Hegele, *Grabbes Dramenform* (Munich: Fink, 1970), p. 47. Benno von Wiese, *Die deutsche Tragödie von Lessing bis Hebbel* (1948; Hamburg: Hoffmann und Campe, 1967), pp. 455–512, refers often to the idyllic limits of historical conflict (*Barbarossa, Napoleon*), to grotesque and irony as limits to the tragic (*Hannibal*), and to *Don Juan und Faust* as a drama of romantic disillusionment.

46. "Whatever is tragic is also merry, and the other way round. How often have I laughed attending a tragic play, and have almost been moved by comedies." Grabbe, *Werke*, II, 238.

47. Grabbe, *Werke*, I, 237. Translations: Grabbe, *Jest, Satire, Irony and Deeper Significance*, trans. and ed. Maurice Edwards (New York: Ungar, 1966).

48. Hegele, *Grabbes Dramenform,* p. 25, underlines that the dictum about inventing character to suit circumstance is particularly suitable in connection with this play.

49. Grabbe, *Werke,* I, 247, in Act I, Scene 3. "By chance you saw yourself in the mirror, and your face striking you as too impossible, you blotted it out" (p. 13).

50. Grabbe, *Werke,* I, 286. "Oh you beautiful, passionate-romantic, never-to-return-again days of the vanished past, when I—" "We *were* Trojans! the golden years of youth are gone!" (pp. 54, 53).

51. "See, there it lies, my home town! Hark, the vesper bell in the grey church steeple is ringing! How pleasant it sounds after three years absence! Even the ancient castle has remained unchanged. Proud and stately it rises there out of the midst of its blooming summer garden, and the first glimmer of the sunset glow makes purple plays of light on its mighty casement windows!" (p. 38); "What a charming woman! One can hear the music of her movements. The unquenchable flames of her eyes sparkle like two volatile naphtha-fires, and her bosom swells gently over her heart like a lake over its wellsprings!" (p. 42).

52. Manfred Schneider, *Destruktion und utopische Gemeinschaft: Zur Thematik und Dramaturgie des Heroischen im Werk Christian Dietrich Grabbes* (Frankfurt: Athenäum, 1973), p. ix.

53. "The Biedermeier variant of problematic humanity." Rudolf Majut, *Studien um Büchner,* Germanische Studien 121 (Berlin: E. Ebering, 1932), p. 70.

54. "The vital breath of innocence and enthusiasm." Friedrich Schlegel, *Lucinde* (1794; Leipzig: Insel, 1919), p. 26. See also, for contrast Ludwig Büttner, *Büchners Bild vom Menschen* (Nürnberg: Hans Carl, 1967), pp. 105–106.

55. Luciano Zagari, *Georg Büchner e la ricerca dello stile dramatico* (Torino: Edizioni dell'Albero, 1956), p. 126.

56. The influence of Musset is generally admitted by the leading commentators. See Herbert Lindenberger, *George Büchner* (Carbondale: Southern Illinois University Press, 1964), pp. 58–59 and 65, or Karl Viëtor, *Georg Büchner. Politik. Dichtung Wissenschaft* (Bern: Francke, 1949), p. 187. More specialized investigations are in Maurice Gravier, "Georg Büchner et Alfred De Musset," *Orbis litterarum,* 9 (1954), 29–44, and Henri Plard, "A propos de *Leonce und Lena;* Musset et Büchner," *Études germaniques,* 9 (1954), 26–36. The earliest works to have pointed to this connection were apparently those of Heinz Lipman, *Georg Büchner und die Romantik* (München: Max Hueber, 1923), and Armin Renker, *Georg Büchner und das Lustspiel der Romantik* (Berlin: Ebering, 1924), pp. 96–108.

57. "L: 'I am deceived' L.: 'I am deceived'. L.: 'Oh, chance!' L. 'Oh,

providence.' " Georg Büchner, *Gesammelte Werke,* ed. K. Edschmid (Munich: Karl Desch, 1948), p. 200.

58. Büttner, *Büchners Bild,* p. 41.

59. Hans Mayer, *Georg Büchner und seine Zeit* (1946; reprint, Wiesbaden: Limes, 1959), pp. 399–460, and, in a very heavy-handed way Gerhard Jancke, *Georg Büchner: Genese und Aktualität seines Werke* (Kronberg: Scriptor, 1975), pp. 253–270, who reduces *Leonce und Lena* to a drama of protest leading to a "paranoide Utopie." To a lesser extent this is the problem of Henry J. Schmidt, *Satire, Caricature and Perspectivism in the Works of George Büchner,* Stanford Studies in Germanics and Slavics 8 (The Hague: Mouton, 1970). Similarly, Maurice Benn, *The Drama of Revolt: A Critical Study of George Büchner* (Cambridge: Cambridge University Press, 1976), p. 162, complains: "for Büchner reality is essentially tragic. Consequently, in tragedy he can be fully realistic, in comedy not so." If the tragicomic is thus conjured away, Benn nevertheless speaks repeatedly of a modification and reduction of reality, and thus admits, I think, that the gap between tragic and comic is often narrowed considerably.

60. Karl Viëtor, *George Büchner,* p. 174.

61. "I am so young and the world is so old"; "the earth is snuggling up fearfully like a child, while phantoms step over its cradle," Büchner, *Gesammelte Werke,* p. 189.

62. "Meanwhile I will lie down in the grass and let my nose blossom up among the grass blades and entertain romantic feelings" Büchner, *Gesammelte Werke,* p. 172.

63. "Man, you are nothing but a lousy pun. You have no father, no mother, the five vowels engendered you between each other"; "you prince are a book with no letters in it, just dashes," Büchner, *Gesammelte Werke,* p. 182.

64. "Jürgen Schröder, *Georg Büchners "Leonce und Lena." Eine verkehrte Komödie* (Munich: Fink, 1966), pp. 199, 53.

65. I disagree with Mario Carlo Abutille, *Angst und Zynismus bei Georg Büchner* (Bern: Francke, 1969), pp. 87–88.

66. Nikolai Gogol, *Polnoe sobranye sotchynenii,* 14 vols. (Moscow: Izdatelstvo Akademyi Nauk, 1937), VI, 157 (in *Dead Souls*) and II, 224. All the translations in the text are mine.

67. Ibid., I, 298, in "Ivan Fedorovich Shponka and His Little Aunt."

68. Ibid., I, 136. A wealth of examples and lucid analyses many of which draw on previous criticism are assembled in Hans Günther, *Das Groteske bei N. V. Gogol. Formen und Funktionen* (Munich: Otto Sagner, 1968).

69. Alexander Pushkin, *Critical Prose,* ed. and trans. Carl Proffer (Bloomington: Indiana University Press, 1969), p. 40.

70. Lee Byron Jennings, *The Ludicrous Demon: Aspects of the Grotesque*

in German Post-Romantic Prose, University of California Publications in Modern Philology Nr. 71 (Berkeley: University of California Press, 1963), p. 166. Günther, *Das Groteske,* pp. 49–65.

71. Wilhelm Michel, *Des Teuflische und das Groteske in der Kunst* (Munich: Piper, 1911), 2nd ed. G. F. W. Hegel, *Sämtliche Werke,* XIII, 301ff. Others who underlined the same features are Johannes Volkelt, *System der Ästhetik,* 3 vols. (Munich: Beck, 1905–1914), II, 412; Theodor Lipps, *Ästhetik* (Hamburg and Leipzig: L. Voss, 1903–1906), I, 504. See also Elli Desalm, *E. T. A. Hoffmann und das Groteske* (Ph.D. diss., University of Bonn, 1930).

72. Günther, *Das Groteske,* pp. 49–65. Alexander Slonimsky, "Technika komicheskogo u Gogolya" (1923) quoted in Robert A. Maguire, ed., *Gogol from the Twentieth Century: Eleven Essays* (Princeton: Princeton University Press, 1974), pp. 338–349, 368–373.

73. Johannes Volkelt, *Ästhetik des Tragischen* (1879; Munich: Beck, 1923), pp. 417–428; also Volkelt, *System der Ästhetik,* II, 558. Virgil Nemoianu, "Tragic și comic la Shakespeare și moderni" in *Calmul Valorilor* (Cluj: Dacia, 1971), p. 74. Oscar Mandel, *A Definition of Tragedy* (New York: New York University Press, 1961) has some subtle comments on "paratragedies" and "prevented tragedies"—a broad category which in my opinion somehow surrounds the area of the tragicomic and is clearly related to the kind of plays discussed in this chapter. The similarity between tragic and comic opposition is also I believe, a basic assumption in Cyrus Hoy, *The Hyacinth Room: An Investigation into the Nature of Comedy, Tragedy and Tragicomedy* (London: Chatto and Windus, 1964). The above-mentioned Solger seems to me the pioneer of this kind of explanation: neatly, a Biedermeier critic provides the theory of the Biedermeier theater.

74. Hoy, *Hyacinth Room,* pp. 21–22.

75. Êrich Auerbach, *Mimesis,* trans. Willard Trask (1968; Princeton, N.J.: Princeton University Press, 1974), p. 325. Even Karl Marx liked to nod approvingly, for example in a comment of April 17, 1854, in the *New York Daily Tribune.* See Marx and Engels, *Werke* (East Berlin: Dietz, 1950–1968), X, 177.

76. Gustav René Hocke, *Manierismus in der Literatur* (1959; Hamburg: Rowohlt, 1963), pp. 210–213. Marianne Thalmann, *Romantik und Manierismus* (Stuttgart: Kohlhammer, 1963), p. 56 and elsewhere.

77. Of course, extremities of his own character may have opened up his mind to tragicomic possibilities. See Toesca, *Musset ou l'amour de la mort,* 245. It is significant that his poems abound in statements such as: "O Muse, que m'importe ou la mort ou la vie?" ("Nuit d'Août", l. 123). In his letters we find statements such as: "Votre lettre est absurde et, par consequent,

charmante" (to Caroline Joubert, 1835); at the beginning of Chapter VIII of *La Confession, sinistre* is equated with *plaisant.*

78. Musset, *La Confession,* p. 57.

6. THE BIEDERMEIER HISTORICAL NOVEL
AND THE DECLINE OF COMPROMISE

1. "Noble human emotion"; "universal convulsion"; "terrible commotion"; "precarious era"; "ownership of staunch goods." J. W. Goethe, *Hermann und Dorothea,* IX, 299–318 in *Gedenkausgabe,* 25 vols. (Zurich: Artemis, 1949), III, 241–243.

2. See Chapters 1 and 2.

3. George Lukács, *The Historical Novel,* trans. Hannah and Stanley Mitchell (London: Merlin, 1960), p. 31. For the antiromantic version, see pp. 63ff.

4. Ibid., pp. 32ff.

5. David Daiches, *A Critical History of English Literature,* 2nd ed. (New York: Ronald, 1970), pp. 831–853.

6. Francis R. Hart, *Scott's Novels* (Charlottesville: University of Virginia Press, 1966).

7. Alistair Duckworth, "Scott's Fiction and the Migration of Settings," *Scottish Literary Journal,* 7 (May 1980), p. 99.

8. Detailed if somewhat primitive enumerations in Walter Freye, "The Influence of 'Gothic' Literature on Sir Walter Scott" (Ph.D. diss., University of Rostock, 1902), and in William Macintosh, *Scott and Goethe: German Influence on the Writings of Sir Walter Scott* (1925; reprint, Port Washington: Kennikat Press, 1970), pp. 94, 101–106, 108, 114–115. Cf. also Edgar Johnson, *Sir Walter Scott* (London: Macmillan, 1970), I, 96, 159, and elsewhere.

9. T. S. Eliot, *Christianity and Culture* (1948; reprint, New York: Harcourt, Brace, 1960), pp. 107–123.

10. Hesketh Pearson, *Sir Walter Scott* (London: Methuen, 1954), pp. 131–132, 240.

11. Johnson, *Sir Walter Scott,* I, 300–301; I, 60–62, 64, 77 (I am referring to his university years); I, 420; I, 238–240; I, 576; II, 1253.

12. Pearson, *Sir Walter Scott,* p. 184.

13. R. C. Gordon, *Under Which King? A Study of the Scottish Waverley Novels* (Edinburgh: Oliver & Boyd, 1969), pp. 12–13.

14. Johnson, *Sir Walter Scott,* I, 411. Hereafter references in parentheses in the text.

15. See also Hart, *Scott's Novels,* pp. 246–337.

16. Walter Scott, *The Antiquary* (Edinburgh: Adam & Charles Black, 1871), Ch. 16. Cf. Gordon, *Under Which King?* p. 38.

17. Scott, *Antiquary,* Ch. 40, pp. 366–367.

18. Ibid., Chs. 5 and 6.

19. Donald Davie, *Sir Walter Scott* (New York: Viking, 1971), p. 99. D. D. Devlin, *The Author of Waverley* (Lewisburg, Pa.: Bucknell University Press, 1971), pp. 114–117, thinks *Redgauntlet* is comic.

20. Scott, *Antiquary,* p. 161 (end of Ch. 17).

21. Christabel Fiske, *Epic Suggestion in the Imagery of the Waverley Novels* (New Haven: Yale University Press, 1940).

22. Gordon, *Under Which King?* pp. 110–130, 24–65, 74–78. See also Russell Kirk, *The Conservative Mind* (Chicago: Henry Regnery, 1953), pp. 106–115.

23. Alexander Welsh, *The Hero of the Waverley Novels* (New Haven: Yale University Press, 1963).

24. Walter Scott, *Redgauntlet*, ed. W. M. Parker (1906; reprint, London and New York: Dent and Dutton, 1970), pp. 38, 40, 44.

25. *Redgauntlet,* pp. 247–248, 342 (Chs. 10 and 18). Hereafter parenthetical references in the text.

26. Hart, *Scott's Novels,* p. 60.

27. Lars Hartveit, *Dream Within a Dream: A Thematic Approach to Scott's Vision of Fictional Reality* (1970; reprint, Oslo: Universitetsforlaget, 1974), p. 250.

28. Ibid., pp. 243–244, 220.

29. Both are men of the sea who try to become men of the land or are involved in affairs of the land. Alan Fairford is led on a voyage of cognition which happens to have a happy ending. The entrails of the earth are in some ways like the resplendent caves of Falun; *The Antiquary* offers similar descents.

30. Cf. the huge anthology Giancarlo Vigorelli, ed., *Manzoni pro e contro* (Milan: Istituto Propaganda Libraria, 1975), III, 32–52, 199ff. It is interesting that Enzo Noé Girardi, *Manzoni "reazionario"* (1966; reprint, Rocca San Casciano: Capelli, 1972), while defending Manzoni, seems to object more to the labeling than to the description.

31. "A book that praises priests and monks and counsels patience, submission, forgivenness"; "submission to servitude, denial of the fatherland, and of any generous civic sentiment." Luigi Settembrini, *Lezioni di letteratura italiana* (1869–1872; Torino: Unione Tipografico-Editrice, 1927), III, 288–340. C. Tronconi, "Delitti," in Vigorelli, *Manzoni pro e contro,* I, 612.

32. Piero Fossi, *La conversione di Alessandro Manzoni* (1933; reprint, Florence: La Nuova Italia, 1974), pp. 109ff.

33. Casare De Lollis, *A. Manzoni e gli storici liberali francesi della Res-*

taurazione (Bari: Laterza, 1926). Cf. also Raffaello Ramat on the influence of Sismondi in Vigorelli, *Manzoni pro e contro,* II, 590–592. See Elena Gabbuti, *Il Manzoni e gli ideologi francesi: Studi sul pensiero e sull'arte di A. Manzoni* (Florence: Sansoni, 1936).

34. Augusto Simonini, *L'ideologia di Alessandro Manzoni* (Ravenna: Longo, 1974), pp. 152–153.

35. Bruna Fazio-Allmayer, *La formazione del pensiero eticostorico del Manzoni* (Florence: Sansoni, 1969).

36. Simonini, *L'ideologia di Alessandro Manzoni,* pp. 110–114, 60.

37. Ibid., pp. 159–162.

38. Archibald Colquhoun, *Manzoni and His Time* (London: Dent and Sons, 1954), pp. 192–195. Alessandro Luzio, *Manzoni e Diderot: La Monaca di Monza e 'La Réligieuse'* (Milan: Dumolard, 1884), pp. 7–9, 85–96. Gaetano Ragonese, *Illuminismo manzoniano* (Palermo: Manfredi, 1968), pp. 21–68.

39. Mario Apollonio, *Studi sul periodizzamento della storiografia letteraria italiana* (Milan: Bietti, 1968), p. 292. There are many studies of influence. For some detailed parallels see Ezio Raimondi, *Il romanzo senza idilio* (Turin: Einaudi, 1974), pp. 290–292, 251, 283, which refers to *Waverley* and *The Antiquary.* See also Ernesto Caserta, *Manzoni's Christian Realism,* Biblioteca dell'Archivum Romanum, 1st ser., 131 (Florence: Olschki, 1977), p. 135.

40. Giovanni Getto, *Manzoni europeo* (Milan: Mursia, 1971), pp. 82–87, 143–180, 183–225, 252 (Hermann und Dorothea), 297 (Scott). The conception)f Joseph Francis De Simone, *Alessandro Manzoni: Esthetics and Literary Criticism* (New York: Venni, 1946), pp. 30–87, heatedly argued, that Manzoni never actually joined romanticism and merely remained a faithful adherent of eighteenth-century forms, which he combined with derivational Catholic aesthetics (p. 33), is untenable. Interesting parallels with Scott in Bruno Stagnito, *Manzoni e la guerra contro il tempo* (Padova: Liviana 1973).

41. Eugenio Camerini established parallels to Diderot's *La Réligieuse* as far back as 1873 in a preface to an edition of *I Promessi Sposi,* according to Vigorelli, *Manzoni pro e contro,* I, 551. See also Luzio (n. 38). On Sade see Mario Praz, *The Romantic Agony* (1933; Oxford, Oxford University Press, 1970), pp. 175–176.

42. Sainte-Beuve was the first to compare *Notre-Dame de Paris* to Manzoni's novel (he also detected similarities to Lamartine). See Dorothée Christesco, *La Fortune de Alexandre Manzoni en France* (Paris: Balzac, 1943), p. 155. Cf. also Mario Mazzucchelli, *La Monaca di Monza* (Milan: Dall'Oglio, 1961), who points to connections with La Harpe.

43. Sandro Guarneri, *Neoclassicismo e classicità in Alessandro Manzoni* (Florence: Antonio Lalli, 1977), pp. 41–47.

44. Carlo Dionisotti, "Manzoni and the Catholic Revival," *Proceedings of the British Academy,* 59 (1973), 1–15, shows the impact of Manzoni's work on Wiseman, as well as on Gladstone and perhaps some of his converted friends, such as Manning and James Hope Scott. He also squarely aligns Manzoni's conversion (that is, his ultimate adjustment to the *Zeitgeist*) with facts such as the Congress of Vienna and the Oxford movement. D'Ovidio and Sailer found seventeen German editions, ten English ones, and nineteen French ones until 1886. Cf. Vigorelli, *Manzoni pro e contro,* I, 668. Vyazemsky and Zhukovsky were in touch with Manzoni; Pushkin knew his work; and Tolstoy's moralistic theory of art may have been inspired by Manzoni. Cf. Vigorelli, *Manzoni pro e contro,* I, 247, and elsewhere. Poe wrote glowing pages on Manzoni in the *Southern Literary Messenger,* 8 (1835), 12. Paris saw in 1828 two simultaneous translations, highly applauded by figures as diverse as Thierry, Villemain, Sismondi, Chateaubriand. Cf. Christesco, *La Fortune,* pp. 83–87. The influence of Manzoni on Reade ("The Cloister and the Hearth") has also been noted.

45. "His mission was that of mediating contraries, not blocking progress," Gianni Scalia, "Manzoni a sinistra," *Italianistica,* 1 (1973), 38–42.

46. "The bourgeois thinks of himself in the form of being, not of becoming or of change," Scalia says, *ibid.* Italo Calvino once called *The Betrothed* a "romanzo dei rapporti di forza." Cf. Vigorelli, *Manzoni pro e contro,* III, 584.

47. That Manzoni's historical research was solid and conscientious stands in no need of further demonstration. Cf. Enzo Noé Girardi and Gabriella Spada, *Manzoni e il seicento lombardo* (Milan: Vita i pensiero, 1977).

48. Fausto Nicolini, *Peste e untori nei 'Promessi Sposi' e nella realtá storica* (Bari: Laterza, 1937). His thesis was criticized, but not really superseded, I believe. He strongly defended the aesthetic justificaton of the plague chapters and answered criticism in *Arte e storia nei 'Promessi Sposi'* (Milan: Ulrico Hoepli, 1939), p. 15.

49. Michele Mazzitelli, *La Peste* (Apuania-Carrara: Bassani, 1941), pp. 161, 170.

50. Emilio Santini, *Storia della critica manzoniana* (Lucca: Lucentia, 1951), p. 52. Francesco de Sanctis, *Il Manzoni: Saggi Critici* (Rome: Garzanti, 1940), pp. 212–228. This observation was made originally in an article published in 1873.

51. Lukács, *Historical Novel,* pp. 70–71.

52. Raimondi, *Il romanzo senza idilio,* pp. 306–307.

53. Enzo Noé Girardi, *Sulla struttura dei 'Promessi Sposi'* (Milan: Celuc, 1971), exaggerates the evolution of Renzo. On the other hand, Claudio

Varese, "La situazione politico-sociale dell'idillio europeo e il Manzoni," *Rassegna della letteratura italiana,* 76, no. 1 (1972), 3–16, erroneously denies that there is a truly idyllic situation at the beginning and at the end; I believe he is right only when he points to Manzoni's dismissal of a predictable moralistic plot.

54. "the (biting) fox hidden under the coat," Angelandrea Zottoli, *Il sistema di Don Abbondio* (Bari: Laterza, 1933).

55. Jacques Goudet, *Catholicisme et poésie dans le roman de Manzoni I Promessi Sposi* (Lyon: Imprimerie Générale du Sud Est, 1961).

56. Elena Sala Di Felice, *Construzione e stile nei 'Promessi Sposi'* (Padova: Liviana, 1977), pp. 47–49.

57. "are absorbed back into the area of style and composition," Giuseppe Raimondi, *Le linee della mano* (Milan: Mondadori, 1972), p. 157.

58. Gina Alani, *La struttura dei 'Promessi Sposi'* (Bern: Franke, 1948).

59. Thus, Benedetto Croce, *Poesia e non poesia* (Bari: Laterza, 1923), pp. 129–130, quoted in Vigorelli, *Manzoni pro e contro,* II, 163, correctly speaks about Don Ferrante and Donna Prassede as "English" figures though he mistakenly attributes them to the influence of Scott.

60. Alessandro Manzoni, *I Promessi Sposi,* ed. Lanfranco Caretti (Bari: Laterza, 1970), p. 329. "The castle of the Unnamed was perched above a dark and narrow valley, on top of a bluff jutting from a rugged chain of mountains, and joined to them or separated from them—it is difficult to say which—by a mass of crags and precipices and a labyrinth of caverns and chasms, extending also down both sides of it . . . From the castle heights, like the eagle from its blood-stained nest, the savage nobleman dominated every spot around where the foot of man could tread, and never saw anyone higher or above him." From the translation of Archibald Colquhoun, Alessandro Manzoni, *The Betrothed* (1951; New York: Dutton, 1961, p. 301). For commentaries on Manzoni's use of onomastics see Lanfranco Caretti, ed., *Manzoni e la Critica* (Bari: Laterza, 1969), pp. 213–219. Thus in the *Nobis Quoque* at the end of the Canon of Consecration we find as a series "(cum) Felicitate, Perpetua, Agatha, Lucia, Agnete, Caecilia, Anastasia." This confers upon the text a liturgical dignity.

61. Alfred Winterstein, *Adalbert Stifter. Persönlichkeit und Werk: Eine tiefenpsychologische Studie* (Vienna: Phönix Verlag, 1946), pp. 334–344. Urban Roedl (Bruno Adler), *Adalbert Stifter Geschichte seines Lebens* (1936, Bern: Francke, 1958).

62. William Johnston, *The Austrian Mind: An Intellectual and Social History, 1848–1938* (Berkeley: The University of California Press, 1974), pp. 86–87, 94–98, 294–295. Curt Hohoff, *Adalbert Stifter* (Düsseldorf: Schwann, 1949), pp. 109–114, seems convinced that Stifter formed his poetic predilections by imbibing in his Benedictine study years the aesthetic ra-

tionalism of Leibniz and Wolff. See Moriz Enzinger, *Adalbert Stifters Studienjahre 1818–1830* (Innsbruck: Österreichische Verlagsanstalt, 1950), p. 63, and Rudolf Jansen, "Die Quellen des *Abdias* in den Entwürfen zur *Scientia Generalis* von Leibniz?" *Adalbert Stifter Institut Vierteljahrschrift*, 13, no. 3–4 (1964), 57–69. Cf. also Adalbert Stifter, *Leben und Werk in Briefen und Dokumenten*, ed. K. G. Fischer (Frankfurt am Main: Insel, 1962), p. 615. Hereafter as *Briefe*.

63. Philip Zoldester, *Adalbert Stifters Weltanschauung* (Bern: Lang, 1970), pp. 166–169.

64. Lukács, *Historical Novel*, pp. 246–249. Günther Müller, "Stifter, der Dichter der Spätromantik," *Jahrbuch des Verbandes der Vereine Katholischer Akademiker zur Pflege der Katholischen Weltanschauung*, 1924, pp. 18–77.

65. Hohoff, *Adalbert Stifter*, pp. 157–158. On biblical and Homeric stylistic formulas, see Franz Hüller, *Adalbert Stifters 'Witiko'* (Eger: Verlag der Adalbert Stifter-Gesellschaft, 1930), pp. 118–122. The most famous reference to Scott is in a letter to Gustav Heckenast of June 8, 1961. Cf. *Briefe*, p. 476.

66. Helmut Pfotenhauer, "Die Zerstörung eines Phantasmas: Zu den historischen Romanen von Stifter und Flaubert," *Germanisch-Romanische Monatsschrift*, 27 (1977), 25–47.

67. The connection between Manzoni and Stifter seems to have remained unobserved. See Mariano Freschi, "Die italienische Stifter-Kritik," *Adalbert Stifter Institut Vierteljahrschrift*, 17, no. 4 (1968), 263–281. To my knowledge only Hohoff, p. 159, noted some stylistic similarities.

68. Zoldester, *Stifter's Weltanschauung*, pp. 162–179.

69. Sepp Domandl, *Adalbert Stifters Lesebuch und die geistigen Strömungen zur Jahrhundertmitte* (Linz: Adalbert Stifter Institut des Landes Oberösterreich, 1976).

70. "All the villainy prevailing in our public circumstances" in letter to Gustav Heckenast, 8 September 1848, in Stifter, *Briefe*, p. 208, and respectively "disorder, despotism and reaction" to the same on 25 May 1848, ibid., pp. 200–202.

71. Zoldester, *Stifters Weltanschauung*, p. 24. Also Carl Schorske, *Fin de siècle Vienna* (New York: Knopf, 1979), pp. 281–311.

72. Stifter, *Briefe*, p. 196.

73. To Gustav Heckenast, 6 March 1849, in Stifter, *Briefe*, p. 220, and to the same 25 May 1848, ibid., pp. 200–201.

74. Knut Pfeiffer, *Kunsttheorie und Kunstkritik im 19ten Jahrhundert: Das Beispiel Adalbert Stifter* (Bochum: Brockmeyer, 1977).

75. Renate Wagner-Rieger, "Adalbert Stifter und die bildende Kunst," in *Neue Beiträge zum Grillparzer- und Stifter-Bild*, Institut für Österreichs-

kunde (Graz: Stiasny, 1965), pp. 136-143. See also Arthur Roessler, *Der unbekannte Stifter* (Vienna: Rohrer, 1946).

76. Horst Albert Glaser, *Die Restauration des Schönen: Stifters 'Nachsommer'* (Stuttgart: J. B. Metzler, 1965), pp. 74-75, 56-57, 23-51, 55.

77. "Restorationist Utopias . . . seek a capitalism rid of all class conflicts," ibid., p. 2.

78. Müller, "Stifter, der Dichter der Spätromantik," pp. 18-77.

79. "The native ground as the vital expression of hierarchical order," Konrad Steffen, *Adalbert Stifter und der Aufbau seiner Weltanschauung* (Zurich: Münster Presse, 1931), pp. 72-109.

80. Emil Kuh, *Adalbert Stifter* (Vienna: n.p., 1868), quoted in Moriz Enzinger, ed., *Adalbert Stifter im Urteil seiner Zeit* (Vienna: Hermann Böhlhaus Nachfolger, 1968), pp. 305-307.

81. Hermann Kunisch, *Adalbert Stifter: Mensch und Wirklichkeit* (Berlin: Dunckler und Humblot, 1950), pp. 101, 71-73, 78-81. There are some signs that younger criticism is overcoming this attitude. See Thomas Keller, *Die Schrift in Stifters 'Nachsommer'. Buchstäblichkeit und Bildlichkeit des Romantextes,* Forum Litterarum 12 (Cologne and Vienna: Böhlau, 1982), pp. 6-10. Hans Joachim Piechotta, *Aleatorische Ordnung* (Giessen: W. Schmitz, 1981), whose book came to my attention after I finished this ms. provides a brilliant interpretation of *Witiko* (with some reference to early short stories). He shows how total aesthetic order returns into aleatory indifference; according to Piechotta, *Witiko* is the earliest modernist work of monotonous seriality and "de-representation" by transcending the author's (and most of the critics') ideological projects.

82. Wendell Frye, *Tradition in Stifters Romane* (Bern: Lang, 1977), p. 129. Walter Schäfer, *Erziehung und Erzieher bei Adalbert Stifter* (Würzburg: Konrad Trittsch, 1936).

83. Christine Oertel Sjogren, *The Marble Statue as Idea,* University of North Carolina Studies in the Germanic Languages and Literatures, 72 (Chapel Hill: University of North Carolina Press, 1972), p. 94 and elsewhere.

84. Kunisch, *Adalbert Stifter,* p. 81.

85. Glaser, *Restauration des Schönen,* pp. 5-12.

86. Stifter, *Der Nachsommer* (1857; Munich: DTV, 1977), pp. 28, 36, 286-296.

87. The anonymous reviewer in the *Westminster Review* (1953) cited by Norbert Fuerst, *The Victorian Age in German Literature* (University Park: Pennsylvania State University Press, 1966), p. 66.

88. Gunther Hertling, "Grenzübergang und Raumverletzung: Zur Zentralthematik in Adalbert Stifters 'Studien,'" *Adalbert Stifter Institut Viertelsjahrschrift,* 16, nos. 3-4 (1967), pp. 61-77.

89. Christine Wohlbrandt, *Der Raum in der Dichtung Adalbert Stifters*, Zürcher Beiträge zur deutschen Literatur und Geistesgeschichte (Zürich: Atlantis, 1967), pp. 65–75.

90. Ibid., pp. 52–55, 49–53.

91. "Standing still, showing and naming: for Stifter these three essentially belong together," Hans Wysling, *Stifter und Gotthelf: Ein Vergleich ihrer Darstellungsweise* (Zürich: Jures Verlag, 1953), p. 59.

92. Ibid., pp. 59–63, 71. Kunisch, *Adalbert Stifter*, p. 91. See an analysis from a Kantian perspective in Wilhelm Dehn, *Ding und Vernunft: Zur Interpretation von Stifters Dichtung* (Bonn: Bouvier, 1969), pp. 9–83. Marianne Ludwig, *Stifter als Realist* (Basel: Benno Schwabe, 1948), concentrates on the forest.

93. Kunisch, *Adalbert Stifter*, p. 186. Cf. Wysling, *Stifter und Gotthelf*, pp. 36–59.

94. Wysling, *Stifter und Gotthelf*, p. 29.

95. Kunisch, *Adalbert Stifter*, p. 46.

96. Michael Johannes Böhler, *Formen und Wandlungen des Schönen: Untersuchungen zum Schönheitsbegriff Adalbert Stifters* (Bern: Lang, 1967), p. 93.

97. Erik Lunding, *Adalbert Stifter* (Copenhagen: NYT Nordisk Forlag Arnold Busck, 1946), p. 90. See specifically the review of K. v. Thaler of the third volume of *Witiko* in *Neue Freie Presse*, 1111, October 4, 1867, quoted in Enzinger, *Adalbert Stifter*, pp. 274–276. See also Rudolf Gottschall, "Adalbert Stifter: Ein Essay," *Unsere Zeit* (1868), pp. 745–766, quoted in Enzinger, *Adalbert Stifter*, p. 342.

98. "The deliberate naivety of *Witiko* springs from romantic philology," Hohoff, *Adalbert Stifter*, p. 165.

99. Lunding, *Adalbert Stifter*, pp. 102–107, 158.

100. Moriz Enzinger, "Witiko-Geographie," *Adalbert Stifter Almanach für 1953* (Innsbruck: Österreichische Verlagsanstalt, 1953), pp. 54–78.

101. Frye, *Tradition in Stifters Romane*, pp. 130, 47.

102. Stifter, *Briefe*, pp. 554, 557. The reference is to an anonymous reviewer in the *Augsburger Allgemeine* of July 1, 1865.

103. "a fully constituted existence that manages to transcend itself without negating the values of its own transition," Steffen, *Stifter und der Aufbau*, p. 99.

104. "That a community can never be organized, but must grow organically, like a garden," Josef Nadler, "Adalbert Stifter, der Dichter des abendländischen Humanismus," *Stifter-Jahrbuch*, 4 (1955), 89–98.

105. "The awesome majesty of the moral law which . . . crushes the perpetrators of high crimes, and snaps like grass blades their plans of violence," Stifter, *Briefe*, p. 460.

106. "Somewhat grittier and higher," Stifter, *Briefe,* p. 646, in the letter to Gustav Heckenast of April 26, 1867.

107. "The present world situation is one of weakness, and so I take refuge in strength and depict strong men and this strengthens myself," Stifter, *Briefe,* p. 464, in the letter to Gustav Heckenast of December 17, 1860.

108. Lunding, *Stifter,* p. 92. He observes that the categories available to a humanist like Stifter were those of cultural ideas, for example, simple forest people ("einfache Waldleute") versus overrefined Viennese cavaliers ("verfeinerte Wiener Ritter").

109. Grete Preuer, *Das Werk Adalbert Stifters und seine Lebensmacht für unsere Zeit* (Linz: Alpenländischer Verlag, 1938), p. 28 and elsewhere.

110. Julius Kuhn, *Die Kunst Adalbert Stifters,* Neue Deutsche Forschungen, Bd. 28 (Berlin: Junker und Dünnhaupt, 1940), pp. 222-223, 245. Cf. also Hans Günther, "Adalbert Stifter und das Reich," *Zeitschrift für Deutschkunde,* 53, no. 5 (1940), or Joachim Müller, "Stifters Witiko und der Reischsgedanke," *Zeitschrift für deutsche Geisteswissenschaft* (1938).

111. "On the basis of companionship, that crucial principle of Germanic law," Adolf von Grolman, *Adalbert Stifters Romane* (Halle/Saale: Max Niemeyer, 1926), p. 87.

112. Walter Epping, "Adalbert Stifters 'Witiko' und das Legitimationsprinzip," *Wissenschaftliche Zeitschrift der Universität Rostock,* 5 (1955-1956), 199-204. Cf. also Georg Weippert, *Stifters Witiko. Vom Wesen des Politischen* (Vienna: Verlag für Geschichte und Politik, 1967), pp. 133, 146-165, 195-212.

113. "Neither a medieval model, nor a Germanic one, nor yet an ideal corporate state is postulated politically" (by Stifter). Erik Wolf, *Der Rechtsgedanke Adalbert Stifters* (Frankfurt am Main: Vittorio Klostermann, 1941), pp. 91-92, 130, 95, 139.

114. "Everything is now multiplied," Grolman, *Adalbert Stifters Romane,* p. 73. Josef Nadler, "Witiko," *Preussiche Jahrbücher,* 188 (1922), 146-166.

115. Marie-Ursula Lindau, *Stifters 'Nachsommer': Ein Roman der verhaltenen Rührung* (Bern: Francke, 1974).

116. Emil Staiger, *Spätzeit. Studien zur deutschen Literatur* (Zürich: Artemis, 1973), pp. 227, 229, 231, 236. The study on Stifter was originally published in 1962.

117. "And all is for the best," Adalbert Stifter, *Witiko* (Leipzig: Insel, 1933), p. 699. Appointment from above and election from below deftly replace each other all the time.

118. Stifter, *Witiko,* pp. 671-673. Actually the future dependents are coming themselves to beg Witiko to let them build his castle.

119. Ibid., pp. 776-778.

120. Ibid., pp. 131–135. There is a similar plea much later by the much revered Benno, p. 690.

121. "Hereabouts, the only overlord is His Highness the Duke, who receives gifts from us, the small people, and who provides us with protection"; "The Duke will be . . . always a friend to the small people, he will live with us, and we will live with him." Stifter, *Witiko,* pp. 556–557.

122. "Your father gave you the advice to relinquish your right to succession as a sovereign over these lands, so that the commonweal not be injured," Stifter, *Witiko,* pp. 248–249.

123. Ibid., pp. 842–847. Cf. Theodor Putz, " 'Witiko' als Urbild des politischen Menschen," *Klassiker der Statskunst,* 7 (Vienna: Wagner und Westphalen, 1950), 42–43.

124. Elisabeth Käni, *Gestaltung und Formen der Zeit im Werk Adalbert Stifters,* Europäische Hochschulschriften, 21 (Bern: Lang, 1969), speaks about "monumentale, steinerne Ruhe." She says that behind all fictional incidents we can recognize time as a law and an abstract frame to which all living things are subordinated.

125. Hüller, *Adalbert Stifters "Witiko,"* p. 109. Hermann Augustin, *Goethes und Stifters Nausikaa-Tragödie. Über die Urphänomene* (Basel: Benno Schwabe, 1941), pp. 17–21.

126. F. Klatt, "Stifter und das Dämonische," *Dichtung und Volkstum (Euphorion),* 40 (1931), 280ff.

127. Jens Tismar, *Gestörte Idyllen* (Munich: Carl Hanser, 1973).

128. Lee Byron Jennings, *The Ludicrous Demon: Aspects of the Grotesque in German Post-Romantic Prose* (Berkeley: University of California Press, 1963), p. 109.

129. Jean-Louis Bandet, *Adalbert Stifter: Introduction à la lecture de ses nouvelles* (Paris: Klincksieck, 1974), pp. 314, 350.

130. Thomas Mann, *Die Entstehung des Doktor Faustus* (1949; reprint, Frankfurt am Main: S. Fischer, 1967), pp. 99ff. See also *Tagebücher,* ed. Peter de Mendelssohn (Frankfurt am Main: S. Fischer, 1977, 1978), I, 33–34; II, 35–36. Cf. Joachim Müller, "Thomas Mann über Adalbert Stifter," *Adalbert Stifter-Institut Vierteljahrschrift,* 12, nos. 1–2 (1963), 60–63.

131. Avrom Fleishman, *The English Historical Novel: Walter Scott to Virginia Woolf* (Baltimore: Johns Hopkins University Press, 1971). Robin Collingwood, *The Idea of History* (Oxford: Oxford University Press, 1946).

132. Leopold v. Ranke, *Weltgeschichte* (Leipzig: Duncker und Humblot, 1881–1888) IX, part 2, pp. 2–5. Also *Sämtliche Werke* (Leipzig: Duncker und Humblot, 1875–1900), vol. 53–54, p. 88 (a letter of 1820 to his brother Heinrich).

133. Herbert Kaiser, *Studien zum deutschen Roman nach 1848,* Duisburger Hochschulbeiträge, 8 (Duisburg: Walter Braun, 1977), p. 166.

134. "The serene happiness of existential appeasement," Lunding, *Stifter,* pp. 94–97.

AFTERWORD

1. See Eda Sagarra, *A Social History of Germany* (New York: Holmes and Meier, 1977), pp. 194–199, 326–332, 380–384, particularly on the status of servants and artisans as well as on leveling. Also E. J. Hobsbawm, *The Age of Revolution, 1789–1848* (New York: Mentor-NAL, 1962), p. 210 and elsewhere. On hometowns see the important book of Mack Walker, *German Home Towns: Community, State and General Estate 1648–1871* (Ithaca: Cornell University Press, 1971).

2. "The hour of the middle-classes with a chance for the predominance of sterling property and cultivation, with legitimate constitutional efforts under liberal slogans, with political revolutions pursuing moderate aims." Hans Freyer, *Weltgeschichte Europas* (1954; reprint, Stuttgart: Deutsche Verlagsanstalt, 1959), p. 559.

3. René Wellek, "Periods and Movements in Literary History," *English Institute Annual 1940* (New York: Columbia University Press, 1941), p. 89. Corrective variants are provided by Gabriel Lanyi, "Further Thoughts on Literary Periods," *Clio,* 8, no. 1 (1978), 15–24, and Claudio Guillen, "Second Thoughts on Currents and Periods" in Peter Demetz, Thomas Greene, Lowry Nelson, eds., *The Disciplines of Criticism* (New Haven: Yale University Press, 1968), pp. 477–509. A refinement of Wellek's theory in a more formal-stylistic direction is in Walter F. Eggers, "The Idea of Literary Periods," *Comparative Literature Studies,* 17, no. 1 (March 1980), 1–15.

4. Jeffrey Barnouw, "The Cognitive Import of Period Concepts," in *Comparative Literature: Proceedings of the VIIth Congress of the I.C.L.A. (Montreal),* (Stuttgart: Erich Bieber, 1979), II, 21–32.

5. Roger Bauer, *Der Idealismus und seine Gegner in Österreich* (Heidelberg: Carl Winter, 1966), p. 9.

6. John Speirs, *Poetry Towards Novel* (New York: New York University Press, 1971). The descriptive arguments here are just and thoughtful.

7. Lilian Furst, *Counterparts: The Dynamics of Franco-German Literary Relationship, 1770–1895* (London: Methuen, 1977), made an excellent case for this kind of connection: the German *Sturm und Drang* corresponds to the French writers of the 1820s and 1830s, the German high romantics to the Parnassians and symbolists.

INDEX

06/01 22:22 5063 INDEX VER-05 BY-RLW DEPTH-111.6" PAGE-291 PUB-ADV

HARVARD STUDIES IN COMPARATIVE LITERATURE

HARVARD STUDIES IN COMPARATIVE LITERATURE